Before Daybreak

The Florida James Joyce Series

UNIVERSITY PRESS OF FLORIDA

Florida A&M University, Tallahassee
Florida Atlantic University, Boca Raton
Florida Gulf Coast University, Ft. Myers
Florida International University, Miami
Florida State University, Tallahassee
New College of Florida, Sarasota
University of Central Florida, Orlando
University of Florida, Gainesville
University of North Florida, Jacksonville
University of South Florida, Tampa
University of West Florida, Pensacola

CÓILÍN OWENS

Before Daybreak
"After the Race" and the Origins of Joyce's Art

Foreword by Sebastian D. G. Knowles, Series Editor

University Press of Florida
Gainesville · Tallahassee · Tampa · Boca Raton
Pensacola · Orlando · Miami · Jacksonville · Ft. Myers · Sarasota

Frontispiece: "Sandycove at Dawn with Joyce Tower." Photograph by Patrick Naughton, June 15, 2010.

Copyright 2013 by Cóilín Owens
All rights reserved
Printed in the United States of America on acid-free paper

First cloth printing, 2013
First paperback printing, 2015

Library of Congress Cataloging-in-Publication Data
Owens, Cóilín.
Before daybreak : "After the Race" and the origins of Joyce's art / Coilin Owens ; foreword by Sebastian D. G. Knowles.
p. cm. — (The Florida James Joyce series)
Includes bibliographical references and index.
ISBN 978-0-8130-4247-3 (cloth: alk. paper)
ISBN 978-0-8130-6094-1 (pbk.)
    1. Joyce, James, 1882–1941—Criticism and interpretation. 2. Joyce, James, 1882–1941. Dubliners. I. Knowles, Sebastian D. G. (Sebastian David Guy) II. Title. III. Title: After the race. IV. Series: Florida James Joyce series.
PR6019.O9Z7474 2012
823'.912—dc23   2012031975

The University Press of Florida is the scholarly publishing agency for the State University System of Florida, comprising Florida A&M University, Florida Atlantic University, Florida Gulf Coast University, Florida International University, Florida State University, New College of Florida, University of Central Florida, University of Florida, University of North Florida, University of South Florida, and University of West Florida.

University Press of Florida
15 Northwest 15th Street
Gainesville, FL 32611-2079
http://www.upf.com

I ndíl-chuimhne ar m'athair, Séamus Mac Eoghain (1913–1981):
"In iochlainn Dé go dtugtar sinn."

[T]he modern mind . . . is interested above all in subtleties, equivocations and the subterranean complexities which dominate the average man and compose his life.
—to Arthur Power, *Conversations with James Joyce*

Contents

List of Figures xi

Foreword xiii

Preface and Acknowledgments xv

List of Abbreviations xxiii

1. Introduction 1
2. The Automobile Age 12
3. The Biographical Crisis 50
4. Arthur Griffith and the Great Game 94
5. Robert Emmet Centennial 142
6. Rhetoric—Modern and Classical 178
7. The Infernal 226
8. Conclusion 267

Appendix: Schema for "After the Race" 273

Notes 277

Bibliography 299

Index 307

Figures

1.1. Joyce in an automobile 4
1.2. Our Weekly Story: "After the Race," by Stephen Daedalus 5
2.1. King Edward VII, a royal automobilist 27
2.2. Camille Jenatzy as the Red Devil 32
3.1. Kingstown Harbour, ca. 1900 76
3.2. Arnold Dolmetsch concert program 86
5.1. M. O'Healy cartoon 148
5.2. Map of route taken by Jimmy Doyle and guests 154
5.3. The 1798 centennial poster 163
5.4. *Freeman's Journal* masthead: "Ireland a Nation" 167
5.5. Fenian sunburst device 175

Foreword

"After the Race" is, after "Eveline," the second shortest story in *Dubliners*, and generally taken to be the slightest. What Cóilín Owens has done is more than rehabilitate this minor story: he has revived the far more important question of Joyce's origins as an artist. *A Portrait of the Artist as a Young Man* never really told us anything about how Joyce learned to become the genius that he was. In *Before Daybreak*, Owens shows us how Joyce took the clay of his material life, whether biographical, philosophical, religious, literary, cultural, technological, or political, and learned to sculpt. Through gloriously close readings of the world of Dublin at the time of the Gordon Bennett Cup Race in 1903, we are given a window into Joyce's creative process, and into Ireland's promise of a new dawn. It is not for nothing that the last line of "After the Race" is "Daybreak, gentlemen!"

"After the Race" is an ur-story, a bronze spearhead in the sand, and Cóilín Owens is our Schliemann, an archaeologist carefully brushing off the dust to reveal a work of telling significance, of proto-Joycean capabilities. With the bravura of Monsieur Dupin in "The Purloined Letter," he shows us that this nexus of Joycean effects has been hiding in plain sight, skipped by generations of critics as a subpar effort on the way to "Two Gallants." He shows us the crucial intersection of the racecourse with the sites with the life and death of Robert Emmet; he tracks the automobilists' wild career over the historical scenes of Irish paralysis; he shows us the implications of the Pauline close to Emmet's famous speech ("I have done"); he displays how the text's obsessive doubling makes it truly a work of "Doublends Jined" (*FW* 20.16); he hears a theosophist hum in the silent ministrations of Villona; and he leads Jimmy Doyle through a Dantean inferno, bringing us out of darkness to admire the stars.

Through this "toptypsical reading" (*FW* 20.15) of "After the Race" and its afterlife in *Ulysses* and *Finnegans Wake*, we are shown the rest of the

Joyce iceberg—the world that lies below the surface of every one of his texts. The fact that any part of that world still remained to be discovered is simply astonishing.

Sebastian D. G. Knowles
Series Editor

Preface and Acknowledgments

When one of his admirers approached James Joyce on a Zurich street and asked to kiss the hand that wrote *Ulysses,* its proprietor declined the offer, saying "It did lots of other things too" (*JJII* 110). His reply (perhaps inflected by the Matthean verse, "If your right hand causes you to sin, cut it off" [5: 30]), might have counted among its inventory of "other things," the denouement of his odd flirtation with Marthe Fleischman during which he "explored the coldest and hottest parts of a woman's body" (*JJII* 451). His remark might also be regarded as pertinent to one of the creations of which he was not proud, the short story of his literary apprenticeship, "After the Race." Estimating it one of his "worst" efforts (*Letters* II: 189), he intended to revisit it (*Letters* II: 151), but apart from some minor changes, left this orphan of his fabulous family to its lowly critical fate.

In the light of the extraordinary literary achievements of his later career, and even between the covers of *Dubliners,* "After the Race" is an apparently minimal work. It has received the least critical attention of all his fiction. This neglect is not unduly troubling to a reader of my years and reticence: there is, indeed, much to be gained from a concentrated study of its genesis and design. One of the first glimmers of the same imagination, the same method, and the same vision that illuminates *A Portrait of the Artist as a Young Man, Ulysses,* and *Finnegans Wake,* its deceptive simplicity and relative aesthetic inferiority are no grounds for critical condescension: none of us is ahead of the proud artificer of even this apprentice work. The scant notice it has garnered affords a unique opportunity for an original reading of a Joycean text that takes us to the surprises that are the trademarks of a master craftsman. This book is a sequel to my similar treatment—in *James Joyce's Painful Case*—of Joyce's other (eponymous) literary embarrassment. It is similarly a synthesis and enlargement of the critical exegesis done thus far by the "Joyce industry."

As an exposé of Joyce's method and vision, it provides for the beginner, a preview, even in its dawning, of the wondrous Joycean firmament.

Joyce's *Dubliners* is an artistic "take" on the society of his birth by a gifted but guarded native son. It is not the mere social reportage for which it is frequently taken. Similarly, the battle-weary clichés about the "paralysis" and "hemiplegia," the putative themes of *Dubliners,* have performed their duty and exhausted their watch. They helped sell the book to a publisher, an unsuspecting public, and three generations of professional readers. In the period between the fall of Parnell and the Easter Rising (1891–1916), filleted of political backbone, there was, by contrast with this popular misperception of the period, an emboldening of the public will for radical change.* As the pressure for political reform—minimally Home Rule and a final resolution of the Land Question—waned, behind it came many factions clamoring for public attention: cultural revivalists, language boosters, Irish Irelanders, Catholic irredentists, and secular Europeanizers. Meanwhile, the old enemy, emigration, evacuated much of the potential energy that might pursue impulses for economic advancement and political change.

To train the spotlight, then, on the more precise "historical moment" providing the occasion of Joyce's "After the Race," this book will begin with the recollection of the events between its author's return from Paris (March 1903) and his departure for Europe (October 1904), the timeframe of most of his *Dubliners* stories and, of course, *Ulysses.* The major public issue during these nineteen months was a continuous and increasingly strident protest against British cultural, economic, and political imperialism. A development of the clubs celebrating the centennial of the 1798 Rebellion, the anti-Boer War movement, and the Robert Emmet commemorative committees, these movements morphed into the irreconcilable Sinn Féin party in 1905. The formidable targets of Arthur Griffith's activism were the hidebound Unionists and the nonstop talk show engaging the Irish Party at Westminster.

The signal value of an attentive historical approach, will, in this instance, become immediately apparent when it emerges that the major subjects of

---

* Patrick Maume's *The Long Gestation: Irish Nationalist Life, 1891–1918,* is the authoritative account of the labyrinthine politics of the period; and Joseph O'Brien's *"Dear, Dirty Dublin": A City in Distress, 1899–1916,* is a magisterial and elegantly expressed account of the conditions of daily life in Joyce's native city.

public debate during the years 1903–4—since faded into semioblivion but then a raging public storm—was the campaign against the official visit of the recently crowned King Edward VII and the celebration of the centennial of Emmet's rebellion, both of which occurred in the same month as the staging of the Gordon Bennett Cup Race (July 1903). What was then a commonplace but has since been erased from the popular memory by the ensuing political tsunamis was the perception that the international car race and the king's visit were two related performances in the political theater designed to upstage the commemoration of Emmet's 1803 rebellion and to impress upon the populace the might and grandeur of the British Empire. The viceregal authorities had already observed—during the course of the raucous 1798 commemorations—the capacity of such celebrations to become rallying points in the propaganda battle between imperialism and the forces of nationalism and awaken violent irredentist aspirations. Subsequent events were to prove them correct.

None of this appears to register with the implied narrator or the characters in "After the Race." But as we shall see, Joyce's understated narrative had a contemporary frisson that is now long lost, the nuances of its language, setting, and action faded from the living memory. To the unhistorical mind, yesterday's sensations seem transparent, inexplicable, opaque, or even ridiculous. What may seem of little moment to us were, nonetheless, palpable contractions in the "long gestation" that brought forth, in time, the "terrible beauty" of a new political order. As this study will demonstrate, they are also significant because they have been mined for some of the materials of the labyrinth designed by one "Stephen Daedalus."

"After the Race" was Joyce's last work written in Dublin. It should come as no surprise, then, that it registers some of the concerns, conflicts, and anxieties attendant upon his imminent departure from the city that was the site of his birth. This decisive point in his early life meant the severance of most of the personal relationships of his youth, especially those with his peers such as Oliver St. John Gogarty, Vincent Cosgrave, and John Francis Byrne. By the same token, it also dramatizes his quarrel with the Irish Literary Revival, whose leaders he had denounced but a month before in his broadside, "The Holy Office." The story was written within the two weeks following his departure (or expulsion) from the Martello tower at Sandycove, a circumstance registered in the setting of its final scene. There are personal reasons, therefore, that ideas of homosocial friendship, betrayal, anxiety about relationships between moneyed clients and Continental entrepreneurs, international political alliances and rivalries, and new technologies, would appear in this, his first swansong.

Joyce came to the writing table well disciplined in classical and modern rhetoric. We know from his school and university curricula and from personal testimonies that he had made it his business to read with diligence the masters: Homer, Ovid, Dante Alighieri, Alexandre Dumas, François Villon, and Henrik Ibsen (all but Homer in his native literary language). More fundamentally, he brought to the task his inimitable genius: his prodigious memory, his avid interest in etymology, his formal compulsions, his fidelity to personal experience, his syntactic and rhetorical punctilio, his amazing capacity for detachment, his concentrated thoughtfulness, and his many peculiar humors. This analysis will argue that as its author readied for physical emigration, "After the Race" registers in many subtle ways the preoccupations of his concealed conscience.

Even though based on largely forgotten events in Irish political and sporting history, and entering Joyce's notice merely as a journalistic opportunity when he was hard up, careful attention to its formal texture reveals much about his development as a young writer. It records, however indirectly, some major events in Joyce's life and refracts some of his permanent interests, values, and conflicts. Careful reconstruction of its design and the circumstances of its coming into being will reveal why Joyce did not revise it, but how, instead, he wove it into his subsequent masterworks, *Ulysses* and *Finnegans Wake*. The study will, then, illuminate not just this early effort, but will show how it is intimately linked with other texts in Joyce's life and work: his brother's diaries, his own epiphanies and stories, his broadside, "The Holy Office," the "Telemachus," "Aeolus," "Cyclops," and "Circe" episodes of *Ulysses,* and the *ricorso* chapter of *Finnegans Wake.*

"Is there one who understands me?"

The approach to "After the Race" is set upon two firm foundations: historical and rhetorical. The historical embraces the circumstances, personal and communal, that surrounded its writing. This includes all references in the story—and there are scores—to figures or events in the public record, as a skim through the index will confirm. The rhetorical embraces the manner in which Joyce's art is informed by his formal education and his wide but eclectic personal reading. This includes many references to and borrowings from the imaginative and intellectual tradition, native, Continental, classical, biblical, and philosophical. In pursuing this study, I employ a variety of critical practices: the synchronization of Joyce's reading and biography with public events on the Irish and world scenes, the exhumation of names and incidents from popular memory and newspaper records, scrupulous attention to Joyce's multilingual resource (his learning, his wit, his pedantry, his appreciation of etymology), profound respect for his intelligence and sense of purpose (his formal control of the voice and design of the narrative), understanding of his aims and worldview (the conflicts of the moment), appreciation of his particular aesthetic (his taste in language, in toponymy, his peculiar allusiveness), and grateful appreciation of the complement of useful commentary on this little story. All of these procedures are informed by an awareness of the genealogy of this text and an appreciation of the high degree of its author's intentionality.

This study, then, proceeds on these informed assumptions: that Joyce's language is never univocal, sometimes equivocal, and always multivalent; that despite appearances, social realism is but one of the many modes of discourse in his early fiction; that it is not reliable or objective history, but an idiosyncratic interpretation of public events; that he is not necessarily speaking with the same voice in his art as he is in his public or private statements; that his disdain of popular nationalist rhetoric and feeling implies that he is not impervious to national feeling; that he approves of "buy Irish" campaigns, and of nationalist resistance to international commerce; that the automobile is not a fact of daily life, but an extravagant luxury; that in liberating the human spirit from reductive religious orthodoxy, repressive moral codes, and political subservience, Joyce is not an advocate of atheism, blasphemy, profligacy, or anarchy; that Joyce's language and ideas require careful historicization if they are not to be misapprehended; that he is not more interested in gender politics than international capitalism and colonialism; that he was not possessed of a coarsened sensibility allowing him to entertain with equanimity gang or homosexual rape as presiding metaphors in his work; in sum, that he does not share any one of a number of subsequent worldviews: that he is not "one of us."

How to Read Joyce

This book will systematically pursue Joyce's method: how he amalgamated his lived and reading experiences and the public events of his day into a deceptively transparent, but densely imagined, and intricately designed story. It will therefore proceed from a commentary on its "plain" sense, and through a series of historicizations and contextualizations—in his biography, reading, and inherited culture, his linguistic sophistication, his partisanship, his personal rivalries, his defensiveness, his paranoia—to an appreciation of the interdependent formal and substantive aspects of his work. While it will be clear that the text bears witness to a high level of intentionality, there is much here that seems subliminal, assimilated from academic training, preserved in its author's capacious preconscious memory, and emerging as expressions of his classical compulsiveness, his "rage for order."

Joyce is a "difficult" writer because he undertakes, even in his stories, to give expression to complex tasks, personal, social, historical, and spiritual. In Joyce's hands, the short story is no longer a mere diversion or entertainment for people who are normally busy with serious things. It is the vehicle of determined reflection endowed with the power of the literary tradition, a meditation on familiar fundamentals: socialization and insight, despair and hope, death and salvation, nature and grace, aspirations always potentially disappointed. For all this impressive list, Joyce is not a social critic, a historian, a philosopher, a theologian, or a psychologist, but first and last, an artist. Thus while on one level his story appears to be absorbed in trivial events, the stuff of the daily news that soon passes into merciful oblivion, careful attention to his language and an awareness of how he came to write it opens up vistas beyond verveless entertainment. The consideration of biographical, and historical, and allegorical, structural, and rhetorical aspects of the work will lead us to an appreciation of his high seriousness.

Joyce is engaged in the examination of questions that have attracted the best minds and unassuaged spirits. He is an intellectually profound poet. In answering the charge that trivial wordplays figured too prominently in his work, Joyce calmly replied that while some of his devices were trivial, more were quadrivial. He understood himself as bearing the exalted name of Saint Augustine and a student of the medieval academy, of the schools of Saint Thomas Aquinas and Dante. Every detail in his work can be accounted for by reference to several simultaneous systems of meaning. The responsible reader, therefore, must be sure that he or she is reading accurately in the light of the lexical and historical records, and prepared to verify these readings scrupulously in consideration of the literary, philosophical, mythological, and theological patrimony that Joyce considered his own. These references need to be sorted, classified, and then arranged in order of relative weight bearing upon any given passage.

The pleasures of reading Joyce derive from the fineness of his language and the design of his labyrinthine structures. His work expresses a vision that never ceases to astonish and humble. Like Bach's, his art expresses a spiritual view of ordinary reality. Joyce is obviously not conventionally pious, but the Gospels are always on his mind, as are the rituals and doctrines of the Catholic Church of Vatican I. He appreciated the historical fact that the Church had captured the high imaginative ground and devised a language and a liturgy to express this for all nations. In usurping some of its claims for himself, he is no hopeless atheist, but a skeptical modern.

I have approached this task from an Irish Catholic background, with firm emotional ties to the Gaelic and nationalist cultural tradition, and a formal training in Catholic theology and English literary history. Much of this—as well as class and gender—I share, from the cradle, so to speak, with James Joyce: having had an education with a similar emphasis on history, classics, English literature, and rhetoric, debate, and religion. When I decided to pursue the study of Joyce as a specialization in graduate school, I looked carefully for the most sophisticated and congenial mentor. In Bernard Benstock, left-wing and secular Jewish American, I found what I needed. He taught me how to read Joyce as might a "frustrated Talmudist." This means knowing which questions to ask, how to go about answering them without presumption or arrogance, attending to the work of others in this field, while remaining undeterred by charges of "elitism."

Forty years later, after a career of teaching students at American public universities how to read with attention and write with expression, I have tried to put into practice what I thought I was teaching them, reminding myself that nothing worthwhile can be done overnight. This has meant that the microcosm of "After the Race" has been the principal tenant of my conscious mind for the past two years.

In grateful memory of three fine readers with whom I have had warm and lively exchanges, Nat Halper (New York City) a passionate harrier through the Joycean thicket, Michael Bryan (Concordia University, Quebec) a learned etymologist, and David Wright (University of Auckland) a careful historical scholar and caring friend. *Requiescant in pace*

Thanks to these generous and attentive reviewers of *James Joyce's Painful Case:* Murray Beja, Stanley Sultan, Marc Conner, Adrian Paterson, Brian Shaffer, Patrick McCarthy, Mary Lowe-Evans, and Roger Lathbury.

Thanks to Patrick Maume for his disgorging some of his encyclopedic grasp of the Edwardian period.

Thanks to Sebastian Knowles, Marc Conner, Chris Griffin, Stephen Whittaker, and Gerry Moloney for their interest, help, and encouragement. Special thanks to Roger Lathbury for the generous application of his editorial and technical skills.

Thanks for the study shelf furnished by the Library of Congress, for the book service of the Washington Research Library Consortium, and especially for the many privileges conferred on me as professor emeritus by George Mason University.

This work could not have been done without my family's loving tolerance of my frequent abstraction and occasional outbursts of enthusiasm. To my wife, Julianne, and our sons, Seamus and Conor, go raibh maith agaibh.

Abbreviations

For almost all of the following abbreviations cited parenthetically in the text I have followed the standard conventions of the *James Joyce Quarterly*. I add several other items that are frequently cited. Unless otherwise noted all references are by page and line.

CDD   Stanislaus Joyce, *The Complete Dublin Diary*, edited by George H. Healey (Ithaca: Cornell University Press, 1971).

CM   James Joyce, *Chamber Music*, edited by William York Tindall (New York: Columbia University Press, 1954).

CW   James Joyce, *The Critical Writing of James Joyce*, edited by Ellsworth Mason and Richard Ellmann (New York: Viking, 1959).

D   James Joyce, *Dubliners*, edited by Robert Scholes with Richard Ellmann (New York: Viking, 1967).

FW   James Joyce, *Finnegans Wake* (New York: Viking, 1939).

JJII   Richard Ellmann, *James Joyce: New and Revised Edition* (New York: Oxford University Press, 1982).

JJA   *The James Joyce Archive*, edited by Michael Groden et al. (New York and London: Garland, 1977–78). I follow the *JJQ* guide for citing volumes and pages.

JJQ   *James Joyce Quarterly*

Letters   James Joyce, *Letters of James Joyce*, vol. I, edited by Stuart Gilbert (New York: Viking, 1966). Volumes II and III, edited by Richard Ellmann (New York: Viking, 1966).

MBK   Stanislaus Joyce, *My Brother's Keeper: James Joyce's Early Years*, edited by Richard Ellmann (New York: Viking, 1969).

P   James Joyce, *A Portrait of the Artist as a Young Man*, corrected text by Chester G. Anderson and edited by Richard Ellmann (New York: Viking, 1968).

SH   James Joyce, *Stephen Hero*, edited by Theodore Spencer, John J. Slocum, and Herbert Cahoon (New York: New Directions, 1963).

U   James Joyce, *Ulysses*, edited by Hans Walter Gabler et al. (New York: Random House, 1986).

1

Introduction

When James Joyce has Leopold Bloom entertain a "[g]ood puzzle" to "cross Dublin without passing a pub" (*U* 4.129–30), he is parodying the remark attributed to Sir Edward Carson that he rejoiced in the thought that he could traverse the city without passing a single shop bearing an Irish Catholic surname. In Edwardian Dublin, almost every major business was owned by the Protestant and unionist ruling class. Nevertheless, the popular imagination was saturated with the pieties of their social inferiors, Irish Catholics: the rebels in the General Post Office prayed the rosary during lulls in the shelling, throngs of women knelt in prayer outside Kilmainham Gaol during the executions within, and more than 50 percent of the adult population were total abstainers from alcoholic beverages.

To the citizens of today's Irish capital, the moral terrain of Edwardian Dublin is "another country." Although the fine Lawrence Collection preserves a hoard of foxed images of period cityscapes, these "fadographs of a yestern scene" are eerily still, their denizens gazing apprehensively into an unknown future that we can effortlessly recollect. To imagine the orders of cloud—cirrus or cumulus—that blew through the minds behind those bland faces, we have to turn to the pages of the *Freeman's Journal*, the *Irish Times*, the *Leader*, and the *United Irishman*. The younger citizens were perhaps most impressed by the sounds of military bands, the splendid sights of royal parades, or the novel odor of automobile exhaust. The older generation could remember the Famine, the Fenian rising, and the several recent outbreaks of typhus.

Those dowdily dressed Dubliners stepping across Grafton or Westmoreland streets in their full dresses or bowler hats, were they to be granted a quick trip forward in time, would be terrified by the series of political earthquakes lying in wait to unbalance their complacency: the 1913 workers' strike that would paralyze the city, the Great War in which tens of thousands of Irishmen would die, the Easter Rising that would rubbish the city center and for seventy years polarize the public mind on the subject of the Anglo-Irish relationship, the influenza epidemic of 1919 that would remove thousands of them from the ranks of the quick, the high hopes and grim struggle of the War of Independence, the bitterness and disappointment that would follow the Treaty and the Civil War, the long Depression, the isolationism and threadbare survival through the Emergency and the stagnant 1950s. The partial success of the independence struggle, the postcolonial partition, the temporary hegemony in the Irish Free State and Republic of an ethos formed out of a concurrence of Gaelic and Catholic cultures, their displacement by the vulgarities of Anglo-American mass media entertainment, eventual European Union membership, a liberalized and then demoralized Catholic Church, hastened by the twenty-year life and sudden demise of the Celtic Tiger.

The passage that today's readers of Joyce can, in comfort and gratitude at our survival, bring to mind—the struggle with Nazism and Communism and through the buoyancy of the decades of consumerism—has taken us further and further from an appreciation of the relatively quotidian but still straitened necessities faced by the Dubliners of a century ago. While we occupy the latest phase of the electronic revolution, they were but making their first acquaintances with the electric age. While today's Dublin is home to thousands of millionaires and a city with one of the highest indices of international transactions in the world, in 1903–4 it had one fifth the population, the largest slums in Europe, a citizenry subject to regular epidemics, constant undercover surveillance, and as manifested by the presence on its streets of squads of uniformed soldiers and police, a center of colonial administration and armed control.

Nevertheless, contrary to the impression that might be derived from reading *Dubliners* out of historical context, the city was far from paralyzed. Between 1898 and 1904, the Irish public was roused by a series of centennial commemorations and exposed to vigorous protests in the streets, in Dublin's City Hall, and in the news media over recruitment for the Boer War and other manifestations of British imperial presumption. These protests were conducted by the Gaelic League, memorial committees, and other fitful or dedicated groups. For example, in April 1902, the production of *The Dandy Fifth*, a comic opera stereotyping Irish characters, ran into raucous protests. Outside the doors of the Theatre Royal, crowds of two to three hundred assembled to sing "The Boys of Wexford," leading to a succession of riots and numerous arrests (*Weekly Irish Times*, April 14). Shortly thereafter, in June 1903, there were near-riotous assemblies at City Hall during the debate over the proposed address to King Edward VII.

The Edwardian years were, in fact, in a continuous ferment of nationalist agitation, much underestimated by cultural commentators with selective interests in the period. Thus, the Abbey Theatre protests of 1907 against John Millington Synge's *Playboy of the Western World* have gotten disproportionate notice in academic histories, much in excess of what they were accorded at the time. Meanwhile, Irish-Ireland organizations mounted a vigorous "buy Irish" campaign that targeted importers of goods competing with native manufacturers. Arthur Griffith engaged in a long-drawn-out propaganda battle over the installation of organs of German manufacture in Irish churches in preference to their Irish-made competitors.[1]

James Joyce wrote his critique of the expensive craze of automobilism, "After the Race," four years before the first Model T rolled off Henry Ford's assembly line. The ways in which this relatively cheap engineering marvel would transform what we now call "lifestyle," was as unforeseen by the author of this little story as the impact in our time of the personal computer. The American Interstate Highway System and the European autobahn, the wonders of the modern world, are the necessary complements to the descendants of Detroit's cheap, mass-market automobile. Today's readers, two to four generations into the automobile age, therefore, live and move among its furniture (the suburb, the motel, the chain store, the recreational vehicle, the air bag, and vacation home) as if by nature itself.

Yet every commentator on Joyce's story, no doubt impressed by its author's reputation as a cultural progressive and literary pioneer, underestimates his instinctive reaction to a technical wonder that is our endowment. Critics seem to assume that the automobile, electric light, and plastics were as familiar to Joyce as they are to us, that he anticipated our valuation of these inventions, or that he could have envisaged the age to come in which his readers would all own cars and could be trained to drive them along reinforced concrete runways at 50 to 70 mph while engaging in casual conversations or entertained by radio programs. While more than 50 percent of Irish households today own at least one automobile, in 1903, there were but a score of car owners in the entire country. The Joyces were not among them. One of the fears admitted by Stephen

Figure 1.1. Joyce, Nora, Lucia, and Lucia's nurse in an automobile, Feldkirch, Switzerland, 1932. Photographer unknown. Courtesy of Beinecke Rare Book and Manuscript Library, Yale University.

Dedalus is "machinery" (*P* 243.18) and the single photograph we have of Joyce in an automobile (in 1932) suggests that his casual appearance was a contrivance (figure 1.1).

Race Commentators

This story originally appeared in the *Irish Homestead* on December 17, 1904, two months after its author's departure for Zurich, Trieste, and Pola (figure 1.2). Despite his subsequent reservations about its quality, he never substantially rewrote "After the Race," making but a few adjustments before submitting it to George Roberts in 1909 as the fifth story in the completed *Dubliners*. This version, with further emendations, is now the standard text, as edited by Robert Scholes. A fine general description of the order of composition and textual history of *Dubliners* and a substantially accurate and complete collation of the text of "After the Race"—comparing the *Irish Homestead,* the 1910 page proofs, and 1914 printings—can be found in the Norton Critical Edition of *Dubliners* (Norris, xv–xliii, 32–38).[2]

By early 1914, the intransigence against Home Rule among Unionist and Conservative MPs and in the House of Lords renewed the prospect of violence, heightened by the Curragh Mutiny/Incident (March 20), the Ulster Volunteer Force gunrunning (April 24), the response in kind by the Irish Volunteers (June 26), and the failure of the Buckingham Palace Conference (July 21–24). In such a rapidly heating political atmosphere, by the time *Dubliners* was eventually published, on June 15 (*JJII* 353), its ironies must have appeared tepid. The anxieties over either a civil war or partition were, in the event, overtaken by the Sarajevo assassination and on August 4 by Britain's declaration of war against Germany. During all of this, the third Home Rule Bill was detained in its accustomed waiting room, to be predictably shelved as Britain moved into battle formation. To radical Irish nationalists, the prologue to the high drama of the Easter Rebellion was being dictated, and Yeats's "terrible beauty" would soon reduce the memory of the propaganda war of July 1903 to a tremulous whisper.

It should come as no surprise, therefore, that the Irish readers on whom Joyce might have counted to understand "After the Race" in 1914 would have, after a decade of rising tensions, regarded with ennui a request to refresh their fading memories of a distant preamble of their current political crisis.[3] To today's readers, fretting over nuclear proliferation, population explosion, and global economic and ecological crises, without the

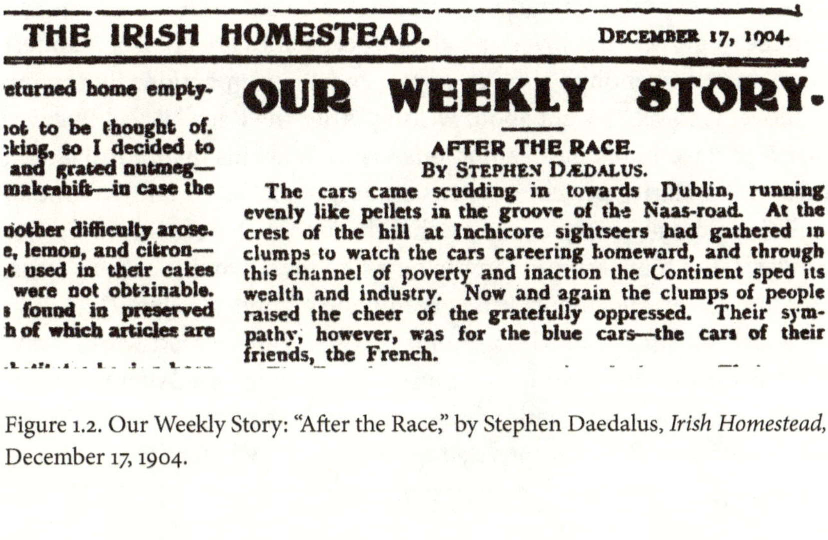

THE IRISH HOMESTEAD. DECEMBER 17, 1904.

eturned home empty-
10t to be thought of.
:king, so I decided to
and grated nutmeg—
makeshift—in case the
nother difficulty arose.
e, lemon, and citron—
t used in their cakes
were not obtainable.
s found in preserved
h of which articles are

OUR WEEKLY STORY.

AFTER THE RACE.

BY STEPHEN DÆDALUS.

The cars came scudding in towards Dublin, running evenly like pellets in the groove of the Naas-road. At the crest of the hill at Inchicore sightseers had gathered in clumps to watch the cars careering homeward, and through this channel of poverty and inaction the Continent sped its wealth and industry. Now and again the clumps of people raised the cheer of the gratefully oppressed. Their sympathy, however, was for the blue cars—the cars of their friends, the French.

Figure 1.2. Our Weekly Story: "After the Race," by Stephen Daedalus, *Irish Homestead*, December 17, 1904.

intervention of scholars and editors, the concerns that provoked this story would appear ephemeral indeed.

The second of the four stories in *Dubliners* that responds to public events,[4] it purports to give an "insider's" view of the news behind the news to which its historical author was diffident and of which he had no firsthand knowledge. Joyce was generally careful to write only about the lower middle class of Dublin society. His characters are drawn from the fifth of the population of Dublin comprising the "commercial class" (and are therefore demographically atypical, not only of Dublin, but more so, of Ireland as a whole).[5] In the case of "After the Race," however, according to the judgment of many scholars (following William York Tindall), Joyce takes a singular misstep in writing about a social and business class with which he was not sufficiently familiar.

Warren Beck, an attentive rhetorical critic, finds that it is "both the sketchiest and the most over-defined" story in the collection (123). Although the exposition and style are too labored, he admits that much of the later narrative exhibits what he terms "the Joycean mode": simple image, subtle implication, detached economy, and deft irony (126–27). Florence Walzl, another distinguished commentator, concurs, noting that "Joyce was too good a self-critic not to recognize the stylistic weaknesses of 'After the Race' in its stereotyped characterizations and confusing plot elements" (195). As I contend, these comments, fair in themselves, have deflected critical appreciation from a profoundly instructive object.

My aims here are to write a scholarly study of an elementary work that will also serve those embarking on their first venture into the Joycean universe. It argues that Joyce's prodigious capacities are ab ovo, manifest if one but takes enough time to apprehend them in action. By tracing his movements as he went about writing "After the Race," it will uncover what is at stake in his more ambitious works. It avoids theoretical jargon and aims for clarity and comprehension. It is not a "Joyce-and-X" kind of book that pursues a single interest that the author shares with Joyce, but one that takes him seriously on the terms he set down: his actual words, their lineage, arrangement, and contemporary import. *Before Daybreak*, therefore, holistically tackles a minor text that can be read without any particular instruction in fifteen minutes. By showing how "After the Race" came to be written and with what equipment its author approached the task, I will unravel its deceptive simplicities and lay before the reader its astounding order, subtlety, complexity, and vision.

This work could not have been done without the explications of a score of fine scholars who have preceded me in this task over the past fifty years. I indicate where I am indebted to these collaborators, and where I demur from or concur with their judgments. If I may appear to have taken more trouble than is warranted, and if some of the procedures may appear wearying or pedantic, I answer that a knockdown exegesis of an amazing text requires no less.

"a commodius vicus"

Chapter 2, "The Automobile Age," will recapitulate the early years of the motor industry, the sports event known as the Gordon Bennett Cup Race of July 3, 1903, and resurrect, from the newspaper record, the hoopla that surrounded its staging in Ireland. Although Joyce was at best indifferent to the event itself, its technology or its outcome, the original readers of "After the Race" were not likely to be so detached. Thus, in order to appreciate the way in which the story might have then been apprehended, the tenor of the public debate surrounding the race requires adequate notice. This chapter, therefore, sets out to "defamiliarize" modern readers from the automobile industry and the public relations, sports, and gambling cultures attendant upon it. These settings allow us to account for the young Joyce's flirtation with this new industry, the hostility of his interview with Henri Fournier, and the selling of his talents to the *Irish Times,* and appreciate his subsequent critique of the competition in "After the Race" in the form of a parody of fashionable sports writing. Joyce's story is countercultural in that rather than producing a conventional sports story, his narrator makes but a few preliminary gestures appreciative of the actual race and focuses instead on the tailgate party. The preposition in the title implies that the Gordon Bennett Cup Race is not about car racing or sports, but a satire on publicity, profits, gambling, and high living.

Chapter 3, "The Biographical Crisis," dilates the personal circumstances, during the late summer of 1904, of Joyce's writing of "After the Race." These are principally his estrangement from his erstwhile male friends, especially Oliver St. John Gogarty. The rivalry with Gogarty had many dimensions—social, temperamental, intellectual, and spiritual— and is reflected in the contrast between the figures of Jimmy Doyle and Villona in the story. This rivalry, which Joyce subsequently developed with great virtuosity in the "Telemachus" episode of *Ulysses,* helps clarify the relationship between this story—its characters, its tensions, and its setting—and the beginning of *Ulysses*. The same biographical reconstruction of these months similarly supports the contention that the figure of Villona is nominally drawn after the French medieval poet François Villon, but more substantively after Arnold Dolmetsch as an expression of Joyce's interest in the music for voice and lute of the English Renaissance. These glosses help us appreciate the first draft of Joyce's self-image as an artist: as a bemused and detached observer of the gross babble of the streets, his inner life conducted in a language luxuriant, refined, and private, concealed behind a mask of silence.

Chapter 4, "Arthur Griffith and the Great Game," examines the political circumstances, domestic and international, surrounding the action of "After the Race." This chapter examines the relationships between the car race and Irish nationalist resentment over the Famine, the contemporary debate over the Wyndham (Land) Act, and the Dublin visit of King Edward. The salient ideologue here is Arthur Griffith, whose weekly newspaper, the *United Irishman,* Joyce intermittently, but with approbation, read. He was, therefore, familiar with Griffith's radical nationalist critique of the imperial political theater featuring the Gordon Bennett Cup Race and the royal visit in July 1903.

When Joyce came to write his story, fifteen months later, Griffith's *Resurrection of Hungary,* a historical dilation of his political strategy to subvert British authority in Ireland, had appeared and was widely discussed in political circles. Based on the model for Hungarian devolution developed by Ferenc Deák, it proposed the disengagement of Irish Members of Parliament from Westminster and the establishment of a dual monarchy like that of the Austro-Hungarian alliance. Through the figure of the Hungarian Villona, Joyce clearly summons an allegorical reference to this devolutionary strategy. This chapter, therefore, implies that "After the Race" is not only the first publication to commemorate a significant benchmark in the evolution of Irish political sentiment before the Easter Rising, but the first to support publicly what was to become the blueprint for the political strategy establishing the Irish Free State. Further, in the figures of Routh and Farley, Joyce is drawing on historical figures representing Anglo-Irish conflict and Irish-American success during the late nineteenth century. Further, the relationship of the story to Halford Mackinder's influential essay, "The Geographical Pivot of History" (April 1904) and Rudyard Kipling's *Kim* (1901), and the Englishman Routh's proposal to end the evening with "one great game" (*D* 48.16) raises suspicion about the part he plays as an intelligence agent in the Great Game for global dominance.

Chapter 5, "Robert Emmet Centennial," expatiates the inimitable ways in which the story commemorates the last phase of the rebellion of the United Irishmen. These include a tacit tour of the sites of the hero's futile rising and execution, citations of his famous speech, and attention to his final request: that he be remembered in a charitable silence. Just as the centennial celebrations of this rebellion reappear in *Ulysses,* so does the major symbol upon which "After the Race" concludes. In having Villona announce the dawn, Joyce is refurbishing a trite symbol from the attic of Irish nationalist symbology. A survey of the contemporary uses of this symbol sets forth how Joyce appropriates it and how this story adumbrates its development in the "Telemachus" episode of *Ulysses* and its full efflorescence in the *ricorso* of *Finnegans Wake.*

Chapter 6, "Rhetoric—Modern and Classical," turns to an analysis of the rhetorical dimensions of the story. While it is superficially a parody of popular sports and adventure journalism, its design and discursive style derive from its author's schooling in the elements of classical literature and rhetoric. A careful analysis of the structure, narrative style, and management of voices demonstrates how, for the beginning of his writing career, Joyce is a sophisticated rhetorician. His subtle handling of free indirect discourse, figurative language, chiasmus, anticlimax, and silence documents his early experimentalism. Joyce's debt to classicism is documented by his management of the mythological parallels between the plot and characterization in the story and Ovid's account of the fall of Phaethon.

Chapter 7, "The Infernal," argues from folkloric, theosophical, Pauline, and Dantean perspectives that the story investigates various claims of access to "the hidden mysteries of nature." Its resemblance to the South Leinster folktale, "Jemmy Doyle and the Fairy Palace," the provenance of the Celtic *bruidhean* [hostel] tale type, suggests that beneath its appearances as a realistic story of commercial relations, it is a redaction of the archetypal adventure in which the shaman descends to and returns enlightened from the Otherworld. At the same time, its septenary design, the motifs of doubling, circles, and cycles, and the many usages of peculiar Hermeticist reference support the contention that it is an allegory of the transition from material to spiritual phases in cosmic evolution (*manvantara* to *pralaya*) and a parody of the literalized spiritual accountancy of contemporary Hermeticism.

The argument uncovers the ways in which the story anticipates several themes in *Ulysses:* metempsychosis, parallax, and (in particular) the lampoon of a séance in "Cyclops." It is therefore a supremely subtle satire on the esoteric claims of the Protestant elites to lead an Irish cultural revival and a criticism of rootless spiritual adventuring from a slightly orthodox Catholic position. This is supported by the sequence of Pauline themes of avarice, Christian hope, and resurrection threading the story under the titular allusion to Saint Paul's boast of his faithful apostleship, "I have run the race" (2 Timothy 4: 7). These themes, along with that of betrayal, appear simultaneously in Canto 34 of Dante's *Inferno*. When Villona announces the dawn, he is thereby analogously signaling the conclusion of the night of the *Inferno,* and figuratively playing the part of Virgil to the bewildered pilgrim, Dante. That this reading accords with Joyce's own intentions is confirmed by his subsequently situating "After the Race" as fifth of the fifteen stories of *Dubliners*.

The argument of the book proceeds, therefore, as Aristotle recommends, from the better to the lesser known. The argument is arranged on the assumption that it will be read sequentially, although it is not necessary to follow that arrangement. Most of the chapters can be read independently, although there is a progressive dependence in the later chapters on the broader and previously adduced evidence in their predecessors. The book concludes with a summary of the argument: that appearances aside, Joyce is at the beginning of his career Emmet's memorialist and Dante's disciple. This seemingly flat and realistic story is intensely wrought. Deeply imagined, it draws selectively on the literary canon and the popular culture of the time, representing ordinary life as comprehended by an imagination that is at once true to objective experience, but also evincing historical, mythological, and anagogical dimensions. It is singularly personal while also drawing sustenance from the mainstream of the cultural tradition of Ireland, which is at once mythological, folkloric, national, and Catholic. "*Scéal a bhfuil údarás ann*" [a story authorized by the cultural tradition], it is singularly magisterial.

From the start, Joyce is writing by the "gold standard": responsive to the classical and popular imaginative traditions of European and Irish culture, he is at once parochial and cosmopolite. The appendix offers a schematic summary of these interpenetrating imaginative spheres—these "correspondences"—and graphically illustrates Joyce's penchant for the elaborate correspondences developed in *Ulysses*. This book will demonstrate in fine detail that, as he departed Ireland for a literary career, Joyce did not misplace his confidence in his own creative genius.

2

The Automobile Age

"Automobilism" was all the rage in Edwardian Britain. Readers of "quality mags" were regularly entertained and instructed in the romance and hazards of this latest bourgeois indulgence. Round the fires at private clubs, gentlemen could read stories that began like this:

> "The Goddess in the Car"
> by C. N. and A. M. Williamson
>
> With a whirr like the beating of mighty wings, the giant automobile rushed through the night along a solitary part of the broad, white road between Paris and Chartres. Its blazing acetylene lights rent the darkness with a blinding glare; behind it traveled a pillar of dust; stones and twigs were swirled into the air-vortex created by its passage. Goggled, masked, clothed all in black leather, Raoul Jullien bent over the steering wheel. Crouched at his feet was a slighter enshrouded figure (like a familiar attending a demon) stop-watch in hand, looking eagerly for the kilometer stones as they flickered by, one every forty seconds.

The heroine then appears: "Her hazel eyes looked black in the reflection of the acetylene lamps, the half-laughing curves of her red lips with an inner sparkle of white teeth was full of resolution, of recklessness, and of humour." Introduced in this way, the representative pair career through a ludicrously melodramatic and implausibly linked sequence of incidents. Underskilled in the art of exposition, the Williamsons have Raoul, even as he hurtles through the countryside, speak past his lover to the readers whose presence he unaccountably assumes: "If I win the race we are in clover again; if I lose, it's bankruptcy at the least—perhaps worse things than that. On this car I have spent all my skill all my experience." As if overstatement trumps unlikelihood, this light diversion blunders on into the dark (*Strand Magazine*, March 1902, 262–71).

Chauvinistic British consumers of such imaginary excursions pictured themselves in a friendly rivalry (once upon the battlefield, now in the automobile trade) with their nearest Continental neighbors. The extravagance of the fiction scarcely concealed the stereotypes of the inherited mutual disdain and jealousy in Anglo-French relations.

Late Victorians had an array of magazines furnishing them fantasies beneath the imperial flag. *Wide World,* for example, was a monthly compilation of tales of adventure, exploration, and sports. It carried illustrated reports of big-game hunting, accounts of colonial exotica, and near escapes from extraordinary natural hazards, wild beasts, and truculent natives. With the commercialization of the automobile (only for the very rich), descriptions of high-speed adventures riding atop of one of these machines were added to the catalogue of sensational stories of physical thrills, spills, and dangers. In September 1902, *Strand Magazine* ran an article entitled "Automobilism" (320–27) that set forth "the infirmities of motor-cars and the foibles of those who drive them" (320). The previous March, one Miss Emily Leslie rendered an account that was both an invitation and a warning to the would-be "automobilists" of the new age ("My First Automobile Ride," 542–48).

Her article celebrates the thrill of bounding along the country roads—unpaved for high-speed travel—at 40 mph. With cheery insincerity, as if she were describing adventures in the remotest colonies, she dramatizes the dangers posed to drivers by unsuspecting peasants and wandering animals. Illustrating the high-speed hazards of this new pastime, she reports an exchange on the topic: "'But the danger,' I protested; 'scarcely a day passes without an accident of some kind: collisions with other vehicles; people knocked down and killed or injured; not to speak of the dreadful accidents which have befallen automobilists on their own account'" (542). Further in the conversation, her French hostess assures her that "Yes, the very best invention of our time; nothing else comes up to it. It's cheaper than horses in the long run—at least, it's just as cheap—and it's safer too, for it can't take fright or run away. You can make it perform the most delicate evolutions when you know how to manage it. Of course, there are plenty of ignorant fools who don't know how to manage it, but *we* always take a mechanic with us, to be on the safe side."

Later, the narrator explains the design of the car, the gears, and in awestruck terms she describes the derring-do of a new species of culture hero: "The upper part of the man's face was concealed by a black visor. This was the driver, or *mécanicien* as he is called in this country" (543). She adds that "I am compelled to admit that the sensation of flying along in an auto-car is certainly one of intoxicating delight" (545), but nonetheless concludes that "for as this is my first automobile ride, so I mean it to be my last—in France, or elsewhere" (548).

These accounts remind today's readers that during the intervening century we have become accustomed to lower risks so that the pleasure of automobile travel is quotidian.

As his title forecasts of his story, James Joyce is not enthralled by the action game of car racing. When he wrote this story he had never ridden in an automobile. The Joyce family, by custom and necessity, conducted their business on foot. Like the vast majority of their contemporary Dubliners, they did not possess even a bicycle (costing £4–5; $30 in 1903) among the ten of them, much less an exotic automobile.

Mechanicians Ascendant

As James Flink's *The Automobile Age* (1988) recounts it, bicycle manufacturers were the first to produce automobiles, and within one generation, too. By 1900, all the leading bicycle manufacturers were producing automobiles: Opel (Germany), Clément and Peugeot (France), Humber, Morris, and Rover (Britain), and in the United States, Pope, Rambler, and Winton (4–6). By then, the internal combustion engine—its power derived from fossil fuel vaporized and under high pressure ignited in a closed chamber—had proven its superiority over its erstwhile rivals, the steam- and electric-driven motors. Although this engine had more moving parts, it generated superior horsepower and was lighter than either of its competitors (Flink, 10–13).

During the 1890s, Paris was the center of the nascent automobile industry and French roads were then the best in the world. Panhard et Levassor began producing motor vehicles in quantity and issued the first regular catalogue advertising motor vehicles in 1892; by 1895 several French firms had followed suit so that the automobile was soon a common sight on the streets of Paris (Flink, 15–17). The Michelin brothers developed the pneumatic tire—invented by Irishman John Dunlop—that quickly became standard.[1] The leading French engineer was Gottlieb Daimler, whose car, based on the Panhard et Levassor model, was the prototype of the modern gasoline-powered automobile. The overall prototype of our vehicle was the 1901 Mercedes, designed for Daimler. In preference to the surrey-influenced design of earlier models, its engine was placed vertically in the front of the chassis instead of under the seats or in the back, which put the crankshaft parallel with the longitudinal line of the car instead of parallel with the axles. This mechanical arrangement accommodated larger and more powerful engines. By 1900 Carl Benz, adopting the engines of Nicolaus Otto and Rudolph Diesel, was competing with the French for the growing market.

France is the home of the automobile: Toulouse Lautrec painted the original recorded motoring portrait, and the first definitive road signs appeared in France. The French, moreover, led the way in sales efforts, using erotic, mythological, and allegorical themes in their advertising. Maurice Maeterlinck, the Belgian philosopher poet, wrote about the automobile as if it were a mystical entity with "its tremblerblade, sparking plugs, and many other organs of which I scarcely dare let myself speak" (*Strand Magazine*, 1903, cited by Pound, 67).

France also gave the world such words as "automobile," "chauffeur," "chassis," and "horseless carriage" [*voiture sans chevaux*], and revived the usage of "mechanicians" (*D* 46.19), which had become otherwise rare in nineteenth-century English usage (*OED*).[2] In a vain effort to swim against the rising tide of fashionable car driving, a London newspaper ridiculed this "new French sporting craze" (cited by Lynch, *Triumph*, 21).

In 1901 there were about 130 manufacturers in France alone—mainly in Paris itself—that dominated the early trade. The largest market for cars in France was among wealthy Parisians, whose acquisitive imaginations the manufacturers stimulated through the advertising device of the auto show. Between 1902 and 1907 France produced more cars than all other European countries combined, and since its output far exceeded its domestic demand, French manufacturers made a concerted effort to develop overseas markets. In this it was but relatively successful: by 1907 it was outproduced by America (Flink, 25).

The Automobile Club of France, the Royal Automobile Club in Great Britain, the Irish Automobile Club (founded in 1902 [O'Brien, 64]), and Automobile Club of America were equivalent organizations among the motoring elite and carried on identical functions—sponsoring tours and tests and lobbying for legislation favorable to motorists (Flink, 27). Annual auto shows and demonstrations at county fairs, but especially exhibitions of long-distance reliability, excited the average person's imagination about the romance of motoring. These clubs and their wealthy members promoted the other major and innovative marketing device: the automobile race. Track and road races, which placed emphasis on speed, were more important for their contributions to automotive technology as tests for weaknesses in design than as publicity for the motorcar (Flink, 30). The 1895 Paris Bordeaux race—which seemed to confirm French superiority in automobile manufacture—stimulated American interest in this new industry.

By 1903–4, American production began to surpass that of France: in France it took three hundred man-days to make a car, whereas in the United States it took but seventy (Flink, 43). Thus when Henry Ford eventually unveiled the Model T in 1908, the French had lost the technological and market edges (25). A lighter and tougher car than its competitors, suspended on arc springs, with an enclosed power plant and transmission and a detachable cylinder head, it was an immediate best buy. By 1914 it could be purchased in Dublin for £100 (O'Brien, 64), or roughly twice the annual income of the average Irish wage-earner.[3]

It contrasted with the heavier European touring car that was identified with the luxury market, and cost three to four times as much (for example, in 1896 the British Humber cost £275, and the Peugeot £395, according to O'Brien, 64). It was easier to drive, handled bad road surfaces and steeper grades better, and had greater engine flexibility than the tourer. Its fuel economy, ease of repair, and high vantage gave it a worldwide appeal (Flink, 38). By these means the Edwardian decade witnessed the dawn of the automobile age.

In the period before the electronic media, the printed press spread the light: newspapers and automobiles sold one another. Reporters were invited to private demonstrations, shown how to operate vehicles, and supplied with press kits. The favorite device in these promotional efforts was the newspaper interview. Manufacturers commonly brought reporters long distances at company expense to be entertained and given a preview of new models in the hope that "free" publicity would ensue (Flink, 30). Newspapers patronized by potential customers were, naturally, the targets of these publicity efforts.

The first buyers of cars came from the same social groups in all countries: wealthy sportsmen, doctors, landlords, businessmen, and engineers. This was an urban class, successors to the landed gentlemen of the previous age who were horsemen or rode in horse-drawn carriages. Outside the city, the profession most susceptible to this new and expensive craze was medicine: in rural areas everywhere the doctor was the first to own a car (Flink, 28). The diction and images attached to today's automobiles bear witness to this succession: "horsepower," "ride," the word "car" itself, and in the design of logos like the Ford mustang and Ferrari's prancing steed. The advertising age has cultivated romantic associations of these animals to stimulate subliminal attachments among potential consumers.

The impact of these dust-producing monsters roaring around the bumpy roads at speeds exceeding 15 mph and endangering the lives of ambulatory citizens, animals, and domestic fowl alike produced a wave of indignant protest. The letters columns of the newspapers of the time record the reactions of correspondents. In Parliament, one Mr. Soares, MP for Barnstable, described motorists as "statutory trespassers on the road... with no inherent right whatever" and Sir Brampton Gurden from Norfolk North spoke in favor of flogging for motoring offenses, while other members supported a speed limit of 6 mph. Baron Montagu of Beaulieu, a patron and historian of motoring, admits that the spirit of the times was, indeed, "anti-motoring" (Montagu, 58–59).

Whereas Edwardian Dubliners walked a great deal more than their descendants, many of them owned bicycles. By the time of the motorcar's arrival, Dublin had, moreover, an excellent tram service. Motorcars arrived in Ireland in 1896—the first a steel-shod and steam-driven car and later that year, the first petrol-driven model purchased by a Dublin physician, Dr. John Colohan. Soon Lord Iveagh and the *Freeman's Journal* editor, M. H. Gillie, had their own models. Horace Plunkett was an early promoter, insisting that the automobile "furnished an ideal combination of business and pleasure" (cited by Lynch, *Triumph*, 26). The first Motor Tour in Ireland took place in July 1900, and at Navan sports the following month, the first contest between mechanically propelled vehicles took place. One Oliver St. John Gogarty participated in the cycle race. Of the poetry in motion he beheld that day he wrote: "Invention needs the same spark from heaven for the man who can bend faith by rhythm, as it does from the man who can transcend the limitations of time and space" (26).

The Royal Irish Automobile Club composed of titled landowners, decorated military men, brewers and distillers was founded in Dublin the next year. The *Freeman's Journal*, the voice of the Catholic bourgeoisie, ardently welcomed the automobile and prophesied that "the motorcar, with its imperative demand for a smooth surface, may prove the chief road reformer of the near future" (25).

It is within these contexts that we move to look at Joyce's interview with the French racing driver and his consequent story.

Fournier Interview

The first Irish publication to promote the Gordon Bennett Cup Race was the *Irish Times*. The semiofficial organ of the Anglo-Irish establishment, its readership would have included almost every motorcar owner of the time. Thanks to the good offices of one Matthew O'Hara, a friend of John Stanislaus on the newspaper staff (*JJII* 119, 127), the editors contacted James Joyce in Paris about a *New York Herald*–style interview with Henri Fournier, one of the prospective French drivers. During his Paris sojourn in the winter and spring of 1903, ostensibly to study medicine, Joyce was ever mindful of Ireland and Irish affairs. He had spent Saint Patrick's Day with the Fenian Joe Casey (the Kevin Egan of *Ulysses*). His review of Lady Gregory's *Poets and Dreamers* appeared on March 26 in the *Daily Express*, around the time of his interview with Fournier for the *Irish Times*. Distasteful though the assignment evidently was, he needed the thirteen shillings and ninepence that the leading Irish unionist paper paid (the interview appeared on April 7, 1903).

It had required three visits to the premises of Paris-Automobile on the Rue d'Anjou (Sunday, April 5) before he was able to pin down the French celebrity (*CW* 106). Unawed by the company, Joyce spares little effort to conceal his irritation: he makes his readers aware of his repeated visits, his long wait, and the intermittent interruptions of the eventual interview by Fournier's "importunate telephone" (*CW* 107). Joyce did not suffer self-important businessmen gladly. Nor did he conceal his disdain for Fournier's clients and readers of the *Irish Times*, the "people of leisure" (*CW* 107).

His first foray into street journalism, Joyce's report gives his *Irish Times* readers an "inside scoop": a face-to-face interview with the chief rival to their presumed hero, Selwyn Edge.[4] Joyce was savvy enough to begin his report by invoking the new language of motor racing, dropping the terms "chauffeur" and "auto," and directing his report of the conversation—despite the diversions into the translation problems attendant upon the equivalencies of kilometers and miles—to the figure of Edge (*CW* 108). The mention of Edge reduces Fournier to silence, either out of competitive anxiety or scorn for the manner of the Englishman's previous victory (owed to massive breakdowns by his competitors in the Paris to Innsbruck race in 1902).

Joyce's arrogance can scarcely conceal the pretence of awe at the horsepower and speeds of which Fournier speaks with such familiarity. Casually mentioning machines in the range of sixty to eighty horsepower, Fournier tells him that his car can be expected to travel at between sixty and eighty-six miles per hour. Garnering these lines of "hype," Joyce quickly steers the conversation to the less reassuring topic of the dubious capacity of Irish roads to accommodate such hot speeds. It is clear from this interview that Joyce was never taken with automobilism or car racing: he is peevish, begrudging, and even insulting to the Frenchman (asking him whether or not he is driving a Mercedes).[5]

In any event, between the April interview and the July race, Fournier was replaced on the French team. For the French automobile industry, which had 180,000 employees at the time, and was turning out 12,000 cars per annum, there was much at stake in the 1903 race (Montagu, 61). Thus, when the Paris-Madrid race (May 1903), anticipated by Joyce and Fournier in the interview (*CW* 107), turned into a debacle, the French industrialists grew alarmed about the impact of a loss in Ireland in July. This infamous May race raised the question of safety to a high pitch. Of the 225 starters in Paris, only 100 reached Bordeaux, with numerous accidents and some fatalities en route, so that the French authorities terminated it there and then. None of the French drivers got that far, although Fernand Gabriel was declared the winner, which forced the racing establishment to substitute Gabriel for Fournier. Another embarrassment would boost the German Mercedes above the French Panhard and Mors (Montagu, 76).

To ensure spectator safety and prevent a possible ban on all racing, the organizers agreed to confine the race to a closed circuit, and the cars were required to make periodic stops and obey the speed limits in the various towns through which the course passed. The race was conducted in the manner of "time trials" rather than as a grand prix event. Although the eventual winner, Camille Jenatzy, averaged 49.2 mph, the five finishers could be viewed careering along the roads at the impressive speeds claimed by Fournier, Jenatzy doing 90 mph downhill (*London Times,* July 4, 1903, 3).

Although Stanislaus Joyce is more severe in his judgment, the brothers were in agreement in assigning the designation "commonplace" to the pastimes of their less gifted acquaintances (*CDD* 55 passim). A recurrent theme in Stanislaus's diary is his condescension to sportsmen. In the entry for October 2, 1904, for example, he writes derisively of a scene at Jones's Road (now Croke Park) in which a number of young men were engaged in competitive cycling. These fellows, he concludes, have minds that are "brutal and low" (*CDD* 107). James is more indulgent here (as on all subjects), borne out by the humorous handling of sports in *Ulysses*—cycling, cricket, bowls, and especially horse racing—each of which signifies in its own relatively trivial way that serious moral calculations are at the center of the novel: the tonal dissonance between the chorus of received ideas and the quiet vitality of "the silent member." We get a crude preview of this in Joyce's report on Fournier, when he expresses his disdain for the ostentatious bourgeoisie represented by this ill-mannered lout who kept his visitor waiting hours: "people of leisure" indeed!

Even if its circumstances were less irritating, the gaunt, underfed, and penniless Joyce would not have struck it off with this swarthy manager of a bustling midcity establishment.[6] He therefore adopted a careless and arrogant attitude toward his subject (Ward, 31), describing Fournier as slow-witted, monosyllabic, and self-absorbed. The editors at the *Irish Times* must, therefore, have received Joyce's report with mixed feelings, since they printed a leader the same day that observed: "[t]he race is now one of the chief topics of conversation in Dublin. There is not a dissentient voice" (cited by Lynch, *Triumph*, 40). Joyce's supercilious and reactionary attitude in this "ironically plain" interview (*CW* 106) seems to arise from his typical stance of intellectual superiority. When Joyce came to write his story some sixteen months later, it reversed this stance into Jimmy's "confused murmur of compliment" (*D* 44.19–20) to the anonymous French driver. More substantial is his conversion of the trope of anticlimax upon which the interview concludes (Fournier's remark on the unreliability of automobiles) into the presiding rhetorical trope of "After the Race." And most significantly, as we shall see, in his story, Joyce transforms his original reactive peevishness into a cunning critique of the Gordon Bennett Cup Race from the perspective of "advanced nationalism."

Joycean Intervention

Joyce's coincidental temporary residence close to the center of this new industry in the winter of 1902 afforded him the opportunity to engage in commercial promotion. Readers of the *Irish Times*—landlords, industrial managers, the Anglo-Irish professional class—constituted the potential market for automobiles in Ireland. Members of this colonial class were the supporters and sponsors of the Gordon Bennett Cup Race, identifying with the British racing team. Popular sentiment (among pedestrians and mere cyclists), for unrelated historical reasons, favored their historical enemy, the French.

The staging of the Gordon Bennett Cup Race in Ireland was followed, whether consequentially or not, by a boost in Irish sales. Whereas on April 1, 1904, only fifty-eight motorcars were registered in the city of Dublin, by September 1905 there were 138 private and nine commercial vehicles registered. With the subsequent reduction of prices forced by American competition, by 1912 the £100 car was on the market, so that by June 1915 over 140 cars were being registered every quarter in the city to add to the 1,500 already in the hands of Dublin residents (O'Brien, 64). As Jimmy's father predicted in 1903, the Irish automobile business was a good investment.

Joyce was at the time personally acquainted with Oliver St. John Gogarty who was among the premier bicyclists in Ireland and subsequently, as a young physician, among the first to acquire a motorcar. Indeed, a factor in Joyce's antagonism to Gogarty would seem, from the evidence of "After the Race" (the only story to mention the vehicle) to be his former friend's enthusiasm for just the kind of expensive dash signified by the automobile. In this respect, Joyce was prophetically correct: in 1907 Gogarty purchased an expensive motorcar: an Argyll. He subsequently switched to a Daimler, in 1912 a Rolls Royce (Ulick O'Connor, 108), and, later, a Mercedes Benz (Gogarty, *Poems and Plays*, 654). Between 1911 and 1914, Gogarty had developed a taste for fast cars, driving the Marquess Conyngham around Ireland at "suicidal speeds" (Ulick O'Connor, 123).

This historical placement of the Fournier interview and "After the Race" shows that these texts were written before Fordism revolutionized the industry, turning a rich man's toy into a virtual civil right. At the time of this interview, the average family income in Dublin was only 22 shillings per week (O'Brien, 167). Before the Model T, cars cost between £200 and £2,500. Thus they were no more than the playthings of the Anglo-Irish establishment, of the butcher-turned-capitalist William Field, or of Oliver St. John Gogarty, MD, and their imaginary counterparts, the Doyles. By 1916, as an established ear, nose, and throat surgeon, Gogarty was able to demand a hundred guineas for an operation, whereas Joyce, with *Dubliners* and *A Portrait* in print, was still scrabbling for students in Trieste.

This historicization shows, further, that Joyce seemed to realize, but disdain, the capitalist wisdom in the investment in the automobile industry: there was, indeed, serious money to be made from cars in Ireland, as elsewhere in Europe and America at the time. Arthur Griffith's and Joyce's articulation of an anticolonial political critique of the Gordon Bennett Cup Race was, nonetheless, an early step in that direction.

It also shows that the rivalry between France, Britain, and Germany (with the United States in the wings) was more immediate and particular than their broad competition on the high seas and in the rush to control African colonies. Centered on the drive to open up the market for private automobiles, it was to become a major global industry during the new century. Multinational automobile logos would soon replace national flags in the movement to capitalist colonialism. Griffith's and Joyce's attitude toward this new development is protectionist and reactionary. "After the Race" is an expression of the step beyond mere pique: the self-reliance promoted by Griffith's Sinn Féin.

The Road Ahead

During the spring of 1903, the daily newspapers reported the continuing guerilla war in the distant Philippines, the massacre of Jews in Kishinev, Russia, and closer to home, the deaths of twenty workers in an explosion at the Woolwich Arsenal. Pope Leo XIII, the longest-reigning Roman pontiff in history, was dying, as was Paul Gauguin (aged fifty-four). Jack London's *The Call of the Wild* was the literary sensation of the spring, while in another spirit, the Irish National Theatre Society was rehearsing Yeats's *The Shadowy Waters*. The communications age was marked by the appearance of the first outdoor telephone kiosk in London, while in America the indefatigable Wright brothers filed a patent for an airplane based on a glider. Ireland was recovering from the effects of February's

Big Wind that brought down one-third of the trees in the entire country, including many ancient oaks in Dublin's Phoenix Park.

The city that Joyce called home had a garrison of 30,000 troops and 2,000 prostitutes (O'Brien, table 22). It had some of the worst tenements in Europe and the highest rate of tuberculosis per thousand of population of any city on the Continent. An English visitor reported of Dubliners:

> they were quite unlike any other English-speaking people with whom I had ever come across (*sic.*). And they appeared altogether lacking in uniformity, tending to go to extremes of ugliness or beauty. Nowhere else had I seen so many giants, so many perfectly formed men and women, and at the same time so many diseased, debased, misshapen, misbegotten or crippled human beings. (cited by Brady and Simms, 237)

Rural Ireland still bore the scars of the Famine, within living memory of half of the population, and every village saw its young—thirty to fifty thousand per annum—disappear overseas, to Britain, Argentina, and the United States. Those who stayed at home rested their hopes on the promise of land reform and Home Rule. Yet this deeply depressed colonial outpost close to the heart of the Empire was making preparations to entertain a lavish international sports event. World Fairs, international festivals, and industrial exhibitions were offering better prospects for international trade, culture, industry, and political relations. The 1900 Olympics in Paris had been a great success (but by the time Joyce wrote "After the Race," the St. Louis Olympics—August 29 to September 3, 1904—had not).

Even as international political tensions between Germany and France, and to some extent between Russia and Britain and Russia and Japan, were mounting—the latter led to the Russo-Japanese war that broke out a year later—the strains that eventually led to World War I were being played out through the formation of various alliances and the sparring known as the "Great Game." The highlight of the summer season in Dublin's parks and gardens was the annual Mirus Bazaar. The spring saw a concerted advertising campaign—featuring a giant balloon floating over the city—for the upcoming major outdoor events of the summer: King Edward's birthday pageant in the Phoenix Park (late June), the Gordon Bennett Cup Race and its motoring sequels (July 2–16), and the king's visit (July 19–27). The birthday pageant was, in any event, rained out (a perennial hazard). These events did not loom even small in the minds of the vast majority of the Irish people: they received scant notice in the nationalist or provincial papers. The pages of the *United Irishman* and other nationalist organs were full of notices of *feiseanna* [festivals], *aeriochtanna* [entertainments], and intercounty football and hurling matches.

Because of Edge's victory in the 1902 Gordon Bennett Cup Race, it fell to the United Kingdom to host its successor. However, England had developed canals and railways at the expense of roads, which featured none of the long stretches available on the Continent. Public concern about road safety had pressed the authorities to impose firm speed limits. There were no racetracks and thus the organizers moved the event to Ireland, where there was less public concern about such matters (Lynch, *Triumph*, 38–39). The speed limit of 12 mph was strictly enforced throughout the United Kingdom, so an Act of Parliament was required before the Gordon Bennett Cup event could be staged on Irish roads. The Honorable John Scott Montagu drafted the Light Locomotives (Ireland) Act, 1903, which exempted cars from any statutory speed limits on the day of the race. The members of the Automobile Club of Great Britain and Ireland (ACGBI)—all gentlemen of business and leisure—organized a full-scale public relations effort: lobbying their MPs and peers, and writing to each of Ireland's county and district councils, city mayors, railway companies (41!), hotels (450), and every national and regional newspaper (300). The thrust of the club's letter was that hosting the race would heighten public awareness of road safety and benefit the Irish economy by at least £20,000 (Montagu, 63).

In any event, both the Irish Party and the Northern Unionists—led respectively by John Redmond, Tim Healy, and Sir Edward Carson—supported the legislation. Of this unusual cooperation, the hardcore unionist newspaper *Northern Whig* commented: "We see a wonderful blending of the Orange and Green" (cited by Lynch, *Triumph*, 39). The bill passed and received Royal Assent on March 27, within a week of its first reading. Given this go-ahead, the organizers set about not only the hosting of the actual race itself, but also an Irish Fortnight (July 1–15)—including speed trials in the Phoenix Park, in counties Cork, Kerry, and Down, an automobile exhibition at Earlsfort Terrace ice rink, and the world's first powerboat race in Cork (*Irish Times*, July 1, 1903, 2; Montagu, 65).

The organizers had at their disposal a road system that, by European standards, was surprisingly advanced. Early in the nineteenth century,

Richard Lovell Edgeworth had improved Irish road surfacing, hastening the transportation revolution. The Board of Works had followed his lead, and, in a historical irony, the onset of the Famine in the 1840s and its Relief building programs bequeathed a sound road system to Edwardian Ireland (Lynch, *Triumph*, 37).

Claude Johnson, secretary of the Automobile Club of Great Britain and Ireland, along with Richard Mecredy, proprietor of the *Irish Motor News*, and Polish Count Eliot Zborowski, selected and designed the route. The course was centered on the town of Athy, and traversed the Leinster counties Kildare, Carlow, and Laois, passing through six towns: Old Kilcullen, Kilcullen, Monasterevan, Stradbally, Athy, and Carlow. It was over a closed circuit (a figure eight), composed of seven laps, and traveling a total distance of 327.5 miles. More than two thousand policemen were drafted in to marshal the racecourse: posted at crossings, they closed off the roads dedicated to the race, and saw to it that farm animals and domestic fowl were kept off. Passing through towns, the cars had to slow down, traveling behind bicycles to comply with the 12 mph speed limit.

Boosters and Skeptics

Irish press reaction to the approaching automobile age and the announcement that Ireland would host the 1903 Gordon Bennett Cup Race was, from the beginning, mixed. When the inaugural Royal Irish Automobile Club's 1,000-mile Tour of Ireland was staged in 1901, the *Freeman's Journal* crowed: the automobile was "a triumph of modern evolution—the Twelfth Centaur" (cited by Lynch, *Triumph*, 26). Long before the race was approved, *An Claidheamh Soluis* [*The Sword of Light*], organ of the Gaelic League, ran a brief editorial (4: 845, February 28, 1903)—in Irish—a mixture of awe, misinformation, and bemusement about this *cóiste-gan-ceann* [headless coach]. It concluded: "*Gluaiseann na mótuir so i bhfad níos luaithe ná traen is ná an ghaoth*" [These cars travel much faster than a train, or, indeed, the wind]. Under its new editor, Patrick Pearse, this weekly took a less indulgent attitude toward the race.

Announcing the Royal Assent, the British *Automotor Journal* trumpeted: "The Irish love a race," adding that the event would stimulate the Irish tourist trade and boost the country's failing economy (Montagu, 60). The first Irish public organ to promote the Gordon Bennett Cup Race was the *Irish Times*. All the major national newspapers—nationalist and unionist alike—fell in line and poured fulsome endorsement on the race. The *Freeman's Journal,* unofficial organ of the Irish Party, editorialized that "[i]n Ireland there is not now, nor never was, the slightest whisper of disapproval of the race" (cited by Lynch, *Triumph,* 50). Dublin's *Motor News* (owned by Mecredy, one of its main sponsors) and the *Daily Mail* (owned by the Dublin-born tycoon Alfred Harmsworth) promoted the event in every issue. Excitement at the new competition stirred sportsmen's blood. The prospect of vehicles hurtling along at 70 mph moved the *Sporting and Dramatic News* to editorialize that it "made the pulses glow, the heartbeats quicken, the breath stand still" (ibid., 155). The nationalist *Evening Herald* (July 1, 1903) rhapsodized that "Ireland . . . is today center of a cosmopolitan interest. It is the playground for the great international game which the Twentieth Century has made its own" (ibid., 17).

Opposition came from cranks, Luddites, and the ancestors of today's Greens for whom "automobilism" was a bad word. An association of antimotorists in Paris cabled King Edward VII, begging him to use his influence to stop the race (Montagu, 76). His Majesty, "a royal automobilist," declined (figure 2.1). A Scottish paper complained that "It necessitates a great waste of petrol," while one Cathcart Watson (MP for Orkney and Shetland) complained in June 1903: "A few people claim the right to drive the public off the roads. Harmless men, women, and children, dogs and cattle, have all got to fly for their lives at the bidding of these slaughtering, stinking engines of iniquity" (cited by Montagu, 59).

Outdoorsmen were outraged. "Dublin is a petrol-smelling Saturnalia!" wrote the *Field.* Even partisans of motorized transport were defensive: *Autocar* editorialized that "they were one and all monstrosities from the average user's point of view" (cited by Montagu, 86). A Limerick magistrate with nativist sympathies testily insisted, "The autocars are the greatest curse Ireland has known since the first batch of English arrived!" (Lynch, *Triumph,* 19). Political "irreconcilables" were even less amicable. The *Irish People* (edited by William O'Brien) protested, "From the outset, we had no love whatever for the project and these death-dealing machines and their drivers, and the hordes of interested speculators and morbid sightseers who follow in their train to this country" (ibid., 47). D. P. Moran's protectionist *Leader* attacked the motor race as a drain on the Irish economy, since there was no Irish manufacturing plant (July 4).

Thus, the *New York Times,* while admitting to some local opposition, was less than candid in reporting that Irish "bewilderment" at the event

Figure 2.1. King Edward VII, a royal automobilist, ca. May 19, 1902. Photograph courtesy of Prints and Photographs Division, Library of Congress.

arose primarily from irritation at the "dislocation of the regular order of things" (July 4, 1903, 3). Comparing the excitement about the city to that generated by the annual August Horse Show, one of the gala events in the Anglo-Irish calendar, the *Irish Times* prophetically rhapsodized that "today the motor-car took the place of the horse." "The sound of the horn is heard in all parts of the city and suburbs," it went on, reporting that "cars fill the streets, and a half-dozen of them are drawn up outside every reputable hotel" (June 30, 12).

It was not lost on nationalist sensitivities like those of the editors of the *Irish People* that the course chosen for this race passed through some of the territory associated with the 1798 Insurrection. The first of the four phases of this insurrection took place in counties Meath, Dublin, Kildare, and Carlow during the week of May 23–30. This popular rebellion against the Anglo-Irish, Protestant, and English colonial landowning class and the garrison that protected their interests had been widely commemorated throughout the country during its centennial, especially in the counties of South Leinster. The revival of revolutionary sentiment that accompanied its centennial celebrations was worrisome to the owners of colonial estates and the managers of businesses concerned about their workers' political reliability. It therefore accorded with the political interest of the ruling elites to make a display of their power, wealth, and status to sponsor an international event like the Gordon Bennett Cup Race even as the Wyndham Act that spelled the end of their power was passing into law. So although much of the press coverage was favorable to, if not enthusiastic about, the race, a survey of newspaper comment from the period argues that this did not typify public sentiment.

A salient example points up the issue. The racecourse passed sites more ancient and historically resonant than the grounds through which the Boys of Wexford and Kildare assaulted the redcoats. It passed the Rock of Dunamase—Fort of the Plains—seat of the O Moores until Cromwell's time. It also passed Kilcullen on the Liffey, with its ninth-century remains, and the monastic ruins of Moone with its famous high cross. The *New Ireland Review* (the publication of the staff of the National University, edited by Fr. Peter Finley, SJ) ran an article in July 1903, "The Motor Cup Course," by one Helen Weldon mounting a sentimental-antiquarian criticism of the race bemoaning the insult to these sacred places. She imagines the dead saints of Leinster (Brigid and Moling), its kings, and heroes "shaking their heads [at] the sight of the pantings and puffings, and the furious zeal of the Daimlers, the Wintons, the Panhards and the De Dions, the monsters which have taken the place of the barouches and the coupés" (284). Heavily larded with toponymical annotation, Naas [fair/meeting place], Kilcullen [Church of the Holly], Timolin [House of Moling], it contrasts Ireland's saintly and scholarly past with the present thoughtless excitement. The ancient virtues of patience, hospitality, decent poverty, and good storytelling are ousted by the modern vices of greed and heartless manipulation—"hype," false friendship, greed—masked under the slogan "the spirit of progress": "the triumph of human ingenuity... making time and space subservient to the needs and enrichment of human nature" (279-80). On the benign side, Weldon concludes that this, too, shall pass, like all else, into the repository of folklore.

Avant La Course

The 1903 Gordon Bennett Cup Race could be described as Ireland's first venture into "high-end tourism." It attracted the sporting aristocrats of Europe, the top drivers representing France, Germany, and Great Britain, along with the first American team to make the transatlantic voyage. It brought thousands of visitors, some of them—as in Joyce's story—driving their own cars. The accompanying extravaganza generated what we would today call "a media frenzy." The baroque trophy—depicting Progress bearing a torch—was on display in West's shop window at 18/19 College Green (Lynch, *Triumph*, 79), and by midsummer the name "Gordon Bennett" passed into popular parlance: in Kildare Town, two guest houses were renamed "Gordon House" and "Bennett House." The Irish "hospitality industry" was born.

The *Pall Mall Gazette* (no friend of motor racing) editorialized that "our sister island is getting such a grand crowd of tourists, as rarely falls to her lot save on occasions of a Royal visit. Whoever loses the race, Ireland will, at any rate, be the winner!" (cited by Lynch, *Triumph*, 40). As the day of the race approached, the supply of hotel rooms quickly ran out. Ireland was flooded with cars: 1,500 in all arrived via the ports of Larne, Waterford, and the Holyhead route (400 passing through Dublin during the week before the race). Dublin's premier hotels were booked by British and European fans: the Scottish Automobile Club members filled the Gresham, while the Shelbourne Hotel was headquarters for the Automobile Club of Great Britain, and (as Joyce's story implies) members of the French automobile clubs (ibid., 79). This hotel was—and remains—Dublin's most prestigious (by contrast, for instance, with the unfashionable and Catholic Finn's Hotel, two blocks away, which employed Nora Barnacle). In 1903 it catered to Dublin's most discriminating visitors, and was staffed by French and German waiters.[7]

Hotelkeepers knew that they were on to a good thing. Roomkeepers and restauranteurs exploited the visitors so that there were many reports of price gouging: £6 for one night in a small room (Montagu, 66). One American, being asked for £7 for such accommodation, protested, "I guess you're making a mistake, my friend. I have more money on me than that!" (cited by Lynch, *Triumph*, 67). By such means was born the "Gordon Bennett!"—an expression of disgust and wonder at being bilked.[8]

Thousands of ordinary citizens lined the streets to see the French team with their fleet of cars disembark at Alexandria Dock (Lynch, *Triumph*, 64). They thrilled to see their favorites with their blue-bloused mechanics and the decks of the three-master, the *Ferdinand de Lesseps*, crammed with cars and spare parts. This chartered boat carried 145 passengers including the leading manufacturers and celebrities, Emile Mors, tire maker André Michelin, and Baron Henri de Rothschild. They received an official welcome: "Three cheers for the first French racers to land on Irish soil!" The French handed out cigarettes and "French pennies" to the children (ibid., 65), and a procession of streamlined Mors cars roared off through the city, their drivers accoutered in grim goggles and billowing dusters. Within hours, French ladies of fashion were parading around the Dublin streets and parks. The newspapers exploited the popular predisposition to romanticize *la relation Française*, whether in anticipation of a French victory, inherited political sentiment, or in admiration of Gallic fashion, they touted the gallant style and sporting bravura of the French team over the gritty Germans and British.

To potential customers the competition was among manufacturers Mors, Panhard, Winton, Napier, and Mercedes. Nonetheless, officially it was between four nations, each represented by three cars: white for Germany, red for the United States, blue for France, and dark green for the United Kingdom (the British "racing green"). Participation in this annual race required that the cars (two-seaters, accommodating driver and mechanic) be manufactured down to the last washer in their respective nation. The drivers in 1903 came from six different nations. The French entry included English and a Belgian-born driver, the U.S. team leader was Scottish, the English favorite was an Australian, and none of the German drivers was a national. The leading German driver and winner was, of course, Camille Jenatzy, a Hungarian-born Belgian (Lynch, *Triumph*, 57). All drivers were professionals and hailed from the ruling class of barons and landowners: *Hochwohlgeboren*. Thus, the language of today's famous instruction, "Gentlemen, start your engines," reveals the aristocratic origins of Grand Prix racing.

These factors help explain the sarcasm of the language in which Joyce's narrator describes the popular acclaim for this exhibition of style, wealth, and status: "the cheer of the gratefully oppressed" (*D* 42.7–8).[9] This sarcasm embraces several issues for which the Irish poor might have been grateful: the benign colonial authorities conceded that Saint Patrick's Day might be celebrated publicly as a national holiday and Dublin Corporation began the bilingual posting of Dublin's street names,[10] and after decades of deadly struggle throughout the country, the Wyndham Act was finally on its way through Parliament. Arthur Griffith's *United Irishman* hammered away on the themes of the illegitimacy of the landlords' claims to property rights, of Westminster to govern Ireland, of the theft of the national patrimony, and of discrimination against Irish Catholics in commercial life.[11] Against these combined forces, he advocated the rejuvenation of native industries and the inculcation of an Ireland of the mind, a nation modeled on Ireland's Celtic Christian Age theorized by Eoin Mac Néill.

The most colorful figure in the race was Jenatzy. He was born to an immigrant Hungarian family who founded Belgium's first rubber factory. A civil engineer, he was the first man to record a speed of over 100 mph, in his racing car, *La Jamais Contente*. The short, leanly built, and red-bearded Jenatzy was a gentleman off the track and a devil on it. He wore light waterproof clothes that billowed behind him and sometimes enveloped his head, giving him, according to the *Morning Post*, "the impression of a satyr." The press corps was so entranced by his surrounding aura that the writer from *Automobile Club Journal* recorded his first roaring into the Athy control as an "avalanche of tremendous reports from the engine, great flames shooting out of the exhaust, suggesting a condensed edition of *The Inferno*" (cited by Montagu, 84). His excitable nature ensured that he quickly became a favorite of Irish race spectators. They were to give him a rousing welcome and a new title, the "Red Devil" (Lynch, *Triumph*, 63) (figure 2.2).

Jenatzy competed the next year for the host Germany (*U* 6.370). He was the popular favorite, as the reference to him in "Oxen of the Sun" reads: "O, get, rev on a gradient one in nine. Live axle drives are souped. Lay you two to one Jenatzy licks him ruddy well hollow" (*U* 14.1558–60). In the event he did not. For our present purposes, however, it is sufficient to observe that glinting amidst this swirl of engineering jargon and Cockney argot—"get rev . . . ruddy well"—are fragments of the name the Irish public had given him in 1903. Similarly, echoing through the cacophony describing the card game in "After the Race," the toasts to the Queens of Hearts and Diamonds, the "flashing" wit, and Villona's piano, we can now discern, as the words "winning," "losing," "win," "lose," and "devils of fellows" (*D* 48.11–26), sound through Jimmy Doyle's dazed inner ear,

Figure 2.2. Camille Jenatzy as the Red Devil. Bosch Magneto advertisement, 1913.

the reverberation of the name by which the day's winner was popularly known, the same "Red Devil."

Before daybreak on July 2, the preparations began. The cars were all in position by 6 a.m., and the first of the twelve (driven by Edge) roared into action precisely at 7 a.m. His eleven competitors took off after him at seven-minute intervals. The course had been well chosen and carefully prepared. The countryside had a relatively low population, was geographically flat, and was readily accessible from Dublin by rail and road. The hedges had been trimmed and the road surfaces steamrolled and laid with Westrumite to control dust (Montagu, 61, 75). Foreign drivers supporting their teams were warned to keep to the left and obey the speed limits. Livestock was banished from the roads, and farmers were compensated for lost fowl. The security precautions paid off: the single fatality, the newspapers reported, was a small boy (85).

The competitors overcame rainstorms and crashes, mud, spills, and overheated engines. Two of the German cars dropped out with broken axles; Edge's tires had failed him so that he had to make several costly changes. Just after 7 p.m., the Race Over card was displayed. Due to the complexities of timing, the staggered starts of the competing vehicles, and the number of objections lodged by several competitors, the organizing committee was obliged to invest several hours of calculation before declaring the official results. It was not until the next morning, July 3, that the final placings were officially announced (*London Times*, July 4, 8). In declaring the results—that the winning car was German and the French were second and third, Joyce's narrator is both inaccurate and premature. The French were "virtual victors" (*D* 42.10) because their three cars finished second, third, and fourth, which earned them the team prize, the Montagu Trophy. This report additionally stretches the historical record in that none of the placings nor the "winning German car" were yet known to anyone as the spectators returned to their Dublin hotels on the evening of the actual race.[12] The "double round of welcome" and "cheer" accorded the French vehicles (*D* 42.13–14, 8) is not of congratulation for their success in the race, as the narrator implies, but from political sympathies originating in French support for the United Irishmen, a theme of the previous five years' centennial commemorations.

Jenatzy covered the course in his Mercedes Simplex in six hours and thirty-nine minutes (Montagu, 82–83). He was followed by the three Frenchmen in two Panhards and a Mors, and then by Edge in his Napier. Only five finished (Lynch tabulates the results [*Triumph*, 171]). None of the American entrants survived past the fifth lap, and two of the British vehicles got no further than the first, Charles Jarrott's Napier ending up in a ditch to be looted by onlookers.

Jenatzy was the first home, confirmed race winner ahead of the three blue cars driven by Rene de Knyff, Henry Farman, Fernand Gabriel, and the green car driven by the fatigued Edge (who was later disqualified). It came down, in the finish, to a competition between Jenatzy and the French: as one journalist summarized it, "The Franco-German war is on again!" (Lynch, *Triumph*, 118). The Red Devil—skidding into bends and accelerating out of them—had lived up to his fearsome reputation. One journalist reported his triumph colorfully: "There is some strange sympathetic likeness between the man and his car. As the Mercedes stands there, its mighty engine panting and straining impotently, while a blue flame flashes from its exhaust, it seems a veritable extract from hell. And Jenatzy fits the Mercedes . . . his red moustache and little red beard add the necessary finishing touch to a figure that seems to be the incarnation of the delirium of speed" (ibid., 131–32).[13]

The Germans celebrated the Mercedes victory, the French their cars. "The nation that wins the Gordon Bennett prize will be the ruler of the international market" crowed the *Allgemeine Automobil-Zeitung*. The German win was the first major international victory for Mercedes and helped boost its sales (Montagu, 86): it cost the Michelin Company alone £350,000–400,000 worth of business per annum in the following years (61). At a special Shelbourne Hotel dinner for the drivers, the French paid generous tribute to the organizers. The Baron de Caters toasted their hosts: "I did not expect such a sporting welcome."

The next day—after a night of celebrations—there was an exhibition of racing and touring cars at Earlsfort Terrace ice rink. To the cheers of the excited onlookers, Jenatzy arrived in the afternoon, driving around Saint Stephen's Green to the Shelbourne. The Phoenix Park speed trial the next day was to become the venue of "motor racing's oldest continuously used road circuit" and of the Irish Grand Prix and Tourist Trophy races (Lynch, *Triumph*, 14). To underline the superior reliability of their vehicles vindicated by their team victory, and after all the auxiliary events, the French drove in a caravan from LeHavre to Paris (ibid.). For his successful management of the entire Irish Fortnight, the Irish Automobile Club president, Horace Plunkett, was subsequently knighted by King Edward VII. This award became a regular object of Arthur Griffith's jibes in the *United Irishman*.

In his comprehensive account of the Gordon Bennett Cup Race, *The Triumph of the Red Devil*, Brendan Lynch concludes that the event "marked an emphatic watershed between Victorian pace and ideas and the brave new world of technology" (17). It should be sufficiently clear that the euphoria celebrated by Lynch (in a book sponsored by the Irish automobile industry) was not shared by radical Irish nationalist opinion, or by James Joyce.

The race did a great deal toward popularizing the motorcar in Ireland (Montagu, 86). The Irish Free State hosted the International Motor Race or Grand Prix in the Phoenix Park in the 1920s. By then everyone accepted the valuable publicity it afforded the new nation. All the major government ministers and over 100,000 people assembled to watch the race in 1928. The victorious Russian, Boris Ivanowski, received the Phoenix Trophy from President W. T. Cosgrave (Cronin, 53–54). A century later, when 90 percent of Irish households own at least one automobile, when the 1903 Gordon Bennett Cup is annually commemorated by an automobile rally, when the presence of multinationals is taken for granted, and Ireland's latter-day prosperity is based on the repudiation of many of Griffith's political and economic values, James Joyce's intervention in the course of Ireland's modernization seems singularly anachronistic.

"solid instincts"

Many readers suspect that Joyce's Jimmy Doyle is cheated by Routh and the Continentals of his money, even of his patrimony.[14] The implication is that the business culture of which they are the representatives does not arrest them in their pursuit of immediate financial advantage over a drunken client, even at the risk of alienating a potential customer. If this reading is sound, it reflects Joyce's anxieties at the time that he wrote the story—late September/early October 1904—as he was preparing to leave for the Continent with Nora. With some trepidation, he conceded to send two guineas to a certain Miss E. Gilford of Market Rasen, Lincs., who claimed to be an agent for the Berlitz schools in German- and French-speaking Europe. His suspicions—which he tried to allay by a telegram to the Market Rasen police—turned out to be correct. As he soon discovered, either she or he was deceived, for when he arrived in Zurich, the school there knew nothing of the arrangements for which Joyce had paid (see *Letters* II: 54–58, 67, and *JJII* 176, 184–85).

Now, the external evidence indicates that Joyce wrote this story sometime between his exit from the Martello tower (September 15, 1904) and October 3 (*Letters* II: 50), submitting it to the *Irish Homestead* the next day (59) just before his departure with Nora on October 8. The story that he was writing during these weeks could reasonably be expected, therefore, to register both his personal aspirations and anxieties. "After the Race" implies Joyce's own exhilaration at the prospect of a new life on the Continent and also his apprehensions about what lay ahead. Aware of his own naiveté, and perhaps foolhardiness, in undertaking this venture, it betrays some of the trepidation that he must have felt about this numinous departure. We can discern, for example, in Jimmy's impressing his parents with "the names of great foreign cities" (*D* 45.28–29) a reverberation of the names of the cities that were the sites of the various Berlitz schools in France, Germany, and Switzerland about which he was in correspondence with Miss Gilford. Much as "Eveline," its immediate predecessor reflects Nora's anxieties about her elopement with Joyce, "After the Race" similarly reflects his apprehensions—justified, as it later turned out—about entrusting his future to Continentals and their presumed English agent.

Like the fictional Jimmy, Joyce was making a risky investment. But unlike Jimmy, Joyce had no inheritance to declare but his genius. Since his temporary job at the Clifton House School, Dalkey, had ended in July (Costello, 223), Joyce had to live by his wits. Richard Ellmann's account of his financial schemes between then and his eventual departure reads like the diary of a confidence man: pawning books, searching for investors and patrons, performing and "borrowing," peddling his translation of Gerhart Hauptmann's play, *Vor Sonnenaufgang* [*Before Sunrise*] and writing the three *Irish Homestead* stories (*JJII* 162–65). However he might disdain the spiritual damage incurred by its acquisition, money was constantly on his mind.

As the story of how the Doyles were the victims of Mammon gestated in his imagination, he was making his last begging rounds upon his Dublin acquaintances. He attempted to extract £5 from Lady Gregory, and smaller amounts from James Cousins, Padraic Colum, AE, Fred Ryan, and Francis Skeffington, and clothes and supplies from James Starkey (*JJII* 178–79). He even risked the suspicion of Nora Barnacle in enquiring about her possible wealth (see letter of September 19, *Letters* II: 55). Joyce betrays his haughty ingratitude toward such benefactors in giving the name of a generous Parisian host and benefactor, Dr. Joseph Rivière, to his personification of Mammon (see *Letters* II: 18n6; *JJII* 112, 183–84).

Faced with the need to maintain his record with a publisher who paid, and to persuade his would-be patrons that he was willing to engage in self-help, he developed his third contribution to the *Irish Homesetead*. Thus, as he pleaded with AE for an advance, he told him that "I gave Mr. Norman my third story 'After the Race' today and I think he will pay me for it tomorrow" (*Letters* II: 59, October 4).[15]

That he was willing to make an effort to meet the *Irish Homestead* readers' expectations is attested by a curious precedent that until recently has been overlooked by students of Joyce's literary beginnings. When AE made the famous offer to entertain submissions from Joyce (ca. July 2, *Letters* II: 43), he had enclosed a sample story that apparently met those expectations. That story was a patently amateur effort, entitled "The Old Watchman" (*Irish Homestead*, July 2, 1903). Entirely forgettable in subject and technique, Berkeley Campbell's story concerns the testimony of an old man about his wasted life. The moral lesson impresses the young boy narrator who infers that the costs of youthful indiscretions are terrifying and incalculable.

As Hans Walter Gabler has noted, Joyce took some cues from this example in imagining the scenario and some of the elements in "The Sisters" (xv–xvi). A couple more made their way into "Eveline." That Joyce still bore this humble example in mind even in late September when thinking of earning his third guinea from A. E. Norman is attested by a brief passage in that story. The old man tells of the failure of his life.

> My father was Dean of St. Patrick's. . . . I was his second son, and was to have gone through Trinity to take my degree and then study for the Bar, but I never got further than my "Little Go," although I was four years in college. I was a bad boy—I know it now—and a great anxiety to my poor old father. . . . I only stayed up to the small hours of the morning drinking and gambling, and losing more money than I could ever hope to pay back. To make a long story short, my father called me into his study one morning and told me he had heard of my doings, and spoke very wisely, and offered me a "start" if I would go to Canada and get away from my bad companions, for he saw I would do no good at home. (*Irish Homestead*, July 2, 1904, 556)

He rejects his father's offer, emigrates, and after many years roaming the world, returns to take whatever job Ireland could offer him. That was serving the Electric Tramway Company as a night watchman. The admission of the disappointment of his life is a salutary lesson to his young auditor. For all the moral and expressive lassitude of the story, it seems to have offered Joyce a useful figure, because he returns as Gumley and D. B. Murphy in the "Eumaeus" episode of *Ulysses,* and in his youthful phase as the Jimmy Doyle of "After the Race."

An earnest lesson in the youthful abuse of inherited social privilege and money, it evidently offered Joyce the opportunity to attach the regretful reminiscence to a story of mishandled opportunities. Joyce would have seen around him scores of fellow students whose drive and talent did not match the economic and social advantages they had over him. And his resentment shows in the portrait of Jimmy Doyle, a young man for whom success in life depends on a combination of networking (Ségouin, whom Jimmy had met at Cambridge, was "well worth knowing" [*D* 43.29–34]) and economics (Jimmy's "respect" for his father's values is attached to the gross image of the "pots of money" to be made in the motor business [*D* 45.3–6]). Although not endowed with the means to acquire it, Jimmy Doyle's vision of life hangs by the "cash nexus."

The artless Jimmy Doyle does not provoke Joyce's full powers of discernment. As social observation, the story is an exposé of the craven grubbing that passed for success among his peers. Stanislaus writes of a career-counseling session (two years before) between his brother and the well-meaning dean of studies at the Royal University. Father Darlington encouraged his young protégé to follow the example of a successful Dublin lawyer who had paid his own way through college by writing leading articles for two newspapers of opposite politics. Joyce replied: "I may not have that gentleman's talents" (*MBK* 188). Regarding the sale of such gifts to the nearest highest bidder, and confident in his own genius, he found in the figure of the spoiled mediocrity, Jimmy Doyle, an easy target. Even as a young man, Joyce did not envy the rich, nor was he deeply moved by appeals on behalf of the poor. His tastes—for opera and dining out—are those appropriate to a man of genius and but accidentally the pabulum of the wealthy. They have by inheritance what his genius needs: the leisure to read as he needed or pleased and write as he saw, without the shackles of ideological commitments. In the figures of the Doyles and their Continental counterparts he may have created an image of the fatuities of a popular culture driven by commercial interests. It is that, and more.

In his second and third sentences, the narrator appears to take an aggressive view of the contrast between the wealth and energy of the Continent and the poverty and passivity of the onlookers at Inchicore. So far as the burden of the subsequent action of the story is concerned, this is something of a misdirection. Whereas the poor do make a couple of subsequent appearances—as awed gazers on Dame Street (*D* 45.16–17) and as making way for the revelers in their evening clothes on Stephen's Green (*D* 46.31–32)—their relationship with Jimmy Doyle or his cohorts is not the subject of the story. The criticism it implies of the Doyles and their Continental friends is not that they are wealthy while their admirers are poor. The story is not born of resentment, envy, or of a desire for social justice. It is rather that as we come to know his mind, we learn that Jimmy Doyle has been raised to think that whatever his engagements, sports, recreation, friendship, education, politics, the marketing of meat or cars, the basis of all serious value is money.

While much of the action of the story is an exposé of the machinations of "conspicuous consumption," its dramatic and poetic design depends on the critical presence of Villona.[16] Whereas Jimmy thinks of his material poverty as "unfortunate" (D 44.2), the place and force in the story given him by the narrator establishes a different principle of opposition. A figure of meditation, judgment, and feeling, marked by detachment, self-containment, and silence, Villona exemplifies the pursuit, not of power or profit, but of that "pearl beyond price," beauty.

Several commentators (Bowen, "'After the Race'"; Somerville, "Money in *Dubliners*"; and Peake, *James Joyce*, 23–25) have made the simplistic summary that "After the Race" is a critique of materialism.[17] C. H. Peake falls into the misreading—based on one or two sentences taken in isolation—that it is concerned with the victimization of the poor by the rich (if it were, it would be a unique Joycean production), even as he concludes that "Jimmy is hamstrung by an inbred absorption in money" (25). He cites Zack Bowen's remark that the word "money" occurs nine times in a few paragraphs and that the story is peppered with related words, such as "rich," "wealth," "sum," et cetera (Bowen, 57–58). It would have been more remarkable in a story about the commercial class, were the word "money" not to appear. These critics overstate the obvious, and taking the story as an example of naturalist art, do not register its technical subtlety.

The word "money," for example, appears with two basic referents: as capital and as disposable cash. On the one hand, it refers to the wealth accumulated by Jimmy's father. The "money" he made (D 43.16, 18) turned him into a man of "substance" (D 44.32). He became "rich enough" (D 43.20) from the meat trade that he can entertain wider investment in the motor business. This "merchant prince" can invest in the business of the "lordly" automobile. Accounts of these activities must, therefore, employ words like "investment" (D 44.34, 45.5), "great sum" (D 44.23–24), and "the capital of the concern" (D 45.2–3). However formally or euphemistically the presiding ethos of these activities may be described—contracts are "secured" and profits are "fortunate" (D 43.19)—in the smoke-filled room where vital decisions are made, the language describing the object of these activities is blunter: of the "pots of money" (D 45.6) to be found. On the other hand, as the gambling scene dramatizes it, Jimmy loses "money" in its narrower and more immediate sense: the contents of his wallet. As the night progresses, he realizes that "he would lose" (D 48.21) not only his pocket money, but that much of his personal bank account would be "written away" (*D* 48.22) via promissory notes, figuratively "paper" (*D* 48.10) and "IOUs" (*D* 48.13).[18]

We are led to understand that just as Jimmy forfeits his disposable cash in the card games of the last scene, so will he lose his capital investment in the motor business of the first. Yet beneath this talk of "monies," we see but two (and sly) references to actual coins: in the reduction of Jimmy's "great sum" of sterling into the biblical "mite" (*D* 45.2) and in the characterization of Jimmy as "the inheritor of solid instincts" (*D* 44.26). While "mite" can refer to any small sum, it originally referred to a Flemish copper coin worth half a farthing (*OED*), and "a solid" is an obsolete English usage for a shilling (originating in the name of the Roman coin, the *solidus*, the weight of twelve silver pennies [*OED*]).

The second of these deserves special notice.

When we first read that "Their team [the French] had finished solidly" (*D* 42.10–11) we accept the journalistic cliché, even if it is a euphemism for defeat. Nonetheless, when we later read that Jimmy "was at heart the inheritor of solid instincts" (*D* 44.25–26) and recognize that it means that he has his eye on the profits to be made from the car business, we have reason to review the force of the second sentence. Just as cars are a business, the race is its advertisement. While ostensibly a compliment—his youthful shenanigans conceal Jimmy's sound character—the force of the word "inheritor," given what we already know about the narrator's estimation of his father, causes us to pause on the oxymoron, "solid instincts." Since the narrator's derision is directed at Jimmy's avarice, the ironical force of the etymological metalepsis on *solidus* hoves into view.

A corollary of the dimensional metaphoric contrasts between "mite" and "solid" is the double paradox of the "immense" but "very poor" Villona who plays the "villain" to these merchants of the "lordly" motor.[19] In what would become a Joycean trademark, the narrator's discretion in handling references to money is the surest sign of its pervasive presence.

The conspicuous material equivalents of invisible capital worth in the story are the high-end hotel, the accoutrements of the young men's evening dress, their cigars and cloaks, Farley's yacht, and especially the cars. It is under these auspices and his reputation as the owner of a chain of French hotels that Ségouin exudes an "unmistakable air of wealth" (*D* 45.7), inflating the image upon which investors' and consumers' confidence reposes. With barely concealed disdain, the narrator invokes the language of business: where "shops" become "motor establishment[s]" (*D* 43.5) and euphemisms like "capital of the concern" and "business matters" conceal the naked greed for "pots of money" (*D* 45.3–6), and a man once asking for public trust uses his position to garner government contracts (larger Dublin butchers styled themselves "victuallers and contractors" [see Jackson and McGinley, 36a]) to become "a merchant prince," and thinks of his role not as advocate but in terms of "control" (*D* 44.18) and "manage[ment]" (*D* 45.1). The narrative is flecked with such ironic borrowings and coinages: overt aspects of the satire on the paralytic effects of the worship of money. The technique of "After the Race" engages finer devices that announce the auspicious arrival of a superior craftsman.[20]

We have, for example, the moment when Jimmy and Villona alight from Ségouin's car. This temporary pause in the action occurs in the middle of the story. Just as the phrase "[n]ear the Bank" (*D* 45.15) indicates where the pair set foot in the center of the city, this same phrase is itself very near to the literal center of the story (its three words preceded by 1,066 words and succeeded by 1,171). This phrase—which refers to the Central Bank—is bracketed by two vivid images describing the manner in which Ségouin's car is characterized: as "human nerves" striving to answer "the swift blue animal" (*D* 45.11–12) and "people . . . pay[ing] homage to the snorting motor" (*D* 45.16–17). By their immediate precedence of and succession to that of the Central Bank, these images enthrone the axial symbol of the story: the idol of Mammon.

By extension, this paramount icon similarly sits between the complementary images upon which the story opens and closes: gambling. As Alain Blayac noted, the phrase, "running evenly like pellets in the groove" conjures up the "implacable determinism that rules the movement of the [roulette] balls, whether in or out of the groove" (44). This image of the channel and calculation reverberates in that upon which the gambling scene ends, of Jimmy Doyle's "counting the beats of his temples" (*D* 48.30–31). In his complementary ordering of these images of car racing and gambling, Joyce exposes their common adulation of a materialist idol.

In a text woven with monetary diction and metaphor, the principal tonal contrast is, as one might expect, between the narrator's ironical uses of financial terms and Jimmy's solemn invocations of the same. Some are patent: the narrator's repeated sarcasm is directed at Jimmy's keeping "his bills within the limits of reasonable recklessness" (*D* 44.28–29) and his father's feeling of "commercial satisfaction" in "having secured for his son qualities often unpurchasable" (*D* 45.32–33), embrace not just the human objects, but in condescension to the financial idioms invoked. In Jimmy's and his father's minds, by contrast, phrases like "a great sum" (*D* 44.23–24) and "pots of money" (*D* 45.6) reverberate in Jimmy's earnest mind. The vulgarity and greed betrayed in his father's metaphor has added piquancy in light of Walter Skeat's recording that the word "pot" is "one of the homely Celtic words" in English usage (Skeat, s.v. "pot"). Similarly, the narrator allows us to savor his irony in reporting Jimmy's "respect for his father's shrewdness in business matters" (*D* 45.3–4) since he has already instanced this "shrewdness" in his "secur[ing] some of the police contracts" (*D* 43.19).

The argument of the story implies a nexus of relationships between class aspirations, business investment, and gambling that requires attention. While the narrator deals with these relationships in a deeply ironical manner, he also engineers the narrative so that they appear within a clearly articulated critique of colonialism.

"gambling gentlemen"

The idea of an international automobile race was the brainchild of James Gordon Bennett Jr. (1841–1918), publisher of the *New York Herald Tribune*. This race was but the most recent foray in his ongoing public relations competition with the Hearst Corporation since the mid-1860s. He had already made a name for himself in New York as a bold and audacious sportsman, highly competitive businessman, and extravagant gambler before he sprang on to the international scene when for a wager of $90,000 he won a transatlantic yacht race from Sandy Hook to the Isle of Wight in 1866. This led to his patronage of the Gordon Bennett Yachting Cup and then to the Motor Cup (1900), so that by 1903, the name Gordon Bennett was synonymous with fast living, public relations stunts, sports for the rich, high-visibility entrepreneurship, and extravagant gambling. Nobody at the time personified and publicized the relationship among business, sports, and gambling like Gordon Bennett. The events of July 3 drew attention to these connections and furnished James Joyce with one of the many themes in his fictional sidebar to the day's main news.

The structure of "After the Race" implies a relationship between the sport of car racing and the pastime of playing cards. Just as the first scene begins with a description of the excitement generated by the car race, the last opens with the fever of excitement generated by the prospect of a night's gambling. Similarly, each of these settings reduces the entertainment value of each activity to a matter of accountancy. The implications in each scene, as many readers have noted, are that just as Jimmy appears to have been cheated at cards—or at least taken advantage of—he will be similarly exploited as an investor in the car business. The story therefore implies an analogy between the diurnal sport of car racing and the nocturnal pastime of card playing. This analogy is rhetorically represented by the repeated "cars . . . cars" of the opening paragraphs and the cry of "Cards! cards!" (*D* 48.4) announcing the action of the last three. Just as the narrative converts the sporting success on the racetrack to the prospect of riches to be won or lost, it subsequently divides the company of card players into winners and losers of cash. The dramatic design of the story therefore implies an analogy between the blandishments, motivations, and impostures of business and gambling.

Now, although he dabbled temporarily in business ventures—exporting Irish woolens to Italy, opening the Volta Cinematograph in Dublin—Joyce was never imbued with the spirit of venture capitalism. Similarly, although he inherited many of his father's talents and a few of his vices, an appetite for gambling was not among them (the word "gambling" appears but once in *Finnegans Wake:* 341.17). John Stanislaus Joyce, never averse to squandering his money and talent, does not appear to have attended the racetrack or to have played cards. When his son came to create Leopold Bloom, he endowed him with a humorously detached view of investment schemes and a singular disinterest in the Ascot Gold Cup. Nevertheless, Bloom remembers playing various card games with the invalided Mrs. Riordan when he resided at the City Arms Hotel (*U* 12.504–7, 17.504, 17.661–62). These games included bézique and nap, which were, at the time, the most popular forms of this friendly pastime.

It is clear from the action of "After the Race" that the game the young men play on *The Belle of Newport* is nap. Of the card games mentioned in *Ulysses*—bézique, twenty-five, beggar my neighbor, spoil five, and nap—the only one that the young men could be playing is nap.[21]

Nap is an uncomplicated trick-taking game that was popular in England at the end of the nineteenth century. It is ideally suited for five to seven participants, each of whom plays for himself. The cards are ranked A-K-Q-J-10 . . . 2, from the standard pack. At the beginning of each trick, each player is dealt five cards. The hand with the highest number of trumps wins the trick. In a manner similar to poker, based on his assessment of the strength of his hand, each player undertakes to predict—and bet on—the number of tricks he expects to win, while matching the bids of his rivals (made in clockwise fashion around the table), or pass. To win four tricks is "nap" (napoleon); five is "wellington;" and to win all five after wellington has been declared is called "blücher." If dealt a particularly weak hand, one can, alternatively, bid to lose all five tricks: called a "mis" (from *misère*), that is, "poverty."[22] If the bidder fails to win the number of tricks he has undertaken, he is obliged to pay each opponent the amount he would have won.

Success in this game, therefore, depends upon good judgment in handling relative fortune. It requires a retentive memory, the ability to deduce the optimal strategy based on one's own hand and the capacity to read the demeanor of one's opponents, and the equanimity to discern, counter, and present bluff. In Joyce's youth, "farthing nap," as it was popularly known, was usually played for minimal stakes in a friendly and familial atmosphere: thus "Grandfarthring nap" (*FW* 202.2–3). The game metaphorically commemorates the greatest moment in nineteenth-century British military history—the Battle of Waterloo—that pitted Arthur Wellesley, the duke of Wellington, and Gebhard Leberecht von Blücher, the Prussian general, against the emperor of the French, Napoleon Bonaparte.

In "After the Race" we read that the game is played between five players—Farley, Doyle, Routh, Rivière, and Ségouin. Their conduct implies an ambiguous mix of social amity (their drinking throughout the games) and serious gambling (their high stakes). We are told that they toast the two queens—of hearts and diamonds—cards that, except for aces and kings, trump all others. The game is described as comprising "tricks" and with a diminishing number of winning participants: beginning with all five, ending with two (Routh and Ségouin), and leaving Jimmy and Farley with the heaviest debits. For his part, as Jimmy's alcoholic intake accrues, so do his financial losses. He becomes progressively disabled from conducting a winning strategy, since "he frequently mistook his cards" (*D* 48.12). His companions are not as friendly as they at first seem: they allow him to gamble while drunk (a violation of gambling's first commandment) even as the stakes "ran high," so that Jimmy's losses soon exceed his actual cash, forcing him to write IOUs.[23] Their concealed hostility to him is conveyed, in addition, by the implications of the verb characterizing the assistance they rendered him in keeping his account: "calculate" (*D* 48.13).

Given the nationalities represented by the players—French, English, Irish, and Irish-American—and the German (or Belgian) victory in the day's car race, it is not hard to see in this figurative re-enactment of the Battle of Waterloo an extension of the allegorical design in "After the Race." Just as Blücher and Wellington, with their Belgian and Dutch allies, won the day on June 18, 1815, over Napoleon's Grand Armée, so do the German driver and the English card-player, Routh, on July 3, 1903. Whatever ambiguities attend the French defeats (Napoleon and Ségouin's "virtual" victories), the consistent losers are the Irish causes. The tripartite relationship between the car race, the card game, and the political allegory that "After the Race" plays out is implied, in turn, by the call—evidently of Routh's—for "one great game" (D 48.16). This implies, in turn, an analogy between the struggle for European hegemony that ended at Waterloo and that between Germany and Britain almost a century later (to be pursued in chapter 4).

This political allegory is amplified in the toasts to "the Queen of Hearts and of the Queen of Diamonds" (D 48.7–8). The subjects of Queen Victoria, on the one hand, had a more affectionate name for their longest-reigning monarch than Maud Gonne's famous insult. Presumably from a widespread sympathy with her heartfelt dedication to the memory of Prince Albert (and beyond *Alice in Wonderland*), she was known as the "Queen of Hearts."[24] Marie Antoinette, consort to Louis XVI, on the other hand, was known as the "Queen of Diamonds." This sobriquet arose from the infamous case of the diamond necklace with which she became embroiled. Justly or not, she was accused of intriguing to purchase an enormously expensive diamond necklace commissioned by Louis XV for his notorious mistress, Madame du Barry. This object became the symbol of her indifference to the sufferings of the poor, and was one of the reasons she went to the guillotine in 1793.[25] There is a heavy irony at the expense of the French entrepreneurs in the narrator's citation of this toast—presumably offered by one of the Frenchmen—in the wake of Ségouin's French Revolutionary toast to "Humanity" but a couple of hours before (D 46.27).

Now, Joyce was neither a Puritan nor a partisan nationalist. Nevertheless, in setting the gambling scene in Kingstown Harbour—named after King George IV, remembered by Irish nationalists as a notorious gambler—he is casting a historically informed slur. Joyce was no more interested in gambling than in competitive sports. Some of his friends from his Dublin years recall his singing of the music-hall song, "The Man

That Broke the Bank at Monte Carlo" (Curran, 41; Colum and Colum, 49–50).[26] Joyce liked it for its expressive swagger rather than the pastime it celebrates. Passing through Monaco thirty years later, he wrote Frank Budgen a letter parodying its opening lines: "I to Monte Carlo went but I never played a cent" (*Letters* III: 302). Yet, for all the relish with which he posed as the gambling gentleman who was the toast of Paris, he was interested enough in linking commercial speculation, gambling, and imperial culture among the targets of his slightly propagandistic art of "After the Race."

One of the tenets of "Irish Irelanders" of Arthur Griffith's and D. P. Moran's stripe was the charge that the British Empire enthralled the colonized by many means more subtle than parades of brute force: the education system that steered them to imperial service, organized sports that turned them into devotees of English pastimes such as cricket and soccer, and especially into clients of horse racing and gambling. In this respect, they were reflecting a widely held view that these latter pastimes weakened the moral fiber of the natives, made them subscribers to British materialist values, and, moreover offered opportunities for the agents of empire to infiltrate the local cultures. In support of this argument, critics of British imperialism pointed to the spread of gambling wherever the Union Jack flew, and to such colonial institutions as the Hong Kong Jockey Club, the Victoria Turf Club, and the Royal Irish Automobile Club (Schwartz, 215–41).

Despite the domestic opposition to gambling within Britain—from the moralistic and work-driven middle-classes and all the churches—gambling flourished throughout the nineteenth century, each according to its means, by the blue-collar and aristocrat. Betting on team sports—first cricket, then horse racing, and then other sports such as boxing and soccer—became more widespread in nineteenth-century England (Schwartz, 175–80). The English were always ambivalent about card playing: adapting both the cards and the games from the despised French, allowing it on certain celebratory occasions, such as Christmas, and under regulation or supervision (Schwartz, 58–65). Similarly, while gambling was, by all accounts, a common vice in Ireland throughout the nineteenth century, it was, like many other normal practices, nominally illegal and disapproved of by Catholic moralists.[27] Horse racing for prizes was illegal since 1740, and a parliamentary act of 1708 made it an offense to play cards or dice for cash (the lord lieutenant's premises were the sole exception in the colony over which he presided). Meanwhile, in America, nominally illegal gambling was accommodated by the thriving riverboat trade, so that the institution of the Mississippi paddleboat (floating on de facto extraterritoriality) was synonymous with lethal fleecings of unsuspecting travelers (Schwartz, 253–56). Joyce's depiction of Jimmy Doyle, the Trinity College law student, losing a substantial portion of his family fortune to a suspect Englishman and on an American boat, yet, is therefore forged from a rich amalgam of historical ironies.

The Irish public was accustomed to such ironies in 1903; for long before he succeeded to the throne, Edward was racing his own Thoroughbreds and making regular gambling trips to the casinos of Hamburg and the French Riviera (Schwartz, 180). He made but a nominal effort to conceal his royal identity while making these excursions under the pseudonyms "Captain White" and "Baron Renfrew" (307). Thus, as we see in the discussion of his character in Joyce's "Ivy Day in the Committee Room," his moral reputation was the subject of much censorious discussion, interpreted by the nationalist press as prima facie evidence of the corrupt influence of British culture on its subject peoples. In the event, the friendly decision of the clerical authorities at Maynooth College on the occasion of his royal visit to drape the Aula Maxima in purple, scarlet, and black, the king's racing colors, gave propagandists such as Griffith a field day. They were able to denounce the Catholic bishops' kowtowing to a Protestant king who officially condescended to their faith as superstition, who at the same time gave scandal by his gambling and extravagance, and whose whole demeanor exuded ostentation and imperial complacency.[28]

Beyond these provincial contexts, which have all but faded into invisibility, Joyce's story refracts the anthropological and historical relationships between gambling and competitive games, sublimations of the hunt, and even of war. While card shuffling and rituals of chance appeal to the primitive mind as offering divination, secret knowledge, or the telling of personal fortunes, they carry with them into modern culture the attraction that risk-taking offers the adventuresome. All the major religions disapprove of gambling, originally because of its associations with pagan divination rites, but historically because for the many for whom it is addictive, it deprives them of the free will essential to human dignity and the capacity to act rationally even in their own self-interest. In a broad sense, business, adventure, sports, banking, and gambling offer the similar sensation of a more intense and thrilling life. Much as the ancient Romans, rich and poor alike, enjoyed betting on amusements in the amphitheatre, including gladiatorial combat and chariot races (Schwartz, 29), betting accounts in large part for the popularity of sports in the twenty-first century. It is not an accident that the Grand Prix motorcar race, of which the 1903 Gordon Bennett Cup Race was a precursor, was taken up by Monaco in the 1920s as a corollary to the main action around the roulette and card tables.

In a broad sense, then, "After the Race" is but another exposé of the speculative obligation laid on aristocrats since the Emperor Nero declared that "true gentlemen always throw their money about" (cited by Schwartz, 28). This was the class in European society to whom adventurers and explorers turned for patronage, promising handsome return on their investment in overseas enterprises. While many family fortunes were made from such speculation, it produced as well several sensational bubbles—rushes of wild investment leading to price collapses and financial ruin.[29] At the time of writing "After the Race," Joyce was in no position to predict whether the Doyle fortune would be enhanced or eviscerated by the promise of an Irish automobile market; but judging by the tenor of this aspect of his story—a minor matter, to be sure—he was not sanguine. His depiction of the circumstances under which the Doyles are inveigled into investing in the Ségouin-Rivière venture is redolent of the atmosphere of the coffeehouses of London in which the prosperous were approached to invest in the East India and South Seas companies, and in which con artists, gamesters, lottery sellers, and dice rollers jostled for the attention of likely gentlemen. In this respect, "After the Race" describes a transition between this informal and serendipitous stage in capital formation and the modern, regulated stock market (the narrator records Mr. Doyle's phrase, "pots of money" [D 45.6], for instance, with an eye to its function in the ensuing card scene).[30]

Looked at in this way, Joyce's story illustrates David B. Schwartz's summary of the perception of investment as another form of gambling: "Stock markets would eventually become legitimate foundations of mercantile capitalism, but as late as the nineteenth century they would be considered by the mainstream as little more than institutionalized bubbles" (122).

In his literary treatment of the relationship between gambling and business, Joyce has a general model in Shakespeare's *Merchant of Venice*. As Schwartz observes, this play interweaves the themes of ship owners' speculation, money lending, and courtship by lottery, implying the mutual relationships between games of chance and the world of business (115). In turning his attention to this broadly similar subject, Joyce manages it in his own inimitable manner. The story begins with the French racing cars and ends with French playing cards. Behind the mask of hilarity in the first and that of "bold adventure" in the second, we are led inexorably to the "cash nexus" that binds them together: the bets that beckon, are hazarded, and are won or lost in the market or at the table. The vortex around which these variously competitive actions revolve in "After the Race" is the Bank of Ireland, situated at the central point—both geographic and narratological—of the story (*D* 45.15).

The international cultural resonance of the link between business and gambling is completed by the accommodation of the gambling on Farley's yacht, *The Belle of Newport*. Among his many accomplishments as newspaperman, publicist, and yachtsman, the same James Gordon Bennett Jr. had established, in 1880, the Newport Casino in Newport, R.I. Although it originated in yet another bet on Bennett's CV, the name "Casino" could have been misleading: it was actually a social and sports center rather than a gambling emporium.[31] Joyce may have been under a misapprehension of the function of this institution in applying the name to the American boat that accommodates extraterritorial gambling in Kingstown Harbour.

These assessments allow us to view "After the Race" as a complex reflection on the displacement of horse racing by Grand Prix car racing in the panorama of occasions for ostentatious gambling. Whereas "the sport of kings" was provided by (and for) those of appropriate breeding, its successor was the product of the ingenuity of *mécaniciens*. The emergence of a class of nouveau-riche businessmen, patrons of this new sport, is one dimension of the fine (and final) irony of the story, in that they are called "gentlemen."

3

The Biographical Crisis

The genesis of *Dubliners* is familiar to every student of Joyce: in AE's famous invitation (July 1904) to write a short story suitable for the *Irish Homestead*. Genial AE asked him if he could submit "anything simple, rural?, livemaking?, [pathetic?] which could be inserted so as not to shock the readers . . . playing to the common understanding and liking for once in a way" (*Letters* II: 43; *JJII* 163). This invitation must have reminded Joyce of a piece of advice he had received from Yeats some eighteen months before, during his Paris sojourn. Attempting to steer his young protégé away from verse, Yeats diplomatically offered an alternative course: "I would strongly recommend you to write some little essays. Impressions of books, or better still, of artistic events about you in Paris, bringing your point of view as much as possible, but taking your text from some existing interest or current event" (December 18, 1902, Yeats, *Collected Letters* 3: 281–82). It was not for twenty months (until mid-September 1904) that Joyce was to produce "After the Race": an alloy of interests that were personal, Parisian, and current. Thus, while heeding the advice of his two eminent mentors, Joyce stumbled into the next stage of his development as a literary artist, the writing of the stories of *Dubliners*.

Between early June 1904 and his departure with Nora Barnacle (October 7), Joyce's life was marked by several axial creative developments. The first of his responses to AE, "The Sisters," appeared in the *Irish Homestead* on August 13 (*JJII* 164). On this, the anniversary of his mother's death, he sent a copy of the story to the woman who replaced her in his life, Nora Barnacle (*Letters* II: 46). The third submission to the *Irish Homestead*, "After the Race," he apparently wrote at the end of September or the first couple of days of October. The personal relationship he had entered into with Nora Barnacle was to replace his heterosexual adventures with prostitutes and displace his unstable friendships with several male friends, J. F. Byrne, John Elwood, Vincent Cosgrave, George Clancy, and (principally) Oliver St. John Gogarty. In Nora's love he had, apparently, found an alternative to both the cynical exploitation of poor women in which he, along with Gogarty, Cosgrave, and others including Elwood had indulged, and a substitute for the mother's love that, with her death, he had lost. He met Nora ten months later and—whether fortuitously or not—in the midst of a search for personal and literary direction, and among various friends, and testing alternatives—music, medicine, journalism—he found a new self-confidence. This assurance appears in his letters to Nora, in the testimony of his brother's diary, and in public documents such as "The Holy Office" (*CW* 149–52).

The main emotional conflicts embroiling Joyce during his last Irish September were the severance of his friendship with Gogarty and the consolidation of his ties to his replacement, Nora Barnacle. While the second story to appear in the *Irish Homestead* (September 10), "Eveline," is a meditation on trust between heterosexual would-be lovers on the brink of emigration, its successor, "After the Race," is a subtle dramatization of the betrayal of homosocial relations and an exposé of the incompatibility of business and artistic personalities. In these (as well as many other) ways, "Eveline" and "After the Race" are companion pieces. As Eveline Hill is a remarkably empathetic portrait drawn on Nora Barnacle (and his sister, Margaret), so is the figure of Jimmy Doyle a caricature of Gogarty. Joyce limns each of these figures by contrast with two cunning self-portraits in the complementary half-named pair: the mysterious exile Frank, and the silent artist, Villona.[1]

During the three months before his departure, Nora Barnacle was supplanting every one of Joyce's close acquaintances. Throughout that summer, between their regular meetings on sunny evenings, they were reading and rereading one another's letters on the rainy ones. Before and during the summer of the Joyces' "walking out," other events were laying claim to public attention: King Edward VII's return visit (April 26 to May 5), the public debate at the Metropole Hotel of Arthur Griffith's Hungarian policy (August 3), the ongoing rivalry between the International and Irish Exhibitions of Industry, and the outbreak of Russo-Japanese hostilities in the Far East.

He courted her as singer, writer, and conventional lover: arranging her attendance at his two public concerts (August 22 and 27), plying her with his own poems along with songs by Henry VIII and Yeats (*Letters* II: 45).

A glance through the surviving letters reveals that for all their physical and emotional intimacies, their relationship was well advanced before he permitted Nora to address him by his Christian name or signed his love letters "Jim" (see 42–52).[2] Joyce's male friends resented the time he devoted to Nora (Maddox, 29). Even as he resided in the Martello tower with Gogarty, he never introduced her to his brilliant friend. As she was known to Gogarty as "the companion" (Maddox, 41–42), Joyce was writing to her that "no human being has ever stood so close to my soul as you stand" (*Letters* II: 49–50, August 29). It is highly significant, then, that on the evening of September 15, immediately after his precipitous vacation of the Martello tower, he asked for, and got, her agreement to "stand beside me in . . . my hazardous life" (53). Just as his friends feared, his relationship with Nora would be the catalyst of his definitive break with Gogarty, whom he had come to regard as the archetypal Irish betrayer.

This break had been coming since Gogarty berated Joyce for his ingratitude in insulting so many of his benefactors in "The Holy Office" (mid-August). This broadside excoriated all the leading Irish revivalists as "Mammon's countless servitors" (*CW* 152), among whom was Gogarty, whose social snobbery betrayed itself in his "preference for a man of tone."[3] Joyce delivers his vituperative denunciation of mediocrities from a position of high-spirited "devilish" abandon (*Letters* II: 51), in the spirit of Arthur Griffith's fearless attacks on place-hunters and flunkeys of the system. His confidence in Nora's love had emboldened him to spurn the protest from two acquaintances (one of whom was evidently Gogarty).[4] While still throbbing from the flare-up, he wrote to Nora, "I offended two men today by leaving them coolly. I wanted to hear your voice, not theirs" (46). Joyce did harbor some regrets about the fissure, nonetheless, as a poem, written at this time, ends: "There is no word not any sign / Can make amend—/ He is a stranger to me now / Who was my friend" (*JJII* 175). For his part, writing of this broadside to an Oxford classmate, Gogarty reported: "I have broken with Joyce. His want of generosity became to me inexcusable. He lampooned Yeats, AE, Padraic Colum, and others to whom he was indebted. A desert was revealed which I did not think existed amid the seeming luxuriance of his soul" (August 16, cited by Ulick O'Connor, 74). The offensive broadside was the beginning of the end of Joyce's friendly relationship with Gogarty: what had begun in a chance encounter at the checkout desk in the National Library in

December–January 1902–3 ended in the Martello tower during the night of September 14–15, 1904.

It is a sign of Gogarty's goodwill toward Joyce, therefore, that even though their relationship was beginning to unravel, he offered him the shelter of the Martello tower in September "to finish his novel" (*Stephen Hero*). Joyce needed a place to work on this manuscript (he had five different addresses between April and September [*Letters* II: lvi]) and Gogarty, no doubt, recommended the tower for its familial remove and natural panorama.[5] It was but a matter of time—a month, to be precise—before the residual enmity between them would resurface and result in a final break. This break is one of the occasions commemorated in *Ulysses* (fictionally backdated by three months). As we shall see, the opening of *Ulysses* revisits the severance first marked in "After the Race."

That this story was slowly taking form in his mind is attested to by several images in "After the Race" that appeared in the letters written during the months preceding its commitment to paper. Writing to Nora on August 29, for example, he cites one of his Paris epiphanies (1902), recalled as he leaned against a lamp-post, smoking, on Grafton Street: "They pass in twos and threes amid the life of the boulevard . . . descending from carriages with a busy stir of garments soft as the voice of the adulterer" (*Letters* II: 49).[6] This passage informs the scene by which Farley enters the action of "After the Race": "The five young men strolled along Stephen's Green in a faint cloud of aromatic smoke. They talked loudly and gaily and their cloaks dangled from their shoulders. The people made way for them. At the corner of Grafton Street a short fat man was putting two handsome ladies on a car in charge of another fat man" (*D* 46.29–34). In this letter he contrasts the original occasion and point of the epiphany: that it was an expression of the fullness of life upon which he had poured the stream of his youth.

Now, almost two years later, when he is "wiser and more controllable," he can reject it and view it from a safe distance. This revaluation of what constituted fullness of life is due, he writes, to the transformative power of Nora's love. This love is for him "a sacrament which left in me a final sense of sorrow and degradation" about the life of the boulevard that he was about to leave forever. Further in the letter he declares himself "an enemy of the ignobleness and slavishness of [Irish] people": a sentiment that appears in the story in the narrator's derisory reference to "the cheer of the gratefully oppressed" (*D* 42.7–8). His discovery that Nora is an exception to this condition enables him to listen with calm disdain to the insults about her that he hears from "certain people."

In this letter, then, we can discern some of the germs of the story that would be written during the succeeding month. While he is explicit in honoring Nora as his redeemer from the influences of his squalid home and his unfeeling reaction to it—consorting with prostitutes and scoffing at social convention—he all but elides the female figure from "After the Race." The story that emerges, while drawing on that epiphany of Parisian decadence, and decorated with snapshots of Irish obsequiousness, is primarily a critique of Jimmy's callowness ("this was seeing life" [*D* 47.28]). It proposes that the socially acceptable activities accommodating male relationships—racing, dining out, and gambling—are vitiated by deception and betrayal. For all their swagger, such relationships are materialistic and exploitative. Viewed from this perspective, fair or unfair, "After the Race" is Joyce's masked au revoir to his relationship with Gogarty, the cheerful cynic, Cosgrave the "solid man" (*Letters* II: 57, September 29), and Byrne, whose Irishness meant to Joyce that "he was false to me" (ibid.: 50, August 29).

Martello Sojourn

While the story was gestating in his imagination, Joyce was living in the Martello tower. Images of that unique pagan aerie and of its contentious denizens—vivid even years later when he came to write "Telemachus"—pulsed in his immediate memory as he wrote the Kingstown Harbour scene of "After the Race."

The Martello tower in Sandycove is one of the twenty-one such squat, tapered, circular granite structures erected at strategic points on the Irish coasts between 1804 and 1806. The alarms raised by the collaboration between the 1798 and 1803 rebels and the French moved the colonial authorities to anticipate a possible Napoleonic invasion. Although Robert Emmet, in his Speech from the Dock, inveighed against the French as among the enemies of Irish liberty, this same speech implied that the United Irishmen were working with the French for the liberation of Ireland; and, moreover, his brother, Thomas Addis, even as Robert was being tried for treason, was attempting to re-engage the same French on behalf of the United Irishmen. The construction of these towers, designed after the impregnable fortresses that the British had encountered in 1794 at Cape Mortella, Corsica, was, therefore, during the Napoleonic wars, a well-advised expedient.

Joyce's stay at the Sandycove tower during its centennial year was not to last long (September 9–15). Nevertheless, the panorama offered by this sterling fastness—perched high on the granite rocks and looking north toward Kingstown Harbour, south to the Muglins and Dalkey Island, and east to the Irish Sea—is bound to leave on any visitor, however brief his sojourn, an indelible impression. So it was with Gogarty: "The seascape is gorgeous," he wrote to G.K.A. Bell (*Many Lines to Thee*, 33). In later life, when he became a man of means, he purchased successive country residences of similar prospect, Dun Guaire Castle, County Clare, and Renvyle House, County Galway, both within earshot of "the lapsing, unsoilable, whispering sea."

During his single week of residence at the Martello tower, Joyce shared it with Samuel Chenevix Trench and Gogarty. The well-known conflict between Gogarty and Joyce over Trench's nightmares and their abrupt parting in the early hours of September 15 was the last exchange between them for two years and therefore, too, the terminus of its relevance to the present enquiry. Whatever the precise circumstances that were the occasion of Joyce's departure from the tower—his fright at the firing of a revolver within the narrow confines of the sleeping quarters, Joyce's paranoia that Gogarty posed a threat to his life, or (more likely), Joyce's emotional shock at the inhumane callousness and spiritual cynicism that Gogarty's cheery wit concealed—he convinced himself that he was put out of the tower.[7]

Staying at this exotic and historical fastness forced Joyce into close living circumstances with adult men, allowed him to proceed with his writing, and introduced him to a stream of visitors. Among them were Arthur Griffith, to swim and discuss politics with Gogarty, AE to paint, and tourist William Bulfin, who has left us an interesting morning vignette. Telling the trio of his travels, he is amused by Gogarty's flashing repartee, and goes on to record: "The other poet [Joyce] listened in silence, and when we went on the roof he disposed himself restfully to drink in the glory of the morning" (*Rambles in Eirinn*, 323). These observations—the contrast between the two "poets," the speechmaker and the silent one, the presence of the Englishman, and the rising sun—corroborate aspects of life in the tower that appear, transmuted, in the final scene of "After the Race."

The Martello tower experience was, for Joyce, cumulative of all of the turbulent events of that summer. It staged and symbolized his imaginative exit from the friendships and the Ireland he had known. An unnamed informant of Bulfin's encouraged him to pay the residence a visit because "the two men living [there] . . . were creating a sensation in the neighborhood. They had assumed a hostile attitude towards the conventions of denationalization, and were, thereby, outraging the feelings of the *seoinini*" (Bulfin, 322).

A bastion of male exclusivity (contiguous to the "gents only" Forty Foot), a marker of Ireland's historical nightmare, and an omphalos of a potentially new culture, it is a powerful symbol of beginnings and endings. Among the immediate and practical concerns that were evidently on Joyce's mind as he wrote this story during the three weeks between his expulsion from the tower and his departure from Ireland, therefore, were his impecuniosity and homelessness. To finance his and Nora's departure, he badgered the same people from whom he had "borrowed" before and had recently satirized (*JJII* 178–79). Yet even as he begged for their support, he was inlaying the text of "After the Race" with similar criticisms arranged to appear soon after he and Nora had sailed out of Dublin Bay.

The hypothesis, then, is that "After the Race" is a heavily disguised fictionalization of Joyce's recent estrangement from his Dublin friends. The events it describes are versions of Joyce's experiences during the final months of his life as a flaneur. It is principally concerned with his relationships with Gogarty and (to a lesser extent) with Trench. The unfolding events of the story draw increasingly on Joyce's experience in the Martello tower. In these respects, the story is a rumination on the connections between ideas of progress, liberty, artistic sincerity, and personal friendship. If Jimmy Doyle is a reductive caricature of Gogarty, and Routh of Trench, Villona is a charcoal sketch of Joyce himself. As a story of this figure's silent detachment from the events that preoccupy the other characters and the citizens of Dublin, his final announcement of the dawn derives from another sphere of experience: from his silent meditation on the dawn over the Irish Sea. In this essential respect, "After the Race" is Joyce's settling of his spiritual account before his imminent departure.

To examine this biographical hypothesis, we must review some of the salient biographical evidence pertaining to Joyce's relationship with Oliver St. John Gogarty.

The Necessary Antagonist

When Joyce remarked to his brother that his distrust of Gogarty would be borne out in Gogarty's betrayal of Sinn Féin (*Letters* II: 187, November 6, 1906), he was implicitly admitting an aspect of the rivalry between them that bears upon the present argument. Gogarty was a regular contributor to Griffith's weekly since its inception in 1899. He wrote commentaries on issues of public health, the theater, and matters of general political and cultural moment: his columns took what was known as the "advanced nationalist" position. Griffith was among Gogarty's regular guests at the tower, where he reveled in Gogarty's witty conversation and excoriation of the clergy. He took Gogarty more seriously than did Joyce. His appreciation of Gogarty's gifts is exemplified in the report that appeared in the *United Irishman* on the Sinn Féin convention on November 28, 1905. The only address cited in full is Gogarty's. One of its passages—illuminating here—reads: "From Leonidas to Emmet the best blood in the world has been shed for the principle we are in danger of forgoing.... We are governed by a force of constabularymen, picked from our own people, spied on by other fellow-countrymen of our own, disgraced in the eyes of the nations of the world" (cited by Ulick O'Connor, 81).

Gogarty returned Griffith's admiration, and became deeply attached to him, becoming, in time, his closest friend. He admired his personal qualities, his courage and discipline ("the spear must be narrow"), and the reticence under which he restrained his political vision (Ulick O'Connor, 86). Griffith apparently divined in Gogarty qualities that Joyce could not; and as James Carens points out, the coldness and emptiness that Joyce claims to discern in him—and depicts with such vehemence in "Telemachus"—were not apparent to either Griffith, AE, Yeats, or indeed Michael Collins, men of very different characters (15). Even as Joyce was to caricaturize Gogarty in his works (*Stephen Hero, Exiles, Ulysses,* and elsewhere), Gogarty was to draw closer to both Collins and Griffith.

In the present context, it is the figure of Griffith that matters, since, as we shall see, "After the Race" is written in the spirit of Griffith's emotional response to Emmet's rebellion and of his anticolonial view of the shenanigans surrounding the July car race. In this respect, it can be viewed as a counterclaim to that made by Joyce's personal antagonist but fellow "advanced nationalist," Oliver St. John Gogarty.

From Joyce's point of view, Gogarty was a simoniac: he wanted to enrich himself by the practice of medicine, a profession in which he was competent but for which he had little passion. His interest in literature was real—he was classically educated, widely read, and had an abundance of wit, or fancy. But Joyce took him seriously enough to admit him to his fiction, portraying him not as a deeply imaginative or spiritual man, but as a *bricoleur*: a fountain of superior wit, besotted with class prejudice, and a snob. Because of his gifts and proximity in age to Joyce, he was Joyce's closest serious rival on the Irish scene. Joyce was emotionally closer to Byrne; but Byrne posed no intellectual or artistic threat as did Gogarty. Gogarty was to Joyce the embodiment of the misuse of imaginative, intellectual, and spiritual gifts, their common heritage as cultivated Irish Catholics. The purposes of Joyce's art require that he be punished with more severity than he would appear to deserve.[8]

Most of us would be very pleased to spend an evening in Gogarty's company. He was a delightful companion in good times and provided Joyce with clothes, money, and accommodation in the bad. And even when publicly offended, he offered hospitality and reconciliation. But Joyce could not tolerate a rival at quarters so close. He knew that his powers were infinitely greater than Gogarty's. But his friend's financial and social position gave him access to the literary/social scene patronized by George Moore, Yeats, Lady Gregory, and AE, from which he was excluded. Joyce, therefore, would imagine him as one of the "mummers" in a social drama written by Anglo-Irish neocolonials. To succeed, he would follow their script; as Gogarty admitted to himself: "there must be something if not of the courtier, then at least of the flunkey, in my composition" (cited by Carens, 118). Such a thought never flitted through Joyce's mind: he would write his own script. To do that, he needed distance, emotional and geographic, from his mercurial confidant.

After his parents and Nora Barnacle, Oliver Gogarty had more personal influence on the author of *Dubliners* than any other living figure. Although Richard Ellmann's estimation of Gogarty as lightweight and meretricious is substantially accurate, in Joyce's imagination he was symbolically valuable as antagonist to the serious artist. His casting of Gogarty in this role helps account for Joyce's unwillingness to accept repeated offers of reconciliation from his quondam friend. Joyce turned the vivid impression that Gogarty had made upon him as a highly charged conduit of the Life Force into a succession of oppositional characters. These "loud-mouthed burly men" (Ellmann's hyperbolic term [*JJII* 219n]) include Corley ("Two Gallants"), Gallaher ("A Little Cloud"), the anonymous cyclist ("Grace"), Goggins (*A Portrait*), Robert Hand (*Exiles*), Doherty in the draft of "Telemachus," Mulligan and Boylan (*Ulysses*), and Shaun (*Finnegans Wake*). Many locutions and incidents, from medical terms that caught his fancy (for example, "phthisis"/"phthisical" [*U* 8.392, 15.994, 17.1252, 1254, 1518]) to memorable witticisms and scenes, can be traced to Gogarty.[9]

Jimmy Gogarty

A perusal of the contents of the story in the light of this selective account of Gogarty's relationship with Joyce demonstrates that it is Joyce's first searching fictionalization of that relationship with particular reference to their sojourn in the Martello tower. The first point here is that, as in "Eveline," its immediate predecessor (which appeared in the *Irish Homestead* during that residency), the story is told not from the Joycean persona's point of view, but from that of the antagonist. Much as Eveline's mysterious Frank is a Joycean mask, in "After the Race," Villona wears the habiliments of a Joycean alter ego.[10]

An examination of the biographical record supports the contention that in many superficial but cumulatively significant ways, the figure of Jimmy Doyle is drawn—vastly reduced, to be sure—after the Oliver St. John Gogarty that Joyce knew. While Jimmy Doyle's talents and character are markedly different from Gogarty's, their *curricula vitarum* are remarkably similar. After Gogarty's example, Jimmy Doyle's inherited wealth enables him to attend "a big Catholic college" (*D* 43.22) (read Gogarty's Stonyhurst) in England, and subsequently Trinity College, Dublin, where, like Gogarty, he "took to bad courses" (*D* 43.24). Nevertheless, the family wealth allowed him to spend some time improving himself socially at Cambridge (as with Gogarty's term at Oxford). The primary prerequisite, at the time, for admission to Cambridge, even for a student who had failed his courses at Trinity College, was his father's ability to pay the tuition. There, again, like Gogarty, he did the requisite social networking: for just as Gogarty returned with tales of his adventures in the social and automobile tracks (*It Isn't This Time*, 73–78), so did Jimmy Doyle. It is apposite, among these connections, to note that Joyce appears to domicile the Doyles at a North Side address that matches that of the Gogartys:

Number 5, Rutland Square East (now Parnell Square East). Further, the scene in the Doyle residence that contrasts Villona's discomfort as Jimmy attends to the punctilio of his evening dress has the tenor of an actual historical incident witnessed by the poorly accoutered Joyce.

If there is one point upon which every acquaintance of Gogarty is agreed, it is on his fussiness about his personal hygiene, his appearance, his grooming, and his clothes: every reader of *Ulysses* encounters this on the first page. Jimmy and Gogarty are practical lookalikes having the same eye and hair color: Jimmy's eyes are grey (*D* 43.14), like Gogarty's, and Buck Mulligan's, which were either "grey" (*U* 1.86) or "smokeblue" (*U* 1.125). Similarly, like the historical Gogarty, Jimmy's hair is "light brown" (*D* 43.13–14) (and Mulligan's "grained and hued like pale oak" [*U* 1.16]). Jimmy is of the same age ("about twenty-six years of age" [*D* 43.13]) as was Gogarty in 1904. Of more salience is Jimmy's and Gogarty's common interest in motor sports and self-images as witty speechmakers and affluent men-about-town.

One can well imagine Joyce's ill-concealed sufferance of Gogarty's tales of derring-do at home and abroad and his reputation as a scintillating conversationalist at Dublin's literary evenings. Thus, in Jimmy's rumination on the image he was cutting among his former friends as he drove through town, his strolling along Stephen's Green in high fashion, his making "a speech, a long speech" to which there is great applause (*D* 47.32–48.2), and his dim impression that the "the wit was flashing" (*D* 48.9), Joyce is privately satirizing Gogarty's reputation as bon vivant, toastmaster, and wit.[11] Joyce's resentment of Gogarty's energy, social profile, and wealth reveals itself in the summary sentence "Rapid motion through space elates one; so does notoriety; so does the possession of money" (*D* 44.14–15). Gogarty had indeed made many motoring friends while in Oxford, and in a letter to one of them, the aforementioned Bell (dated July 22, 1904) rejoices that his "restless sprite will be allured . . . with motors when my friend Burke returns" (*Many Lines to Thee*, 24).

Simon Dedalus (no less) corroborates the second virtue, Gogarty's "notoriety," in adding that "[h]is names stinks all over Dublin" (*U* 6.64–65). Again, and more bitterly, in giving the prosaic Jimmy a fleeting self-image as a poet (as he "conceived the lively youth of the Frenchmen twined elegantly upon the firm framework of the Englishman's manner" [*D* 46.9–11]), Joyce is making a mildly disdainful reference to Gogarty's aspiration to be the creator of "a graceful image . . . and a just one" (*D*

46.11–12), and nothing more than a mocking jester. The most acidic aspect of this taste of Gogarty, however, comes in the imputation that this scion of an "advanced Nationalist" is putting his own financial and social ambitions ahead of that inheritance, and is only roused to action when in his cups and confronting Routh, who as we shall see, is a ghost from one of the darkest passages in the nightmare of the history that is Ireland's. This contretemps does not prevent him from taking his place at the card table and collaborating with and losing to Ireland's historical enemy. This accords with Joyce's "final view of [Gogarty's] character": that "if he gets the chance and the moment comes, he will play the part of MacNally and Reynolds" (*Letters* II: 187). This is to all appearances an unjust judgment, but one with which the "die-hard" Irish republicans, attempting to assassinate the then Senator Gogarty and incinerate his vacation residence in Renvyle (1922), subscribed.

More evident, as some commentators have sensed, is Joyce's identification with Villona. This impoverished émigré, a cultivated musician, a silent and self-contained man who, although he can roister when the occasion is right, rises to passionate expostulation in the company of philistines. Villona is the first fictionalization of his self-portrait as a "fantastic idealist," who invoking "isolation . . . the first principle of artistic economy," bemusedly observes the "mimic hunt" of the field sports. With but the "regiment of the winds" for company, he would represent the enthusiasms of "younglings" as emblems of "the frailty of all things."[12] Like the later Stephen Dedalus of *A Portrait* and "Telemachus," Villona looks to the natural world as an adequate mirror of his interior life. His preoccupations are not technological, financial, or athletic, but aesthetic.

"The Holy Office"

Sometime during the first fortnight of August 1904, whatever its immediate provocation, Joyce made his first public declaration of his decision to embark on a literary career. This intemperate outburst against men of small talent, unworthy usurpers of his Irish Catholic inheritance, was the broadside, "The Holy Office." Failing to pay the printer, he took with him a few copies that he distributed to his friends before departing with Nora in October.[13]

In Joyce's time, the Holy Office was the title by which the ecclesiastical tribunal for the suppression of heresy and the punishment of heretics was known in the Roman Catholic Church (*OED*, s.v. "Holy Office," 8 d). The name by which it was previously known—from the thirteenth to the nineteenth centuries—was the Inquisition, and today is known as Congregatio pro Doctrina Fidei [Congregation for the Doctrine of the Faith] or CDF. It is with a certain degree of respect to the office charged with assessing the orthodoxy of theologians or preachers of the Gospel, then, that Joyce is making a tongue-in-cheek comparison.[14] The primary irony of the title is the sphere of reference implied by a secondary meaning of "office" (singular): as a privy, outhouse, or "office of ease" (*OED*, 9), or in Hiberno-English usage, "out office." Joyce's usage here, therefore, combines these two denotations to accommodate his particular effect of contrasting theological and scatological reference.[15] This play of religious orthodoxy, artistic integrity, and sanitation against heretical contamination, the service of Mammon, and the function of the sewer bears the central imaginative load of Joyce's satire on the mediocrity of the Irish Literary Revival. It is thereby his first invocation of what was for him the key image drawn from his reading of the poems of François Villon: "*ordure*."

The Irish Literary Revival was led by mystical claimants—Yeats and AE—whose spiritual instincts were reactive to ordinary experience. When conjoined with nationalist sentiments, it became a "movement," and was joined by practitioners of no particular talent or vision, but the sakes of Narcissus, Mammon, or the Occult. For Joyce, the imaginative life and the sex drive are in constant tension with the restrictions of formal life (Power, 74). This is the force of his sardonic remark that the single English invention of note is the water closet (*JJII* 217): just as it sanitizes the home and purifies the air, it engineers away the ordure and represses our awareness of the presence of brutality and decay in our daily lives. The creative figure for whom the ordure of life—poverty, gambling, whoring, drinking, thieving, hunger, pain, and the exercise and satisfaction of the human orifices—was always present was François Villon. Therefore, when Joyce wrote "The Holy Office" and when he appealed to Grant Richards that "It is not my fault that the odour of ashpits and old weeds and offal hangs round my stories" (*Letters* I: 63–64, June 23, 1906), he was invoking the spirit of Villon's forthright bodily realism, artistic accomplishment, and literary vision.

In "The Holy Office," then, Joyce adopts the stance of an inquisitor who is exposing the cultural heretics of the Irish Revival and expelling them from the sacred realm of artistic excellence. Posing as the *censor deputatus*, he liberates Parnassus of its baser claimants. As vicar-general in an office of ease, he performs the self-assigned role of vicar general of the Holy Office, and in a gesture with double qualification—as agent of purgation and expeller of heretics—he transforms himself from "the sewer of their clique" into a position of exaltation whereby they, and not he, are expelled. Thus, as the Church is relieved of its heretics and the body of its feces, so is the Irish Parnassus purified of its false claimants, those who confuse Mammon with true exaltation of soul.

Donning the robes of an inquisitor and physician, the persona exposes the heretical pretenders to the orthodoxy of true art and diagnoses the need to purge the Irish cultural establishment of its faint-heartedness. On behalf of "the eternal qualities of the imagination and the sexual instinct," he argues that the Irish revivalists have allowed their partiality to the formal life to suppress both of these instincts out of which a fully expressive human art can be produced (Power, 74).

The persona in Joyce's poem turns the tables on his opposition: whereas he has been expelled by their small-spirited clique, he is declaring them outside of the Parnassus built from systematic Aristotle, mystical Dante, and steely minded Aquinas. The persona is therefore setting the parochial Irish against the canonical tradition, intellectual and spiritual. The persona appropriates the voice of the Catholic tradition—which combines mysticism and intelligence—against the "frivolities" of the Celtic and pagan past and an inherited class privilege that the Anglo-Irish Literary Revival has claimed as its province and property. He is prepared to deal with the "lower" spheres, eliminative or erotic. While pretending to high-mindedness, these fellows actually serve Mammon; while paying obeisance to false idols, he stands by his own talent and pride, kowtowing to nobody. Invoking the language of excommunication, he declares them anathematized. The soul is purified by the laxative procedures he prescribes for them and for the Irish movement. The language is confrontational: by metaphorically conjoining the heretical and the fecal, it violently yokes the provinces of soul, mind, and body.

Posing as a hybrid of pedant, ecclesiastical bureaucrat, enema-administering physician, and custodian of intellectual, spiritual, and artistic standards, Joyce vents a hilarious catalogue of Swiftian vituperation, in the tradition of *Hudibras* or *The Dunciad*. Had his education acquainted him with Brian Merriman's *Cúirt an Mheán Oíche* [*The Midnight Court*], he would have had a native model for his bravura outburst. But it did not:

a Jesuit education was not partial to Gaelic culture. He had a continental precedent in the Villon, whose collection of satirical poems, *Le Lais* [*The Legacy*] is the proximate model for "The Holy Office."

"The Holy Office" is a Villonian exercise in a pseudoclerical expunging of spiritual ordure. In every major way, Joyce's persona in "The Holy Office" is modeled on that adopted by Villon in *Le Lais*. The more specific literary prototype of *Le Lais* and *Le Testament* is the mock testament, a medieval form in which a dying testator bequeaths his several body parts to various individuals (Villon, xiv); and "The Holy Office," as a document distributing appropriate encomia to his would-be relict, is a (somewhat premature) literary testament.

Joyce's denunciations are both general and specific, *urbe et orbe:* without extenuation naming the offenses and identifying the offenders. Nothing that Joyce wrote is closer to the spirit of Villon than this outburst of vituperation. Just as in his *Le Lais,* Villon mixes the erotic and mock ritual, so does Joyce in this broadside, "To sister mummers one and all / I act as vicar-general, / And for each maiden, shy and nervous, / I do a similar kind service" (*CW* 151). Like Villon, he strikes the pose of a rake, profligate, and of a university-educated rhetorician: "I, who disheveled ways forsook / To hold the poets' grammar-book, / Bringing to tavern and to brothel / The mind of witty Aristotle" (*CW* 149: the "brothel"/"Aristotle" rhyme is quintessentially Villonian). Again, in his citation of emetic references—for their shock value as well as their serious assault on sensibilities circumscribed by the luxuries of bourgeois life—Joyce owes a direct debt to Villon's barrage of insults to personal acquaintances, police and law officers, and the rich and powerful of fifteenth-century Paris. As Villon indicts hypocritical clergy, gluttonous administrators, and protectors of unearned wealth, Joyce denounces prissy Synge, precious Yeats, frivolous women (Ella Young and Susan Mitchell), superior Gogarty, and obsequious Padraic Colum.[16] The Hazelhatch millionaire to whom Colum kowtows is the same Thomas Hughes Kelly: our man Farley.

And again, as Villon dons the mantle of a cleric, Joyce pretends to "act as vicar-general" with the authority to dispense plenary indulgences, and as Villon engages in scatological humor, Joyce figures himself as offering the services of an enema ("purg[ing] a bellyful"). And much as Villon's *Lais* is couched as a will containing a list of itemized endowments upon his various enemies—each one targeting their respective failings (corruption, gluttony, stupidity, et cetera) Joyce designs "The Holy Office" as his envoi to those who are unfit to share his exalted company, identifying their respective disqualifications (pusillanimity, sentimentality, piety, et cetera). And as Villon wrote his *Lais* on the eve of his banishment from Paris to Angers, imagining himself persecuted by unworthy adversaries, so Joyce wrote "The Holy Office" in one of his bouts of paranoia, imagining that he had been an outcast from the social-intellectual community behind the Revival, "the sewer of their clique." And as Villon saw himself an intellectual son of Aristotle and Aquinas, so does Joyce, in a gesture of defiant reverse snobbery directed at the Anglo-Irish Protestant leadership of the Revival, describe himself as "steeled in the school of old Aquinas" (and subsequently, therefore, equipped to "forge" the true conscience of the Irish race). They each strike a similar stance of the disdainful, detached, and superior poet: as Villon, conscious of his *"bruit"* [fame] (*Lais*, line 69), condescends to his fellow masters of arts, Guillaume Cotin and Thibault de Victry (for example) as *"Paisibles enfans sans estry / Humbles, bien chantans lu lectry"* [Peaceable boys, easygoing / Meek, sweet singers at the pulpit] (*Lais*, 220–21), Joyce's soul shall spurn John Eglinton and George Roberts evermore because "they have crouched and crawled and prayed" (*CW* 152).

Both angry young men, Villon and Joyce, in their respective expostulations, *Le Lais* and "The Holy Office," disgorge a stream of scurrilous charges, gossip, in-jokes, and double entendres. While they lacerate their enemies, each performs a kind of striptease: throwing off the social proprieties one by one, they engage in a paradoxical game of self-pity and excoriation. Much as Villon's *Le Lais* is by turns libelous, humorous, and acidic, Joyce's is wounding and personal, saved only by its brilliance. Both are devil-may-care and scabrous, barreling along in rollicking rhythms and riveted with oxymoronic rhymes.

"The Holy Office" was the beginning of the end of the Gogarty-Joyce relationship, which was to last but another month. When Joyce turned to write "After the Race" following his departure from the Martello tower, he was to invoke, again, in the figure of Villona, the image of François Villon and in Jimmy Doyle (as we shall see) the scion of an offal-producing butcher. But this time, he was not to dip his pen in the poet's well of venom, but to wear his mask of disdain, detachment, and near-silence. Thus, as Villon adapted his persona from the extraversion of *Le Lais* and the more measured tonalities of *Le Testament*—Joyce, perhaps chastened by the hostile reception accorded his broadside, learned to channel the flood of "The Holy Office" into the narrow gorge of "After the Race." The result was the scarcely more than nominal presence of Villona, the lone man of sensibility among a throng of "intensities." In the figure of the artistically talented and bemused would-be playboy, Villona is not captivated by the fast life. Like Villon, he is in a position to write of it with some intimacy; but he's no profligate. Rather, his position is not moral superiority, but aesthetic detachment.

Clearly, then, if the vehemence of Villon's *Le Lais* informs the vituperation of "The Holy Office," Joyce's invocation of Villon in "After the Race" is more eclectic, circumspect, and irenic. Nevertheless, his purpose in endowing his Hungarian poet with Villon's name insinuates something about the "inner life" of the poet beyond the limitations of short fiction. The figure of Villona, the detached and largely silent poet, if seen in relationship with Villon, signifies something about the richness of the life of the mind that would reach its fullness in the Stephen Dedalus of *Ulysses*. The relationship between Villona and Villon, then, is one indication of the direction Joyce's spirit was taking, as when he admitted to a nationalist friend that his mind was more interesting to him than the whole of Ireland whose case was being advanced with such clamor in the streets.

Poor Villona

A corollary of the identification of Jimmy with Gogarty, then, is that Jimmy's relationship with Villona is a recasting of Gogarty's with Joyce. Just as Villona's optimism and talent are an expression of Joyce's faith in his own gifts, so does the parenthetical comment (Jimmy's about Villona), "but, unfortunately, very poor" (*D* 44.2), admit Joyce's defensiveness about his poverty when in Gogarty's company (*JJII* 143–44).[17] Nevertheless, their linking arms and singing of "*Cadet Roussel*" and perambulations around Stephen's Green are a direct allusion to their shared recreation during the summer of 1904 (Ulick O'Connor, 62).[18] This originally sentimental marching ditty about a naive but patriotic soldier became a drinking song, inviting parody and salacious improvisation, jocular specialties of both Gogarty and Joyce (*MBK* 213). Indeed, Joyce performed it so often at house parties that "Cadet Roussel" (along with "Kinch," "Dublin's Dante," "the artist," and "the hatter") was added to the nicknames by which Joyce was known among his friends and rivals at the time. The interplay between Francophilia, faux-naiveté, and derisory or obscene parody is an aspect of Joyce's reverse portrayal of the worldly wise Gogarty into the gullible Jimmy Doyle.

The exchanges between Joyce and Gogarty while Gogarty was at Oxford document their shared interest, informed by Arnold Dolmetsch, in Elizabethan songs for voice and lute, and their condescension to the vulgarity of popular English musical taste (Ulick O'Connor, 67). This appears in the story as Villona's diplomatically controlled indignation at Routh's ignorance of the glories of his country's cultural inheritance. The narrator's diction, as if in sympathy with the historical perspective raised by Villona, invokes occasional obsolete usages—"remonstrative" (*D* 43.28) and "discover to" (*D* 46.15)—is reminiscent of the penchant for archaisms employed by Joyce and Gogarty in their correspondence. As Ulick O'Connor notes, their letters about the prospect of a possible collaboration as performers of Elizabethan ayres were genteel and antique. For example, Gogarty wrote, "Inform me how thou liltest; at present I wind the pastoral pipe. By the Christ's crust I am sorry I cannot make haste to help you. Let me know if thou wouldst fain travel." To this pose of robust archaic gentility, Joyce responded in kind: "You will not have me faithfully. Adieu then inconsequent" (64–65). The tone of this diction—superior but playful—did not survive their estrangement: their subsequent communications are oblique and diplomatically formal.

The tension between Jimmy and Villona is the counterpart of that between Gogarty and Joyce. This can be observed in Jimmy's delivery of a long and drunken speech that is loudly applauded by the boisterous revelers (*D* 47.32–48.2): surely a backhanded compliment to Gogarty's reputation for disingenuous and narcissistic speechmaking. Its narrative corollary, Jimmy's recurrent irritation with Villona's silences—in the car, at the Doyle home, and during the card games—is surely Joyce's acknowledgment of the effect his condescending silences were having on Gogarty' rhetorical flourishes, especially during their occupation of the Martello tower. Joyce's passive aggression made its mark: writing fifty years later, Gogarty remembered that his "constant air of reprobation and his reserves and silences annoyed me" (*It Isn't This Time*, 91).

Yet another way in which the story reflects the estrangement of these erstwhile friends is Villona's resistance to the culture of alcohol in the hotel and aboard *The Belle of Newport*. It appears that Joyce had a justifiable fear of alcoholism and had resolved, following his mother's death, to abstain permanently. The mutual competitiveness that entered their relationship led Gogarty to tell Elwood that he would cause Joyce to renege on this pledge, thereby breaking his spirit. It was in Gogarty's company that Joyce commenced a period of heavy drinking from which Stanislaus eventually rescued him.[19] When Joyce discerned that such a threat (seriously intended or not) had been made, he formed a negative view of Gogarty's character that persisted through the rest of his life (*JJII* 131–32). Further, in providing a rationale for Routh's presence by way of the Cambridge connection, Joyce is borrowing from the social links that Gogarty made while at Oxford—with Bell, Samuel Chenevix Trench, and many others mentioned in his autobiography (see especially 73–83).[20] Finally, in giving Villona a Hungarian nationality (his rare Calabrian surname notwithstanding) and having him announce the dawn—in contrast with Jimmy's complicity an exploitative multinational enterprise—Joyce is (a little unfairly) appropriating to his own account credit for the Sinn Féin strategy with which the residents of the tower must have concurred with Griffith.

There is no evidence that Gogarty recognized himself in this contemptuous portrayal.[21] Gogarty had lost his father in 1888 when he was but ten years old (Ulick O'Connor, 13), whereas the historical William J. Field, the model for Jimmy's father, was a bachelor, and had no son.[22] So in creating James Doyle Sr., Joyce marries Field to Gogarty's widowed mother! The merciless transformation of Dr. Gogarty Sr., surgeon, into the butcher Doyle and of Oliver Gogarty, aspiring medical man into Jimmy, the potential car dealer, was apparently beneath Gogarty's notice. It should not have been, however, since the Mulligan of *Ulysses,* the aspiring surgeon whose preoccupation with anatomy causes him to think of life's values very like a butcher: "And what is death, he asked, your mother's or yours or my own? You saw only your mother die. I see them pop off every day in the Mater and Richmond and cut up into tripes in the dissectingroom. It's a beastly thing and nothing else. It simply doesn't matter" (*U* 1.204–7). This genealogy helps account for Simon Dedalus's otherwise puzzling insult, that Mulligan is "[a] counterjumper's son" (*U* 6.70–71). It also helps account for Mulligan's return in "Scylla and Charybdis" to interrupt and mock Stephen's disquisition on paternity (*U* 9.482ff.). Thus in *Ulysses,* Joyce casts aspersions on Gogarty's parentage by having Simon swear to "tickle [the] catastrophe" of this "bastard of a nephew" (*U* 6.65–70) and have Mulligan, in behalf of the material facts of life and death ("tripes"), defensively deride all parenting.

Therefore, in underlining the contrast of Villona's musical talent, cultural taste, and unfortunate poverty with Jimmy's naiveté, fecklessness, and wealth, Joyce is expressing his own sense of superiority to his pampered friend and rival. Gogarty was complex, spirited, and, indeed magnanimous; but he was not subtle-minded. He would have been much ahead of his time to appreciate the full range and power, even at this its first stage, of Joyce's command of literary language and form, and devious literary subterfuges of revenge. Once triangulated, the relationship between the text of "After the Race" and the circumstances under which it was composed points to a theme that lies at its heart: the betrayal of friendship. In the figures of Jimmy Doyle and Villona we have a heavily masked image of the relationship between Gogarty and Joyce. Jimmy's presumption and greed lead him to a dubious investment in the French motor enterprise. Even as he jeopardizes his birthright, he betrays his country. In this way, the casting of Jimmy Doyle as Ireland's betrayer to Anglo-French interests, against Villona, whose voice announces the reawakening of Ireland's deeper European heritage, is Joyce's first dilation of his lifelong personal conflict with Oliver St. John Gogarty.

Prenatal Telemachus

Despite his repeatedly expressed dissatisfaction with "After the Race," and his aspiration to revise it (*Letters* II: 151, 189, August–November 1906), Joyce never pursued that desire in ink. The story remains, with a few emendations, as it originally appeared in the *Irish Homestead* on December 17, 1904. By the time he was ready to start the writing of *Ulysses* (1914–15), and having in the meantime written *A Portrait,* he had devised other uses for the materials in this story. Although it has not been remarked by any critic, it should have been relatively easy to see that in writing the opening episode, "Telemachus," Joyce makes heavy use of the same materials, transforming them into a wholly new and superior creation.

He drew up the original schema and made the preliminary sketches for *Ulysses* in Trieste, before leaving for Zurich, in mid-1915 (Litz, 142). While staying at Locarno in 1917, he wrote the first three episodes. Claude Sykes received the first of these on November 10, 1917 (*JJII* 420), and "Telemachus" appeared in the March 1918 issue of the *Little Review* (3–22). It was quickly recognized as masterly: Yeats thought that the Martello tower episode displayed "our Irish cruelty and also our kind of strength . . . [and was] full of beauty" (*JJII* 531). No doubt, Yeats was reacting to the invidious portrait of Gogarty in "Telemachus." But Joyce's larger purposes show that this projection is not motivated by personal spite so much as from the high seriousness of his aims for the work as a whole. "Telemachus" is clearly a revisitation of the scene sketched in "After the Race," embracing a radical transformation of many of the details of that story.

It is a commonplace that *Ulysses* is a sequel to *A Portrait*—Stephen having returned from his first foray into Continental freedom to stake his claim as the poet of the emerging Irish nation. There are many thematic and imagistic links between the diary entries of *A Portrait* and "Telemachus" (Benstock, 4). "Telemachus" is, too, a narrative sequel to Villona's announcement of the new day breaking over Sandycove, Kingstown, and the surrounding mountains. It features a trio of characters who represent the same triad of forces with which "After the Race" is concerned: the colonizer, Ireland's betrayer, and the visionary poet. Like "After the Race," "Telemachus" abides by the Aristotelian unities of time, place, and action; but beyond the limitations of its predecessor, it puts its readers in the presence of three characters who are identified and developed, each of them complex and conflicted. Unlike the ciphers, Jimmy Doyle, Villona, and Routh, these characters are brilliantly rendered, individuated, and rounded. Each of these works examines the relationship of Ireland with its colonial master and identifies the claimants vying to set its future course. Whereas the primary themes of "After the Race" are apparently technological and economic, they are substantively sprung with imaginative and spiritual tensions. Those are more express in "Telemachus," where Mulligan, the voice of the scientific and objective mind, derides the spiritual. Stephen, as Bernard Benstock rightly points out, is deeply skeptical about Mulligan's aggressive agnosticism. He allies himself with the brilliant heretics of his tradition, repudiating "the mockers, Mulligan's ancestors . . . [and] glorying in the heritage of both the defenders of the faith and the sincere detractors, Stephen allows himself to be carried away with secret pride, until his sense of irony deflates his rhetorical overenthusiasm" (8). By contrast with this deep and penetrating portrait, the limning of Villona's silences and Jimmy Doyle's callow impulses is preliminary.

The brilliant narrative technique of "Telemachus" makes a substantial advance on the nuanced, but limited, use of free indirect discourse we encounter in "After the Race." As in the earlier text, the narrator is detached from the action. But in addition to allowing the characters to speak for themselves, he intimates their presence by admitting their mental idioms into his discourse. The most dramatic advance is the way in which the narrator exposes us to Stephen Dedalus's high intelligence. Whereas Villona's humming, silences, and occasional remonstrations indicate the hidden presence of a developed sensibility close to the center of "After the Race," readers of "Telemachus" encounter Stephen's colorfully tessellated mind: its stock of Hamletisms, ecclesiastical and Homeric analogues, and vivid immediate observations all illumine his existential anguish. This is the first indication of one of Joyce's major innovations in *Ulysses*: the revelation of Stephen Dedalus's stream of consciousness ("The proud potent titles clanged over Stephen's memory the triumph of their brazen bells: *et unam sanctam catholicam et apostolicam ecclesiam:* the slow growth and change of rite and dogma like his own rare thoughts, a chemistry of stars" [*U* 1.650–53]).

Whereas the main conflict in "After the Race" is between Jimmy and his automobilist friends (with Villona as an all-but-mute chorus), "Telemachus" shifts the readers' attention to the contest between Stephen and Mulligan over the key to the tower and the milk woman's attention, with Haines as the bemused choral voice. The contrast between the joking friends and the silent Villona morphs into that between the joking Mulligan and the "moody brooding" Stephen (*U* 1.235–36). The Stephen Dedalus of "Telemachus" is drawn after Villona's inwardness and Jimmy's youth and selfishness. The "Telemachus" episode exploits Gogarty's account of his British academic sojourn, especially in his description of the ragging of Clive Kempthorpe (*U* 1.165–71). The clarity of this scene—with its effete English figures ("their moneyed voices")—expands on the portrait of Mulligan as Stephen's true antagonist, and not the attendant Haines. The silence of Villona's exile is enlarged into Stephen's reticence in the face of Mulligan's jaunty disrespect and his expulsion from the tower, which in itself lays claim to a place of original rebirth for Ireland.

As a transformation of the "torpid" Routh, the rather slow-witted Haines is another "ponderous Saxon."[23] His class bias against the impecunious and disheveled Dedalus has infected Mulligan, who thinks that Stephen is "not a gentleman" (*U* 1.52). His daylight affability euphemizes as "rather unfair" his nation's historical exploitation of the Irish, even as the avenging panther pursues him through the dark. Thus, the relatively obscure figure of the Englishman Routh becomes, in the figure of Haines, a personification of the "auld enemy" responsible for the nightmare of the imagined Irish past. By registering Stephen's "rising colour" in the face of Haines's polite evasiveness, Joyce is refining the images attending Jimmy's spat with Routh in the narrative of "After the Race."

In Joyce's collection of preliminary notes made in 1904 for his projected autobiographical novel, there is a character named Doherty (Gorman, 136; Scholes and Kain, 85, 107–8; Fragment A, Litz, 132–33). In this note, entitled "Dr. Doherty and the Holy City," he appears "standing on the steps of his house the night before" and blaspheming the Mass. Given the date and the subject, it evidently draws on a historical memory of Oliver St. John Gogarty at his home at 5 East Rutland Square, which eventually transferred to the tower scene in "Telemachus" where it receives its full embellishment (*JJII* 379). In view of the context established by the action of "After the Race," particularly the interlude at the Doyle home, we are able to see how the historical Gogarty is the basis for the succession of fictional figures in the rhythmically echoing hallway of names: Doyle, Doherty, Goggins, and finally, the stage-Irish Mulligan.[24] In this same scene, the image of Jimmy giving "equation" to his dress tie—drawn, as we have seen, from Joyce's observation of Gogarty's punctilio about his appearance (and habit of addressing inanimate objects)—is rephrased into Mulligan's "[P]utting on his stiff collar and rebellious tie [as] he spoke to them . . ." (*U* 1.513–14). Mulligan's rivalry with Stephen (heeding the Irish superstition of the devil's presumed antipathy to holy water) has him pretend to see the devil in Stephen's disheveled appearance and his antipathy to physical cleanliness. Stephen mentally returns the insult, hearing in the "gurgling in his throat" (*U* 1.12) Mulligan's empty, soulless jesting images of his bestiality and the medical specialty that was to become Gogarty's, ENT. He is so decadent that he devalues the prideful integrity of Stephen's soulful rebellion. (It is significant that during his tower sojourn, the image of the skull and hell's torments haunted Joyce's dreams, as his letter to Nora of October 3 reveals [*Letters* II: 50].) For his part, Mulligan is a mocker of the priesthood and of Stephen's trembling satanic gesture of defiance. Stephen's retort to this taunt is internal: he imagines Mulligan as prehensile. These contending forms of rebellion against the "narrow sense of the word," as Stephen puts it, are complex developments of the demonic images that present themselves to Jimmy Doyle in the final scene of "After the Race": "They were devils of fellows but he wished they would stop . . . [their] terrible game" (*D* 48.13–18).

These devices are extensions of the attribution of "dirt" to the group led by the pointedly named Ségouin. As we saw in the previous chapter, cars were synonymous with the first air-pollutant of the automobile age, dust.²⁵ Whereas Ségouin is a materialist to whom Jimmy sells his soul, the Stephen of "Telemachus" is dirty of body and soul playing to the cleanly shaved swimmer, Mulligan. The themes of dirt in "Telemachus"—Stephen's dirty handkerchief, his secondhand breeks, his disdain of bathing, his superstitious dread of baptismal reminders, the image of Lady MacBeth's sleepwalking through the arena of his mind ("Yet here's a spot" [*U* 1.482])—are all reactive developments of the figure named Ségouin, symbolic of avarice and deception and materialism, and to Stephen's superior spiritual conscience and capacity, supersaturated with residual religious scruple, committing simony. We can catch a corollary development of the image of Jimmy Doyle's "giving a last equation to the bows of his dress tie" (*D* 45.31) of which the implied narrator observes that "Jimmy, too, looked very well when he was dressed" (*D* 45.29–30), precisely the terms in which Mulligan compliments Stephen, as he offers him gray pants: "You'll look spiffing in them. I'm not joking, Kinch. You look damn well when you're dressed" (*U* 1.118–19). Mulligan's concern with the social etiquette he can afford is a foil to Stephen's preoccupation with rules of conscience. He is a blasphemer, mocks the Mass, has a tail, is a hypocrite, has a devious temper, advises lying, mocks serious effort (Stephen's Hamlet theory). and plays the part of Satan in the three temptations of Christ (Luke 4: 1–15).

References to Hamlet and Claudius, hero and usurper, thicken the contrast between these antagonists. Their antagonism is vividly imaged in Stephen's brooding on the contrast between his rotten teeth and those of Mulligan, which are gold-filled: images of the contrast between Christ and Chrystostomos, savior and simoniac, Christ and Judas (of the proverbial yellow gown), true poet and usurper. Jimmy Doyle, admirer of toothy grins, and Buck Mulligan, the possessor of one, are both "gay betrayers" of Ireland's cause. A significant contribution to the contemporary usage in 1904 was Arthur Griffith's characteristic designation of members of the Irish Party, because of their willingness to attend Westminster despite the illegality of the Act of Union, as "usurpers" (prominent among which was the Kingstown butcher, William Field). The final word in "Telemachus," "usurper," therefore makes multiple references to betrayers of loyalties: whether Antinous, Judas, Claudius, Doyle, or Mulligan.

Mulligan's blasphemous "Ballad of Joking Jesus" (*U* 1.584–99) is a crude, if witty, misuse of poetic gifts: contrasting Stephen's ruminating on lines from Yeats's poem of King Fergus who forgoes political power for the sake of poetry (*U* 1.239–41). He thus "rules the brazen cars" not by ownership but by meditative imaginings. In this reference as well as in Mulligan's to Royce (*U* 1.257) (Gogarty owned a Rolls Royce when Joyce began *Ulysses*), "Telemachus" registers some verbal and thematic reverberations of "After the Race." The link between the demonic, the bestial, and the automobile suggested by the phrases as "the bounding courses of the swift blue animal" (*D* 45.12) and "pay[ing] homage to the snorting motor" (*D* 45.17), resurface in "Telemachus." There they are conjoined in the portrait of the beastly minded Mulligan: the Buck with the equine head, whose ambitions with the lancet are parallel to those of the Doyles with the cleaver. They all exhibit, in Joyce's terms, inauthentic "B-attitudes" (see Owens, "Joyce's Farrington"). In these images, embracing the conflict between technology and art, cynical iconoclasm and principled dissent, we can therefore see how they are grounded in Joyce's personal rivalry with Gogarty.

A comparison of a fascinating passage in "Telemachus" with its relatively transparent antecedent in "After the Race" is illuminative of both works and of the persistence of some images in Joyce's imagination: "Woodshadows floated silently by through the morning peace from the stairhead seaward where he gazed. Inshore and farther out the mirror of water whitened, spurned by lightshod hurrying feet. White breast of the dim sea. The twining stresses, two by two. A hand plucking the harpstrings, merging their twining chords. Wavewhite wedded words shimmering on the dim tide" (*U* 1.242–47). This passage exemplifies one of the dominant narrative strategies of *Ulysses*: opening with the narrator's objective description, it quickly modulates into the character's—in this case, Stephen's—stream of consciousness. It is therefore comparable with what we can imagine in "After the Race" behind his long silences and intermittent exclamations of Villona's inner voice. What can this cultivated man, possessed of an appetite for life, looking at his friends' zest for physical and financial risks, be thinking? Does he brood on his exile? Does he read their noisy energy with envy, or is he a bemused tourist? We can infer that he masks his boredom at the "great game" by his polite exit to revisit a scene he had a few hours before proclaimed "beautiful!" And gazing over the bay and the sea as the dawn broke, he is rewarded with another moment of joy—at once natural and immediate, but also archetypal and immemorial. Whatever preoccupies him, the images the narrator employs to represent his mental life—the "darkened mirror" (*D* 47.15–16) and "daybreak" (*D* 48.33)—surely register the contest between his values and those at stake below deck.

Thus, when the image and symbol of the "darkened mirror" of Kingstown Harbour recurs in "Telemachus," it has metamorphosed from a generalized Pauline or Platonic figuration (to be expatiated in chapter 7) into a collection of more particular references within Stephen's experience. The stream of associations begins with Mulligan's shaving mirror, pinched (like Corley's coin) from his household skivvy. Stephen's literary mind at once converts it, via Hamlet and Wilde, into an emblem of the rural sentiment favored by the Abbey Theatre at the time: from Joyce's point of view too expressly patriotic and compromised by reactionary anticolonialism. The image of the sea as a mirror—as it would have appeared on calm mornings from the tower balustrade—reminds Stephen of his mother's love ("its breast"), her bitter death ("a bowl of bitter waters"), of Swinburne's deification ("Our great sweet mother"), and of Mulligan's jocund intervention as cynical medical and devotee of Swinburne. Stephen cannot be alone in his personal grief ("white breast") and spiritual bewilderment ("the dim sea"): Mulligan's mocking voice continues to break in. Thus, when in indignation at Stephen's brooding, he exclaims, "Look at the sea. What does it care about offenses? Chuck Loyola, Kinch, and come on down," he wishes him free of superstition, a residuum of his religious faith. This remark is a rebuttal of the Platonic image of the sea as the dark mirror of the eternal world that appears in "After the Race" raising before the mind's eye Saint Paul's image of the "dark glass" (Corinthians 1: 13). To Stephen, seen within the confines of Dublin Bay, the sea becomes a bowl of bitter waters reflecting "love's bitter mystery," the theme of Saint Paul's letters that Mulligan is asking Stephen Dedalus to abandon (figure 3.1).

Another complex transformation of a passage from "After the Race" appears in the next two incomplete sentences, "The twining stresses, two by two. A hand plucking the harpstrings, merging their twining chords" (*U* 1.245–46). This metaphoric rumination is Stephen's way of imagining himself as an Irish bardic poet, accompanying himself on the national instrument, the harp. This is an expansion of the metaphor underlying the sentence, "Jimmy, whose imagination was kindling, conceived the lively youth of the Frenchmen twined elegantly upon the firm framework of the

Figure 3.1. Kingstown Harbour, ca. 1900. Photograph courtesy of Prints and Photographs Division, Library of Congress.

Englishman's manner" (*D* 46.9–11). His perception of the cultural differences between the stolid and philistine ("torpid") Routh, and the energetic, diplomatic, and refined Ségouin, is conveyed in the contrast between the frame and strings of a musical instrument.

In a paragraph devoted to one of the "musical circles" within which Jimmy moved, the narrator appropriately imbues his description with images of vocal and instrumental performance: "volubly," "tongues loosened," "madrigal," "old instruments," "dexterity," "spurious lutes," and "resonant voice." As one of that circle, Jimmy's metaphor would, therefore, appear trite. His self-congratulation—"A graceful image of his . . . and a just one" (*D* 46.11–12)—the narrator records, with mild irony.[26]

If we notice that the image reappears in "Telemachus," and in a much more complex form, we are in a better position to appreciate its original purpose and force in "After the Race." The "graceful image" has subliminally struck upon a symbol buried in the midden of Ireland's history. The harp, symbol of Ireland's aristocratic cultural tradition, with which the ancient Irish *fili* accompanied himself in the performance of his poems, is conjured up by the double image of the elegant "twining" of the hands as they rotate in drawing the chords from the strings stretched on the "firm framework" of the instrument. Thus, whereas the Villona figure laments the loss of the Renaissance lute, the dramatic, imagistic, and political context—Jimmy's chauvinism awakened by the dour and firm Englishman—encourages readers to consider that the greater regret is the loss of the grand symbol of Irish high culture to English vulgarity, a centuries-old plaint in Gaelic culture: "the harp that once." Therefore, the justness of his own "graceful image" is lost upon Jimmy, as—without the supporting gloss afforded by "Telemachus"—it has been upon the readers of "After the Race."

In conjuring up the mental image of the "twining stresses," therefore, Stephen is imagining himself the true heir to Ireland's poetic tradition. This sharply contrasts with the image of elegant twining kindled within Jimmy Doyle's imagination (D 46.9). If Stephen's metaphor is more historically informed than Jimmy's, it is also more responsive to the present circumstances. He has just been observing Mulligan shaving, and the images of the instruments—bowl, razor, and brush—have passed into his consciousness; and they become the media of his anguished spiritual musings. Gogarty's historical brush, made of ivory and inlaid with gold filigree, was the pride of his well-provided personal toilet.[27] One step in his campaign to Hellenize Ireland was his giving this brush the appropriate name, "chryselephantine" (the narrator of "Circe" borrows Gogarty's word to describe the papal standard [U 15.1410]). In thinking of Mulligan as "Chrysostomos" (U 1.27), Stephen is returning a complex compliment then: not only is "Chrysostomos" a double reference to Mulligan's gold fillings (his gold-and-ivory teeth, by contrast with Stephen's rotten ones) and to the "golden-tongued" Saint John Chrysostomos, it is as well a reference to Mulligan's "chryselephantine" shaving brush.

The recollection that Joyce's experience in the Martello tower was the biographical basis of both "After the Race" and "Telemachus" produces some interesting additional corollaries. The displacement of the setting of the final scene of "After the Race" to Farley's yacht retains the geographic and historical vantage points: the perspectives on the sea and morning, and the relationships with British imperial interests in Ireland from the point at which an Irish alliance with France became a particular threat. A few notes on Joyce's handling of these elements will suffice.

First, that the Martello tower was constructed "when the French were on the sea" helps account for the presence of the milk woman, the Shan Van Vocht in "Telemachus." Farley's *Belle of Newport* moored in Kingstown Harbour offers a symbolic checkmate to this haven constructed and named after King George III. This Irish-American's trophy—an emblem of his success when outside the thrall of empire—bears a name that completes the symbolic transformation represented in nationalist poetry: of the Old Woman into the beautiful queen, the Belle.

Second, Bulfin's account of Joyce standing on the parapet of the Martello tower to behold the rising sun (323) affords an independent perspective on striking images in each scene. There is a relationship between Villona's appearance at the conclusion of "After the Race" "standing in a shaft of grey light" (*D* 48.32), viewed from below deck, and the description of Stephen at the tower stair head in "Telemachus," where the narrator tells us that "Two shafts of soft daylight fell across the flagged floor from the high barbacans" (*U* 1.314–15).

Third, the unique sight offered by the Martello tower, admired by Joyce and Gogarty in historical accounts, was the glory of the morning sun. As we have seen, it is to Villona's good taste that this particular pleasure accrues; and (as we shall see) his report of it bears complex political and mythological burdens that embrace Fenian and Sinn Féin aspirations and the morning goddess Ussa. In "Telemachus," it undergoes a further development and transformation in that it links Swinburne's Mighty Mother, the Shan Van Vocht of Irish popular political tradition, as well as Athena. In addition, we have to take into account that whereas for the milk woman, the rising sun manifests the glory of God (whom she thanks for it), to Mulligan this is but an example of Irish folklore that he pretends to elucidate for the researcher, Haines.

Fourth, there are several minor elements that link the texts with the historical record and with one another. The financial arrangements between Gogarty and Joyce for the running of the tower have been the subject of some argument—both between their accounts and between commentators. The gambling debts and the "passing of paper" record this in "After the Race" as does the settling of the milk woman's account in "Telemachus." Similarly, as already noted, Joyce's suspicion of Gogarty's intentions to turn him into a drunkard appears in the contrast between Jimmy's inebriation and Villona's sobriety on the one hand, and Mulligan's promise of a "royal drunk" on the other.[28] Mulligan's citation of the "Coronation

Day" song, a topical reference to that of Edward VII, is remembered in both texts from 1902 (Gifford, 19), but with a zest that does not derive from the spirit of imperial loyalty.

The sunrise is the most dramatic aspect of the setting in each case—witnessed by Villona and Stephen respectively—and in the "Telemachus" episode, its transformation into a sunburst: "A cloud began to cover the sun slowly" (*U* 1.248). Its linkage with the "deeper green" of the sea in the subsequent sentence underlines its political connotations from the Fenian period.

Trinity Gentleman

As we have seen, the rivalry between Joyce and Gogarty is primarily based on differences of personality, moral values, and imaginative depth. From a social perspective, then, since they sprang from virtually identical social roots, their differences lay in the ways in which they imagined their social aspirations. The key term in this context is the relationship, as understood at the time, between social class, the study of classics, and the usages of the story's ultimate word, "gentlemen" (*D* 48.33).

The high respect in which classics were held in elite schools of the late Victorian period led to the denigration of the study of other languages (especially French), the sciences, and (most of all) business studies, or commerce. The schoolmasters of the time derided the study of French as lacking in academic rigor, and moreover, since it was the native language of a people who could not be counted upon to be "gentlemen," was regarded as a "tinpot" subject fit only for those of lower taste, indifferent talent (Honey, 135), or women (Colum and Colum, 13). Such was the cultural rivalry and reverse snobbery in Anglo-French relations at the time that many English resisted affecting French pronunciations—of such words as "Monsieur" (mon-sewer) and "fillet" (fill it)—lest they be viewed as stooping to Frenchified affectation. (A small irony in all of this is that the name "gentleman" itself entered the English tongue from Norman-French, as Walter W. Skeat notes, s.v. "gentle".) In Ireland, efforts to insert the Irish language into the intermediate school curricula encountered similar charges from classicists, as the exchange between Douglas Hyde and Professor Mahaffy of Trinity College made infamous (Dunleavy and Dunleavy, 210–11). A similar bias affected those who aspired to the serious study of science or of business. Whereas scientific activities were estimated as mere mechanics, business was beneath the dignity of a man of culture, a gentleman (Honey, 137).

More important than this curricular matter, however, was the way in which classical education in England (and at its premier colonial outpost, Trinity College) was connected to the idea of a gentleman. We have Arthur Hugh Clough's word for it that "the one great purpose for which boys are sent to Public Schools [was] . . . to prepare themselves by study for the station of a gentleman" (cited by Honey, 133). To the late Victorians, to maintain the comfortable and respectable station of a gentleman, one was expected, when the occasion arose, to be able to at the very least invoke an appropriate classical allusion. This was a sign of one's "conspicuous education," the acquisition of which met the primary purpose of social display and the assertion of status, and was of no intrinsic or utilitarian value whatsoever (134). The study of the "Greats" was regarded as conferring "character," whereas it was more obviously a class marker par excellence. While pretending to a defense against the evils of industrialization, voracious materialism, and the purely utilitarian tendencies in education and society, the study of the useless accomplishment of classics was largely the preserve of gentlemen who were considered too rich to work (Cathorne-Hardy, 138). Thus by virtue of his having studied the "Greats," the literature of the most civilized, profound, powerful, and subtle minds the world had known, the gentleman was expected to be wiser, more civilized, more profound, and therefore most fit to take seriously his role in governing the nation and empire (139). These presumptions comprise the object of D. P. Moran's derision in a phrase he popularized, "a Trinity gentleman."

By the end of the nineteenth century, the traditional idea of the "gentleman" had therefore metamorphosed from its original, feudal, roots. Although historically designating a man of noble birth (though not necessarily of the high nobility), it had passed into general use as describing a man of noble character and cultivated tastes. Such a man could not, therefore, be consumed with the technical tedium or time constraints of a trade. Whatever the sources of his wealth, he had to be a man of leisure who could devote much of his personal energies to the pursuit of the higher virtues of public service, political leadership, or cultural endeavors. The gentleman was therefore deemed to be above petty self-interest and be a man of honor. When called upon, his chivalric character was expected to emerge: he was presumed to be personally courageous, urbane, well-spoken, and a good conversationalist. He was serious-minded, kept his own counsel when appropriate, and never engaged in acrimonious argument, coarse language, or personal insult.[29]

Clearly, it was upon these narrow grounds that the duel between Joyce and Gogarty was paced. While both were of Irish Catholic middle-class background, Gogarty's education (at Trinity College and Oxford) and aspirations (to become a man of means) were comprehensively shaped by the English notion of a gentleman, whereas Joyce's alliance with and antipathy to Gogarty arose from their differences of family background and education rather than their disparities of talent or temperament. They both came from urban Parnellite families and were supporters of Griffith's Sinn Féin movement and his more radical form of nationalism, and both were hostile—though in different degrees—to physical force republicanism, the Church's influence in Irish life, and the aspects of the Revival that favored rural culture, especially that of the Irish language. Their acute rivalry arose partly from these similarities and their awareness of their superior gifts that their different temperaments and courses of education accentuated.

Gogarty's education followed the agenda by which an English gentleman was socialized: he took pride in his command of Greek and Latin, was a highly accomplished speaker, a man of fashion, a champion sportsman, adventuresome and valorous, humble and generous, public-spirited and quick to make friends. By virtue of his education at Trinity College and Oxford, therefore, his conception of himself as a gentleman allowed him to disdain the lower social orders—rude-accented Irish Catholics and devious Jews—and to be unmerciful to those of lesser talent whom he lampooned mercilessly. Except for the fact that he was an Irish Catholic, Gogarty embodied the ideal of the English gentleman: a brilliant amateur in all things, even entertaining his patients with spontaneous verse.

Joyce had a more introverted personality than his friend, was educated at the Royal University, and was possessed of little physical courage but of vastly greater spiritual fortitude. Joyce made much more of his relatively limited education. He was acutely aware that by contrast with Gogarty, he had no money and no Greek.[30] He did not qualify for admission to the ranks of English gentlemen, although he deported himself throughout his life as if he were one. He was always courteous, quiet-spoken, avoided contentious argument, and when he could afford it, dressed his wife like a lady, and tipped waiters like a man of means. What Gogarty would achieve through his public persona—as senator in the Irish Free State, as daredevil driver of a Rolls, resident at a premier Dublin City address, and owner of an elegant Connemara home—Joyce would through understatement, apparent withdrawal, and the inscription of his rivalry with Gogarty in a series of literary representations of increasing moment.

Thus, in having the Doyle family's investment in Jimmy's "conspicuous education" along the lines laid down by Gogarty's mother, Joyce is burlesquing the manner in which they attempt to make a gentleman out of Jimmy. Jimmy meets none of the social or intellectual requirements of that station: the son of an Irish Catholic victualler, possessed of the twelfth commonest Irish surname, the best he could have done at Cambridge was to accept his designation as a "gentleman commoner." Jimmy doesn't appear to know much French, still less Latin or Greek. He was left to exploit the social network that, we understand, exploited him: "gentlemen" do not beggar their drunken friends. Considering, too, the Francophobic reverse snobbery embraced by the culture of the Oxbridge gentlemen, Jimmy's consorting with French automobilists is a further indication of his unworthiness to enter that particular club. Yet another irony in Joyce's handling of this culture is that Routh, the one figure in the story who might qualify for social reasons for the rank of gentleman, is exposed as ignorant of the cultural achievement of the Elizabethan period, the single phase of English cultural history that gave the term its particular meaning as a sophisticated courtier.

This leaves us with Villona, who as a singular man of courtesy and cultivation, despite the limitations of his ethnicity, and the paronomasia of his name, qualifies for moral regard. In this man's addressing all of those who do not merit the sobriquet "gentlemen"—Irish, Irish-American, French, Franco-Canadian, and English—is, of course, the story's final irony.

Villona

Villona is a uniquely attractive character in the story. A man with an artistic temperament among businessmen and sportsmen, he is out of place. The narrator insinuates that he has found himself at the race by virtue of his membership in a Cambridge musical circle attended by Jimmy. He is in Dublin, then, as a guest of the Doyle household, is three times identified as Jimmy's "friend" (*D* 44.5, 45.16, 45.34) sharing the back seat of Ségouin's car.

Villona is a genial and grateful guest. He is fond of food and good company, open and spontaneous in his appreciation of quality: to the natural setting of Kingstown Harbour he exclaims "It is beautiful!" (*D* 47.23) and to Jimmy's speech, *"Hear! hear!"* (*D* 47.33). He has a buoyant personality: the narrator remarks that despite his extreme poverty, he is in "good humor," is possessed of an "entertaining" presence, "excellent spirits," and of a natural "optimism." Musically talented, he has a resonant bass voice and is a "brilliant pianist." The narrator makes it clear, moreover, that when the others are engaged in animated discussions of cars, investments, and cards, he is preoccupied with questions of aesthetics. He is the one character in the story with an inner life. Whereas Jimmy's partiality to the repose of art is unbalanced by the exhilaration of fast travel, Villona is constantly humming to himself; while Jimmy and his friends are gambling, he plays the piano; and as the cabin shakes with the cheering that greets the climax of the evening's excitement, he is gazing at the silent sunrise over the Irish Sea. He embodies the Joycean artistic ideal—that of the culturally informed, politically neutral, déclassé, detached observer: alert to the natural beauty of the world, yet also possessed of a rich interior life, revealing itself in the language of the soul, music.

Villona is, therefore, an antagonist to the main action of the story. The narrator appears to treat him with some condescension ("he had a very satisfactory luncheon" [*D* 43.10]); or as an afterthought: the word "besides" recurs in his observations about this outsider ("besides he was an optimist by nature" [*D* 43.10–11], and "Besides Villona's humming would confuse anybody" [*D* 44.12–13]). Nevertheless, Villona takes the lead three times in the night's proceedings: in the after-dinner conversation (*D* 46.15ff.), in playing the waltzes for the dancing (*D* 47.24ff.), and in the voluntaries to accompany the card-playing (*D* 48.5ff.). His gradual disengagement from the spirit of the occasion can be traced by contrasting the earnestness and vehemence of his discussion of art at the dinner table (*D* 46.15–21) with the fine antanaclasis contrasting his "play[ing] voluntaries for ... [t]he other men [who] played game after game" (*D* 48.5–6), and his disappearance from the action—indicated by the silent piano (*D* 48.17)—until his annunciation of "Daybreak, gentlemen!" (*D* 48.33). This abrupt and anticlimactic line, coming from a character that has been "forgotten" from the page describing the most exciting action of the story, is the dramatic culmination of the narrator's tack of relegating Villona and treating his interventions as belated. The sequence that links Villona's presence, gradual disappearance, and sudden return matches the formal pattern of the images of the day, the night, and the dawn that correspond, in turn, to the dramatic structure of the story.

Masking incidentals aside, the figure of Villona resembles Joyce himself at that time: a musician, poet, and aesthete, detached from the car racing and the gambling, a penniless wanderer, wont to avail himself of brief lodgings in the homes of various friends (*Letters* II: lvi), and the herald of the dawn. To render his self-image in the figure of Villona, Joyce drew on an impressive figure in the contemporary arts. To recover this genesis requires a historical excursus.

"a deep bass hum of melody"

Although the narrator is clear in his depiction of the contrast between Villona's tastes and temperament and those of his companions, he is notably reticent about conveying the quality of Villona's inner life. The most pregnant clues come in the passage describing the dinner conversation at the hotel. Twice, it appears, Villona intervenes in the discussion about the talk of the town, "the triumph of the French mechanicians" (*D* 46.18–19), to swing the topic toward the arts and a proper regard for the past: "Villona, with immense respect, began to discover to the mildly surprised Englishman the beauties of the English madrigal, deploring the loss of old instruments.... The resonant voice of the Hungarian was about to prevail in ridicule of the spurious lutes of the romantic painters" (*D* 46.15–21). This passage attributes to Villona some of Joyce's own interests during the summer of 1904. He had, indeed, "discovered" for himself the beauties of the English madrigal and of the repertoire of the English Renaissance lute, especially the work of John Dowland and Henry VIII. The contemporary patron of this discovery, honored by his partial inscription in "After the Race," is none but Arnold Dolmetsch.

Arnold Dolmetsch (1858–1940) was the pioneer in the revival of performances of early music of England (before Purcell), particularly on period instruments. This migrant to London came from a family of mixed French, German, Swiss, and Bohemian origin (the name may be Hungarian [Margaret Campbell, 27n18]), who were for generations instrument makers, scholars, and performers of early music. Dolmetsch has had a great influence on late-nineteenth and twentieth-century attitudes toward scholarship and performing practices particularly through the reconstruction and development of obsolete instruments (the viols, the clavichord, keyboard, and the recorder). A contemporary program illustrates the period of his musical interests and the instruments of its sensibility (figure 3.2).

In 1889, while looking for music for the viola d'amore, Dolmetsch first came upon English fantasies for viols in the Royal College of Music and in the British Museum. To play this long-neglected music, he began to acquire and restore early instruments, and in 1890–92, with his daughter Hélène, he gave a series of public concerts on viols and harpsichord. Beginning in 1893, he made his own lute, and soon acquired a high reputation as craftsman, performer, and propagandist for music of Renaissance England. He championed the cause of "small music" against the loud and full sound that filled London's concert halls in the 1890s, the "big sound" of Richard Wagner, Franz Liszt, and Hector Berlioz, which, gathering through the century, was then eminently fashionable. His clavichords—producers of subtle, intimate, and metallic percussive sounds—which he also manufactured from the 1890s, bore his slogan, "*Plus fait douceur que violence*" [Sweetness does better than vehemence].

It was his good fortune to rediscover for the English public the abundant musical literature for viols: fantasies, ayres, galliards, pavans, "sparking with the dance-rhythms of those superb amateurs, the Elizabethans" (Margaret Campbell, 21). He also set himself the task of researching and acquiring the proper historical technique for playing these works on accurately reconstructed instruments. Thus at the beginning of the twentieth century, the name of Dolmetsch became associated with "the authentic interpretation of early music on the instruments for which it was written" (23). In making this argument, he became a critic of piano culture, which, he proposed, elevated sonority and the commercialized requirements of Victorian furniture over the musical values of refined expression, rhythmic complexity, and tonal nuance. He claimed, for example, that Johann Sebastian Bach's keyboard works should only be played on a harpsichord. A coiner of aggressive epigrams in heavily accented French, he excoriated popular taste: for example, "in music, the survival of the loudest has been the law of the past hundred years" (161).

He had in the beginning to overcome fierce prejudice (Queen Victoria

Manhattan Theatre

HARRISON GREY FISKE, Manager.

MONDAY AFTERNOON, JANUARY 19, 1903,
AT 3 O'CLOCK.

SECOND CONCERT OF OLD MUSIC
BY
ARNOLD DOLMETSCH
MRS. ARNOLD DOLMETSCH
AND
MISS MABEL JOHNSTON.

Management   - - - -   W. N. LAWRENCE.

PROGRAMME

1. Extracts from Playford's Introduction to "The Skill of Musick."
   The fourth edition, 1664
   I. A TUNE FOR THE BASS VIOL..Anon
   II. ALMANE FOR TREBLE AND BASS VIOLS......................Alph. Ferabosa
   III. FOUR TUNES FOR THE TREBLE VIOLIN...............................Anon

2. Song, accompanied by the Lute,
   "THE PRIMROSE" (Words by Robert Herrick).............Henry Lawes, c. 1650

3. Four Dance Tunes for Two Viols and Harpsichord,
   I. ALMAIN, II. CORANT, III. SARABAND, IV. JIGG.....William Lawes, c. 1650

4. A Song, with Violin Obligato and Harpsichord accompaniment,
   "O LET ME WEEP"..Henry Purcell, c. 1680

5. Prelude and Saraband for the Viola da Gamba, accompanied by the Harpsichord,
   Marin Marais, 1686

6. "Les Fastes de la Grande et Ancienne Mxnxstrxndxsx," for the Harpsichord,
   PREMIER ACTE.   "LES NOTABLES ET JURÉS MXNXSTRXNDXUS"
   SECOND ACTE.   "LES VIÉLEUX, ET LES GUEUX"
   TROISIÈME ACTE.   "LES JONGLEURS, SAUTEURS ET SALTIMBANQUES, AVEC LES OURS ET LES SINGES"
   QUATRIÈME ACTE.   "LES INVALIDES OU GENS ESTROPIÉS AU SERVICE DE LA GRANDE MXNXSTRXNDXSX"
   CINQUIÈME ACTE.   "DÉSORDRE ET DÉROUTE DE TOUTE LA TROUPE; CAUSÉS PAR LES YVROGNES, LES SINGES ET LES OURS"
   François Couperin, 1716

7. Prelude for the Clavichord..J. S. Bach, 1722

8. Chacone for the Harpsichord.....................................G. F. Handel, 1721
   PERFORMERS:
   MRS. ELODIE DOLMETSCH, MR. ARNOLD DOLMETSCH
   AND MISS MABEL JOHNSTON.

Figure 3.2. Arnold Dolmetsch concert program, January 19, 1903. Courtesy of Music Division, Library of Congress.

publicly expressed her dislike of his sound [Margaret Campbell, 30]), but his dogged persistence—despite his abrasiveness—won him many admirers among cultural elites including William Morris, George Bernard Shaw, Arthur Symonds, and George Moore.[31] Dolmetsch's great gift was that, in a period when early music was virtually ignored except for academic study, he had the will and musicianship to take work out of the museum and make it intelligible to a modern audience (*New Grove Dictionary*, s.v. "Dolmetsch").

Joyce's interest in Elizabethan music did not arise from any direct contact with Dolmetsch (who never visited Dublin). Ellmann's informants recall his sweet renditions of songs by Dowland and Henry VIII between 1896 and 1902 (*JJII* 52), the years when Dolmetsch's reputation and influence was on a steep rise, and would seem to correspond, moreover, with the time when he is most likely to have read Moore's *Evelyn Innes* (its first two editions appeared in 1898 and 1901). He may have read Arthur Symons's essay, "A Reflection at a Dolmetsch Concert," delighting in the "return to this happy music, into which beauty shall come without the selfishness of desire" (17). It is clear, in any event, that before he wrote "After the Race" (September 1904), Joyce had read *Evelyn Innes*, since "Eveline," written the previous July, exhibits a number of details with analogues in Moore's novel.

Joyce, in any event, knew of Yeats's purchase of a psaltery from Dolmetsch to accompany his collaboration with Florence Farr (1901–2). Dolmetsch had made a psaltery—a lute-like instrument—for Yeats and Farr, so that they could pursue their plans to chant poems backed by the lute (*JJII* 154–55; Foster, *Yeats*, 257–58). He had by then a cultivated feeling for the songs of John Dowland and Henry VIII, which he would perform accompanying himself on the piano. This he found unsatisfactory, and contemplating the prospect of a vocal career, he wrote to Gogarty proposing that they commission a lute from Dolmetsch in order to tour English summer resorts from Falmouth to Margate performing the songs of Dowland, William Byrd, and John Bull (*Letters* I: 54, June 3). Meanwhile, he was gaining a reputation as a performer of Irish and Elizabethan songs at the Sheehy and Cousins homes. Among his favorites were "Turpin Hero" and "Pastime and good company" (the latter the best known composition of Henry VIII). In his diary entry recording one such evening (June 8), Joseph Holloway writes that Joyce sang these "dainty ballads most artistically and pleasingly," accompanying himself on the piano (40; Bauerle, 18–19; see also Curran, 41; and *JJII* 51–52).

For his part, Joyce was sufficiently reassured by the reception among his friends that on the morning of June 16 (which we remember for other reasons), he wrote to Dolmetsch inquiring about the prospect of the manufacture of an authentic lute. Dolmetsch's response to this request was diplomatic but negative: he cautioned Joyce about his underestimation of the cost of the instrument and the difficulty of mastering playing technique. For a larger appreciation of these matters, he advised Joyce to read his two essays that had recently appeared in the April and May issues of *The Connoisseur*.

The April issue gets right to the first of these topics. Dolmetsch launches immediately into an attack on faddists within his movement to revive the lute: "Even modern poets use the word on account of its poetical associations, though they hardly understand what it means." Noting that authentic instruments are very rare, he insists that "spurious 'property' lutes manufactured by clever, if unscrupulous, Italians for the benefit of later-day collectors, are far more numerous than genuine specimens, even in public museums. He goes on to criticize not only inauthentic reproductions but uninformed representations of them in art galleries: "The modern painter who wishes to introduce a lute into one of his works, a fashionable thing nowadays, has every chance of reproducing some impossible model, perhaps a complete forgery, worse still, some partly genuine instrument, which through the successive 'restorations' and 'improvements' of ignorant admirers has become completely transformed." He therefore advises would-be lutenists to proceed with caution: "A careful examination of the lutes so frequently to be met with in old pictures would be a safer guide to the understanding of the various forms of this instrument; for the older masters well understood its beauties, and, unlike their descendants, their paintings were technically accurate" (213). Dolmetsch goes on to illustrate, from the pictorial record (a painting by the Venetian Vittore Carpaccio, ca. 1450–1525) and with photographs of Renaissance instruments, the genuine article (http://www.klassikitar.net/carpaccio-thepresentationdetail.html).

The authentic Renaissance lute, he argued, "attained its greatest perfection in Western Europe between 1500 and 1650, then quickly lost its popularity, and only left with us a very degenerate offspring—the mandolin" (214). Its halcyon days were in Northern Italy—Venice and Padua—about

1550. This lute, "incapable of loudness," went out of fashion when full sound became the desideratum in music (215). Therefore, in subsequent centuries its design was altered, leading to the misrepresentations of subsequent painters.

Reading this essay a century later—during which the lute has become a familiar instrument in consorts and from the performances and recordings of masters of the instrument like Julian Bream—it appears to be unduly preemptory. The genuine instrument had not been heard or seen for several centuries. He thus saw the necessity to distinguish between the lute as general term for stringed instruments having a body with a neck whose strings are plucked, and the true Renaissance instrument. The lute proper is a plucked stringed instrument with a round body in the shape of a halved pear, a flat neck with seven or more frets, and a separate pegbox set perpendicularly to the neck. The Renaissance instrument had eleven strings. It is not easily tuned and is notoriously sensitive to temperature and humidity (*New Grove Dictionary*, s.v. "lute").

Dolmetsch's second essay gives fair warning of these obstacles as he offers instructions on playing the instrument. It is accompanied by many historical illustrations and scores from the Renaissance.

Very likely convinced by Dolmetsch's arguments in these pieces, Joyce abandoned the project.[32] In any case, Dolmetsch declined to comply with the order—no doubt because he suspected (rightly) that he would not be paid the sixty-five guineas he required (*U* 16.1760–769). Joyce continued throughout his life, however, to regard Dowland's ayres with undiminished respect. In his essay on Mangan (February 1902), he praised an unnamed lyric of Dowland's as "immortal" (*CW* 80); and writing to Harriet Weaver twenty-four years later, he estimated Dowland's songs as "beyond question. I could never sing them but I could listen to them all day. . . . I hope something I have written may bear comparison with *Come silent night*" (*Letters* III: 138).[33]

The reader of this survey of the Joyce-Dolmetsch relationship will no doubt recognize that in the figure of Villona, Joyce emulates Moore's fictionalization of Dolmetsch. Villona's detached superiority to his sporting friends, his general cultivation, his musical talent, and especially his antiquarian musical tastes, are clearly drawn on the Arnold Dolmetsch with whom Joyce had been in correspondence but three months before.

The fictional Hungarian and Englishman bearing the names "Villona" and "Routh" are apparently drawn—at least nominally—from two historical companions of unnamed national origins whom Joyce met at a café in the Carrefour de l'Odeon in the company of other Bohemians and expatriates from Italy and Germany (Gorman, 100–101). The language through which this ur-European Union Assembly conducted its literary and intellectual arguments was, by Joyce's report, Latin. Joyce's recherché invocation of the "spurious lutes of the romantic painters" (*D* 46.20–21) may well be drawn on his memory of one of the culturally competitive conversations among these émigrés.[34]

True to form, Joyce's depiction of Villona borrows many subtle hues from Dolmetsch's well-known character. This impoverished French-speaking gourmand and occasionally contentious musician is the voice of reflection, refinement, and art in a loud and mechanical world. Much as in the first scenes of the story where his persistent humming blocks out the noise of the car engine, in the last he attempts to insulate himself from his companions' vacuous hilarity, their bold toasts and jests, by "return[ing] quietly to his piano and play[ing] voluntaries for them" (*D* 48.4–5). "Voluntaries" are organ pieces originating in the church music of the English Renaissance; and the yacht piano is an instrument of reduced size resembling the clavichord with which Dolmetsch (and his quiet spirit) were then associated. The playing of either, therefore, requires "returning." The scene in which Villona is crouched over the yacht piano playing dance music for the company, which the narrator declares "Bohemian" (*D* 47.31), surely reveals a characteristic Joycean watermark identifying Dolmetsch's ethnic origins and partiality to music for courtly dances.[35]

These are but instances in the major scheme by which the aesthete Villona is drawn on Dolmetsch. The ironies in the sentence "Villona, with immense respect, began to discover to the mildly surprised Englishman the beauties of the English madrigal" (*D* 46.15–16) are worthy of comment. The narrator's phrase, "with immense respect," is apt in view of Villona's corporeal bulk and by contrast with the usage—just one page before—of the word "respect" to characterize Jimmy's view of his father's business acumen (*D* 45.3–4). It reflects, too, Villona's finesse by contrast with his robust companions (he applies the word "beauty" to different objects), Dolmetsch's "discoveries" in the British Museum and his condescension to the English public (and Moore's attribution of the same to Innes). In employing the verb "discover to," Joyce has his narrator employ an Elizabethan usage, meaning "to disclose to view" (*OED*). With respect to its primary object, this is nicely appropriate. It reveals as well Joyce's own contempt for popular English taste. The usage also recalls the narrator's lingering amusement at his own paronomasia, three pages before, in the verb describing how Jimmy came to view the "line of shining white teeth" of the French competitor: when his "swarthy face . . . disclosed" them (*D* 44.20–21). Villona, as a Hungarian, like the Irishman Joyce, would have had to "discover" the beauties of the English madrigal for himself, since they were not part of his cultural inheritance. Hungary had no contact with the madrigals, and Ireland—except for providing, as Joyce thought, Dowland a birthplace—had none either. Joyce seems to have developed an appreciation of madrigals through Dublin's Palestrina choir (see Bauerle's note on Dowland's "Weep You No More, Sad Fountains," 22). Joyce, like Villona, is an incipient modernist *deraciné:* from the margins of empire a penniless transplant.

Villona's browbeating of Routh with his "ridicule of the spurious lutes of the romantic painters" (*D* 46.20–21) is a synopsis of and partial quotation from the first of Dolmetsch's two essays in the *Connoisseur* to which he had in July directed Joyce's attention. In that same essay, as we have seen, Dolmetsch criticized the modifications made to the original Renaissance lute—for convenience of manufacture and maintenance, and to overcome the technical challenges posed by the older instrument—as well as the resulting historical misrepresentations of the lute by nineteenth-century painters, offering in rebuttal an accurate contemporary example from Carpaccio. Neither Dolmetsch nor Villona identify the offending painters, whether out of diplomacy or because of the good judgment of the editors of the *Connoisseur* or the implied narrator of "After the Race." Joyce's narrator may have in mind, however, the confusion arising from the usage "harp lute" that arose around 1800. This instrument, according to the *New Grove Dictionary,* "is mentioned on a few title pages dating from about 1800 as the 'lute' was in actual fact the harp-lute, whose music shows no discernible relationship with the real lute" (s.v. "lute: repertory: England"; and see illustration).[36]

These contextualizations allow us to appreciate yet another and perhaps more oblique set of references to emerge from Joyce's apparently bland account of a dissolute evening. As we have seen, Joyce's desire to give an authentic historical rendering of the songs of the English Renaissance impelled him to seek out Dolmetsch's patronage. During his last three months in Ireland (June–September 1904), the songs of Henry VIII, which Dolmetsch had done much to revive and recommend (Margaret

Campbell, 39, 57, 68), were on his mind. He transcribed "Ah, the sighs that come from the heart" for Nora Barnacle, sending it to her in early September. He regrets that it was written "by a brutal and lustful king." Yet, no doubt thinking about his own impoverished and even sordid circumstances he wrote: "The song is so sweet and fresh and seems to have come from such a simple grieving heart that I sent it to you, hoping it may please you. It is strange from what muddy pools the angels call forth a spirit of beauty. The words express very delicately and musically the vague and tired loneliness which I feel. It is a song written for the lute" (*Letters* II: 44–45; Bauerle, 20–21).

The Henry VIII song that he performed for the gathering in the Cousins's drawing room is less intimate, but especially interesting in the present investigation of the ambience of "After the Race." It concludes:

> Company with honeste,
> is vertu, vices to ffle;
> Company is good & ill,
> but evry man hath hys fre wyll:
> the best ensew,
> the worst eschew,
> my mynde schalbe;
> Vertu to use,
> vice to refuse,
> thus schall I use me. (Bauerle, 19)

A product of Henry's youth (it appears in the Henry VIII manuscript, ca. 1520), this is the best known of the thirty-four compositions attributed to him. Musically and lyrically simple—its poetic and musical phrases are repeated—it was apparently intended for amateur performance.[37] It celebrates the "goodly sports" of youth, taking an indulgent attitude toward the partiality of young gentlemen to spend their time in pursuit of pleasure. They can develop an appreciation of the social virtues by participating in the group activities of the hunt, the song, and the dance. These pastimes are preferable to idleness, the seedbed of vice.

In choosing to perform this particular song for his Dublin friends, Joyce is paying them the gracious tribute implied by its title. There is some internal evidence that it was still on his mind when, some three months later, he sat down to write "After the Race." First, "the goodly sport" and "pastance" (pastime) that youth pursues—are the ostensible common objects of song and story: the "hunte, syng & dance" of the song, the racing, *Cadet Roussel,* and square dancing of "After the Race." Just as the persona in the song celebrates the "dalliance" of "Youthe," the implied narrator of the story describes Jimmy's excitement at "the cargo of hilarious youth" (*D* 44.3) rejoicing in the "lively youth of the Frenchmen" (*D* 46.10). Similarly, as the song celebrates "good company," Jimmy is proud that his Dublin friends would have seen him "in the company of these Continentals" (*D* 44.17), and subsequently exclaiming to himself "What good company they were!" (*D* 48.3). They are not, however, "good" in a moral sense. In view of the evident exploitation of the callow Jimmy Doyle, this song's earnest advocacy of the moral benefits deriving from liberality in youth adds another dimension to an ironic story. In having its fling, naive youth is likely to be thrown.[38] Finally, since the song derives from the repertoire recommended by Villona, a man who is "an optimist by nature" (*D* 43.11), it further sets the meditative poet apart from his superficial and dishonest company. Villona gives the story resonance and depth.

Villona's relationship with the historical Arnold Dolmetsch would seem, finally, to include a homophonic allusion to the instrument that Dolmetsch had done most to revive during the 1890s: the viola de gamba, commonly known as the bass. Thus there is a formal analogy between the implied narrator's insetting of a Tudor song in a story of modern technological competition and his recording of the dissonance between Villona's "deep bass hum" (*D* 44.6) and "the noise of the car" (*D* 44.13). And in yet another refiguration, the narrator presents this relationship as the geometric intersection of "musical and motoring circles" (*D* 43.26).

4

Arthur Griffith and the Great Game

The Issue

During Joyce's first sojourn in Paris (December 1902 to April 1903), a series of political events was evolving that, after his return to Dublin, would approach a temporary convergence and bear upon his first imaginative efforts. In January 1903, a Land Conference between landlords and tenants produced a report on the reform of the system by which Ireland's primary natural resource, agricultural land, had been owned and managed for ten generations. This report became the basis of a bill that was set before the House of Commons on March 25. The ensuing recriminatory debate discussed the complex terms by which it proposed to restore to the long-dispossessed tenantry the legal right to their ancestral lands. The prospect of overcoming centuries of animosity (or as the *London Times* reported it, "misunderstanding") between colonial and native interests strained tensions within the Irish Party, renewing the familiar charges between radicals and moderates of intransigence and betrayal. From April to July, this historical legislation was the first item of the daily news; and with the passage of its first iteration it became known as the Wyndham Act.

The beginning of this debate happened to coincide with two other, apparently unrelated, events. On March 27, 1903, the proposal to stage the Gordon Bennett Cup Race in Ireland received Royal Assent, and four days later came the announcement that King Edward VII would make his first official visit to Ireland. This last provoked an immediate and predictable controversy. Recalling the protests over the visit of Queen Victoria but two years previously and the refusal of the Irish Party to participate in the ceremonies that marked the coronation of her son (1902), Irish public opinion became stridently divided, especially in Dublin.[1] In "advanced nationalist" circles, just as the queen's visit was seen as a ploy to recruit soldiers for the Boer War, and attendance at the coronation implied loyalty to an illegitimate sovereign power, so would the political allegiance of Dublin Corporation be put to an uncomfortable public test (*London Times,* April 2, 1903: 6c).

The debate on the particular issue of whether or not to offer a formal address of welcome to the king became a hot topic around dinner tables, in bars, and at every public meeting between March and late July. While the visit was public and official, proponents of a statement of respect (led by the Lord Lieutenant Dudley) resorted to appeals for common courtesy and to traditions of Irish hospitality (*London Times,* May 3). Moderate opinion held that it was in Ireland's interest to cultivate the benignity of the royal couple: by declaring his intention to visit, Edward was signaling his approval of the Land Act on its way through Parliament (and he was, moreover, rumored to personally favor even Home Rule). Radical (or as the *London Times* termed them "professional") nationalists took the view that all of these arrangements, ceremonial, sporting, and legislative (arranged in March, predicted for July) were constituents of a coordinated program in the imperial cajoling of the public will. Arranged to coincide with and upstage nationalist plans to mark the centennial of Emmet's rebellion (July 1903), their political purpose was to renew in the minds and hearts of the Irish the pride in and gratitude for their membership in the world's greatest empire and a loyalty to its genial monarch.

The diffidence that marked Joyce's interview with Henri Fournier might, therefore, be inflected by more than his personal indifference to automobile racing. That he was unable to play the game as the publishers of the *Irish Times* would have wished, suggests that his animosity toward the event was affected by the rising tension at the time (April 7) over the perceived links between the race, the king's visit, and the effort to soften nationalist reservations about the terms of the Land Act. In the minds of "advanced nationalists," these ceremonials were designed to project a halo of benignity around an arrangement whereby the tenants were allowed to redeem their natural inheritance.

Within days of his arrival in Dublin (April 12) to attend his seriously ill mother's bedside, Joyce must therefore have read with attention this editorial in the *United Irishman* attacking the plans to stage the Gordon Bennett Cup Race:

We are to have a motor race in Ireland this year, and that the event—which might have been harmless in itself—will be used to further Anglicize and debauch the population of a large tract of the country, is evident from the manner in which the projectors are already openly deriding the national feeling and religious instincts of the people. In the issue of *Motoring Illustrated* of April 4, we find the following passages in a description of the race course: "The grave of the builder of Castledermot lies under the shelter of a roofless broken-down abbey wall, not many yards from the high road on which the competition for the Gordon-Bennett Cup will speed. It is even likely that the shaking of the road will jar the bones of the fine old Saint. His ghost, which it is supposed lives in the ivy-covered tower, will be startled at the sight of these latter-day machines, descending the road made sacred by the footsteps of good old Irish monks—men who spoke another language 'entirely,' and whose spirits will stand amazed at the polyglot procession making sixty miles an hour, of Britons, Frenchmen, Germans, and Americans. When their bones were planted in the cemetery of the Abbey, there was no America so far as they knew, no Germany as we know it, and England was a very uncertain quantity indeed. Each village in Ireland had some sort of a king who sallied forth as often as the wounds which he had received in the last battle were healed up, to hack and chop and hew at his neighbours."

In another passage we read: "Ireland has had many hundreds of kings, each of whom, I understand, killed his predecessors in mortal combat, and seized the throne, this being the *modus operandi* of accession."

The people of Ireland will be, at least, interested to see how those motoring cads can hold them up to the world as a species of Fiji Islanders, and how their dead saints and kings and the graves of their ancestors are made subjects for the derision of ignorant bourgeoisie. In the latest issue of the publication the insults and jibes are continued—one cemetery is described as so full of Irish kings that there is not room for even a little prince and his "regally nourished" grass of this cemetery is stated to be protected by a stone wall from the browsing of pigs and cattle, or something to the effect. The motor cads are endeavoring to put the Irish people under a great compliment for this race, and are expecting that the "peasants"—yea, and the County Councilors—will be only too glad to undertake the patrolling of the course for a piece of ribbon (especially if the ribbon be a *green* one, as the *Times* correspondent remarked), just as savages would be willing to render valuable services to the civilized donors of a few glass beads. The compliment, however, is all on the other side and the public of Leinster should not allow themselves to be deceived about it. The automobile racers would not be allowed on the English roads by the local authorities, and they could not get a bill passed to legalize their race in England. Ireland, now that she has consented, wisely or unwisely, to have this race held here, should insist on proper respect being paid to her people, her past, and her historical landmarks by the English bounders whom she is accommodating. The most timorous mammon-worshippers need not fear the consequences of any such assertion of Irish dignity, for it will only make the Bruisers all the more ready to pay fairly for their accommodation. Unless the cads are taught to correct their manner at present, it will be impossible to withstand the on-rush of puppyism which will take place later on. (*United Irishman,* April 18, 1903, 4: 1–2)

Arthur Griffith's intemperate editorial went much further than the skepticism Joyce expressed in the pages of the *Irish Times* by underlining the role of the race in the program of imperial propaganda. Griffith's trenchant attack on the event, however crudely it stacked the political, historical, social, and religious cards, furnished a political rationale for Joyce's peevishness with Fournier.

Although sixteen months were to pass before Joyce would return to the subject of the Gordon Bennett Cup Race, several of Griffith's points of critical intervention seem to have registered with him: the organizers' condescension to Irish peasants, the inevitably succeeding "puppyism," the disrespect for Irish customs, and the encouragement of even "the most timorous mammon-worshippers." Joyce may not have shared all of Griffith's political and cultural values, but in this editorial (and its sequel two months later) he encountered a radical point of view that he would later recast as a sympathetic Dantean fiction. By then he had read Griffith's expatiation of his political ideas and strategy in *The Resurrection of Hungary* (1904). As we shall see, "After the Race" is a work of subtle art that not only embraces Griffith's critique of the Gordon Bennett Cup Race, but also invokes Griffith's visionary alternative for a regenerated Ireland.

Just as he had done in 1900, Griffith took the lead in protesting the royal visit of 1903 (July 21 to August 1 and repeated the next year, April 26 to May 6). He not only linked this visit to the Gordon Bennett Cup Race (July 2, 1903), but argued that both were designed to trump the Emmet centennial celebration (July 23). The public campaign against the address of welcome was initiated by Edward Martyn in a letter to the *Freeman's Journal* (April 4), with which Yeats concurred (April 9). In language that applied equally to the euphoria promoted by sponsors of the car race, Yeats vigorously rebuked the hype surrounding royal visits, which "with their pageantry, their false rumours of concessions, their appeal to all that is superficial and trivial in society, are part of the hypnotic illusion by which England seeks to take captive the imagination of this country, and appeal to what are chiefly money interests" (Yeats, *Collected Letters* 3: 346). The most dramatic moment in the campaign of resistance was the public meeting of May 18 at the Rotunda that resulted in a famous mêlée (Ó Lúing, 111). Known as "The Battle of the Rotunda," it pitted Maud Gonne, Griffith, and Edward Martyn against Tim Harrington (Lord Mayor of Dublin), and John Redmond and his followers in the Irish Party (including William Field). Maud Gonne took over the proceedings, demanding that no address be made; but after her persistent protestations were declared out of order, the meeting broke up in disarray.

Of these two issues—the staging of the race and the welcoming of the king—the latter was the more contentious: whereas nationalist Ireland was inclined to ignore the car race, it was roused to anger by the prospect of according, under duress, an official welcome. On the evening of July 3—the day after the event—as the Continental and American visitors wined and dined around town, the attention of ordinary Dubliners was drawn to a second acrimonious public debate that once again pitted Maud Gonne, Edward Martyn, and their noisy entourage against the Unionist and Irish Party members of Dublin Corporation. Thus, even as it reported the news of the car race, disappointing, no doubt to its British readers, the *London Times* felt it necessary to include an account of this affair, bemoaning the "professional nationalists . . . the self-constituted leaders of the party of extreme disloyalty" who forced the meeting into suspension (July 4: 8f). Eventually, by a slim margin of three, the Corporation voted against the address. In commenting on the long series of meetings preceding the visit, Griffith vigorously excoriated Irish Party members who admitted any partiality to welcoming the king or ducked the deciding vote.

Similarly, during the three months leading up to the Gordon Bennett Cup Race, as the mainline newspapers—unionist and nationalist alike—acquiesced in reproducing the Royal Irish Automobile Club hype, Griffith reiterated his dissenting line. In the June 13 issue of the *United Irishman*, for example, we read:

> The Motor Race is one of the symbols of that "union of hearts" which, according to the newspapers, we are now witnessing in Ireland; perhaps the smell which the motor-car leaves behind is symbolic, too. But the example of rich men's law which this motor race furnishes is worth noting. For the purpose of accommodating a few wealthy men in their fad, the British Parliament passed a law giving up to them the complete use of twenty or thirty miles of road in Kildare, and ordered that no other traffic be permitted on these roads on the day of the race. In addition to this, the services of thousands of policemen and soldiers, paid by the whole community, will be placed at the disposal of the motorists, the County Councils and the Urban Councils are bothered with Local Government Orders and have to circularize the inhabitants along the course, who in turn are incommoded, and to some extent endangered. As the Paris-Madrid race shows, the risk of serious injury and grave loss of life is very great. Yet every newspaper, from pink to buff, is zealously retailing the sophistries of the Automobile Club, and arguing that there is a vast difference between a motor race in France and one in Ireland, though the machines and men will be the very same. In France they do things so badly: the French people are so inconsiderate that men going on machines at eighty or ninety miles an hour dash into trees and ditches. The Automobile Club—an aristocratic collection of motorists and motor manufacturers—is issuing statements as to the harmlessness of a pastime which has already killed ten people. This motor race would not to-day be permitted in England. And outside its danger, its only other effect will be to attract a horde of undesirable immigrants who will do the country no good.

> At the bottom of all this motor racing, however, there is not even any kind of sporting feeling, such as it is. It is simply a commercial venture between rival manufacturers, and one of the inspired statements issued to the Irish Press recommends the thing on the ground that if an English-made car wins, it will greatly stimulate the motor industry in "this country." The geography of the Automobile Club is like Lord Charles Beresford's history. But in this sentence we have an indication of what is at the basis of the whole business. (5)

In challenging the mercantile elites who promoted the race, Griffith was taking extraordinary risks. It is salutary for twenty-first-century readers to bear in mind that Unionism was a respectable and commercially effective presence in Edwardian Dublin. During the course of the nineteenth century, the power base in Dublin Corporation devolved from the self-perpetuating Protestant and Unionist oligarchy to a Catholic middle class, composed of publicans and grocers. It should be borne in mind that since voting rights were extended only to men of property, few Dublin citizens participated in municipal elections.[2] Since Daniel O'Connell's mayoralty (1840–41), when this shift first announced itself, Corporation politics became increasingly polarized and more frequently in conflict with the British colonial administration. These conflicts came to the notice of even the politically unengaged members of the public in the bitter disputes over the naming of streets and the official recognition of royal visits.[3]

The city's main industry was the colonial administration for all of Ireland, employing a loyal staff and running a competent surveillance system. All but a few of the major businesses had Protestant-Unionist owners. These same interests controlled the major newspapers, which when failing to suppress dissent through ridicule, could count on the support of the administration and police. In this orderly garrison city, as contemporary photographs illustrate, the police and army were constantly visible on the streets. Dublin, in fact, had the highest proportion of police to citizens of any city in the United Kingdom—1 to every 330 of its citizens—despite the absence of professional criminals and the (largely effective) campaigns of temperance movements to curb unpremeditated offenses resulting from alcoholism.[4] Nationalists of various degrees of advancement were thereby forced to make their peace with these adverse circumstances. Only radicals like Griffith (who owned but one pair of shoes), or Maud Gonne (who was independently wealthy) could afford persistent opposition to loyalist hegemony. For the pugnacity of its columns, Griffith's newspaper ran the risk of suits for libel, its occasional suppression, and the smashing of his printing press.

Gryffygryffygryffs (*FW* 358.22)

Arthur Griffith (1871–1922) grew up in poverty on Dominick Street in Dublin's inner city. There he witnessed levels of deprivation, degradation, and overcrowding that are outside the range of Joyce's fiction. A childhood disease left him with a permanent limp that, in addition to his diminutive stature, steeled him with an extraordinary level of personal discipline, willfulness, and moral courage. One of the formative images of his youth was an old woman's eyewitness account of Robert Emmet's execution. The cruelty and pathos of the scene left an indelible effect upon his conscience (which he described in the *United Irishman* on September 19, 1903, the centennial of that event). He was confirmed in his anti-British attitudes while temporarily living in South Africa shortly before the outbreak of the Boer War (1899–1902). While editing for a time the Transvaal newspaper, the *Middleburg Courant*, he was impressed by the parallels between the plight of the Boers and that of the Irish. Upon his return to Dublin, with William Rooney he founded the *United Irishman* to disseminate propaganda on behalf of the Irish Transvaal Committee. This committee, which included Maud Gonne, W. B. Yeats, and James Connolly among its members, supported the two Transvaal brigades. Their four hundred volunteers were raised in protest against the recruiting of about 28,000 Irishmen for the British forces in that latest colonial war. These efforts took the activities of the 1798 centennial committees beyond ceremonies and memorials and into practical political action, reinvigorating the Irish separatist movement.

Profiting from the popular opposition to the war, and partially financed by Clann na Gael in America, Griffith's and Rooney's pugnacious newspaper ran weekly for seven years (Glandon, 18–19). In its inaugural issue (March 15, 1899), Griffith envisioned "an Ireland leading the world against the bloody, rapacious, and soul-shivering imperialism of England." In the Irish Party's moderate demand for Home Rule and indulgence in endless talks he saw but acquiescence in "the turpitude of the British Empire."

He wrote his dissident political journalism after the spirit of Jonathan Swift and John Mitchel under the masthead borrowed from this Young Irelander's newspaper of the 1840s.

Griffith was to urban artisans as the Land League was to farmers. Inheriting the nationalist tradition of 1798, 1848, and 1867, and rejecting the Anglo-Irish compromises of Grattan's Parliament, he advocated an egalitarian and nonsectarian republic. He was sympathetic to French republicanism (he took the oath of the Irish Republican Brotherhood [IRB]) and was guarded about clerical claims on Ireland's conscience. Griffith's Irish nationality was historical rather than linguistic, genetic, or sectarian: he regarded Cuchulain, and not St. Patrick, as the foundational icon of Irish civilization (Maume, 54).

An economic pragmatist, he advocated the freedom of Irish manufacturers from trade restrictions imposed by London and legislation protecting Irish industry from foreign competition. He promoted "buy Irish" campaigns, and "praised the Continental model of protectionism and an interventionist state" (Maume, 49). Griffith's nationalism therefore appealed to artisan traditions of self-help. He advanced a classical republican ethos of self-sacrifice for the nation—as against "enlightened self-interest." Any sacrifice was justified in creating a national state; and the cultivation of the indigenous arts, crafts, sports, and language was justified inasmuch as it served that end (55).

In the spirit of Young Ireland, Griffith and Rooney ran regular columns on Irish history and mythology to instruct the Irish people in their own history and culture. His newspaper provided surveys of Irish literature, encouraged the cultivation of Irish music and language, and gave notice of affairs sponsored by the Gaelic League, the Young Ireland Society, the Anti-Treating League, and the Gaelic Athletic Association (Ó Lúing, 94, 107). The pages of his paper featured letters and articles by figures as diverse as Yeats, Douglas Hyde, Thomas Kettle, Patrick Pearse, Eoin MacNéill, many clerical figures, and Frederick Ryan, the leading socialist and agnostic in Dublin. For all that, under a variety of pseudonyms, Griffith wrote most of each issue himself. Although the *United Irishman* had a modest circulation, its readers included all the influential figures in the advanced nationalist circles of the time—those faithful to the memory of Charles Stewart Parnell (Glandon, 13).

Griffith was first of all a pragmatic nationalist ideologue. He had little appreciation of the arts apart from their political usefulness: they were a higher form of political propaganda and useful in overcoming the banality and corruption of English influences permeating Irish society. He was a vehement opponent of Anglicization, denouncing both the prurience and jingoism of the music hall and the "respectability" of genteel West Britonism. He was convinced that sentimental and immoral literature abetted colonial designs. They degraded the lower classes and made them amenable to capitalist exploitation. He thought that Britain suppressed Irish industries and exploited her natural resources. The British enticed Irish entrepreneurs (such as Dunlop) to leave Ireland and invest Irish capital in the "mainland." He viewed unrestricted commercialism as leading to the degradation of the populace by a tyrannical elite and its mercenaries. He therefore inveighed against "respectable" shopkeepers and professionals who served Dublin Castle and ignored the slums: they were no better than Irish women consorting with British soldiers. He dismissed William Martin Murphy's *Irish Independent* as a near-tabloid purveyor of British decadence (Maume, 50–53).

The vehemence (or intemperance) of his denigration of the queen as a patron of suppression and prison led him to publish Maud Gonne's inflammatory broadside giving Queen Victoria the insulting sobriquet, the "Famine Queen" (*United Irishman,* April 14, 1900: 5). This insult to the monarch earned for Griffith a month's incarceration and the temporary closure of his weekly.[5]

Griffith was a courageous, energetic, impatient, obstinate, and occasionally witty journalist. He enunciated his positions in a highly colored and dramatic style, alternating between sarcastic and heroic epithet. He specialized in rousing invective, calling the events of 1845–48 "the Great Artificial Famine" (*Resurrection of Hungary,* xviii), terming the Irish public schools "the stultification system" (xxi), and ridiculing the "brass band" of "the denationalized nobles" of Austria (xxii). He excoriated the acquiescence of the Irish Party in the rule of Westminster. He claimed that the net result of the Union was "three rebellions, four major famines, twenty-seven minor famines, thirteen major industries closed down, the abolition of the Irish Exchequer and Customs, a five-fold increase in Irish taxation, a 25 percent decrease in the population, the exile from Ireland of five million people, and the change over to grazing of 80 percent of the tillage land of Ireland" (cited by McCartney, 38). The vehemence with which he held his positions earned him censure from Pearse, and his severe reservations about the political usefulness of the language revival injected tension into his public relationship with Hyde. Similarly, he clashed with Yeats over the role of the theater in the renewal of national life, and with Connolly over his declared skepticism about the prospect of a worldwide socialist fraternity.

In 1900, Griffith founded Cumann na nGaedhal to advance Irish national independence through cultivating industries, Gaelic culture, physical education, and the nationalization of public boards. Cumann na nGaedhal opposed physical force except as a last resort in achieving these ends. This led to the formation of a National Council (1903), originally to oppose the king's visit, but evolving into a forum for advanced nationalists to discuss their common cause. This organization evolved into the Sinn Féin party (January 1904), which after 1906 formed the main opposition to the Unionists in Dublin Corporation (Ó Lúing, 132–33). During the summer of that year, Griffith focused his efforts on two issues: the International Exhibition, and *The Resurrection of Hungary*. A committee of industrial and commercial elites, led by William Martin Murphy and the Earl of Drogheda, organized a trade fair exhibiting the latest advances in British and Continental technology. Griffith organized a protectionist counter attraction, an Irish Industries Show based on the slogan, "buy Irish" (154–55).

Following his return from Paris and for several years afterward, James Joyce was among Griffith's regular readers (*MBK* 168–70). Over the succeeding eighteen months, Joyce attended to Griffith's propaganda, concurring with much of it: the necessity to combine Irish nationalist aspirations with the encouragement of free enterprise, of offering passive resistance to British efforts at co-option, and the boycott of Westminster. Joyce had some disagreements with Griffith: over the Irish language policy, over his criticism of Yeats's theater, and, as Tekla Mecsnóber points out, over sexual mores. Griffith had denounced British "venereal excess" in Ireland, to which Joyce replied that waxing about "pure men and pure women and spiritual love . . . [was] lying drivel" (*Letters* II: 191–92).

In viewing "After the Race" as a development of the Fournier interview, therefore, these stirring public events and Griffith's prominent part in them must be taken into account. The story embraces in various ways the staging of the race itself, the adverse press reaction to it, the larger protests against the king's visit that followed hard upon, and the subsequent Emmet centennial in September. These contentions were resuscitated the following year with King Edward's second visit, the massive display of British naval power during the Horse Show Week (both July),[6] and Griffith's cumulative publication of *The Resurrection of Hungary* (September). That Joyce was sympathetic to Griffith's efforts is borne out by his contribution to the concert on August 27, 1904, which was part of Griffith's Irish Industries Show, in contention with William Martin Murphy's International Exhibition. It is the subject of "A Mother," in which Griffith appears, unkindly cast as Hoppy Holohan.

Joyce and Griffith

In James Joyce's small pantheon of Irish political leaders, Arthur Griffith came second only to Charles Stewart Parnell. This evaluation Griffith earned the hard way, to judge by the contrast between Joyce's youthful remarks and those of his maturity. Their relationship began with the launching of the *United Irishman* (1899) and ended only with Griffith's death in 1922. To judge by Stanislaus's admittedly unreliable remarks, Joyce might well have been initially attracted to Griffith's paper because it came in for castigation by the Jesuits at Belvedere and the indifference of his classmates at the National University to its politics (*MBK* 168–69). The relationship started badly with Joyce's dismissive estimation of William Rooney's *Poems and Ballads* (*JJII* 112). In that review, Joyce had not only made a crucial distinction between political and literary sincerity (he assailed the carelessness and meanness of spirit in the collection), but described its attempt at poetic rhetoric as "issued from headquarters" (*CW* 84–85, December 11, 1902). This was a thrust at Griffith, who used that jibe repeatedly in his own criticism of writers he claimed were "Castle Catholics." Griffith had wit enough to cite one of Joyce's own phrases ("one of those big words [patriotism] which make us so unhappy") in advertising Rooney's book in the next issue (December 20) of the *United Irishman* (*JJII* 112). It took some years before Griffith forgave Joyce for that offense to the memory of Rooney whom he estimated the noblest man he knew (Ó Lúing, 98). To Joyce, however, the issue was not moral character, but literary judgment, a matter about which they differed sharply (Mecsnóber, 342). For Griffith, politics subsumed art, whereas for Joyce, it was the reverse.[7] Whereas Griffith preached against "the false lights of cosmopolitanism," Joyce criticized the Irish and Gaelic revivals for their indiscipline and parochialism.

Joyce was on social terms with many of Griffith's political acquaintances during his years at the Royal University, as the two long paragraphs in *Stephen Hero* indicate (61–62). In Cooney's tobacco-shop on Friday nights, the leading members of "the irreconcilable party" assembled under the leadership of Michael Cusack and Arthur Griffith. Joyce took a sardonic view of those discussions, thinking them purblind and politically naive. Their enthusiasm for the Hungarian precedent was excessive and socially misjudged in that it left undisturbed the despotic rule of the Magyar elites over the majority Slavic and Teutonic descendants of the former villains. These passages confirm that Joyce was at least an occasional reader of the *United Irishman*, since it did indeed carry regular reports on "any signs of Philocelticism . . . in the Paris newspapers," notices of Gaelic Athletic Association activities, and the dispute between the GAA and Dublin Corporation over the use of the Phoenix Park for hurling and Gaelic football matches. Unionist members of the Corporation had contended that hurling was a danger to health, whereas Griffith had poured derision on their patronage of polo (*United Irishman*, June 13, 1903: 5).

For his part, Griffith approved of the recreational advantages of hiking over physical contact sports. Given his own predispositions toward walking as a means of healthful familiarization with his surroundings, Joyce would certainly have approved of one of Griffith's subsequent columns in which he advocated the cultural advantages of walking or cycling over automobile driving. Automobile drivers, these "scorchers and record-breakers," were in too much of a hurry to appreciate the scenery or the historical associations of the places visited (ibid., March 26, 1904). Griffith was a regular visitor to the Martello tower, cycling out from the city and taking a vigorous thirty-minute swim at the Forty Foot, and sunning himself on the rocks (*JJII* 172). That Griffith was acquainted with Joyce from around this time is attested by William Bulfin's report of a seventy-mile bicycle ride in Griffith's company one weekend in August–September 1904 (322–24). Griffith's historical presence at this edifice, within the line of sight of an observer standing on the deck of a yacht moored in Kingstown Harbour to view the rising sun, at the time his *Resurrection of Hungary* was being publicly debated suggests, therefore, that his contribution to the political myth of national deliverance underwrites both the opening chapter of *Ulysses* and the last line of "After the Race."

For all his reservations about Griffith, Joyce's letters to his brother document his persistent interest in the pages of the *United Irishman* after his departure to Trieste, and even after it was reconstituted as *Sinn Féin* (1906).[8] As Mecsnóber writes, Joyce's critical attitude toward the Austro-Hungarian control of Trieste was affected by his reading of Griffith's critique of this particular example of imperialism in action (341).

It is abundantly clear from this correspondence (and from Stanislaus's writings) that on the subject of contemporary Irish politics, the first name that always came to Joyce's mind was Griffith's. "Poor little U.I.: indignant little chap," he wrote on March 15, 1905, evidently in response to the most recent issue of the newspaper Stanislaus had forwarded (*Letters* II: 85). "Ivy Day in the Committee Room," Joyce's story most concerned with contemporary politics (written that midsummer), is informed by Griffith's loyalty to Parnell, his critique of the Irish Party, of the socialists, the Unionists, and takes up one of Griffith's crusades: his opposition to "loyal addressers" on the occasion of the king's visit in 1903 (Jackson and Costello, 246–48).

In all of this correspondence, it is clear that Joyce favored Griffith's over his father's Irish Party. He was kept abreast of the development of Griffith's political organization and ideas as reported in the pages of *Sinn Féin*. At the second annual convention of the National Council (September 1906), Griffith made the keynote speech calling for the boycott of certain British goods, for a scheme of primary and secondary education conducted on national principles, for the creation of a national banking system, and for the establishment of a national civil service. This elicited from Joyce his most comprehensive assessment of Griffith:

> [S]o far as my knowledge of Irish affairs goes, he was the first person in Ireland to revive the separatist idea on modern lines nine years ago. He wants the creation of an Irish consular service abroad, and of an Irish bank at home. . . . A great deal of his programme perhaps is absurd but at least it tries to inaugurate some commercial life for Ireland and to tell you the truth once or twice in Trieste I felt myself humiliated when I heard the little Galatti girl sneering at my impoverished country. You may remember that on my arrival in Trieste I actually "took some steps" to secure an agency for Foxford tweeds there. What I object to most of all in his paper is that it is educating the people of Ireland on the old pap of racial hatred whereas anyone

can see that if the Irish question exists, it exists for the Irish proletariat chiefly. (*Letters* II: 167)

This passage attests to Joyce's admiration of and reservations about Griffith. While he shares his national feelings, he keeps a socialist's distance from his chauvinism. At the same time, he sees his own efforts to import Irish woolens into Trieste as an expression of just the modern, practical, patriotism advocated by Griffith. The passage also implies that the kind of entrepreneurship of which he approves is the antithesis of that embodied by the fictional Doyles.

Two months later, in a sequence of letters to Stanislaus, with whom he evidently had a disagreement about Griffith's newly formed Sinn Féin Party, Joyce repeated his approval of the policy of abstention from Westminster in favor of practical trade and economic measures. In a remarkable volte-face from the condescension of *Stephen Hero* four years before, he admitted that "either *Sinn Fein* or Imperialism will conquer the present Ireland" (*Letters* II: 187). In this same letter he professes to admire Griffith's "intelligence and directness," although he is skeptical about the prospects of achieving a secular society free of the moral and linguistic agendas of the Catholic Church and of the Gaelic League, respectively. Similarly, while he approves of Griffith's persistence in exposing "the odour of corruption" hanging over the Irish Party, he is repelled by his reactionary Anglophobia and sexual repression (191; *MBK* 168–69).

When Joyce ran into intractable problems with George Roberts over the prospect of a Dublin publication of *Dubliners* in 1911, he wrote his "Curious History," a letter protesting his ill treatment by Maunsel's manager. Although he sent it to numerous newspapers, only Griffith's *Sinn Féin* ran it in full (*Letters* II: 291–93; *JJII* 334–35), where it appeared in the August 17 issue. When Joyce visited Dublin twelve months later, Griffith received him "very kindly," and advised him that Roberts's fear of libel was not unrealistic. In publishing this letter including the reference to Edward VII's profligate life, Griffith was acknowledging that he had given Joyce the lead in this matter and recognized in Joyce his own protégé. As the present investigation holds, Joyce writes as a disciple of Griffith not only in "Ivy Day in the Committee Room," but in "After the Race" as well. A glance at Joyce's essays, "Home Rule Comes of Age" (1907; *CW* 193–96) and "The Home Rule Comet" (1910; *CW* 209–13), shows them to be expansions of Griffith's famous witticism about this ever-postponed promise of the Irish Party: "[I]f this be liberty the lexicographers have deceived us."

By the time that Joyce undertook the writing of *Ulysses,* Griffith had become the most popular figure in the Irish nationalist movement, ahead of Eoin MacNéill and Patrick Pearse. His newspaper was one of the principal organs responsible for creating the intellectual atmosphere that made the 1916 rebellion possible, although he sided with MacNéill in attempting to dissuade its leaders from proceeding into military action. Nevertheless, as subsequent events transpired, the 1916 Rising became known as the Sinn Féin Rebellion, catapulting his small party into the forefront of the War of Independence after the 1919 election, so that when the Free State was eventually established, it pursued the principles laid down in the *Resurrection of Hungary* fifteen years before (McCartney, 47). For his part, as the writing of *Ulysses* progressed, Joyce inscribes but one contemporary politician: Arthur Griffith. He appears in the minds of the narrators of two episodes (*U* 12.1574, 15.4685) and in the thoughts of each of the main three characters: Stephen's (*U* 3.227); as the patron of Bloom's nationalist politics, which are proactively Home Rule, Land League, entrepreneurial, and nonviolent (*U* 4.101, 5.71, 8.462); and twice in the last episode, in Molly's skepticism about her husband's associations with "that little man" (*U* 18.383–88) (anticipating the creation of Sinn Féin by sixteen months). It is historically significant, moreover, that as Joyce was writing these pages in Paris, Griffith was undertaking the negotiation of the terms of Ireland's political future. *Ulysses* was published in February 1922, six weeks after Griffith signed the Anglo-Irish Treaty, establishing the Irish Free State.

Joyce was happy to know that when *Ulysses* appeared, Griffith was the first president of the Irish Free State (*JJII* 533). This insignificant-looking man had none of Parnell's glamour, but embodied something beyond his pragmatic politics and persistence: personal courage. A member of the British delegation was later to write, "a braver man than Arthur Griffith I never met." Similarly, Griffith left an indelible impression on Joyce's imagination.

In the triple invocation "Gryffygryffygryffs," then, Joyce mythologizes Arthur Griffith as a gryphon. Consecrated to the sun, this ferocious enemy of the horse is the doughty guard of the treasure hidden in its native mountains. Its square stance and defiant brow betoken intelligence and fortitude. For his moral courage in defending Ireland's industries and natural resources against imperial horsepower (and his publication of "A Curious History"), Joyce confers upon Griffith a sterling heraldic escutcheon. Its motto, an echochamber of affectionate street cry, minatory growl, and resplendent declamation, reverberates with some of the tones first struck in the story that ends at dawn.

"the odour of offal"

How, then, does "After the Race" express Joyce's debt to Arthur Griffith's vision of Irish politics?

As many commentators (for example, Bowen, "After the Race," 57–58; Walzl, 194–95) have observed, the naturalistic action of the story gives us Joyce's only take on members of the Irish commercial class. Under the pretense of amity and style, they exploit one another. Both the race and its aftermath tell the same flat story: how the Irish are political and business losers to the English and the Continentals. The story makes it clear that the peasants and ordinary Dubliners are awed onlookers at a display of foreign wealth and power. The story, moreover, is not about the attraction of foreign investment in Ireland, but about capital flight.

The Doyles personify the corruption of the Irish Party, the father a formerly "advanced Nationalist" (*D* 43.15) whose business success is based on service to the Crown, and the son who has invested his inheritance in a frivolous foreign business enterprise. Only in his cups does the ghost of Jimmy's *mauvais foi* rise to accuse his conscience and provoke atavistic acrimony. These aspects of the fortunes of the Doyle family reflect some themes in Griffith's more personal attacks on members of the Irish Party: besides the ineffectuality of their participation in the illegal "talking shop" of Westminster, it was a recurrent theme in his criticism of individual members that since the death of Parnell they abandoned the dedication to the pursuit of Home Rule, directing their energies to self-enrichment through their political and business networking, betraying the cause of Ireland by foreign investment, and engaging in business pursuits indifferent to the interests of the Irish proletariat.

As is well known, the career of Jimmy Doyle's father is drawn on that of William Field, a successful Dublin victualler. He was a prominent Nationalist from Blackrock, County Dublin, a member of the Dublin Corporation, and MP for St. Patrick's Division from 1892 to 1918. Field's father was a Young Irelander at the time of the Famine, and his own political career began during the agitation supporting amnesty for imprisoned Fenians in the 1870s. His business ascent commenced from his butcher's shop at Number 6, Main Street, Blackrock, and expanded over the next two decades into a chain of similar establishments all over the city (Jackson and Costello, 169). He was a personal acquaintance of John Stanislaus Joyce from the time of the Joyce domicile on Carysfort Avenue, Blackrock, 1892–93 (Costello, 106), subsequently leading the Nationalist capture of Blackrock urban district council from the Unionists. The combination of this trade and his personal eccentricities—he went about town with shoulder-length hair, a black broad-brimmed hat, and a long black cloak—earned him the name "Hamlet" in the Joyce household.[9]

Field helped organize Parnell commemorations, the 1798 centennial, and was on the platform during the Emmet centennial in September 1903. His extensive personal contacts among the Dublin working class made him one of the few members of Parliament impervious to the constant criticism leveled at the Irish Party by Griffith in the pages of the *United Irishman* and *Sinn Féin*. Griffith attacked Field for using his position for self advancement, and as a member of the Irish Party, for participating in Westminster debates. He called, instead, on voters "to repudiate forever . . . the sham miscalled 'constitutional action'" (*United Irishman*, 1899, cited by McGee, 274). Field's supporters responded with a public address and presentation. In its report of the occasion, the *Daily Independent* praised Field for his leadership and generosity: he was highly reputed by all "ites," as "unpurchasable." Griffith was not deterred by such rebuttals. We find him, therefore, four years later, calling on all Irishmen to cease supporting Westminster MPs of any kind. He quipped that the term "advanced nationalism" that the Irish Party journalists had always used to describe the politics of the supposed "extreme Fenian party" made no literal sense ("nationalism cannot be any more or less advanced than nationalism") and was simply a ploy designed to confuse the public mind and hide the fact that Westminster MPs were not in any sense Irish nationalists (*United Irishman*, May 22, 1903). William Field was again among those upon whom he poured his disdain in June 1903, at the height of the controversy over the royal address, calling him a "flunkey" of the Crown (Jackson and McGinley, 35u).

A vigorous urban Nationalist MP, Field argued strenuously in Westminster for legislation making urban landlords accountable for the upkeep of their properties and for rent control. William Field is therefore no easier a target for Joyce's satire in "After the Race" than he was in the pages of the *United Irishman.* A leading figure in the Irish Cattle Traders and Stockowners' Association (Costello, 299), his proprietary interest in foot-and-mouth disease is a likely source of Joyce's citation of this agricultural matter in *Ulysses*.[10]

There is no specific evidence that Field's fortune derived from police contracts. It would have been difficult for him to retain his political reputation as a leading Nationalist were it so or so bruited about. The fictional charge conveys a complex irony that would, in time, become recognizable as characteristically Joycean. This early sighting calls for a brief dilation.

In the city of Joyce's youth, the Dublin Metropolitan Police (DMP) were a formidable presence. Their high visibility on the streets was undoubtedly due to political considerations: the felt need to discourage subversion, particularly in view of the unrest surrounding the commemorations of the 1798 Rebellion, the Boer War, and the succession of protests over the visits of Austen Chamberlain and royalty. Consequently, the charge that the ratepayers of Dublin were paying for their political repression even by their own people was one of the refrains in the nationalist press (O'Brien, 243).[11] A force of 1,100 men selected for their physical size and housed in seventeen barracks plus the Training Depot on Kevin Street, they bulked large in the consciousness even of apolitical citizens. The DMP went about their business unarmed, and were therefore not regarded as posing the same degree of imperial intimidation as their counterparts in the provinces, the Royal Irish Constabulary. Recruited from among the sons of provincial Irish small farmers, they were regarded by Dubliners as uncouth and "harmless" dupes of empire rather than as enemies of the people. This is, indeed, the way they appear in Joyce's story, "Grace," where the trainees appear but one step removed from the cabbage flung in their direction at dinnertime: "65, catch your cabbage!" (*D* 161.4). Similarly, in *Ulysses,* Leopold Bloom thinks of them in connection with fat soup, beef, bacon, and drilling (*U* 8.406–13). They were regarded as enforcing the law not by force of arms but by their embodiment of beef and brawn. Supplying their official premises with meat was thus both the essential means by which law and order was maintained in the City of Dublin and a lucrative business. Since the valuable contracts governing this supply to the eighteen police facilities were subject to political patronage, they became a real, if unpublicized, issue at every election to the Dublin Corporation.[12]

Now, among the duties assigned the DMP, next to the arrest of drunks and domestic abusers (statistically high in their annual reports), came the inspection of premises that might pose a hazard to public health (O'Brien, 183–87). This duty was of vital public importance because during the last quarter of the nineteenth century, Dublin exhibited the most elevated mortality rates among major towns and cities of Britain and Ireland (ibid., 22; Daly, 274); and there was general suspicion that this high incidence was due to overcrowded tenements, poor sanitation, malnutrition, and virtually unregulated private slaughterhouses (Daly, 271–75). Recognizing the salience of this last factor, the Dublin Corporation attempted to abolish all private slaughterhouses in favor of a municipal abattoir.

But when this facility was constructed in 1881 outside the city boundary (and beyond the jurisdiction of the Corporation) it posed no official threat to private operators. The result was that fully three quarters of the 3,000 animals slaughtered each week in the city in 1900 were dispatched in the sixty-seven private facilities serving 137 butchers. Hence the usual spectacle of hundreds of cattle being driven from the pens at the market where they were bought, not across the street to the abattoir but in wayward procession through the city to the various private yards in residential areas—even in the heart of the city (O'Brien, 123). Many of these yards were in wretched condition with ramshackle huts and shanties, their floors stained with the residue of blood, offal, and entrails. The infected—or what Bloom calls "dicky"—meat (U 6.397) produced by these unsanitary yards often ended up in the markets. This also meant that only the most exclusive neighborhoods were free of the stench of offal drifting down laneways and between the residences. This situation therefore posed both a serious public health hazard and an odious offense. Not surprisingly, there were frequent outbreaks of infectious diseases.

Historians of the period report the ongoing campaign of the Dublin Corporation and the Sanitary Committee to deodorize the city. These authorities tried to have the constabulary make rigorous inspection of overcrowded tenements and their sanitary facilities (outdoor toilets and ashpits), suspected houses of prostitution, and the scores of dairies and slaughterhouses. Throughout the last quarter of the nineteenth century, the victuallers association (second only to the licensed vintners in political clout) stoutly resisted the regulation of this last category. The chief spokesman for this powerful lobby arguing against restrictions on free trade was a victualler who won every election to Dublin Corporation between 1895 and 1916: none other than William J. Field MP (Daly, 262–63).

In turning the historical Field into the fictional Doyle, then, Joyce is imputing another level of corruption and conflict of interest to the figure that otherwise does not appear in the explicit text of his story. Doyle is supplying victuals to the force charged with supervising the conditions under which his meat is slaughtered and the offal disposed. The contemporary records admit that the health code was poorly enforced, and inspecting constables often turned a blind eye to breaches of the regulations. Indeed, as if it were a purposeful dimension of their training, the supernumeraries in the police Training Depot were required to endure daily reminders of a notoriously smelly knacker's yard in the adjoining premises on Kevin Street.

Therefore, when Joyce wrote to Grant Richards to defend *Dubliners* against the charge of indecency, and indignantly insisted that "It is not my fault that the odour of ashpits and old weeds and offal hangs round my stories" (*Letters* I: 63–64, June 23, 1906), he was not merely flailing the metaphorical air. At least with respect to "After the Race," we are entitled to take him at his literal word.[13] These inferences from the text and silences of "After the Race" are supported by one historical and two fictional witnesses: the agitprop playwright, Oliver St. John Gogarty and the medical student Malachi Mulligan, the immortal citizen, Leopold Bloom.

Oliver Gogarty, MD, took public health seriously enough to write a stage play dramatizing the dire conditions in the city's tenements. *Blight: The Tragedy of Dublin* was a sensation when produced at the Abbey in 1917. His criticism of the milk and meat business appears in the voice of Stanislaus Tully, who calls the milk of the city "liquid filth," and the knackers' yards on Saint Patrick's Street and Bull Alley as driving the poor to drink (cited by Ulick O'Connor, 137). In the spirit of Arthur Griffith, he attacks the complacency of the middle classes who refuse to face up to the prevalence of the sickness and poverty in their midst. The original "slum play" in the Abbey tradition, it anticipated Seán O'Casey's celebrated trilogy on inner-city life.

In *Ulysses*, both Mulligan and Bloom express concern about the ways in which the dairy and slaughterhouse businesses imperiled public health. Mulligan, "her medicineman" (*U* 1.419) compliments the "milkwoman" (*U* 1.498) on the quality of her Sandycove milk.[14] Were everyone to have such a reliable supply, he argues, "we wouldn't have the country full of rotten teeth and rotten guts. Living in a bogswamp, eating cheap foods and the streets paved with dust, horsedung and consumptives' spits" (*U* 1.411–14). This social critique lodges in Stephen's mind, and when summoned three hours later, it has become typically internalized as, "Dead breaths I living breathe, tread dead dust, devour a ruinous offal from all dead" (*U* 3.479–80). For his part, Bloom extrapolates the familiar Dublin complaint and fear to a fantasy about Glasnevin Cemetery: "infernal lot of bad gas . . . one whiff of that and you're a doner" (*U* 6.607–12). Joining the discussion of the diseases of animals in Barney Kiernan's, he is reported as twice going beyond either of the young men, taking action in the spirit of responsible citizenship: "Because he was up one time in a knacker's yard. Walking about with his book and pencil . . . Joe Cuffe gave him the order of the boot for giving lip to a grazier. Mister Knowall . . . [advocating] [h]umane methods [of slaughter]" (*U* 12.835–43).

These issues were, therefore, very likely the subject of discussion between Joyce and Gogarty before or during the Martello tower sojourn, and just ripple the surface of "After the Race." Joyce's portrayal of the Doyle fortune as based on a butchery business catering for the Dublin Metropolitan Police does not appear to have brought Field to the minds of either the editors of the *Irish Homestead* or Maunsel and Company, even though George Roberts and his printer were apprehensive about potential libel. The fictional Doyle has a son and heir, whereas the historical Field—but one of the 135 butchers in Dublin at the time—died without issue in 1935.[15]

Joyce's antipathy to Field may derive from some aspect of his father's relationship with his fellow Parnellite. The critique of mercantilism in "After the Race" is partially owing to Griffith. The narrator's superior attitude toward money is not Griffith's. Neither did Griffith moralize about what made one "genuinely happy" (*D* 43.12). He was a pragmatic nationalist whose rhetoric could range from mild sarcasm to vituperation. Therefore, while some of the narrator's heavy ironies—"modified his views early" (*D* 43.16), "fortunate enough to secure some of the police contracts" (*D* 43.19), "merchant prince" (*D* 43.21), "advanced Nationalist" (*D* 43.15), and "unpurchasable" (*D* 45.33)—are informed by Griffith's lexicon, the narrator's critical stance is more supercilious, condescending, and understated than anything flowing from Griffith's forthright pen.

Griffith's positions can sometimes be discerned in Joyce's stance in some of these early stories. On the one hand, behind the attribution of

"English accents" to the purveyors of porcelain vases at the "Araby" bazaar, we can read Griffith's repeated criticism of such bazaars and *cafés chantants* as "un-Irish" (for example, see *United Irishman,* March 18, 1899). On the other, as a political allegory, "After the Race" is a critique of race-based nationalism. Griffith and others at the time (D. P. Moran and some Gaelic Leaguers) were inclined—based upon the notion of an original Milesian/Celtic substratum—to objectify Irishness. That Joyce objected to this aspect of Griffith's thinking or propaganda is one of the major political themes of *Ulysses;* but it is obliquely adumbrated in this story. From this perspective, the title can be translated as "after nationalism." Once the claims of race are set aside, the resurrection of Ireland can follow. In the light of the universal sun, Ireland can, like Hungary, take her place among the nations of the earth.

There is a significant contemporary irony, then, in Ségouin's "shepherd[ing] his party into politics [because] [H]ere was congenial ground for all" (*D* 46.21–22) in the hotel dining room on the night of July 2, 1903, when the very next evening, Arthur Griffith, in the chambers of City Hall, was leading a bitter attack on members of the Dublin Corporation, Unionists and Nationalists alike (among whom was William Field), for even debating the prospect of offering an address of welcome to King Edward VII.[16] The larger political irony resides in the analogy between the "greens" of the two Saints Stephen: the first Christian martyr and the patron of Hungary.

Magyars Reimagined

The Resurrection of Hungary appeared in the *United Irishman* in serial form (27 articles, January 21 to July 24, 1904), and then in book form (99 pages) on September 29, 1904, as Joyce was working on "After the Race. It was an instant best seller: 20,000 copies in three months (Ó Lúing, 121–25). This success was mainly due to its dramatic conclusion: the proposal that, pursuant to the Hungarian precedent, elected Irish MPs, rather than attending Westminster, should themselves unilaterally constitute a governing body for Ireland.

Griffith justifies this move on two grounds: the illegality of the Act of Union (1800) and the century of material and moral disasters that befell Ireland since the passage of this legislation. Citing the Renunciation Act of 1783 through which the British Parliament had abrogated its right to legislate for Ireland, he held that the Union was illegitimate, and that the Irish Party's presence in Westminster was illegal. They should therefore cease to attend Parliament. This strategy in attacking the Union was not new: Daniel O'Connell, Thomas Davis, and John Mitchel had advocated similar courses. Griffith renewed the argument after the tactics that had recently proved effective in other sectors: Parnell's filibuster, Michael Davitt's boycott, the Gaelic Athletic Association's ban on foreign games, and Douglas Hyde's program of de-Anglicization (McCartney, 34).

Taking the position that devolution within the Austro-Hungarian Empire remediated Hungary's former political debility, Griffith holds that, given the historical parallels in Anglo-Irish relations, a similar move would benefit Ireland. Despite the dignity of its native languages and cultures, Hungary was Germanicized as Ireland was Anglicized. Despite their abundant natural resources and native talent, the Hungarians were treated prejudicially within the empire: like the Irish in the British Empire, their continued service to that alliance was not in their own best interest. The Austrians put it about that "Hungarians were nothing better than ignorant boors, drunken, immoral, and intractable, whom Austria was compelled to occasionally punish in the best interests of civilization" (*United Irishman*, June 3–5, 1904). In chapter 15 of *Resurrection*, Griffith argues that the negative caricature of the Hungarians as "Magyar Miska" [Michaels] was paralleled in British caricatures of the Irish as lazy, disorganized, and feckless. Through the pages of his newspaper, Griffith sought to explode the image of the Hungarians and of the Irish as impulsive liars, of these "white Turks" and "Oriental Paddies" whose territory was "simply the most backward country in Europe." Instead, he attempted to reinstate the image of the "heroic ... brave [and] ... gallant Hungarians" (cited by Mecsnóber, 343). His frequently reiterated view that the power of the imperial press to justify continued British exploitation of Ireland militated against Ireland's ability to lay its just cause before the world's conscience is the theme taken up by Joyce in his trenchant 1907 contributions to *Il Piccolo della Sera*, especially "Ireland at the Bar" (*CW* 197–200) and, with more dispassionate art, in the story "Counterparts" (see Owens, "Joyce's Farrington").

Both Hungarian and Irish resistances to imperialism were inspired by the nationalism sweeping Europe in the first half of the nineteenth century. Like Hungary, Ireland should recognize that her enemy's difficulty presented her with an opportunity: Austria's conflict with Germany and

Britain's with the Boers presented Hungary and Ireland with similar political opportunities.

The Hungarian precedent offered several models to Irish separatists: the rejection of physical force in favor of passive resistance (Ferenc Deák), the revival of an Irish monarchy after the precedent of the dual monarchy (1867), and the establishment of an Irish Dáil in Dublin like the Council of Three Hundred in Budapest (Lajos Kossuth). Ireland should establish her own trading network, legal system, and education program that would inculcate pride in her own language and history. Beyond these separate interests, the "common factors"—foreign affairs, defense, and finance—should be preserved. Under a common flag acknowledging a dual monarchy, as Hungary is "for the Hungarians," Ireland would be "for the Irish." Griffith recounts the revival of pride in Hungarian folklore, music, native traditions, and the language and literature of the Magyars, ridiculing at the same time the "brass band" of Austrian propaganda and the mystique of the Esterhazy family.[17]

With the controversy over the address to King Edward still in the public mind, Griffith developed the parallel circumstances attendant upon an axial incident in Austro-Hungarian relations. Ferenc Deák took advantage of a similar opportunity presented by the emperor's visit to Budapest, to make the public case for Hungarian Home Rule. Deák's "First Address of the Hungarian Diet of 1861 to His Imperial Majesty Francis Josef, Emperor of Austria" converted a formality into a bold political stroke. "In this great document," Griffith wrote, "every line breathing manliness, patriotism, and resolution, Deák stated the case of Hungary, not for Francis Josef only, but for all the world. The Loyal-Addresses, as we know them in Ireland, had ceased to exist in the Hungary of 1861" (19, chapter 4). Deák stated the case for Hungary's claim to constitutional devolution from Austria, concluding, "therefore, we declare that we will take part neither in the Imperial Parliament nor in any other assembly whatsoever of the representatives of the Empire; and, further, that we cannot recognize the right of the said Imperial Parliament to legislate on the affairs of Hungary" (21).

In chapter 8, "The Royal Visit of 1865" (37–38, *United Irishman,* February 20, 1904), Griffith addresses an incident in Austro-Hungarian relations that was topical in Ireland nine months before. In this stage of his historical reconstruction of Austro-Hungarian relations, Griffith recounts the visit of the Emperor Francis Josef to Budapest in 1865—ostensibly to attend the races—but politically to cement Austrian control over her "weaker" sister. The chapter begins with these ironic sentences:

> It is to be clearly understood that the visit of his Imperial Majesty, the Emperor Francis Josef, to Pesth, the capital of disloyal Hungary, on the 6th of June, 1865, was wholly unconnected with politics, and was in no wise prompted by the fact that war between Austria and Prussia appeared inevitable. His Majesty went to Pesth for the purpose of seeing the races. . . . At the same time, however, it was thought well, in order to cut the claws of seditious and noisy persons, to insert paragraphs in the newspapers recalling to the recollection [*sic*.] of the Hungarians the kind words His Majesty had on more than one occasion used about Hungary, and the chief journal in Vienna even went so far as to say that His Majesty was so fond of the Hungarians that, but for certain ministers, he would long since have abolished military law and settled the Hungarian question satisfactorily. "The monarch," remarked this Vienna journal profoundly, "is equally the monarch of Hungarians and Austrians, and loyalty to the sovereign is as incumbent on the Hungarian as on the Austrian. Hungary can have no grievances against the sovereign, whatever faults she may find with his ministers." (38)

Griffith's sarcastic recounting of this incident from Austro-Hungarian relations reminds his readers of the rationale of his and Maud Gonne's protest against an address of welcome to King Edward the previous summer. It once again draws attention to the ways in which imperialism—Austrian or British—renders its subjects amenable to its rapine. In historicizing this incident in the long struggle of the Hungarians to rid themselves of Austrian control, Griffith is showing how relatively minor gestures of impoliteness could produce substantial results and how a strategy of passive resistance provided alternatives to abject compliance and violent rebellion. He is reminding his readers that events like the Gordon Bennett Cup Race and King Edward's visit were not only linked one to the other, but were both part of the political propaganda campaign that sought to turn the Irish into "little Englanders." Just as such propaganda had succeeded in recruiting tens of thousands of Irishmen to fight in the Boer War, it would do so the next time England found herself in a political crisis. By the time *The Resurrection of Hungary* appeared in its second edition (1918), Griffith would have been proved right again—and with vastly greater consequences. In drawing out this incident, then, Griffith is arguing that Hungarian diffidence to Austria's military problems in preparing for the Austro-Prussian war was paralleled by Ireland's detachment from England's difficulties in the Boer War and World War I.

This extended analogy with the Hungarian peaceful separatist movement was widely discussed at the time in the press and public platforms. It appealed to advanced nationalists who desired an alternative to the armed rebellion that had been the focus of so much recent celebration. Its publication drove the Irish Party to mend its internal divisions in the face of this new contender of its willingness to participate in what was to become widely thought of as an illegal and ineffectual talk shop. The Hungarian Policy was discussed at an all-day open conference at the Metropole Hotel on August 4, 1904, with delegates from London, Belfast, and the Irish provinces. They debated the merits of passive resistance, the expectation of American political and financial support, the prospect of the establishment of local arbitration courts independent of statute authority, and of the resuscitation of the native royal lineage.

Official response from Irish nationalist opinion-makers was slow to appear. Tom Kettle replied in February 1905, and Terence McSwiney in December, each granting its merits but querying its practicality. In response to D. P. Moran's derision (in the *Leader*) of the "Green Hungarian Band," Griffith published a sequel in the May-June issues of the *United Irishman*. For his part, Joyce wondered privately how cogent it was to present Hungarian separatism as a useful paradigm for the Irish proletariat since the Magyar landed gentry survived by subjecting the Slavs and Rumanians after 1867 (*Letters* II: 167; Manganiello, 121).

In this context, it is clear from his treatment of the subject of the address of welcome to the king in "Ivy Day in the Committee Room"—his favorite story—that Joyce was personally invested in Griffith's campaign. This reconstruction of Griffith's chronology supports the contention that just as Deák's subversion of the address of loyalty (1861) has a bearing on "Ivy Day," so does Deák's subsequent attack on the exploitation of royal visit and an apparently friendly day at the races (1865) have a similar bearing on "After the Race." This story, conceived and written in the midst of the public debate over Griffith's *Resurrection of Hungary* with its critique of the machinations of imperial propaganda justifies his invocation of the Hungarian connection in this story. Villona, a man endowed with no rank but with sensibility (he speaks for the arts of music and painting), the most fetching figure in the story, is a rebuttal of the stereotypically uncouth and slovenly Hungarian. For all his personal reservations about Griffith's ideas, this means that Joyce's "After the Race" is the first expression of approval of the Hungarian policy to appear in print in Ireland. Finally, in forging the Hungarian connection within his story, Joyce is stretching a point of verisimilitude.[18] Since Hungarian phonetics stresses the first syllable, his name constitutes a near homophone with "villain," the social class in Hungary that Joyce saw in need of liberation both from Austrian and Magyar exploitation. In giving his alter ego this unlikely name, then, Joyce is implying a fine sympathy with the Hungarianism espoused by Griffith.

"with linked arms"

Villona's announcement of daybreak is an express invocation of the talk of the town in late summer 1904, Griffith's *Resurrection of Hungary*. The nationality of Joyce's Hungarian was not drawn from life (although Joyce remembered his artistic Parisian friend as "enormous" [Gorman, 100]). As Tekla Mecsnóber observes, "he seems to be a perfect fit for the more attractive nationality traits that Griffith attributes to Hungarians" (343).[19] She adds that "the unabashedly physical and artistic Hungarian Villona and the repressed Irishman Jimmy seem to symbolize their national stereotypes; both of them truly take 'after the race' of their forefathers" (348). Perhaps, but Joyce's designs are always nicer than the uses of caricature.

Clearly, Jimmy Doyle is more closely linked to Villona (his "friend" [D 44.5, 45.16, 19]) than any other character in the story. The political implications of this relationship are conveyed in the sentences describing their after-dinner stroll ("the city wore the mask of a capital. The five young men strolled along Stephen's Green in a faint cloud of aromatic smoke. They talked loudly and gaily and their cloaks dangled from their shoulders. The people made way for them" [D 46.29–32]), and the one describing their later proceeding toward Kingstown Harbour ("with linked arms" [D 47.16–17]). These sentences have been inadequately glossed. First, when before the Act of Union, Dublin was (in a manner of speaking) a capital city, the street along which these twentieth-century bons vivants stroll—between the Shelbourne Hotel and the top of Grafton Street— Saint Stephen's Green North, was known as Beaux' Walk (Bennett, s.v. "St.

Stephen's Green"). Their swagger and style conjure images from Georgian Dublin when it was the capital city of a colony and noted for the opulence and style of the classes who lived along its elegant streets.

As Griffith argues in *The Resurrection of Hungary,* the substance of Budapest's protest against the hegemony of Vienna had been that it was not estimated an equal capital in a dual arrangement of mutual respect. At the time of the writing of "After the Race," the Austro-Hungarian flag represented the dual monarchy in a complex arrangement of colors and arms. In 1904 the Austro-Hungarian flag consisted of three equal and horizontal stripes depicting the red, white, and red of Austria, and the red, white, and green of Hungary. It also bore the two crowns above the arms of the dukes of Austria and those of the royal succession of Hungary. The latter was composed, in turn, of the double cross of Saint Stephen mounted upon a green base, and beneath that base, the green horizontal half-stripe representing Hungary. This emblem was familiar enough to Irish readers in 1904 for D. P. Moran to deride Griffith's followers as "the green Hungarian band" (a multiple reference to Griffith's jibe at the pomp and ceremony—the "brass bands"—of the Esterhazys, the Hungarian color, and the Cumann na nGaedhal/Sinn Féin movement).

The narrator of "After the Race," therefore, invokes a complex synecdoche of two greens and two Stephens. First, green is the national color of both Ireland and Hungary, in contrast with the red of Britain and Austria. Second, the narrator offers Dublin's Saint Stephen's Green as an amenity that would give the impression that Dublin was a capital, whereas it but wears a mask (as the equestrian statue of King George II on St. Stephen's Green would have reminded any stroller in 1903).[20] The "Green" in the place name is not adjectival, however, but a substantive in the sense recorded by the *OED* (12 b): "a piece of public or common ground in or near a village," and consistent with the Hiberno-English usage of a public garden or park (as the example cited from 1888 by the *OED* records). This particular Dublin Green (there are others at Trinity College and Sandymount) is named after the Hellenizer of early Christianity, better known as the protomartyr (Acts 6–7). He is the patron saint of Stephen Dedalus, the reason he calls it "my green" (*P* 249.10). The patron saint of Hungary (977–1038) bearing the same name, whose double cross stands upon the Hungarian green, was the Magyar king and founder of Christian Hungary, in the wake of the Battle of Veszprem (998). A wise and humble man, he traveled about the country he had just founded disguised as a beggar. He was canonized in 1083. When Hungary's claim to sovereignty was made in the nineteenth century, he became the patron of Hungarian nationalism.

The motif of the two kings or dual monarchy appears parodically in the last scenes of the story. When the young men resume their walk ("with linked arms") to Kingstown Harbour, the political symbolism of this location would not have been lost on literate Irish nationalist readers of the time. The succession of royal visits to Ireland—beginning with George IV in 1821, including Victoria's three (1849, 1861, 1900), and most recently, Edward VII's (1903, 1904)—linked the name with British imperial royalty. The royal cavalcade that opened each of these visits was the ritual ride from Kingstown to the Viceregal Lodge in the Phoenix Park; its complement, on the conclusion, was the return to the same Kingstown (O'Brien, 246–47). Before King George's visit it bore the name of *Dún Laoghaire* [Fortress of King Leary], after the fifth-century king of Tara who had a fort there. The name was restored after the victory of Griffith's Sinn Féin Party in the 1918 general election.

The motif of dual political and cultural allegiances represented in the Irish/British Hungarian/Austrian links permeates the yacht scene of "After the Race." Villona, the Hungarian pianist, plays a waltz (associated with Vienna); the revelry is described as "Bohemian" (*D* 47.31; one of the Hungarians' complaints against the Austrian administration was what they perceived as the Germanization—especially under Alexander Bach—of the bureaucracy). Again, the toasts celebrate the native countries of all the revelers, including Hungary (but neither Austro-Hungary nor Canada). The second round of toasts, moreover—to "the health of the Queen of Hearts and of the Queen of Diamonds" (*D* 48.7–8)—implies, besides good luck, the dual monarchs of love and wealth. In the context of the political allegory pursued by the story, however, this pair of reds celebrates the duality of the imperial powers of Vienna and London.

It is a measure of Joyce's debt to Griffith's imagining the restoration of the Irish high kingship (via the surviving lineage of O'Conor Donn) that he has a Hungarian Irish Jew, Leopold Bloom, accept the crown of Ireland in the "Circe" episode of *Ulysses* (see Robert Tracy).

These reflections help account for the appearance and roles of two minor figures in the story: Routh and Farley. Respective emblems of political enmity and alliance with Ireland's political interests, they are, as we shall see, consistent with Griffith's Anglophobia and Columbiaphily, respectively.

Routh

More than half way through the action of the story, a minor character makes a casual entry. We read that he is "a young Englishman" (*D* 46.5-6) who has been a student at Cambridge. Although bearing the distinguished English patronymic, he is ignorant of one of his nation's finer achievements in the arts: the vocal and instrumental music of the English Renaissance. He is apparently in Dublin to support the British drivers in the day's race, is apparently staying at the Shelbourne, and knows how to gamble. He has a stereotypically reserved manner, but is roused from his torpidity when his national honor is impugned. He trumps Jimmy Doyle's Anglophobia by announcing the final round of cards—which he wins—with a reference to the larger arena that would justify his British triumphalism: the Great Game (*D* 48.16). What are we to make of this *nouveau arriviste*?

Like Villona, he is named after one of Joyce's acquaintances in Paris, one Eugene Routh of indeterminate nationality (Gorman, 100; *JJII* 123). Of these historical characters Joyce divulged no more to Gorman. There must be some account for political antagonism that the fictional Routh arouses: he cannot be allowed to plead the Fifth Amendment.

Of the many Rouths in the *Dictionary of National Biography*, the obvious object of Joyce's reference here is Sir Randolph Routh (1785–1858), director of the Relief Commission for Ireland during the Famine (1845–48). In this capacity he executed the noninterventionist policies of Sir Robert Peel (1845–46) and Lord John Russell (1846–48), who made relief monies available on the condition that they did not interfere with normal commerce.

During his three years in Ireland as the chief commissioner in charge of the procurement and distribution of food for the starving population, he had Indian corn (maize) imported from the United States. He published recipes for the proper preparation of this unfamiliar and unpalatable commodity known as "Peel's Brimstone" (Kinealy, 64). For what was officially regarded as highly efficient work in the face of an escalating disaster, he was subsequently made a Knight Commander of the Bath.

Among his Irish dependents he won no such accolades. During the first two years of the Famine, he administered relief schemes that, in retrospect, were woefully inadequate. He allowed the landlords and their agents to proceed with thousands of evictions, affecting to see in these population-reducing actions the very hand of Providence. He therefore defended the export of grain in 1846, protecting the ports with troops to ensure that these commodities—which paid the rents—were safely shipped. As an administrator of Lord Charles Edward Trevelyan's laissez faire policies, he is partially blamed for the fact that these exports continued throughout his tenure, even as the people starved. Of the potato upon which the majority of the poor depended for their sustenance, he said that the ease of its cultivation left "the people to indolence and all kinds of vice . . . [and that] it is very probable that we may derive much advantage from this present calamity" (cited by Kinealy, 51). On the inadequacy of the ports in the west of Ireland to facilitate the importation of Indian meal, he remarked that "it is annoying that all these harbours are so insignificant. It shows Providence never intended Ireland to be a great nation" (cited by Woodham-Smith, 67). Late in the day, as the calamity escalated, he modified his theology, and shifted the burden of blame to some of the more adamantine landlords (163–64). Alarmed that further starvation could lead to rebellion, he moved with a greater sense of urgency to open the storehouses.

A fair reading of the record would conclude that Routh does not deserve the negative reputation accorded him by Irish nationalists: his name was a lightning rod for criticism of draconian policies that he had privately sought to adjust. In the verdict of popular opinion, nonetheless, he is indicted for defending the land system, the root cause of the Famine, and for the grudging response that allowed a crisis to become a catastrophe (Kinealy, 82). In the native oral tradition—which no doubt the Joyce family shared—the name of Routh was associated with Lord Trevelyan's famous vision of the Famine as the hand of God: "The great evil with which we have to contend is not the physical evil of the famine but the moral evil of the selfish, perverse and turbulent character of the people." Nationalists viewed the Famine as the result of the dispossession and systematic impoverishment of the people fully implemented after the Williamite War (1689–91) so that they were reduced to subsisting on a single, cheap, plentiful, but unstable crop. The Famine was therefore a predictable effect of Ireland's colonial exploitation. In John Mitchel's famous summary, "The Almighty, indeed, sent the potato blight, but the English created the Famine" (cited by Kinealy, 6).

Such sentiments were never far beneath the surface in political conversations concerning the Land Question in late-nineteenth-century Ireland. The British government and the Irish landlords, patronized by Queen Victoria herself, were viewed as the real villains of the Famine years (Kinealy, 14). Recriminations over the Famine received a renewed public airing in Maud Gonne's inflammatory broadside on the occasion of the queen's visit in 1900 and again during the first half of 1903, during the Westminster debate on the Wyndham Act. Advanced nationalists like Griffith saw this, the tenth in the series, as yet another version of the original Land Act of 1860 that secured the landlords' legal rights at the tenants' expense.

In 1860, there were 13,000 landlords, one-third of whom were absentees; three hundred of these estates exceeded 10,000 acres each. There were 500,000 tenants, 400,000 of whom had no written leases and were subject to short-notice eviction at any time. The 1903 Land Act instituted a massive government scheme of land purchase. This meant that landlords were invited to sell their land holdings for more than their fair market value; and tenants were thereby enabled to convert their rents into reduced payments that now became mortgages spread over 68 ½ years. The Wyndham Act thereby brought to an end the bitter Land War of the previous decade and greatly accelerated the pace of land transfer. It meant that the landlords were compensated for their surrendered lands, their power truncated to their demesnes, while more than half of the land passed into the proprietorship of the former peasantry. However contended at the time, these acts eventually remediated the most acrimonious ground-level issue in Ireland after the Famine.

The 1903 Land Act was supported by a majority of the Irish Party, led by William O'Brien, who accepted that it was not a decoy for Home Rule, but a firm step in that direction. The King's visit to Ireland was officially his acknowledgment of that historic compromise, although, as we have seen, Irish nationalist irreconcilables did not see it that way. When James Joyce returned from Paris in the spring of 1903, the debate over the principles, aims, and terms of this historic agreement were in the daily news. He was again struck by the poverty of his exploited country. In his subsequent attempts to explain this poverty to Europeans, he points to the causal links between English colonialism, Irish poverty, and starvation. Writing for the Triestines in 1907, he put it this way: "Ireland is poor because English laws ruined the country's industries, especially the wool industry, because the neglect of the English government in the years of the potato famine allowed the best of the population to die from hunger" (*CW* 167). Here he is thinking of Sir Randolph Routh, the British administrator specifically charged with managing the colony on behalf of the crown.

He was to enter into *Ulysses* the name of the 1860 Act protecting property over human rights into the annals of infamy: the Deasy Act. Ventriloquized through the more inflammatory tones of the Citizen, Joyce amplifies the charge:

> They were driven out of house and home in the black '47. Their mudcabins and their shielings by the roadside were laid low by the batteringram and the *Times* rubbed its hands and told the whitelivered Saxons there would soon be as few Irish in Ireland as redskins in America. Even the Grand Turk sent us his piastres. But the Sassenach tried to starve the nation at home while the land was full of crops that the British hyenas bought and sold in Rio de Janeiro. Ay, they drove out the peasants in hordes. Twenty thousand of them died in the coffinships. (*U* 12.1365–72)

The language is drawn from John Mitchel, Michael Davitt, D. P. Moran, and familiar to anyone attuned to popular expressions of nationalist sentiment including the pages of Griffith's paper. The term "Sassenach" [Saxon] implies personal references to Lords John Russell and Charles Trevelyn. But the primary reference, fair or not, is to the Sassenach on the spot, Sir Randolph Routh.

Thus, when Ségouin attempts to deflect the after-dinner conversation in the hotel dining room from art to politics, he fails to reach the desired "congenial ground" (*D* 46.22). Feeling that umbrage might be taken at Villona's derisory remarks about the vulgarity of English musical taste and the historical incompetence of latter-day painters, he steers the conversation from cultural contention to pacific politics. Both visitor and host, he is in a delicate position. By the evening of July 2, 1903, the debate over the Wyndham Act had exhausted all but the most dedicated or fanatical citizens. A politically naive visiting Englishman bearing the name of an ancestor who was knighted for his service in Ireland might expect at least a circumspect regard. For Jimmy Doyle (recently returned from Cambridge), the presence of an Englishman with the name that has for so long been demonized in Irish nationalist rhetoric, was sooner or later bound to emerge from the shadows. The "generous influences" of Irish whiskey were likely to inflame an already "kindled" imagination and release a drunken version of the "buried zeal" of his formerly "advanced Nationalist" father who was a child when Sir Randolph Routh was a household name (William Field was born in 1843), so that it is not surprising that it turns nasty.[21] That the argument invoked Sir Randolph's name is conveyed by the terms in which the narrator makes his diplomatic exit from this disquieting scene: "there was even danger of personal spite" (D 46.26).

We are therefore expected to infer that Jimmy Doyle's quarrel with Routh arises from resentments unremediated in Ireland since the Famine. His apparently spontaneous argument is, moreover, a mask for Joyce's own inherited feelings and another indication of the subscription of "After the Race" to the anticolonial agenda of Arthur Griffith's *United Irishman*. Finally, the images of Dublin's "[wearing] the mask of a capital" (D 46.29) and of Jimmy's "linked arms" (D 47.17) with Routh ironically summon the grand symbol of the Union of Britain and its Irish colony, the Union Jack: embracing the arms of the crosses of Saints George, Andrew, David, and Patrick.

"one great game" (D 48.16)

"After the Race" is the only story in *Dubliners* with an international cast of characters: the only one in which an American appears. As several commentators have noted, the Gordon Bennett Cup Race expresses an allegory of the international political situation, the relations between the leading world powers at the time (for example, Bowen, "Hungarian Politics in 'After the Race'" and Fairhall, "Big-Power Politics and Colonial Economics").[22] The competition between the automobiles flying the colors of Germany, France, Britain, and the United States is a pageant enacting the rising tensions between these powers for dominance of the serious geopolitical arena.[23] Late in the night's revelry and far into its gambling, as Jimmy Doyle sinks deeper into his cups, he "knew that he was losing" (D 48.11). Then "someone" among his friendly rivals proposes a final round: "one great game for a finish" (D 48.16). Entering this last round, Jimmy understands that "he would lose, of course" (D 48.21). With the elimination of himself and Farley, "the heaviest losers" (D 48.26), then, the outcome "lay between Routh and Ségouin" (D 48.20). Routh wins this final "terrible game" (*D* 48.18, 23). The language describing this international competition, therefore, carries both retrospective and prospective historical implications: of Waterloo and Apocalypse. In the language of the times, however, it had a force that Joyce might have hoped would not be lost upon his readers.

In his ostensibly casual reference to "one great game," the narrator is evidently citing one of the players. Since the "Great Game" was a fairly familiar expression from the lexicon of British imperialism that had received a renewed currency during the summer of 1904, the safe money is on Routh.

Between 1813 and 1907, the strategic rivalry between Britain and Tsarist Russia over the control of Central Asia was known in Russia as the "Tournament of Shadows," and in Britain as the "Great Game." The British feared that the Russians would filch India, "the jewel in the crown," and thereby acquire a strategic warm-water port. The ensuing tension overtopped less confrontational maneuverings into the First and Second Anglo-Afghan Wars (1839–42, 1878–80), and concluded with the Anglo-Russian Convention in 1907 that divided Afghanistan between them. This agreement was the official whistle ending the Great Game. More broadly, the term referred to the competition between the major political actors at the end of the nineteenth century for global dominance. It apparently originated in Otto von Bismarck's metaphor for the "party of three on the European chessboard," by which he meant that the isolation of Russia and Austria-Hungary would leave him with just France and Britain as serious rivals for superpower status. By 1900, however, the term embraced both Britain and its transatlantic cousin, the United States, as competitors for geopolitical hegemony. With the collapse of Spanish power in the Philippines, the United States found itself, reluctantly or not, charged with containing the imminent German presence and less immediate Chinese threat in that region. More specifically, the term referred to the common interests of France, Britain, and the United States to contain the growing power of Germany and its potential for a takeover of the Asiatic landmass dominated by Czarist Russia.

The publication of Halford J. Mackinder's "The Geographical Pivot of History" in the April 1904 issue of the *Geographical Journal* renewed the urgency of the term. In his terse essay, this political geographer advanced the argument that unless circumscribed, a single political entity could use the manpower and natural resources of Eurasia to dominate the rest of the world. It was therefore in the interests of Britain to cooperate with France and the United States in obstructing a potential German-Russian alliance and the tactical consequences of the construction of the Trans-Siberian Railroad (1891–1913). It consequently proposed the strategy of supporting a number of buffer states from the Mediterranean, through the Middle East, and through the Indian subcontinent to limit the access of this potential superpower to the practical means of achieving this dominance: the oceans.

This paper gave higher profile to the overseas campaigns in which Britain had been engaged during the previous half-century from the Crimea to Afghanistan, and in South Africa. Mackinder's analysis surveyed the conditions that subsequently led to World War I, the rising tensions between Germany and Britain and their respective allies.[24] His essay took a long historical survey of the pattern of invasions from the Asiatic "Heartland" from the dawn of history through the Mongols in the fourteenth century, leading to the European exploration and colonization of the Americas, Australasia, and South Africa. Holding that 1900 marked "the end of the Columbian epoch," he argued that "we are witnessing the last moves of the game first played by the horsemen of Yorkmack the Cossack and the shipmen of Vasco de Gama" (421). The political systems bearing the names of various nations were products of the interplay between geography, demography, and resources: just as the idea of European civilization was the outcome of the secular struggle against Asiatic invasion, so was the idea of the nation states—of Germany, France, England, the United States—the result of resistance to external barbarism (423).

Observing that the steppes between the Urals and the Caspian Sea left Europe defenseless, and mixing his metaphors with abandon, Mackinder drew a terrible picture of the "clouds of ruthless and idealess horsemen sweeping war over the unimpeded plain—a blow, as it were, from the great Asiatic hammer striking freely through the vacant space" (427). In the meantime, the rivals to these Mongols, Magyars, and Goths were "the Vikings in their boats" (427) pillaging Europe along its theretofore undefended western ocean frontier. "Thus the steeled peoples of Europe lay gripped between two pressures—that of the Asiatic nomads from the east, and on the other three sides that of the pirates from the sea" (428).

The only traces of the earlier inhabitants of Europe—the Celts—were a few of their topographical inscriptions, as witnessed by the names of the great rivers the Don, Dneiper, Dneister, and Danube. In the contemporary world, Russia had replaced the Mongol Empire; and with its vast resources of manpower, food, and minerals, and its inaccessibility to naval power, it posed a similar threat to European, and specifically, British political culture. This "pivot region," therefore, the Eurasian "World Island," required concerted containment; and the nation-state that succeeded in that containment could lay claim to world leadership and power.

The chief claimants to that leadership were Germany, France, Britain, and the United States. Lesser players—Afghanistan, Hungary, India, the Philippines, Ireland—would have to take their places as determined by the interests of the major powers. The complex strategy of espionage and exploration, threats and alliances (secret and announced), feints and feigned insults, diplomatic incidents, advantageous regional disputes, the fomentation and support of proxy wars, the staging of royal visits, the patronization of international sports events, and the promotion of them through the loyal press, were one and all, then, discernable as strategic moves in the Great Game.

Mackinder's analysis, was, naturally, based on the assumption of the superiority of British civilization and its corollary right to control the resources of peoples of lesser power or presumed endowment. One of the darker ironies here is that Mackinder's paper appeared during the British expedition to Lhasa (April–September 1904) and within a week of the Tibetan massacre at Guru (March 31) that was not reported in the *London Times*.

It is worth noting at this point, that as Joyce was writing "After the Race"—during the last week of September 1904—the newspapers were reporting the British evacuation of the newest member of their crescent of buffer states, Tibet. This dramatic public reminder of the currency and geographic reach of the players in the Great Game might well have brought to Joyce's mind its most celebrated fictionalization, Rudyard Kipling's *Kim* (1901). As Joyce was finishing "After the Race" (October 3), he wrote to Nora that his brother Stanislaus was "reading a book and talking softly to himself: 'Curse this fellow'—the writer of the book—'Who in the devil's name said this book was good' 'The stupid fuzzy-headed fool!' 'I wonder are the English the stupidest race on God's earth' 'Curse this English fool' etc etc" (*Letters* II: 51). Now, in Stanislaus's diary (the entries for October 2 and 13), we learn that he was reading Kipling's *Plain Tales from the Hills* (*CDD* 136–38). It is the author of this volume and of *Kim* (which the Joyce brothers had already read and discussed) that Stanislaus judges an

"English fool." James did not share his brother's estimation, however: he respected Kipling's fidelity to objective fact, and his Trieste library contained a copy of *Kim* (*Letters* II: 205; Ellmann, 115).

The hero of this novel, Kimball O'Hara, is the orphan son of a British soldier in British India. His quest for truth takes him through many adventures from Lahore to the Arrow River. In the course of these travels, he is torn between two cultures and educations: official and unofficial, British and Indian. Sent away to a boarding school, he is educated in mathematics, map-making, and classics that equip him for a role as a British agent in the Great Game. A Tibetan lama undertakes to liberate him from the Wheel of Life in the pursuit of a translation from the condition of sin and into that of spiritual enlightenment.

During his imperial service, Kim becomes doubly acculturated as an Anglo-Indian, reflecting his parallel education in the life of action and of the spirit. Thus, the originally naive boy is inducted both as a subaltern of the British Empire and as a chela [disciple] of the oriental guru. Finally, with his awakening by the River Arrow, he has achieved both maturity in the world of tricks—as a spy in the Great Game—and as a chela of the Great Wheel.

This all-male epic tale of tricks and enlightenment could well have constituted a precedent for Joyce's story. Both feature a naive Irish boy who is educated as a servant of Empire (at Trinity College Dublin and Cambridge University), and is subsequently initiated into the trickery of the Great Game (through his inheritance of his father's fortune and his participation in the race). At the same time, the shamanic figure of Villona offers him the option of spiritual detachment. Like Kim, Jimmy vacillates between defending his subject race (his rising to the argument with Routh, his response to the rising sun) and his fascination with the baubles of power (his elation at the feelings of speed, power, and wealth exuded by his swaggering companions). The emblem that Kipling dangles before Kim, the red bull on a field of green (the imaginary Irish regiment, the Mavericks), might have prompted Joyce's more covert and adroit emblematic use of Dublin's Stephen's Green as Hungarian flag. Kipling's rather heavy-handed treatment of the dual themes of political and spiritual quests may have provided Joyce with a precedent for some aspects of the subtle thematic structure of "After the Race." In the mysterious figure of Routh, a match for the profile of a spy, we may have a Joycean gesture toward one of Kim's roles in the "Great Game."[25] In view of the contemporary celebration of Britain's latest apparently successful venture in Tibet and Mackinder's recent rationalization of global realpolitik, Joyce must have derived some satisfaction from his understated subversion of what Edward Said calls this "masterwork of imperialism" (Kipling, 45).

Mackinder's sophisticated delineation of historical and technical issues elides the counterclaims—political, economic, moral—of colonized peoples. Closer to home, where Mackinder's assumptions appeared axiomatic, nationalist ideologues such as Arthur Griffith persistently attacked efforts to naturalize such imperial presumptions. In concert with Griffith's broad propaganda, therefore, Joyce's implied narrator, ventriloquizing Routh's imperial phrasing as he commences the final fleecing, makes a sly rejoinder.

The force of the allusion in "After the Race" is therefore clear: the final prize is neither the day's cup nor the night's bag. The real race is between the imperial powers for domination in the "post-Columbian" age. The car race is a proxy game. From the point of view of a resistant member of the colonized, the British, French, and German mechanicians striking awe and inducing compliance in the hearts of the plain people of Ireland as they roar over the plains of Kildare, through the streets of Dublin, and in and out of the pockets of its subaltern Doyles replicates Mackinder's image of the idealess horsemen thundering over the plains of Hungary and through the streets of Vienna and Rome.

If one is disposed to concede that the Doyles—father and son—are apparently complicit in this hegemonic enterprise, they are true descendants of the seaborne counterparts of the Asiatic hordes that reduced the Celtic Europe of Mackinder's thesis to a few place names, the Vikings (Doyle is a Norse patronymic). Similarly cast by the vicissitudes of history, the Hungarians and Irish are alike: pawns on the big board. They can, like Villona, remain but as spectators of the main action which engages their political superiors, or, like Jimmy, stake their patrimony on the outcome of the game. Neither option will make them winners: the choice is between detachment and loss.

Although Mackinder's diagnosis of geopolitical relations was in some respects prophetic, it had several blind spots: to the role that air force and oil would play in making the United States the major power. He did not take on board the implications of the first flight at Kitty Hawk (December 17, 1903), nor indeed the economic and political consequences of the recent inventions of the automobile and radio. Similarly, neither the consumer revolution about to be wrought by the mass production of the automobile nor the rise to world power of the United States must have been apparent to the author of "After the Race." Consistent with this impression, then, Farley's role in the story, corresponding to the poor American performance in the car race, is to share with Jimmy Doyle the heaviest loss at cards. The final exhibit in the day's display of conspicuous consumption, his *Belle of Newport*, if it impresses Villona ("It is beautiful!" [D 47.23]), it does not the narrator. As if taking their cue from Thorstein Veblen's recent critique, this symbol of elevated pecuniary taste the envious Europeans cynically toast.

These international political circumstances have, therefore, a clear bearing on the story, supporting its status as a political allegory of the contention for global supremacy in the automobile age. A closer look at a couple of the characters bears this out in some surprising ways.

"the spy of three castles" (*FW* 101.22–23)

His surname aside, there is something of a mystery about the figure of Routh. His appearance, demeanor, and role in the story suggest that he may be the first in a series of figures in Joyce's fiction who, while playing one role in the life of the city of three castles, are also agents of the Dublin Castle. The evidence, while not conclusive, is, well, intriguing.

Since the time of the United Irishmen, the British authorities in Ireland had successfully thwarted military threats to their colonial regime. This was accomplished by an informal intelligence apparatus, paid informers, vastly superior military organization, brutal repression, and what Griffith called "a wall of paper" around Ireland. The names of Leonard MacNally, Red Jim MacDermott, Francis Higgins, and Richard Piggott rang in the political memories of Irish nationalists as among Americans does that of Benedict Arnold.

So it was in the Joyce household. John Stanislaus Joyce, the son of a Whiteboy, was sympathetic with the IRB (see Jackson and Costello, 153–54). Whatever his reservations about his father's politics, James retained an abiding paranoia about spies, informers, and betrayers personal and political. He had good reason to, for the movements of all figures with known radical political sympathies were watched, especially in the major cities of Cork and Dublin. The police file photograph of John Kelly

(Jackson and Costello, *inter* 214 and 215) substantiates this point about one political activist for whom Joyce had a warm personal feeling. Just as he admired—although he did not share its intensity—the patriotism of George Clancy, he was suspicious of Oliver St. John Gogarty's professed allegiance to Griffith and Sinn Féin. He wrote to Stanislaus that Gogarty, given the chance, "will play the part of MacNally and Reynolds" (*Letters* II: 187, November 6, 1906), paid informers on the United Irishmen. Writing about "Fenianism" some months later (March 1907), Joyce informs his Triestine readers that James Stephens's organization of the IRB in a network of independent cells was "eminently fitted to the Irish character because it reduces to a minimum the possibility of betrayal" (*CW* 189). Nevertheless, despite Stephens's precautions, there were paid informers in the ranks of the Fenians, which led to his own arrest along with Jeremiah O'Donovan Rossa and John O'Leary before the rising of 1867.

For all their success in Ireland, the British intelligence apparatus was run in an amateur fashion until about the time Joyce is writing "After the Race." Throughout the century, British military and police were unofficially free to open all domestic and foreign mail. The British experience during the Boer War revealed the need for a permanent, professional approach to intelligence and counterintelligence (Polmar and Allen, s.v. "England–Great Britain–United Kingdom"). Following Robert (later Major General and Sir) Baden-Powell's successes in intelligence gathering in South Africa, and the valuable information gleaned from the fields of British India, the colonial authorities recognized that this aspect of the manner in which they conducted the Great Game needed professionalization. They began the systematic recruitment of intelligence officers from among the ranks of the Oxbridge graduates: giving them military training, providing them with suitable "covers," and insinuating them into critical outposts in the developing conflict with Germany. They soon had a system of "observers" (paid local informers), "carriers" (travelers and tourists), and "collectors" (analysts at the headquarters in London). From these beginnings in 1901 developed the Secret Service Bureau of 1909, and subsequently, under the War Office and Admiralty, M15 and M16, respectively.

The well-organized opposition to the Boer War was not only the major public political issue during Joyce's student days at the Royal University, but was, in retrospect, one of the turning points in modern Irish history.

In R. F. Foster's view (*Modern Ireland*, 431, 456; enlarged by Maume), this agitation woke Irish political sentiment from the passivity of the decade after the fall of Parnell, and the energies it released—via the figure of Arthur Griffith—eventually led to the Rising of 1916, the antirecruitment campaigns of the next year, and the triumph of Sinn Féin in the 1918 general election. The colonial authorities were well advised, therefore, to pay close attention to the activities of political and patriotic cultural clubs at the time of the staging of the Gordon Bennett Cup Race in 1903.

The authorities had an extensive intelligence network throughout Ireland and scores of informers in Dublin City (see McGee). In Dublin, the G Division of the DMP was charged with coordinating the surveillance that reported on the movements of known agitators. Accordingly, its functionaries observed the movement of the patrons of railway stations, bars, clubs, meetings, and especially funerals. A survey of the "S" Files of the Chief Secretary's Office for the years 1899–1904 makes it clear that there were numerous informers throughout the country supplying the authorities with information on expressions of disloyalty overheard at meetings of the United Irish League, the IRB, the Transvaal Committee, the Parnell Commemorations, meetings of the Manchester Martyrs commemorative committees, and the Gaelic Athletic Association. In 1899, Commissioner J. J. Jones of the DMP informed Dublin Castle that "The Irish Republican Socialists are a bad lot. . . . The Irish Transvaal Committee embraces all that is dangerous in Dublin" (cited by O'Brien, 243). While many are identified by name, some are known by pseudonyms, such as "Whiskey" (for an informer named Fagan who worked in a distillery). Prominent figures like Maud Gonne and Arthur Griffith were trailed and their associations noted (for example, the report of October 10, 1901, on Griffith's visit to Paris).[26]

Well aware of this, Joyce slips into *Ulysses* several figures that he allows us to suspect as performing for the state some surveillance service. In the "Circe" episode Bloom thinks of himself as traversing a territory over which spies from both sides of the colonial divide contended (the "Gaelic league spy" [*U* 15.220] versus the navvy [*U* 15.518]); and the name of a notorious betrayer of the Fenians, Red Jim MacDermott, appears in the ironic catalogue of Ireland's heroes (*U* 12.179). Bloom is right: Corny Kelleher, the undertaker's assistant, while working for Henry J. O'Neill, carriage maker and undertaker, is an "observor" on behalf of the DMP.

This job affords him opportunity to track political activists who, in accordance with Irish custom honoring dead patriots or subversives, would only appear in public and allow themselves to be identified at funerals. Thus, while in charge of Paddy Dignam's obsequies on June 16, to his "contact," Constable 57 C, Corny reports, "I seen that particular party last evening" (*U* 10.225). His surveillance role causes him to resurface in the "Wandering Rocks" and "Circe" episodes, where his good terms with the policemen accrue to Stephen's advantage.

The mysterious man in the macintosh may well be another "observor" of Paddy Dignam's funeral. A further player in the spy game is Piper. An acquaintance of the characters in "Syclla and Charybdis," he is doing some work on Shakespeare's Stratford background in support of "the Rutland theory" of authorship (*U* 9.1073–76) and he is expected to attend a literary evening (*U* 9.274–76). The only grounds upon which to suspect him he shares with Haines: both Englishman are temporarily engaged in Irish cultural affairs at which they might encounter potential political élites. Beyond this the text of *Ulysses* does not go. Yet, a search for the historical Piper has produced a palpable hit. There was, indeed, in Dublin at that time one J. Stanton Pyper (1868–1941).[27] Whether Joyce—or his annotators—knew that he was a British spy, they do not admit it (Gifford, 210). Nevertheless, as Alf MacLochlainn discovered, he was sending reports to British intelligence from the Dublin circles he frequented ("*Pyper? Un homme de pois!*").

For these reasons, suspicion ought to descend upon the Routh of "After the Race" as an intelligence officer. First, he is an Englishman who although he has been to that nursery of M15 Cambridge, is not particularly cultivated, and has the firm manner of a man with military training. He appears at the hotel dinner without explanation, except that he was a university acquaintance of Rivière's. Routh does not evince any interest in the car racing itself, nor does he participate in the discussion of automobiles at the dinner. Attendance at the race, then, may well be the pretext under which he makes an entry on to the Irish scene. He seems to be making a good start on his assignment, since he immediately engages with the scion of an "advanced Nationalist": therefore someone who can potentially uncover leads in the identification and pursuit of subversives, members of the IRB (as was suspected of the historical William Field; see Maume, 228).

There are two clues (besides his name) that Routh is in Dublin on an intelligence mission: going beyond polite political conversation, and apparently under the influence of alcohol, he sheds some of his proverbial British reserve and raises Jimmy's Anglophobic hackles. Were it not for French diplomacy, which soothes the conflict, he might have blown his "cover." Routh, moreover, evidently comes to Dublin with sufficient finance; and although we do not know who calls for cards—he is the most probable candidate there—almost certainly the "someone [who] proposed one great game" to finish the night's entertainment (*D* 48.16). This contention is supported by two pieces of evidence: he is the eventual winner, and he is the only one of the company for whom the phrase would have been a familiar part of his lexicon. The reference summons up, as we have seen, Kipling's *Kim*, a novel of political intrigue, exotic foreign travel, double crossings, disguises, and espionage in defense of the British Empire.

As we know from subsequent developments, the British failure in Ireland after 1914 is in large part due to deficiencies in intelligence. Had the authorities even one competent mole operating among the conspirators, there would have been no Easter Rising. Further failures in intelligence during the Anglo-Irish War were due to faulty security and irresponsible political direction, and lack of Dublin-London cooperation (Gudgin, 52). In a reversal of precedent, the success of the Sinn Féin activists during the Anglo-Irish War was largely due to the penetration by their agents into the headquarters of both the Royal Irish Constabulary and the Dublin Metropolitan Police, and the failure of the British to recruit any informers within the Irish Republican Army. Under Michael Collins's forthright leadership, swift and brutal action was taken against informers. His ability to win the intelligence war persuaded the British decision to enter into formal negotiations in 1921.

As the sponsor and winner in the "great game" of cards that concludes the night's entertainment, and at the principal expense of Jimmy and Farley, Routh is a worthy agent of British interests. Not only has he personally profited from the evening, he has begun the infiltration of the Irish-American connection, which since the foundation of the IRB to the sponsorship of the *United Irishman* has been a vital link in mounting an effective resistance to British power in Ireland. Routh, therefore, is the most likely subject of the otherwise inexplicable entry in Joyce's notes for *Dubliners* (1904): "To take the part of England and her tradition against Irish-America" (Gorman, 138). This takes us to Farley.

Surprising Farley

The presence of a well-off Irish-American in Dublin on the occasion of the Gordon Bennett Cup Race is justified on the historical grounds that many Americans made the transatlantic crossing in support of Alexander Winton and his teammates. Of all the foreign visitors, the Americans were the most popular (*London Times,* July 3: 11a). They left behind them in Ireland a reputation for unequalled largesse (Lynch, *Triumph,* 69). Joyce's Farley registers this positive image.

Farley's presence represents the Irish-American alliance invoked as a political and financial booster to Irish nationalist aspirations from the Fenians to Sinn Féin. By 1900, American flags were standard in nationalist parades and demonstrations. That an Irish-American Catholic is successful enough in 1903 to dock his yacht in Kingstown Harbour, the preserve of Ireland's premier clubs (the Royal Irish, the Royal St. George, and the National Yacht Clubs), is Joyce's nod to the hoped-for source of economic and political changes in Ireland.[28]

This particular version of the "returned Yank," a familiar type in Irish life and fiction, is drawn on at least three prominent Irish-Americans within Joyce's ambit: James Gordon Bennett Jr., Thomas Hughes Kelly, and John Cardinal Farley.

James Gordon Bennett Jr., after whom the race was named, was one of the most famous Irish Americans of the time (his mother was from Meath). He was known in Ireland for his work among the poor of New York and for his establishment of an Irish relief fund in 1882. During his flamboyant lifetime—he was a bachelor until 1914, his seventy-third year—he spent $30 million on lavish adventures. His visit to Cobh (then Queenstown) in his large yacht *Lysistrata* in 1890 got much press notice at the time (he did not return in July 1903). His reputation as "the beau ideal of the man of the world and all-round daredevil," bequeathed to British slang the name "a Gordon Bennett" to an outrageous stunt (see Richard O'Connor; *American National Biography,* s.v. "Gordon Bennett").

This Irish-American philanthropist appears to have made a discreet appearance in Joyce's story. Like his historical model—who never attended any of the events he sponsored, and never drove a car—Farley enters the story well removed from the race, and in an otherwise all-male narrative, in the company of women (like this precedent, Joyce's Farley apparently prefers pressing the flesh to pressing the pedal). This autocratic, erratic, but charitable Irish-American yachtsman and newsman (known to his friends as "Jimmy") is thus the obliquely inscribed figure behind the circumstances that brought together James Joyce, the historical Frenchman Fournier (who was not there either), and the imaginary Farley (who was) in an imaginary sequel to the 1903 Gordon Bennett Cup Race.

Joyce was not acquainted with the said Jimmy Bennett (although he undoubtedly read his *Paris Herald* during his four-month sojourn in the French capital).[29] There was, however, another Irish-American millionaire and philanthropist residing in Ireland at the time whom Joyce knew socially, and on whose account, by a circuitous route, the figure in "After the Race" is given the name Farley: Thomas Hughes Kelly (1865–1933).

With his substantial inheritance as support, Kelly moved to Ireland and lived in a stately manor, Halezhatch, in Celbridge, County Kildare. He offered to continue his Tyrone-born father's philanthropy and interest in Irish cultural causes, endowing several young Irish writers, including Padraic Colum, with generous annual subsidies (Mary Colum, 241). This encouraged Joyce to make a determined—but futile—effort to secure similar support for himself (*JJII* 141, December 1903).

Now, this Thomas Hughes Kelly was a nephew of perhaps the most prominent Irish-American in nineteenth-century America: Archbishop John Joseph Hughes of the Archdiocese of New York. His successor to this exclusively Irish see in 1903 was John Cardinal Farley. On arriving in America in 1864, this native of County Armagh had simplified (from Farrelly) the spelling of his surname. His contemporary international reputation turned on his involvement in the Catholic Modernist controversy and his strong support of Irish causes: he vowed not to visit Ireland in 1912 until Home Rule was granted (*Encyclopedia of the Irish in America*, s.v. "Farley, John Murphy Cardinal"). Along with Thomas Hughes Kelly, he was an honorary vice-president of the New York Irish Literary Society, a sister organization to Yeats's Dublin organization, launched by lawyer John Quinn in 1902. The controversy surrounding *The Countess Cathleen* (1899) soon embroiled the Archbishop: he could not appear to patronize an anticlerical work and so resigned in June 1903 (Reid, 12–14). This minor controversy would have reminded Joyce of his own refusal to join in the protest against *The Countess Cathleen* (*JJII* 66–67) and of a curious coincidence of clerical names.

The name "Farley" is a variation of Farrelly—Ó *Fairceallaigh*—a Breffny sept associated with counties Meath and Cavan, the particular spelling a borrowing of a common English name (MacLysaght, 140).[30] In imagining this bearer of the name as "a short fat man" (*D* 46.33), Joyce shows himself, once again, as a trader in fine ironies (in this case what the ancient rhetoricians termed an "*adnominatio*"), since *fairceallach* means "chunky, or strongly-built." When the Joyce brothers attended Belvedere in the 1890s, they knew a Father Charles Farley, a member of the Jesuit community (Bradley, 94–96). He was characterized by Stanislaus as "scatter-brained" (*MBK* 53). The fictional Father Farley earns higher marks from Leopold Bloom: recalling his efforts to get Molly into the choir, he reflects that this particular priest "looked a fool but wasn't" (*U* 5.333). When the same Father Farley offers his estimation of Leopold the First of Dublin, he sounds like the Archbishop of New York who took exception to Yeats as an ambassador for Irish culture: "He is an episcopalian, an agnostic, an anythingarian seeking to overthrow our holy faith" (*U* 15.1712–13). The Irish-American millionaire who bore the name of the then Archbishop Farley's predecessor, Hughes, would have suggested to the young James Joyce a name associated with Irish-American success and with patronage of Irish cultural enterprise. In the name "Farley," therefore, we have a complex invocation of worldly success, ethnic pride, religious orthodoxy, and patriotism.

On the rhetorical level, Farley's belated and surprising appearance in the story ("It's Farley!" [*D* 47.4]) leads a parade of sixteen exclamation marks along the narrative line. By announcing him in this manner, and since in Middle English, "Ferly" means "surprising" or "strange," Joyce demonstrates that his partiality to etymological paronomasia is resourceful, humorous, and an active ingredient in his earliest work. There are therefore multiple historical, symbolic, and rhetorical justifications for Farley's brief presence in the story.

5

Robert Emmet Centennial

Robert Emmet was a son of Dublin City. He was born, bred, educated, and executed there. His life, rebellion, and death took place on the same streets along which Joyce walked and sent his imaginary cars in "After the Race." Emmet and Joyce passed their youths between the same façades, trod the same granite flagstones, and uttered (in slightly different accents) the same familiar names: Suffolk Place, Granby Row, Sydney Parade. Were chance to bring them together in another world, they would feel that together they were at home.[1]

Emmet was born on March 4, 1778, at 109/110 Saint Stephen's Green: the west side; his memorial statue stands opposite. The seventeenth child of Dr. Robert and his wife, Elizabeth Mason, from his earliest years, Robert and his older brother, Thomas Addis, were with their daily bread, raised on dangerous political opinions. News of the American Revolution thrilled their passionate father with the prospect of a similar freedom on behalf of England's first colony. Even though he was state physician, Dr. Emmet was a vehement proponent of Irish political independence, leading Thomas Addis into the United Irishmen and soon into its leadership. Robert was educated at Samuel Whyte's English Grammar School at 75 Grafton Street, where he distinguished himself in public speaking. At age fifteen he entered Trinity College Dublin, and studied to become a barrister at King's Inns. When Thomas Addis was arrested and jailed for membership in United Irishmen in 1798, suspicion fell upon Robert, who promptly left Trinity without completing his studies.

He departed for the Continent, and in accordance with the plans of the United Irishmen for military action in behalf of Irish liberation, had several meetings with Napoleon Bonaparte and Charles Maurice de Talleyrand in 1801. He quickly became disenchanted with them: they were at the time seeking accommodation with the English, and thereafter Emmet was uncompromising in his opposition to any collaboration with the French. In taking this position, he was at odds with many of the United Irishmen in Paris as well as with his brother who was then in jail. The peace treaty (Amiens) between England and France in 1802 confirmed him in his view that no hope could be entertained on Ireland's behalf from *le quartier Français*.

Returning to Dublin, therefore, he invested his personal inheritance of £2,000 in a conspiracy with some radical Dublin merchants to stage an independent rising. He recruited rebels in the city and contiguous counties. He signed contracts for the manufacture of pistols, blunderbusses, rocket launchers, and hinged pikes, setting up two arms depots in the Thomas Street area of Dublin City: on Patrick Street and Marshalsea Lane (codename "Kildare"). To protect himself against discovery, he corresponded in several different handwriting styles under various pseudonyms, "Robert Ellis," "Hewitt," "Cunningham," and "Trebor."[2] His plan was to capture the Pigeon House Fort, the Islandbridge and Cork Street barracks, and Dublin Castle itself.

The resumption of Anglo-French hostilities (May 18, 1803) and an accidental explosion at the Patrick Street depot (July 16) forced him into premature action. Thus, before he could finalize his arrangements with his allies in Wicklow and Kildare, and assure himself of adequate manpower and funding, he had to take to the streets. Aware of Dublin Castle's aroused suspicions, he decided to go ahead with the rebellion on July 23. In the event, only a fraction of the Kildaremen made their way, via Naas Road, to the city that morning.

An undermanned and poorly prepared retinue—only about eighty out of the hundreds expected—assembled at the Marshalsea Lane depot. During their march along Thomas Street, Emmet realized that he had but about a dozen armed and competent followers, and decided to call off the rebellion. After the attack was aborted, however, a mob assembled on Thomas Street and waylaid the carriage of Lord Kilwarden, the chief justice, and his nephew, murdering both. The army was called out and promptly quelled the flourish. Emmet fled to the Wicklow Mountains but soon returned to Dublin to visit his sweetheart, Sarah Curran, where he was arrested by Major Henry Sirr.

His one-day trial for high treason was staged on September 19. Nineteen witnesses testified against him, none on his behalf, and after no more than a few minutes of deliberation, Emmet was found guilty. He was sentenced by Lord Norbury to be hanged and beheaded. His last night was spent in Kilmainham Gaol. He was executed on September 20, 1803, at 1 p.m. near Saint Catherine's Church at the intersection with Bridgefoot Street.

Robert Emmet was the most famous of the last eighteen members of the United Irishmen who suffered this fate in 1803. An Irish separatist, his vision of political liberty was shaped by his Continental republicanism and his personal relationships with Dublin city merchants and artisans. Although he had formed military alliances with rural rebels in counties Kildare, Meath, Wicklow, and Wexford, he expressed no interest in land reform, the major issue outside the city. In this respect he is the essential patriotic Dubliner. His fame rests on his distinction of character, the idealism of his youth, his romance with Sarah Curran, the heroism of his servant, Anne Devlin, and the eloquence of his speech from the dock. His foolhardy escapade set an example for rebels who in succeeding generations would take his view that given the imbalance of power between rightful Irish claims and overwhelming British power, participation in conventional politics so disconcerted the popular national will that only a military coup (even if unsuccessful) could furnish an embarrassment and an emboldening example. To awaken Ireland from its pacified slumber, the expiation of a bloody sacrifice in arms was the ambition and vocation of Robert Emmet.

"The darling of Erin"

Throughout the nineteenth century, Robert Emmet was the sanctified personification of romantic Irish nationalism: the inspiration of the Young Ireland movement, the Ribbonmen, the Fenians, and Patrick Pearse. His memory entered sentimental nationalist culture through the many songs in Thomas Moore's *Irish Melodies* (5 volumes, 1808–34; Moore was a fellow student of Emmet's at Trinity), especially "She Is far from the Land," "When He Who Adores Thee," and "Oh! Breathe Not His Name" (familiar to households less musical than the Joyces). The rebirth of the radical Irish republican spirit that the 1798 centenary commemorations were designed to effect appropriately began March 4, 1897. For the next five years, the Robert Emmet 1798 Centenary Club held his heroic virtues and sacrifice before the public through open meetings, staged funerals at the site of his execution on Thomas Street, wreath-layings at his presumed grave in

Saint Michan's, and the inclusion of songs and recitations in his memory at concerts, *aeríochtanna*, and *feiseanna*. Dramatic productions of his life and trial and fund-raising efforts were mounted to erect a suitable memorial. All but a few of the hundreds of poems and songs originating in this period disappeared after brief lives, while others like "God Save Ireland" and "Bold Robert Emmet," are familiar items a century later in the repertoire of Irish republican balladeers.

A. M. Sullivan's *The Story of Ireland* (1867) and *Speeches from the Dock* (1878), read in Catholic Young Men's Societies and Land League reading rooms, became a late-nineteenth-century best seller (Elliott, 176). By the time the centennial of Emmet's rising arrived, there were several biographies of the hero in print,[3] and a torrent of commemorative posters, pictures, songbooks, plays and pageants, press reports, and other Emmet centenary–related publications gushed from patriotic presses in the same centenary year. This led to an even greater level of enthusiasm, so that more books on Emmet appeared during the next decade than in the entire preceding century, all reproducing the same romantic and sentimental image, and all drawing in one degree or another on R. R. Madden's work. In each of these representations, Emmet was canonized as Ireland's patriotic saint. His youth, gifts, and sincerity made even his enemies squirm. Again and again, patriotic rhetoric pitted "the godlike young patriot" against "the drunken, sanguinary Norbury . . . that ruffianly minion of the English tyranny" (cited by Elliott, 174–75). By 1903, the names of Castlereagh, Sirr, Norbury, and McNally were bywords for villainy.

Leonard McNally was a Dublin barrister who was one of the original members of the Society of United Irishmen, and a confidante of Wolfe Tone, Napper Tandy, and many others in the leadership. A talented poet and playwright and grotesque in appearance, this "good-natured, hospitable, dirty fellow" was the principal defense attorney for many patriots, including Robert Emmet. McNally was the last to attend on Emmet in his cell the next morning in Kilmainham Gaol as he prepared for death.

For his services he got a patriot's funeral in 1820. When an heir applied for the continuation of his Secret Service pension of £300 per annum, an enquiry was made into his father's activities. This brought to light the astonishing news that McNally was, all along, a government informer. Even as he accepted legal fees from Emmet and other United Irishmen, he was on the payroll of Dublin Castle. Emmet's ordeal is, therefore, a classic instance of the political show trial (Hardiman, 227–28). Even by the standards of the day, there were grounds not only for an appeal (excluded from the sentence), but for the declaration of a mistrial and Emmet's release. In a letter to Stanislaus (November 6, 1906), Joyce compares Oliver St. John Gogarty to McNally, "a very native Irish growth" (*Letters* II: 187). To Joyce, who saw analogies between his personal life, that of the nation, and of Jesus Christ, the figures of Oliver Gogarty, Cosgrave (and for a time J. F. Byrne), had their analogues in Thomas Reynolds, Higgins ("The Sham Squire"), and Leonard McNally, whose famous kiss linked him with the immemorial Judas. This particular instance implies a private identification—that may surprise many—with Emmet.

A significant factor in the elevation of Emmet as the embodiment of the nobility of Irish political aspirations was the cult of this last United Irishman among Irish-Americans. The safe harbor given to most of the original leadership, especially Thomas Addis Emmet, by the American authorities, helps account for this. They exerted substantial influence in elite political circles, while among the poorer classes fleeing the succession of famines the conscious invocation of Emmet's example, promoted by the Emmet Monument Association, led to the foundation of the Fenians in New York (Elliott, 178). A familiar icon in Irish-American homes, as Charles Fanning reports, was a Currier and Ives lithograph of Emmet before his bewigged judges (148), while in Irish homes, as Yeats recalled, his image was elevated alongside the icons of Saint Patrick and the Blessed Virgin (Frayne and Johnson, 319). Meanwhile, Emmet's speech from the dock was widely admired and emulated outside in the wider culture. The most famous Fenian ballad, T. D. Sullivan's "God Save Ireland," makes clear the links between the fate of the Manchester Martyrs and Emmet. As Fenianism cultivated patriotic fervor in two generations of young men by public commemorations, his story captivated young women because of his tragic love affair with Sarah Curran and the exemplary fortitude of Anne Devlin (Elliott, 181). So even though some nationalist historians, such as A. M. Sullivan, censured "the criminal hopelessness of his scheme," they extolled "his extreme youth, his pure and gentle nature, his lofty and noble aims, his beautiful and touching speech from the dock, and his tragic death upon the scaffold" (cited by Elliott, 177).

The public protests against recruitment for the Boer War (1898–1901) inflamed the anticolonial fervor fanned into life by the 1798 commemorations. The result of these propaganda campaigns was a heightened public sensitivity to the devices of British hegemony in Irish life and a reinvestment in the image of Emmet as a catalyst of resistant emotion. The broad appeal of this campaign manifested itself in the formation of an Emmet's football or hurling club in almost every county in Ireland, and the production of patriotic tableaus and dramatizations of the romance, rebellion, trial, and oration of Emmet. Although such Irish-Irelanders as D. P. Moran (*Leader*), Arthur Griffith (*United Irishman*), and Patrick Pearse (*Claidheamh Soluis*) were acerbic in their criticism of "the kind of 'lip-rebellion' that accompanied recreational Fenianism," they were more vituperative in their denunciations of the pusillanimity of the Irish Party, West-Britonism in social and recreational spheres (for example, music-hall vulgarity), and carnivals celebrating British imperial culture, such as royal visits, society events at Dublin Castle, viceregally sponsored bazaars, and sporting events such as polo tournaments.

These opinion-makers were therefore unanimous in their opposition to the Gordon Bennett Cup Race and the visit of King Edward VII, which they viewed as plotted events, arranged in order to defuse the rising public sentiment surrounding the drama of July and September 1803. When, in the event, on Thursday, July 23, the precise centennial of Emmet's rising, the royal party traveled in state from the Viceregal Lodge via Kilmainham and Thomas Street to a formal reception in Dublin Castle, even the skeptics could not misinterpret official intentions. The radical nationalists, therefore, were vindicated in their disdain of the Gordon Bennett Cup Race. They were chiefly exercised in the long-running debate over the kind of welcome that would be accorded King Edward. Since his ascent to the Crown in January 1901, he had desired an Irish visit; but it was impossible until the Boer War ended (with the Treaty of Vereeniging in May 1902), and the public temper had sufficiently cooled.

If the authorities were forward enough to stage the king's visit to coincide with the centennial of Emmet's rebellion while putting it forth that His Majesty wished to honor the passing of the Wyndham Act, they were diplomatic enough to avoid confrontation with the arrangements to celebrate that centennial scheduled for the weekend closest to his execution, the following September. Thus, both events (and their preamble, the Gordon Bennett Cup Race) could go off without exposing public order to too great a risk. There is no hint of dissent observable from the royal carriage. As George Wyndham wrote of loyal Dubliners on July 26: "They worked themselves into an ecstasy and all sang 'God Save the King.' The Queen kept pointing to this or that tatterdemalion saying 'the poorer they are,

Figure 5.1. M. O'Healy cartoon. *The Leader,* July 11, 1903.

Mr. Wyndham, the louder they cheer.' There was ever and always the same intense emotion.... here was a whole population in hysteria" (Wyndham, *Letters* 2: 73). For his part, Griffith, who was to make a byword of Queen Alexandra's remark, greeted King Edward by reiterating a theme lost upon the royal party: "It was not for a Land Bill Emmet died" (*United Irishman,* July 25).

These tensions between Unionists and Nationalists and the linkages in the radical nationalist press are the subject of a cartoon by M. O'Healy that appeared in D. P. Moran's *Leader* on July 11, 1903: between the Gordon Bennett Cup Race and King Edward's arrival. Although graphically crude, it captures the tenor of the public mood during that month (figure 5.1).

The one-eyed porcine huckster with his tray of knickknacks caricatures the editorial values purveyed by William Martin Murphy's *Irish Daily Independent*. This newspaper, a rival to the Parnellite *Freeman's Journal* along with the Unionist *Irish Times* and the "advanced nationalist" press, is accused of the advantageous selling of baubles to the rabble of all parties.

Appearing in the issue for the week between the Gordon Bennett Cup Race and the king's visit, it satirizes the hypocrisy and opportunism of the mainstream national media. The emblems of his shamrock-designed cravat and Union Jack represent the irreconcilable opposition between the counterclaims of nation and empire. This week's featured emblem—in anticipation of the royal visit—is a desktop bust of King Edward. The hawker's Loyalist customers, on the one hand, can also purchase surplus badges manufactured for the Gordon Bennett Cup Race. His Irish-Irelander clients, on the other, can buy green or harp-and-sunburst flags.

Whether his customers support the International Industries Exhibition or the rival Home (or Our) Industries Exhibition, he can accommodate their tastes and principles. They can choose between "Robert Emmet Costumes" or the "Latest London Fashions." If they are inclined to international wantonness, he will sell them *Sapho* badges or an exposé of its decadence, "Studies in Blue."[4] If they are partial to the arts of the Gaelic Revival, he will sell them lapel pins with Celtic harp design. And if they are disposed to public parades, he can assure a supply of 1798 tin pikes ("tinpikery" meant fair-weather patriotism). The transparent fraudulence of these symbols of the defense of national sovereignty is attested by their German origins.[5] The multiplicity of political and social allegiances that this mercantilist will accommodate is symbolized by the display of hats: the king's crown, DMP helmets, 1798 Centennial slouch hats, Loyalist bowlers, RIC cadet pillbox hats, and army officer caps. The vendor's customers are cultivated by the competing speechmakers of the nationalist-republican alliance and of the Loyalist-Unionist faithful, readers of "Society Notes": to the one he sells icons of the 1798 commemorations (pikes and spades), and to the other Union Jack pennants. Even as the vendor sells the rotating flags of the United States and the United Kingdom, he purveys too, depending on the climate, those of the Irish-Irelanders and of the Catholic Church. Images of the competing ideologies appear in the elevated speechmakers and the pendant of King Edward set across from the image of the hanged man: Robert Emmet.

Blunt though it is, this cartoon exposes us to the squall of images bruiting through the public mind during the summer of 1903. It is a graphic summary of the argument mounted here: that the staging of the Gordon Bennett Cup Race was perceived as an event designed to enhance the British imperial image and promote internationalism at the expense of historical patriotic commemoration and the protection of native culture and industry. The cartoon is, therefore, critically useful in that it summarizes the conflicting and associated loyalties that were aroused by the exhibitions, the race, the commemorations, and the visit. Finally, in its criticism of the commodification of all ideologies by the *Irish Daily Independent,* it shares some of the ground occupied by the author of "After the Race."

In the aftermath of the king's departure, Griffith typically editorialized:

> His Britannic Majesty came to Ireland in the Emmet centenary year to show the world the spectacle of a nation selling its own soul and dishonouring its dead. The date of his visit was fixed to synchronise with the centennial date of Emmet's insurrection—even as the English in the Transvaal deliberately fixed the anniversary day of the Boer independence for proclaiming the Boer a serf.... He was to celebrate the actual centenary of the defeat of Emmet by a ball in the Castle, and then he was to triumphantly tour Ireland, receiving the homage of its four provinces. (*United Irishman,* August 8)

In the event, the procession marking the centennial of Emmet's execution had close to 100,000 participants, drawing at least that many spectators thronging the sidewalks. Recognizing that the population of Dublin City and its suburbs at the time was around 375,000, this was an enormous public show (O'Brien, appendix B). It was a vastly greater number than those cheering King Edward's cavalcade on the same streets three months before. Led by dozens of Gaelic Athletic Association clubs with their *camáin* (including the Bray Emmets football club, which had just won the Dublin championship that year), they included the *cumainn* of the Gaelic League, Cumann na nGaedhal, and the Daughters of Erin. Squadrons of schoolchildren wearing sashes and green hats, blowing bugles and tin whistles, bore pictures of Emmet and scenes from his life. The Irish National Foresters and the "Robert Emmet Costume Association" carried tin pikes. Seventy-two trade union and tradesmen's associations marched under their guild banners, one of them bearing aloft Emmet's death mask. This two-mile-long procession enacted, in the words of one commentator, "a pilgrimage... from Emmet's cradle to his grave—from his birth-place at Saint Stephen's Green to the scene of his execution at Thomas Street" (*Derry People* cited by Elliott, 194). For six hours the streets of Dublin rang with the strains of "The Memory of the Dead" and "A Nation Once Again."

Extreme nationalists were not pleased with the frivolity of too many of the participants: it was insufficiently solemn. Griffith thought that it was tawdry (the marchers did not keep step and many of the banners he thought shoddy), and too compromising to the hacks of the Irish Parliamentary Party (one of whom, William Field, was on the reviewing stand [*United Irishman*, September 19]). Those who paid lip service to Emmet's ideals—"tinpikery," humbug, and sham—were merely masquerading, engaging in a hideous farce that chiefly benefited the railways (which had laid on "specials" to transport participants from the provinces) and "Bung" (the Jamesons and Ardilauns). He recalled with contempt the cheers he had heard from these same sidewalks for the visiting King Edward in the very week of the rising's centenary. As the royal cortege passed near Saint Michan's he imagined the martyr's "silent" reproach to the cheering of the *seóiníní* (*United Irishman*, October 3). Moran's *Leader* took the view that they were stupidly pretending to be rebels, wasting time mourning over the grave of Emmet while encouraging the real men of violence to claim that they were furthering the national cause.

Joyce—who seems to have been among the throng that day—immortalized the scene in "the last farewell" passage in "Cyclops" (*U* 12.525–678): a bravura expansion of Griffith's comments on the display and a similar conflation of newspaper accounts of the royal visit and the centennial commemorations of 1903. This parody of a newspaper feature story, force-fed with society-page clichés, draws on newspaper accounts of the royal visit and the centennial commemorations of 1903. The references to the "assembled multitude which numbered at the lowest computation five hundred thousand persons" (*U* 12.533–34), the "[s]pecial quick excursion trains" (*U* 12.539), and the brass and reed band playing patriotic melodies (*U* 12.536–39) are drawn from newspaper accounts of the Emmet centennial parade. Similarly, the list of foreign dignitaries comprising the Friends of the Emerald Isle (FOTEI) (*U* 12.554–71) burlesques the display made of the appearance of French and American delegations with their flags at the Emmet centennial and the burlesque of the execution of "the hero martyr" (*U* 12.609), draw for several details on accounts of the assembly on Thomas Street on the precise centennial date. The hilarious humor of this passage arises from the rhetorical incongruities in the reporter's baroque euphemization of an exemplary imperial cruelty. Joyce's fierce satire is therefore not directed at Emmet's sacrifice but at the manner of its memorialization.

In this same passage he manages a brief reprise of the main point in "After the Race." The sentence, "Considerable amusement was caused by the favourite Dublin streetsingers L-n-h-n and M-ll-g-n who sang *The Night before Larry Was Stretched* in their usual mirthprovoking fashion. Our two inimitable drolls did a roaring trade with their broadsheets among the lovers of the comedy element and nobody who has a corner in his heart for real Irish fun without vulgarity will grudge them their hardearned pennies" (*U* 12.541–46). These cadgers on a patriotic cause, the "blacklegs of literature" of whom Joyce complained elsewhere, like Jimmy Doyle, exploit national interests for personal gain. The excerpt illustrates his point to the Triestines at the death of John O'Leary, that the Irish "even though they break the hearts of those who sacrifice their lives for their native land, never fail to show great respect for the dead" (*CW* 192).

This and similar demonstrations of patriotic fervor produced varying responses in nationalist Ireland. The actor Brandon Tynan, who had made his name playing Emmet across the United States, presented himself as the model for the famous Jerome Connor's statue catching Emmet in a pose of gallant resilience (completed in 1912). Meanwhile, back in Dublin, the play that captured the mood of the time was Henry Connell Mangan's *Robert Emmet,* performed at the Molesworth Hall in October 31, 1903 (Ellis-Fermor, 216). Dudley Digges's rendition of the thrilling oration dissolved audiences in tears. More determined nationalists concurred with Griffith's call for moral regeneration and de-Anglicization in promoting "Emmet's Days": avoiding carnivals and sports for the sake of respect, silence, reflection, mourning, and practical resolution (*United Irishman,* September 19, 1903). These commemorations, however, contributed to the formation of a renewed revolutionary movement imbued with the idea that Emmet's example required another grand gesture of redemptive sacrifice. Thus Patrick Pearse claimed that just as Emmet redeemed Ireland from the Union, another staging of his rebellion would redeem the treachery of the parliamentarians.

It is therefore within this spectrum of cultural and literary debate over the appropriate response of nationalist Ireland to the Land Act, the Gordon Bennett Cup Race, and the royal visit that Joyce's venture into the controversy should be viewed when, more than a year later, he pondered how he would transform his ill-tempered interview with Henri Fournier and its chain of sequels into political art. The Martello tower at Sandycove, in which this story was conceived, was a concrete historical response to the Emmet rebellion (1903 was its centennial). The resulting story matured as he gazed across the parapet northwest into Kingstown Harbour and behind it Dublin's skyline, or east across the Irish Sea, the only residence from which he could behold the glory of the sunrise. If we bear these biographical, geographic, and historical circumstances in mind, we may be in a position to appreciate how "After the Race" is a beveled memorial to a famous Dubliner.

In looking at these potent voices and symbols, we should recall that Joyce's evolving attitude toward history was moving away from Thomas Carlyle's belief that a nation's history is the story of its heroes, and toward Friedrich Nietzsche's, that it is more accurately understood as an indeterminate network of seemingly indifferent events: an infinite tale of mediocrity, distraction, and boredom. It is my hypothesis that "After the Race" is most fruitfully read with a clear sense of the tension between acclaimed events and the unremarkable business of daily living.

Through the City

Turning to Joyce's story, then, we can see from the title alone that it assumes a stance resistant to the media hype surrounding the Gordon Bennett Cup Race. Its implied narrator is less interested in the contest than in its aftermath, and less in the course than in its "tailgaters." The map of Dublin City and its environs—with which he apparently expects his readers to be familiar—does not even mention the route pursued by the celebrated contestants, but describes specifically or by implication those pursued by the high-rolling revelers.

We first learn of their approach to the city from the southwest: from County Kildare via the Naas Road. From there they are obligated to follow Tyrconnell Road, passing Goldenbridge at Inchicore (*D* 41.4). For the next three pages (until *D* 45.13) we are treated, via the narrator's free indirect discourse, to some essential exposition and a taste of the mind of Jimmy Doyle. Only when the tourists reach College Green six kilometers later does the narrator identify their surroundings (figure 5.2).

Our otherwise precise geographic guide has fallen silent as Ségouin's car travels between Inchicore and the Bank of Ireland. We can see from the map that this reticence intervenes once the vehicle enters Emmet Road (as it was named since the 1880s; and appropriately, since Emmet was especially the hero of the artisans of Inchicore). Crossing the South Circular Road, it passes Kilmainham Gaol and Mount Brown, proceeds

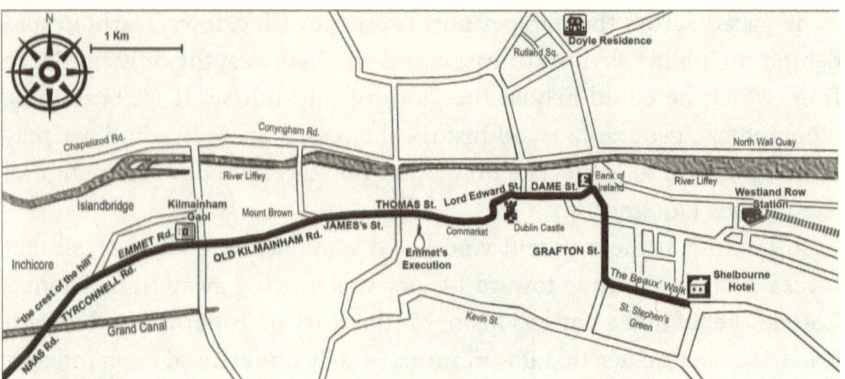

Figure 5.2. Route taken by Jimmy Doyle and guests. Digital map by Arjun Sheoran, 2009.

along James's Street; and from there steers along Thomas Street, High and Lord Edward streets past Dublin Castle, and into Dame Street. The car stops in front of the Bank of Ireland at College Green to dispatch Jimmy Doyle and Villona and then continues around into Grafton Street, heading for Saint Stephen's Green where Ségouin and Rivière are lodging. Now, while the main public events of the day have by this time concluded through provincial Leinster, and the evening's entertainments are accommodated between Saint Stephen's Green and Kingstown Harbour, these disparate and frivolous activities are linked by a topography charged with a ritually reinforced energy that Joyce (vainly) hoped would register with his Dublin readers.

The narrator allows, without comment, Ségouin's car to pass all of the points associated with the Emmet rebellion. First, they retread the road taken by Emmet's Kildaremen on the morning of July 23, 1803: via the Naas Road past Rathcoole to Inchicore (passing the future site of the infamous Red Cow Roundabout a century before conception). They pass Kilmainham Gaol where Emmet was imprisoned between his capture and execution. Gliding along Thomas Street, they traverse the streets on which the insurrection was planned (the depots at Marshalsea Lane and Patrick Street), where it occurred (Thomas Street itself), and past the most revered place of all, the scene of Emmet's execution (outside Saint Catherine's Church at the intersection with Bridgefoot Street where today an inscribed marble plaque and plinth mark the spot). Without apparent pause, the automobile pursues the route taken by Emmet and his partisans toward Dublin Castle before the rebellion fizzled out at the scene of the Kilwarden murders. The riders pass the sentried gate of the castle, the hub of British colonial administration and intelligence (the repository of McNally's reports), the main target of Emmet's and other abortive risings. From there along Cornmarket, High Street, Christchurch Place, doglegging at Werburgh Street, and via Lord Edward Street (named after the United Irishman Lord Edward Fitzgerald in 1886), they make their way to Dame Street. It is at this point—after a lapse of three pages—that the narrator's auto-censorship ceases and he identifies the riders' terminus: "Near the Bank" (*D* 45.15).

The car halts at the east end of Dame Street. The narrator focuses our attention on the awe in which ordinary citizens hold the visitors, reinforced by the references to Dame Street, the Bank of Ireland, and Grafton Street, the vortex of Ireland's financial, insurance, and fashion industries. It is clear, however, from the foregoing catalogue of omissions that Jimmy and his French friends halt between three significant monuments signifying the forces against which Emmet's rebellion was mounted: the Union of Great Britain and Ireland, represented by the Bank of Ireland that replaced the Irish Parliament in 1801 (thereby warranting the narrator's remark that Dublin "wears the mask of a capital" [*D* 46.29]); the colony's think-tank, Trinity College, which expelled Emmet in 1798 for his republicanism; and the Anglo-Irish Protestant Ascendancy, figured by the bronze statue of King William III. The image of "[a] little knot of people on the footpath paying homage to the snorting motor" (*D* 45.16–17) nicely compares Ségouin's automobile beneath this triumphalist equestrian statue to Protestant hegemony in a double image of colonial horsepower, new and old.[6]

We have been conducted in stiff-lipped silence, then, through the streets of Emmet's constituency (blue-collar Inchicore and the Liberties), and whose stones have recently echoed to the popular acclaim of his futile rising, eloquent speech, and barbaric execution.[7] For the rest of the evening, we are brought on a tour of moneyed and fashionable Dublin: from the Bank of Ireland, through Grafton Street, the fictional simulacrum of the Shelbourne Hotel, and along Saint Stephen's Green, the watering-holes and airing promenades of those whose sophisticated tastes are furnished by the spoils of empire. Jimmy conducts his friends along the north side of the Green, past the imposing statue of George II, between the hotel and Grafton Street—the Beaux' Walk—turning before they reach Emmet's birthplace on the west side. Similarly, the train southeast from Westland Row (named for a property magnate) to Kingstown (named for George IV) represents the imperial imprint firmly pressed into Dublin's toponymy. It traces, most immediately, the recent coming and going of his grandnephew Edward VII, Kingstown pier bearing first and last the pressure of his royal corpulence. These all flash subliminally by in the story as Jimmy loses track of the time, the place, and the cards.

By having his caddish automobilists career in hilarious abandon past the landmarks of Dublin's pathetic and cruel history, then, Joyce is brilliantly fictionalizing Griffith's characterization of the Gordon Bennett Cup Race as a device to camouflage the source of Irish paralysis. When Griffith charged that the race dishonored the bones of the Irish kings and saints entombed by the roads of Kildare and Carlow, he provided Joyce with the cue for this satirical story of a raffish crew of weekend tourists ignorant of and indifferent to the blood shed on the stones of Old Dublin. Were Jimmy not so awed by and anxious to ingratiate himself with these dashing fellows, he might have leaned forward and instructed them. Since she plays host to the Gordon Bennett Cup Race in England's name, as if she had no claim to a nationhood to call her own, Ireland has not "taken her place among the nations of the earth." Thus by ironic analogy, in Joyce's eloquent restraint—another gnomonic figuration in *Dubliners*—we have an apt expression of his respect for Robert Emmet's last request: to render him honor in accordance with the injunction, by "the charity of its silence."

Jemmety

In the light of this essential historical intelligence about the Emmet rebellion, all commonplaces at the time of its writing, it is a short step to the observation that the naive Jimmy Doyle is a parodic version of this national hero whose idealistic rebellion Joyce thought "foolish" (*CW* 189). On some apparently trivial biographical counts, they are at least superficially similar. Both Jimmy and Emmet are young Dubliners of approximately the same age: Jimmy is "about twenty-six years of age" (*D* 43.13), and Emmet (March 4, 1778 to September 20, 1903) was executed six-and-a-half months before his twenty-sixth birthday. Jimmy's father was "an advanced Nationalist" (*D* 43.15) who nonetheless managed to make his fortune from "police contracts" (*D* 43.19). Emmet's father, Dr. Robert, was state physician for Ireland, an official appointment that made him a prominent and wealthy man. Despite his colonial position, he was an open admirer of the American Revolution, an outspoken Patriot, and in time a radical (Geoghegan, 53–57). Both Emmet and Jimmy were temporary law students at Dublin University: Emmet dropped out because of the suspicion that had fallen upon him over his engagement in unapproved political activities on the premises, and Jimmy because he "took to bad courses" (*D* 43.24). Each of them then went abroad and intrigued with "their friends, the French" (*D* 42.9) in competition with their common enemy, the English. Each inherited a handsome personal fortune from his father that on the assumption of French assistance, he is persuaded "to stake the great part of his substance" (*D* 44.32) on a speculative venture.

One of the charges against Emmet was his fastidiousness in dress. The prospective liberator of his nation should be properly attired. The Emmet costume, therefore, was flamboyant: white waistcoat and white pantaloons, a sash and a pair of new black boots, a green military jacket with gold lace on the sleeves and several gold epaulettes as might accouter a general, a sword, a pair of pistols, and large cocked hat (Geoghegan, 174). It must have been with a feeling of grim humor, then, that Joyce (anticipating O'Casey's Uncle Peter of *The Plough and the Stars*) wrote "Jimmy, too, looked very well when he was dressed and, as he stood in the hall giving a last equation to the bows of his dress tie" (*D* 45.29–31) before having him sally forth to meet his destiny.

Reveling in the "notoriety" (*D* 44.14) his venture will earn, each is borne along to the "limits of reasonable recklessness" (*D* 44.28–29) into a venture that was a "serious thing for him" (*D* 44.32–33). The experience is disillusioning, however. Whereas the naive and idealistic Emmet learned to distrust the French, Jimmy Doyle (with the "rather innocent-looking grey eyes" [*D* 43.14]) finds, late in the game, that he is one of the "heaviest losers" (*D* 48.26). Each young man finds himself out of his depth and is exploited and betrayed by collaborators. These analogues between their stories accord with Joyce's incisive remark about the Emmet rebellion that it was "one of those flashes of Celtic temperament that lighten the shadows for a moment and leave behind a darkness blacker than before" (*CW* 189). This is apposite to his decision to conclude "After the Race" with the irony of Villona's announcement, "Daybreak, gentlemen!"(*D* 48.33).

From the Dock

The climax of Robert Emmet's rebellion, and the reason for which it is literally recalled, is his famous speech from the dock. Having stood before Lord Norbury for the thirteen hours of his trial for treason—during which the testimony of nineteen Crown witnesses and none in defense was heard—he delivered an hour-long, and apparently extempore, oration, ending shortly before midnight on September 19, 1803. The final minutes of this speech have entered the rhetorical canon at home and abroad: from Texas to New York, aspiring public speakers receiving educations as diverse from one another as Abraham Lincoln, Robert E. Lee, and Terence Winch could extemporize its conclusion (Fanning, 141), and even the *London Times*, the major organ of imperialism, printed the speech in full on September 26, 1903 (3a). Its final paragraph reads:

> My lord, you are impatient for the sacrifice. The blood which you seek is not congealed by the artificial terrors which surround your victim—it circulates warmly and unruffled through its channels, and in a short time it will cry to heaven. Be yet patient! I have but a few words to say: my ministry is now ended. I am going to my cold and silent grave; my lamp of life is nearly extinguished. I have parted with everything that was dear to me in this life for my country's cause, and abandoned another idol I adored in my heart, the object of my affections. My race is run—the grave opens to receive me, and I sink into its bosom. I am ready to die—I have not been allowed to vindicate my character. I have but one request to ask at my departure from this world—it is *the charity of its silence*. Let no man write my epitaph; for as no man who knows my motives dares now vindicate them, let not prejudice or ignorance asperse them. Let them rest in obscurity and peace: my memory be left in oblivion and my tomb remain uninscribed, until other times and other men can do justice to my character. When my country takes her place among the nations of the earth, then, and not till then, let my epitaph be written. I have done. (John J. Reynolds, 117)

In vindication of his moral character that the Crown had impugned, this thrilling speech moves between sentences of alternating length, parallelism, and suspended syntactic design. In its high-minded identification of nation and moral righteousness, it is the *locus classicus* of Irish patriotic rhetoric. It draws on biblical images of worship, blood sacrifice, sacrament, and adoration, contrasting his sacred ministry with the bloodthirsty impatience of his powerful enemies. Invoking Pauline images ("to the unknown god," "my race is run," and "the greatest of these is charity"), it alludes to the encomium of Jesus, "greater love hath no man than to lay down his life for his friend," His silence before Pontius Pilate, and His last words ("*Consummatum est*").

The Pauline text to which it bears the most developed reference is the Apostle's conclusion to the Second Letter to Timothy where we have one of Saint Paul's most personal statements: "For I am already being poured out like a libation, and the time of my departure is at hand. I have competed well; I have finished the race; I have kept the faith. From now on the crown of righteousness awaits me, which the Lord, the just judge, will award to me on that day, and not only to me, but to all who have longed for his appearance" (4: 6–8). In this sequence of images—of the pouring of his blood, the completing of his race, the analogy between the martyr's crown and the athlete's wreath, and the day of liberation to come—we have evidence that Emmet saw himself as a Christian martyr and that Ireland's cause was an expression of Christian witness. All of those who in the Irish patriotic and nationalist rhetorical tradition recite these famous lines implicitly invoke the allusions, sacred and secular.

The full speech made three main assertions: the vindication of his moral character (seven times mentioned), the autonomy of the insurrection from French interests, and its political justification to attain the independence of Ireland. The first of these arose from the charge that he was responsible for the Lord Kilwarden murders: he denied this on the grounds that he had abandoned the rebellion when these outrages occurred. On the substantial point, the charge of treason, Emmet acknowledged his having taken the United Irish oath and planning the overthrow of British administration in Ireland.

The presiding judge, Lord Norbury, interrupted Emmet's oration at several points to remind him that he was abusing the privilege of the court by preaching treason (Geoghegan records the speech and the exchanges [3–15]). Turning once again to Joyce's text, we read that "Jimmy made a speech, a long speech, Villona saying *Hear! hear!* whenever there was a pause. There was a great clapping of hands when he sat down. It must have been a good speech. Farley clapped him on the back and laughed loudly" (*D* 47.32–48.2). First, this evidently echoes both the historical circumstances of the speech (its length and interruptions) and its status in Irish and Irish-American culture during the century since its declamation. Second, the dramatic context raises significant questions about not only Ireland's traditional enemy (personified by Routh), but also about those whom the "gratefully oppressed" Irish have regarded as "their friends, the French" (D 42.8–9). Both, Jimmy concludes late in the night, are "devils of fellows" (D 48.14). Third, the images from the opening paragraph of Joyce's story, "running evenly like pellets in the groove" (D 42.2–3) and "through this channel" (D 42.5) would appear to echo the terms in which Emmet began the last sally in his famous speech: "The blood which you seek . . . circulates warmly and unruffled through its channels." Fourth, the image of the young patriot and lover, with his high rhetoric and magnanimity even in the face of imminent death that has so transfixed popular national sentiment, is parodically reproduced in the rhetorical phrase, "gallantly the machinery of human nerves" (D 45.11), describing Jimmy's callow excitement. Fifth, Emmet's acceptance of his fate and the bravado of his desire for an uninscribed burial are reflected in Jimmy's being "glad of the rest, glad of the dark stupor" (D 48.28) as the long night drew to a close, and the prospect that his folly would be covered up (D 48.28–29). Most revealingly, however, is the manner in which Jimmy counts the beats of his temples (D 48.30–31)—the rhythm of his circulating blood—and the title of Joyce's story cites that most emotional of Pauline images in which Emmet concluded his speech: "My race is run." In these respects, "After the Race" is a polite, reserved, but respectful tribute to Emmet, if not as a patriot, at least as an exemplary epideitic performer.[8]

The passionate eloquence of his speech astonished even Emmet's most vehement enemies and moved his supporters to high emotion. In a grand gesture that has passed down through the oral tradition, his defense attorney, Leonard McNally, as if in emulation of Judas Iscariot, "leaned over and kissed him theatrically on the forehead" (Geoghegan, 15).

Finally, then, this evidence supports the claim that the technique of "After the Race," in its sly citations from Emmet's high rhetoric and the series of oblique allusions to the historical events of 1803, contends with the popular clamor that marked the centennial. It implies, too, in its restraint and silences, it records in Joyce's inimitable manner, an expression of loyalty to one whose name is not given breath.[9] If, on the one hand, the ceremonies celebrating the Gordon Bennett Cup Race and the visit of King Edward were indeed designed to outperform the commemorations of Emmet's rebellion, they would seem to have failed. If, on the other, romantic Irish nationalist rhetoric was wont to respond to Emmet's appeal with "blatherskite," Joyce's story answers both with a peculiar form of artistic reticence. In this respect, it is a specialized exercise for connoisseurs of poetic justice.

"I have done"

This reading of "After the Race" queries, once again, the apparently derogatory treatment of Robert Emmet in the "Sirens" and "Cyclops" episodes of *Ulysses* (*U* 11.1269–94; 12.525–678). At the conclusion of "Sirens," recalling the final sentence of Emmet's oration, and without explicit comment, Bloom reduces his colonic pressure. On the common assumption that Bloom is here also—in a manner of speaking—giving voice to his creator's view of Emmet, Irish nationalists have taken offense. It seems to confirm the impression that Joyce harbors a condescending view of the Irish patriot and his admirers. This is a common misreading (for example, by Luke Gibbons), and a simplification that underestimates the density of the historical moment, the dialogical design of *Ulysses,* and the technical complexity of Joyce's literary methods.[10]

As the narrator tells us that Bloom, exiting from the Ormond Hotel, "viewed a gallant pictured hero in Lionel Marks's window," Bloom's thoughts, "Robert Emmet's last words" (*U* 11.1274–75), cut him off. Readers have deduced that the picture of Robert Emmet in the shop window has reminded him of the last two sentences of his famous speech. The inference is satisfactory enough, supported as it is by his association of these twenty words with the seven last words of Jesus, the subject of Saverio Mercadante's oratorio (Bloom has momentarily confused Giacomo Meyerbeer with Mercadante [as Gifford notes, 311]). Bloom's memory lapse and his subsequent apparent disdain for these words have distracted readers from recognizing the association between the executions of Jesus and Emmet. Their puzzlement is easy to appreciate, for at this point in the story, the narrator appears confused. The words of Ben Dollard's pathetic 1798 ballad ("The youth has entered a lonely hall") interfere in the narrator's description of something the blind stripling is doing, to produce the sentence "A youth entered a lonely Ormond hall" (*U* 11.1273), which is quickly clarified by the subsequent observation that "An unseeing stripling stood in the door" (*U* 11.1281). The blind stripling has tapped his way to the Ormond Hotel entrance through which Bloom has exited but a moment before. As the reader is sorting the coincidences of "Ormond" (the name of the hotel, the location of Lionel Marks's shop, and the region in which the 1798 Rebellion occurred), Bloom is thinking of another youth who has confessed to his patriotic excess in another hostile hall, and approaches the final loneliness of death by execution: Robert Emmet.

To unwind the skeins of association and argument, it should first be observed that Bloom is not merely summoning the familiar cadences of Emmet's last words. Were he so doing, he would be like the narrator who has conflated the visual and audio images from Dollard's song and the stripling entering the door of the Ormond Hotel. But Bloom is at the same time reading the words of Emmet's last speech in the window of the antique shop at 16 Ormond Quay Upper. This particular aspect of the moment neither the blind stripling nor the narrator registers. This moment requires a small historical intervention.

One of the prize patriotic memorabilia from the period was the expensively produced 1798 centennial poster commemorating what was the last major incident in that rebellion: Robert Emmet's insurrection, speech, and execution in 1803. This poster retailed at 2/6, and (even after six years) holds pride of place in this antique dealer's: enough to hold Leopold Bloom's attention over the display of musical instruments, candlesticks, and bric-a-brac (figure 5.3).

Its central image is the profile of the intense hero. Marianne Elliott points out that it is not historical, but seems more like "a cross between typical pictures of young priests and those of the young Napoleon" (184). Perhaps so: but as with the inherited version of the speech, it is the received popular tradition that concerns us. At the top of the poster is a frieze of national symbols, a round tower, Irish wolfhound, dolmen and Celtic cross, centered on an angel surrounded by an array of pikes above those of shattered canons and broken chains. A border of intertwined shamrocks frames three texts: a brief preface, Emmet's entire speech (with Lord Norbury's interruptions), and a paragraph describing the morning of Emmet's execution.

The introduction sets the scene in the Green Street Courthouse. His request for a delay in the proceedings having been rejected, "Emmet, upon the instant, exhausted as he was by the trial . . . [delivered] the following speech which may safely be pronounced to be one of the most splendid

Figure 5.3. The 1798 centennial poster. Courtesy of National Library of Ireland, Prints and Drawings, HP6.

and powerful effusions of impassioned eloquence and patriotic devotion which ever fell impromptu from the lips of man." Then it prints the entire speech from "What have I to say why sentence of death should not be pronounced on me according to law?" to the final "I have done." The text is rendered in four dense newspaper columns, impossible to read except at close range. In all of this, the singular phrase—because it appears in capital letters—appears in the final paragraph: "THE CHARITY OF ITS SILENCE."

That Bloom would have encountered this poster commemorating Emmet's role in the rebellion of the United Irishmen and celebrating his idealism and eloquence just after the applause for Dollard's performance of "The Croppy Boy" establishes the historical links between the two kinds of patriotic rhetoric—the ballad and the speech—from the same political movement. That the chapter managed in the spirit of music should end in a speech in enjoining the tribute of silence is poetically apt. The narrator's response, and, indeed, Bloom's—despite his rebellious colon—are in the spirit enjoined by Emmet, whose country had not yet taken her place among the nations of the earth, an appropriate silence.

The poster (and this argument) is not yet done, however. It closes with a description of the day of execution, taken, it seems, from one of the many patriotic embellishments of the Emmet legend. It begins: "Day dawns through the prison bars. Emmet, rousing from his reverie, lifts his eyes to Heaven; and on bended knees, whilst offering up his young life as a willing sacrifice for that country which he loves so dearly, calls down blessings upon its martyred people." It concludes with the comment that as the aggravated sentence is carried out, "England's vengeance" and "brutality" are "satiated." Neither Elliott's unsympathetic commentary nor the implied narrator of "Sirens" who reports Bloom's thoughts on the poster of "a gallant pictured hero" observes the salient emblem that links this paragraph with the image presiding over the entire graphic. In the middle of the flourish of the arms of the United Irishmen stands a pensive angel amidst the rays of the rising sun.

The designer of the poster records, therefore, the powerful imaginative relationships between Emmet's deliberate self-effacement and the dawn of a nation for which he was giving his life. The prospect of the end of this "nightmare of history" recurs in *Ulysses* in the minds of both Stephen and Bloom. Bloom had already reflected on this emblem (*U* 4.100), and would again (*U* 15.1469), under which the United Irishmen rebelled in 1798 and

1803, and which animated their recently celebrated centennials. Its appearance at the conclusion of "After the Race," as a story of silent tribute to the memory of Emmet, is historically in accord with the kind of refined national feeling we might expect from Joyce.

We have seen the manner in which "After the Race" reviews, in cunning silence, the events of the rebellion and the rhetorical tropes of Emmet's speech. This centennial poster, cited at the conclusion of "Cyclops," supports the contention that it also underlies the denouement of "After the Race." Just as Emmet's last morning on earth—after his betrayal and fateful sentence—promised political daybreak for Ireland, so does Villona's announcement, as he stood "in a shaft of grey light" (*D* 48.32), bring Jimmy Doyle to a relief from his terrible night, and announce the day during which he will realize that he has been at least exploited, if not scammed. Invoking in this way the complex icon of national awakening, Joyce's story is a literary equivalent to the poster: their daybreaks both literal and politically visionary. The invocation of this poster in *Ulysses* is further evidence that the "truth" of that work lies not in Bloom's involuntary release of gas, but in the network of relationships between what the narrator hears but does not see and what Bloom reads but the narrator does not record. In this instance of Joyce's commitment to "silence," he is honoring the hero's last request.[11]

The Emmet rebellion is but one instance in a series of executions and funerals in the city of the Danes (Emmet's execution takes place in the city center of Danish Dublin). The larger context is the recurring rebellion of sons against fathers, itself a historical manifestation of the eternal warfare between the angels and God's "awethorrorty" (*FW* 516.19).

These historically instructed observations allow us to return, finally, to a recapitulation of the trips taken by Jimmy Doyle and his French friends. We are now in a position to observe that the three phases of the day's "careering" have a tripartite schematic historical correspondence with the Emmet rebellion. Just as the route of the Gordon Bennett Cup Race took the drivers through the geography of the first phase of the 1798 Rebellion, through Kildare and Carlow,[12] the second takes us along the string of spots associated with Robert Emmet's rebellion in 1903, and the third takes us to his paradoxical last request, his execution, and the reassertion of imperial hegemony. Whereas on the naturalistic level our attention is drawn to the conspicuous consumerism surrounding the Gordon Bennett Cup Race and the elation produced by "[r]apid motion through space" (*D*

44.14), the narrative strategies that Joyce invokes take the reader in reverse gear through time and into historical remembrance. Joyce's imaginative retrogression is thus a nuanced rebuke both of the disingenuous display made by the centennial parade and of the exploitation of a sports event to advance colonial interests. The story is therefore a brilliant subscription to Arthur Griffith's political criticism of the Gordon Bennett Cup Race. The astonishing understatement of "After the Race," written on the eve of his departure into exile, documents Joyce's capacity to pledge, through its cunning silences, his unique hope.

"by dawnybreak in Aira" (FW 353.31–32)

"After the Race" ends with Villona's anticlimactic announcement of daybreak. As we can infer from the probable circumstances of its conception, it might well have been conceived as its author beheld daybreak from the parapet of the Martello tower at Sandycove. William Bulfin's report, cited in chapter 3, assists us in the entertainment of the relevant scenario. Unique among Joyce's residences, the Martello tower afforded a spectacular view of the daily sunrise: he must have risen early at least once to enjoy the tower's singular prospect. Since this panorama illumines both the conclusion of this story and the opening of *Ulysses*, it clearly left a permanent impression in Joyce's visual memory.

Joyce would have therefore been in a position, from firsthand experience, to know that on July 3, 1903, the sun rose within a couple of minutes of 3:30 a.m.[13] Jimmy and his companions, absorbed in their "great game," have missed the view. In concluding his story this way, Joyce is not inventing anything: as R. B. Kershner has noted, "the dramatic arrival of daybreak after a night-long indulgence was a popular convention, and Joyce was well aware of it" (79).[14] The irony is both larger and finer than this because of the symbolic status of sunrise in the iconography of the culture represented in the story.

The sunrise (or sunburst) is part of the common stock of European symbolism, and although widely used in the flags of the seventeenth and eighteenth centuries, the *scál ghréine* was assumed by Irish nationalists of the nineteenth century to be a native icon of some antiquity. In his searching study of Irish flags, Gerald Hayes-McCoy traces the image from the membership card of the Irish Volunteers in 1782 through its appearances in Moore's Irish melody "The Wine Cup is Circling" (1834), the pages

Figure 5.4. *Freeman's Journal* masthead: "Ireland a Nation."

of the *Nation* (1843), and the banners of Irish Republican Brotherhood (1867) (155–56). It appeared on Land League banners (176–77) and after Joyce's Dublin had passed into history. The First Battalion of the Dublin Regiment of the Irish Volunteers, in 1914, adopted the rising sun with its nine rays signifying the coming of Lugh, the sun god of Irish antiquity, out of the kingdom of Manannan—the sea—to rescue Ireland from the Fomorians, subsequently forming "the standard of Finn MacCumhall" (200). The adoption of this flag—in preference to the more conventional harp with the maiden—was the subject of controversy in 1914, when the sunburst was viewed as "too Oriental" (201). The image survives in Irish iconography: on postage stamps and the flag of the Irish cadet school (230).

The icon of the rising sun was a more familiar image in Irish popular culture a century ago than it is today (where it has largely receded into the image behind the Sinn Féin/IRA slogan, *Tiocfhaidh Ár Lá* [Our Day Will Come]). It adorned the masthead of the leading nationalist daily newspaper, the *Freeman's Journal* (figure 5.4). "*Fáinne Gheal an Lae*" [The Dawning of the Day] was (and remains) a familiar Irish song, and *Fáinne an Lae* was the title of the Gaelic League publication (1898–1900) (before it became *An Claidheamh Soluis*) founded and edited by one Bernard Doyle and with a masthead of the rising sun. It was therefore one of the more tired clichés of nationalist propaganda, art, and drama.[15] Even as Joyce's manuscript of "After the Race" lay on AE's desk at the *Irish Homestead*, Maud Gonne's patriotic melodrama, *Dawn,* appeared in the pages of the *United Irishman* (October 29, 1904).

Of the scores of verses and songs that the high feeling of the 1798 centennial generated, one song, then familiar, but now long forgotten, appears to have a verifiable proximate relationship with the manner in which Joyce executed the closure of "After the Race." It went:

> When shall the day break in Erin?
> When shall her daystar arise?
> Out of the east resplendent
> To flood on straining eyes.
> When shall her wrongs become righted
> And the sad past forgotten be?
> That time may be distant, what matters
> It shall be her destiny.
> Chorus:
> Ireland is Ireland through joy and through tears;
> Hope never dies through the long weary years;
> Each age has seen countless brave hearts pass away,
> But their spirit still lives on in the men of today.

The music critic of the *Weekly Irish Times* (May 25, 1901, p. 3, col. 5) called this "a stirring patriotic song with a choral refrain . . . in *tempo di Marcia,* easily singable. . . . a very successful song at a popular Theatre Royal pantomime some short time ago . . . [with a] swing and spirit that cannot be missed." This song is of interest here because of its iconographic and patriotic reverberations in Villona's hearalding of the new day. Its entirely unremarkable words and woodenly martial music gave it but a short life, so that despite its temporary success, it was not reprinted after 1901. John McCormack made two recordings of the song, however.[16] The records of the Edison and Gramophone and Typewriter Company (G&T), in London, indicate that McCormack made these recordings circa September 12, 1904 (with orchestral accompaniment), and (with piano) on September 23, 1904. They were not released at the time, or ever re-recorded; but fortunately, the originals have survived. They were finally released on CD in 1991.[17]

As is well known (even if often imprecisely reported), John McCormack and James Joyce were acquainted, and had in some respects, at that time, similar talents and led parallel lives. McCormack had won the gold medal for solo tenor at the Feis Ceoil in 1903, and encouraged Joyce to enter the competition the following year (May 16), where he was awarded but the bronze on account of his inability to sight read (*JJII* 150–52). Later that summer (August 27) they appeared together at the Antient Concert Rooms. This was a memorable occasion on two counts: it marked the height of Joyce's short musical career, and it was the end of the early phase of McCormack's long one. Within six weeks they both left Ireland on their separate artistic and international ways. With respect to the present investigation, however, it has two further points of significance. The concert was organized in support of the Irish Industrial Exhibition, and was thus part of the "buy Irish" campaign promoted by the Gaelic League and Griffith.[18] The dominant character of the evening's songs was sentimental and nostalgic ("The Old Green Isle," "The Green Isle of Erin," "The Ould Plaid Shawl," "The Irishman," and "Killarney"). Joyce's performance of "The Croppy Boy"—which the *Freeman's Journal* reported as "sweet" and "pathetic" (*JJII* 168n)—was, in fact, the single expressly political selection on the "Programme" (Jackson and McGinley, 131), and an evocation of the recent commemorations of the 1798 and Emmet rebellions.

Between September 11 and 23, McCormack was in London to make a series of recordings of Irish songs (twenty-seven in all), the first of a famous career in vocal recording. Today's listener can discern—despite the acoustic limitations of the wax cylinders—the sweetness, clarity, power, and articulation of his as yet undeveloped voice. It is perhaps not a coincidence that as McCormack was committing this song to the permanent record, Joyce, resident in the Martello tower, was gazing at the sunrise on the Irish Sea and recalling this temporary favorite of Dublin audiences that he had heard his friend and rival sing but weeks before. This trite topical song did not survive very long after the fervor generated by the 1798 centennial had waned, and McCormack had judgment enough never to record it again. The author of *Finnegans Wake* remembered it, however, as the intermediate title above reveals. In any event, "When Shall the Day Break in Erin?" seems to be among the topical materials memorializing, however ineptly, the United Irishmen that Joyce was gathering into the text of "After the Race."

When Joyce imagined Villona elevating the image of the rising sun to iconographic status at the anticlimactic denouement of the story then, there was a well-established link between it and the aspiration to Home Rule. To readers of the daily *Freeman's Journal*, with its Parnellite icon of the sun rising over the former Irish House of Parliament, Villona's announcement would have been seen to complete the allegorical motif that threads through the narrative: from the image of the cars topping "the crest of the hill ... careering homeward" (*D* 42.3–5), drawing up near the Bank of Ireland (*D* 45.15), and of Dublin's wearing "the mask of a capital" (*D* 46.29), cumulatively proffering the hope of Home Rule. By inference, therefore, there is an analogy between Jimmy's distracted night and the terrors of the seven hundred years of Irish suffering. There is, indeed, a correspondence between the political sympathies of the historians who term the events of 1798, 1803, 1848, 1867 (and, of course, 1916), "rebellions" or "risings" and this persistent and subliminal icon. In Joyce's work, the image of daybreak or dawn draws on that same reservoir of images promising the renewal of Irish political life. This Fenian or Home Rule motif first appears in "An Encounter," with Fr. Butler's prodding Leo Dillon to rise from his schoolboy's indulgence in English comics to the recitation of his homework assignment. In calling on the boy to begin with "*Hardly had the day dawned,*" Joyce is slyly suggesting that the leader of the anti-Parnellite faction in the Irish Parliamentary Party, John Dillon (1851–1927), prefers a comic book named *The Union Jack* to the production of the serious assignment headed with the logo of the Parnellite paper, the *Freeman's Journal* ("An Encounter" [*D* 20.17–18]).

The opening scene of *Ulysses* returns to Villona's morning purview at the conclusion of "After the Race." The Martello tower was within his line of sight as he gazed, eleven and a half months (and three hours) earlier, at the eastern horizon. This scene offers several contrasting articulations of a new dawn for Irish culture. First, Mulligan, Stephen, and the narrator concur in personifying the natural scene: the Irish Sea as "a great sweet mother. . . . The scrotumtightening sea" (*U* 1.77–78) surrounding "the awaking [Dublin and Wicklow] mountains" (*U* 1.10–11). Under the aegis of this symbol, this scene offers contrasting schemes for Irish cultural and political renewal: Mulligan's Hellenization, Haines's Anglo-Irish patronization, Hydes's De-Anglicization, and Stephen's Europeanization. Then, in a paradigm switch, Ireland becomes transformed into the "milk woman," the subject of a string of allegorical epithets from the *aisling* [vision] tradition, "Old and secret. . . . Silk of the kine and poor old woman" (*U* 1.399–404). A Christianized personification of Ireland, she sees in the morning sun the glory of God (*U* 1.390). Among the young men, Mulligan is the object of her attention. Besides her payment, he offers to Hellenize her and Stephen: by paganizing her and teaching Stephen Greek ("*Epi oinipa ponton* . . . *Thalatta!* . . . *omphalos*" [*U* 1.78–80, 176]). He has begun his paganization by his pantomimic assumption of the priest's role: blaspheming the Mass and the Holy Spirit, even as he counsels Stephen to a pretense of religious observance. Mulligan offers the liberation of scientific materialism, the very siren that hails and inveigles Jimmy Doyle. Haines is Routh *redivivus:* an English liberal with a bad conscience. He is "[t]he seas' ruler" (*U* 1.574): the Royal Navy ensures that on its empire, beginning with the sea and land bearing Mother Ireland's name, the sun never sets.[19] The onetime challenge presented by the French navy ("when the French were on the sea") echoes "Billy Pitt's" decision to fortify his mastery over the first colony by the construction of the tower in which they now billet and banter (*U* 1.543–44). Haines recognizes, but euphemizes, England's guilt: offering but the characteristic Oxbridge understatement (and implied narrator's litotes), "We feel in England that we have treated you rather unfairly" (*U* 1.648).

While his nightmares testify to his repressed historical guilt, they terrify Stephen, who as the descendant of its victims, suffers more than their perpetrator. Like Villona, the appalled Stephen stands aside, brooding over the mystery of his mother's removal and his service of three masters. The nearest embodiment of Ireland's conscience, he is calumniated as the "dreadful bard" (*U* 1.134) even if endowed with "more spirit than any of them" (*U* 1.151). But his present spiritual and existential crisis causes him to disparage the images by which Irish nationalists are roused to action: "I see little hope . . . from her or from him" (*U* 1.501).

Behind the entire scene, praised by the milk woman, blasphemed by Mulligan, unimaginable to Haines, and appalling to Stephen is the image of the Holy Spirit. The object of Mulligan's breezy mockery ("switch off the current, will you?" [*U* 1.28–29]), Stephen's tremulous skepticism ("The void awaits surely all them that weave the wind" [*U* 1.661–62]), Haines's clumsy denial ("Personally I couldn't stomach the idea of a personal God" [*U* 1.623]), and the object of the milk woman's inherited hope, the Spirit is (mayhap) enjoyed by the departed soul of Stephen's dead mother. The central mystical relationship around which this, the opening chapter of *Ulysses,* is fabricated, with its prospects of political, cultural, material, or spiritual renewal (like "the mild morning air"), is that represented by the image from the Irish imaginative tradition of the milk woman, her cow, and "daybreak in the lush field" (*U* 1.401). In these respects, it is an expatiation of the understated climax and the themes latent in "After the Race."

Later in *Ulysses*, Bloom ruefully remarks on Arthur Griffith's disparagement of the careful politics of the same newspaper: "Sunburst on the titlepage . . . a homerule sun rising up in the northwest" (*U* 4.100–102). The subsequent stage direction ("Circe": *"Bloom's weather. A sunburst appears in the northwest"* [*U* 15.1469]) accompanying Bloom's fantasy of himself as King Leopold the First implies the grandiose power not only to liberate Ireland from Britain but even from the oppression of Seasonal Affective Disorder. This motif reaches its transnational expansion in the *ricorso* of *Finnegans Wake* (593–604).

Ricorso

Continuous daylight illuminates but two of the *Dubliners* stories: "An Encounter" and "The Boarding House." Twelve take us through twilight or into darkness. Only one—"After the Race"—takes us all through the night. It pursues Jimmy Doyle's passage through a sleepless and dreamless night in a miasma of manic partying. He undergoes a hazing, an allegorical revisitation of "the nightmare of [Irish] history" in which he witnesses the betrayal of Ireland's national interests in which he is familially and personally implicated. "After the Race" is a story announcing the beginning of a century of major technological change as the gasoline-powered cars fill the daylight hours with noise and fumes. Similarly, the "electric candle-lamps" (*D* 46.8) illuminating the celebratory dinner at the fashionable Shelbourne Hotel forecast the coming electric age that banishes the darkness of the night.[20] "After the Race" is the one story in *Dubliners* in which both the automobile and electricity appear. These complementary images of the triumph of rationalism, science, and technological progress that the race and its revelries celebrate are dramatically upstaged, however, in the story's denouement, as the impassive poet and musician, Villona, the only character in the story with a sense of history, announces the perpetually recurrent daybreak.

This herald of the rising sun enters a caution about the enthusiasm with which we celebrate technological advance by offering a reminder that such apparent progress is enfolded by the immemorial myth of the eternal return. A narrative that begins with four figurative horsemen and ends with the dawn's dispersal of confusion and delirium conveys intimations of apocalypse. A pursuit of these hints leads to some interesting reconsiderations. Just as there are "four young men" in the French car (*D* 42.18–19), there are four teams in the Gordon Bennett Cup Race: signs that we may be entering a Viconian new age. By diverting his account from the newsworthy events of the day to the perennial sunrise, Joyce is symbolically indicating the chimera that Jimmy and his father entertain, that with proper investment, this era can be his. It falls to Villona, however, to announce the true epiphany of the story: that this is but one manifestation of the energy—atomic or divine—that burns in all things, enabling their renewal through all the cycles of the human, cosmological, and spiritual systems.

In his heralding of daybreak we have, therefore, the germ of the *ricorso* of *Finnegans Wake*. Even as the Doyle parents—like the Earwickers, Dublin Danes—approach the end of their night's rest on Rutland Square, the miscommunication between Villona and Jimmy on the other side of the sleeping city adumbrates the eternal rivalry between Shem and Shaun. Approaching the conclusion of what was to be his last work, Joyce returned to this slight beginning and to an archetypal moment he developed to its full efflorescence in *Finnegans Wake* (593–604).

Daybreak opens chapter IV, the final chapter. A pivotal moment in the text, on the literal level it looks both backward at the night that has just ended, and forward to the new day. It simultaneously marks the emergence of the Irish Free State from the thrall of its most recent invaders. On the larger millennial scale, as it invokes shades from the primeval penumbra, it announces the advent of the Viconian divine age. In celebrating the turning of each of these temporal circles, the language of the text invokes images from the holy books of the Buddhists, Hindus, and Egyptians, the Hebrew and Christian scriptures, and Celtic archeology, grounded in multifarious vocabularies of heavily marked Sanskrit etymology.

Its most proximate plane of interpretation is based on the biorhythmic premise that all solar and resurrection myths are unconscious inferences from the experience of the diurnal alternations of sleeping and waking to which the human species has adapted by virtue of the revolving earth's solar dependence. The energy—physical and psychological—required for the activities of the daylight hours derives from the apparent passivity of nightly repose. Adequate daily functioning requires our descent into a "cycological" underworld (Bishop, 76–77). Not the least of Jimmy Doyle's youthful complacencies is his attempt to deny the claims of his unconscious (and conscience): to manage without sleep. Villona's announcement comes as a reprieve from the resultant waking nightmare, and not as a summons to renewal.

At the same time, it invokes the major turning points in Irish history, from Saint Patrick's vanquishing the druid in a test of powers to the recent triumph of Sinn Féin in finally establishing the Irish Free State. This revolution on the national scene replicates locally the prospect that Giambattista Vico predicted on the grand, or millennial, stage, the "new orther" (*FW* 593.11) of the divine age. The axial historical enactment of this new creation is Christ's Easter resurrection announced with references to earlier self-manifestations of the transcendent First Cause "Oyes! Oyeses! Oyesesyeses! . . . I yam as I yam" (*FW* 604.22–23).

Whirling within this maelstrom of references to the apocalyptic summation of all history, language, and culture are numerous reverberations of the themes of "After the Race." The dramatic realism of Villona'a announcement of dawn in Kingstown to Jimmy, Routh, and their fairweather friends is transformed, in the allegorical phantasmagoria of *Finnegans Wake,* into the "matin a fact" intoned in "leery subs of dub" to "the sousenugh" [and] "one of the two or three forefivest fellows a bloke could in holiday crowd encounter" (*FW* 596.05–17). On the literal level, the daybreak that Villona announces becomes the universal "six o'clock shark" (*FW* 558.18) (as well as the hour of the author's birth [*JJII* 642; Hart, 73]). What was a prophecy, moreover, in Villona's voice, had become, by the time of *Finnegans Wake*'s appearance, an accomplished fact. "Daybreak" became "Calling all downs. Calling all downs to dayne" (*FW* 593.2), and "Calling all daynes. Calling all daynes to dawn" (*FW* 593.11). Joyce ingeniously marks the links in this "newera's day" (*FW* 623.7) between the millennium of the vanquishing of the Danes and the contemporary vanquishing of the British by the native Celts.

The family name of Doyle, which originated from the descriptor *dubhghall,* "dark foreigner," is not among Gaelic genealogies, and appears most frequently in areas adjacent to the eastern seaboard where the Norse settled (MacLysaght, 128–29). The Doyles, like the Earwickers, are Norsemen or Scandinavians: all endowed with a zeal that is appropriately "ancient."[21] "Calling all daynes to dawn," therefore, as it addresses HCE and his sons, Shem and Shaun, echoes Villona's rousing of Jimmy, scion of the Doyles. As Shem and Shaun step into the inheritance of the sleeping HCE, Villona

Figure 5.5. Sunburst device adopted by the Fenians (Hayes-McCoy, 155).

and Jimmy take joint, if unsteady, charge of the Doyle estate. The variant "Calling all downs," as several commentators have indicated, also picks up the phrase "calling all cars" from the argot of modern police work. Since the word "car" appears elsewhere in *Finnegans Wake* (308.08) as a kabbalistic code word for "four" [Ir. *Ceathar*], it links the car with the announcement of the Viconian fourth age.

From this mystical perspective, then, Villona's exclamation is the Word of the new aeon: the automobile age is but a material shadow of the fourth Viconian age.[22] Again, on the political level, *Finnegans Wake* emulates "After the Race" in linking Ireland's dawn with Sinn Féin ("Sonne feine, somme feehn avaunt! Guld modning" [*FW* 593.8–9]) and King Arthur with Arthur Griffith, the first President of the Irish Free State ("Arcthuris comeing.... We elect for thee, Tirtangel" [*FW* 594.2–4]). The self-government, absent though desired in "After the Race," achieved and celebrated in *Finnegans Wake*, implies the revivification of the spirit of the medieval Fenians among the nations of the modern world: "The old breeding bradsted culminwillth of natures to Foyne MacHooligan" (*FW* 593.12–13). The contextual citation of the crest of the family Finnegan—"A hand from the cloud ... holding a chart expanded" (*FW* 593.19; see Rose and O'Hanlon, 290)—is a double emblem of the unwritten text of the future and of the sunburst flag of the latter-day Fenians (figure 5.5).

This millennial renewal, this "newera's day" (*FW* 623.7), this reversal of the historical darkness making men new and one, is blessed by a mystical light: Newman's "light kindling light" dispels the "dimdom done" uniting "kithagain with kinagain" (*FW* 594.3–6). Thus these pages of *Finnegans Wake* reprocess the images that received their first airing in "After the Race" and reappeared in the envoi of Joyce's lecture, "Ireland, Island of Saints and Sages": "One thing alone seems clear to me. It is well past time for Ireland to have done once and for all with failure. If she is truly capable of reviving, let her awake" (*CW* 174).

The "shaft of grey light" entering the cabin door of Farley's yacht, by the time it reaches *Finnegans Wake,* illuminates the "langscape" of Dublin—from Lambay Island to Chapelizod—and floods across the counties of Ireland: from "limericks [to] kilalooly" (*FW* 595.12–17) (Farley's vessel reconfigured as the boat of Amen-Ra). The liturgical invocation that announces the entire passage—"Sandhyas! Sandhyas! Sandhyas!" (*FW* 593.1), in its simultaneous embrace of *Sanctus* (L. "holy"), *samdhi* (Skt. "twilight of dawn" and "peace")—brings to mind that Joycean *omphalos* within Villona's line of sight toward the rising sun: Sandycove.

Villona is the original "Eireweeker" (*FW* 593.03). He comprises, *in potentia,* the figures who announce the new age: the Celtic sun-god Lúgh Lámhfhada ("Lamfadar's arm" [*FW* 597.1]) who presides over midsummer fires, lights the Wicklow mountains and the Hill of Allen, and inspires the wonder of Stonehenge (Joyce did not know of Newgrange), Saint Patrick ("firethere the sun in his halo cast" [*FW* 612.30]), and Ireland's sun-king ("Solsking the Frist" [*FW* 607.28]). The narrative dissonance between Villona and Jimmy Doyle prefigures the duos of Little Chandler and Ignatius Gallaher ("A Little Cloud"), Lenehan and Corley ("Two Gallants"), and, metamorphosing into the rivalries between Stephen and Mulligan in the opening scene of *Ulysses,* between Ireland's brooding but rightful poet and her unworthy son and gay betrayer. The brilliant and bitter satire of this scene makes explicit the understated ironies of "After the Race." The temporary exuberance of the *Ricorso* passage reprocessing the same imaginative stock soon settles into a resigned, even Buddhist, murmur. As Joseph Campbell and Henry Morton Robinson write, "The mood of the last pages of *Finnegans Wake* is very nearly that of the vastly disillusioned yet profoundly acquiescent, and even subtly joyful East" (340n1).

In these ways, the rearview mirror of the *Ricorso* in *Finnegans Wake* catches fleeting glimpses of Villona's annunciation of Jimmy Doyle's tomorrow. The *Wake*'s *ricorso* is a protracted meditation on the roots of civilization, as the human family rises from the chaos of primeval darkness, responds to an immanent divinity, and confronts in hope the indeterminate future.²³ They also provide an autobiographical note of pride and promise, that despite his reservations about its quality, Joyce recognized in "After the Race" his last work written before his departure from Irish soil, the promise represented by this "Tobecontinued's tale" (*FW* 626.18). In the figure of Villona, indifferent to the engines that were firing the mechanical age, Joyce was, to coin a phrase, projecting an image of himself sailing off into the sunrise.

6

Rhetoric—Modern and Classical

"After the Race" is a broad satire on the subject and a parody of the style of the stories read by British gentlemen during the reign of the King Edward VII. As ironically implied by Villona's term of address on which it ends, it satirizes the expectations aroused by an account of the Gordon Bennett Cup Race among the presumed readers of a glossy monthly such as the *Blackwood's Magazine,* the *Strand,* or the *Gentleman's Magazine. Blackwood's* (1820–1980), known as "The Maga," was the standard-bearer of British Victorian values. The stereotypical pabulum of British colonial life, it claimed to offer its readers at home and abroad sound criticism and Tory political commentary. Each issue carried articles on the management of the empire ("British Interests in Siam," "Russia and Japan: Navies," "Army Shooting and Its Improvement," "Foreign Undesirables"); sports ("Cricket Reform," "Sport and Politics"); and adventures in exotic climes. And (for the ladies): "My House in the West Indies," "Bridge," and "Dogs I Have Known and Loved."

A score of magazines competed for the middle to lowbrow readership. They took sports and big-game hunting more seriously than they deserve; but operating on the assumption that the world was the young Briton's playground, they recounted humorous and romantic tales of speed, risk, wonder, and adventure. Told in breathless style, such tales were lubricated with exclamatory phrases like "intoxicating, exhilarating, and perfectly charming!" As described in chapter 2, motoring stories appeared frequently, either celebrating the new satisfactions of high-speed motion or expatiating on "the infirmities of motor-cars and the foibles of those who drive them" (James Walter Smith, "Automobilism," *Strand,* September 1901: 318). As the joke had it, "*l'automoblesse n'oblige pas*" (324).

The narrator of "After the Race" enters these lists by invoking some of the clichés from stories of such derring-do in the popular press; thus the somewhat reserved and skeptical emphasis, in his opening paragraphs, on the high or excellent spirits, hilarity, good humor, high stakes, and "careering" automobilists and the awe in which he represents their regard by the anonymous bystanders. Also, in his characterization of the motion of the automobiles as "scudding" (*D* 42.2) and "bounding" (*D* 45.12), the narrator is rendering a graphically accurate image of the dangers and discomforts endured by motorists bouncing over roads designed for horse-drawn carriages that did not exceed 10 mph. And again, when he makes the sententious pronouncement, "Rapid motion through space elates one," and follows it immediately with the deflationary qualifiers "so does notoriety; so does the possession of money" (*D* 44.14–15), he is inditing a trope long honored in the Irish literary tradition, the undercutting triad.[1] The narrative exhibits many examples of clumsy or imprecise writing, such as "well above the level of successful Gallicism" (*D* 42.17–18), the pleonasm "an optimist by nature" (*D* 43.11), lazy euphemisms like "did not study very earnestly" (*D* 43.24), unintentional puns such as "fortunate enough" (*D* 43.19),[2] thoughtless metaphors like the mercantile "cargo" (*D* 44.3), the idolatrous "pay homage to the snorting motor" (*D* 45.17), and the irony in Jimmy's trite phrases, "to see a little life" (*D* 43.27) and "seen so much of the world" (*D* 43.32). These are the more explicit signs of a parodist at work on the approximate rhetoric of the recreational journalism of the time designed for the gentleman consumer.

It is not hard to imagine Joyce endowing his narrator with a sense of superiority over sentimental vulgarians earned in a school that—like Clongowes and Belvedere—trained its students in classical rhetoric. The elementary classical studies to which the young Joyce was exposed required a lot of memorization—first of vocabulary and grammar, and then of long passages from Virgil, Ovid, and Horace. Beginning students in Jesuit schools used an edition of Emmanuel Alvares's *Prosodia* and as they advanced (*P* 179.21–24), they were required to produce exact translations of assigned passages in each class, and then, occasionally to render that literal translation into elegant English. They were required to master Latin prosody, grammar, and rhetoric; and were therefore examined on their ability to scan poetic texts, "parse" individual elements in the language (write precise syntactic notes), and to tag figures of speech with their classical names.[3] To develop proficiency in these skills, students were given nightly assignment accompanied by "prelection," in which the teacher previewed the passage by highlighting significant or tricky items. This included assigning the use of figures of speech, idiomatic usages, and unusual grammatical constructions.

The text of "After the Race" is rich with subtleties deriving from this training that distance the narrator both from popular journalism and from the vulgarians who are his subject. Take, for instance, his treatment of *The Belle of Newport*. Large enough to make the three-thousand-mile voyage from Rhode Island to Kingstown for this occasion, it must have been an impressive sight. For all he tells us of the prospect, nevertheless, the narrator is apparently underwhelmed. He admits that it is furnished with a kitchen, a wine supply, a yacht piano, and a crew, and is normally berthed in the most exclusive port in the United States. Much as he passed over in near silence the momentary appearance of Farley's "handsome ladies," he grants but fleeting notice to his *Belle of Newport*. He seems more pleased with the gendered jingle between "a music of merry bells" (*D* 47.10), this nautical *belle*, and those naughty *belles*. He does not seem any more impressed by this trophy from the New World than he is by the Continental cars. The narrator responds to these wonders of engineering not as one of the wayside gazers, but as a poet, intent upon the apposite tones of his own account. In this way, by opening his story under a slim pennant of nautical images—"scudding," "crest," "channel" (*D* 42.2-5)—he has prepared us for the sight of distant Newport.

By such means—the contrasts of apparent incompetence with keen technical control—the implied narrator parodies writing that accommodates itself to readers in search of a little diversion. This aspect of "After the Race" anticipates the more pungent satire of Leopold Bloom's entertaining the notion that he might contribute something to *Titbits* following the example of Philip Beaufoy's "*Matcham's Masterstroke*" (*U* 4.502-36). The concealed narrator of "Calypso" is more direct than the narrator of "After the Race": suggesting that even moved by the promise of one guinea per column, Bloom was not likely to produce even bathroom reading. In a deftly understated passage rich with verbal humor, he depicts Bloom "seated calm above his own rising smell," assessing his ability to produce columns composed of necrotic prose like "*Matcham often thinks of the masterstroke by which he won the laughing witch*" (*U* 4.513-14).

Therefore, Warren Beck—an astute reader of the literary style of "After the Race"—may be correct in identifying its weaknesses in the superficial characterization of Jimmy and the sketchiness of the scenes (123). But he censures the clumsiness of the clause, "whose spirits seemed to be at present well above the level of successful Gallicism" (126; *D* 42.17–18), not recognizing it as a Joycean parody of equivalent pretentiousness found in the pages of "the Maga." He underestimates Joyce's rhetorical resource, and misjudges his devious methods.

Classic Structure

Of the *Dubliners* stories, only "Eveline" is shorter than "After the Race." "After the Race" extends through but 6 ½ pages of the text, its 134 sentences and seventeen paragraphs totaling 2,243 words. Beginning his story in medias res, the concealed narrator pursues a direct time sequence interrupted by one long expositional pause. The story has a classic tripartite structure: its seven scenes arranged in a sequence of three clusters separated by two interludes.[4] The story observes the unities of time, space, and action: it occurs within a twenty-four-hour period, between the western and eastern borders of the City of Dublin, and it accounts for Jimmy's pathetic fall as an immediate consequence of his engagement in a pressure game beyond his soft priming.

This sequence of scenes pursues the drive from Inchicore to College Green, the dinner at the Stephen's Green hotel, and the all-night party in Kingstown Harbour. The narrative conveying the action of these major episodes is punctuated by two transitions: at the Doyle family home, and the travel sequence from the hotel to *The Belle of Newport*. As several readers have noted (for example, Bowen, "'After the Race,'" 54–55; Rafroidi, 30), the major device governing this structural arrangement is the ascent to an apparent climax, followed by a prompt drop into bathos. A closer inspection of the narrative structure discovers some finely purposeful variations—foreshadowings, flashbacks, disjunctions, misdirections, and apparent faux pas—belied by the deceptive simplicity of the narrative organization.

> Scene 1: paragraphs 1–6 (*D* 42.2–45.12)
> Interlude 1: paragraphs 7, 8 (*D* 45.13–46.3)
> Scene 2: paragraph 9 (*D* 46.4–28)
> Interlude 2: paragraphs 10, 11–13 (*D* 46.29–47.23)[5]
> Scene 3: paragraphs 14–17 (*D* 47.24–48.33)

Scene 1 revolves around the thesis sentence, "Rapid motion through space elates one; so does notoriety; so does the possession of money" (*D*

44.14–15). It is appreciably a parody of the thrills-and-spills stories from popular journalism. But it is more than that. If, on completing the story, its readers reflect that its three stages make the case for the new sensation of automobile travel (scene 1), for the satisfactions of conspicuous consumption (scene 2, interlude 2), and for the pleasures of gambling (scene 3), they will recognize that the narrator has cunningly summed up this thematic progression in a sentence that is notable for its tongue-in-cheek portentousness and abrupt bathos. In its content, structure, tone, and technique, it is a brilliant paradigm of the entire story.

Scene 1 is composed of the first seven paragraphs (1–7). Its primary purpose is expositional: the depiction of Jimmy Doyle within his circle of motoring friends. It does this by funneling the setting of the race through the company of Frenchmen to their Irish host (paragraphs 1–2). Paragraph 3 gives us the narrator's exposition on Jimmy's credentials, moving from a detached and objective rendering to a closer and more personal account of Jimmy's perspective. Paragraph 4 returns briefly to the public action—the passage of the vehicle through the (unnamed) streets—before returning to the privacy of Jimmy's thoughts. These are the exclusive subject of paragraphs 5 and 6, until the end of 6. Here we are returned to Jimmy's physical consciousness of his immediate surroundings as the car arrives at College Green. Paragraph 7 concerns itself with the division of the party into the two pairs of riders and walkers.

The only notice that this paragraph takes of emotion or value is the "curious feeling of disappointment" that attends Villona's and Jimmy's walk home. Thus, the line of development in this first scene of the story can be traced through its epigrammatic theme sentence, "Rapid motion through space elates one; so does notoriety; so does the possession of money" (*D* 44.14–15), to its hyperbolic apex, "The journey laid a magical finger on the genuine pulse of life and gallantly the machinery of human nerves strove to answer the bounding courses of the swift blue animal" (*D* 45.10–12),[6] to its anticlimactic conclusion on a note of disappointment. This structural pattern—the raising and lowering of expectations, the misdirection of the reader's attention, the plummet into anticlimax—all of which its title implies—is the narratological paradigm for the structure and rhetoric of "After the Race."

We encounter this trope in several ways in the first few sentences of the story. It appears right off in the paradoxes describing the Irish as "the gratefully oppressed" (*D* 42.8) and the French as "virtual victors" (*D*

42.10). These curious phrases are immediately followed by the anomaly of a "welcome" (*D* 42.15) accorded the cars "careering homeward" (*D* 42.5). These curiosities—or solecisms to which newspaper readers are accustomed—are immediately followed by a misdirection that subsequently proves instructive. In introducing these cars—identified by their blue paint—the narrator elides the distinction between the competing vehicles and those of their supporters, so that unless readers already know that the former were two-seaters, we will have accepted the description of Charles Ségouin and his three companions without realizing that these four young men are not competitors in the race, but investors in what it advertises.

In paragraphs 1 and 2, then, the narrator directs our attention to the admiration of the Irish public for the achievements of the French competitiveness and enterprise. But again, this is a misdirection, because as his story unfolds, we realize that he is impervious to the press clamor surrounding the race. He pretends to share in the public excitement by characterizing Jimmy Doyle and his Hungarian guest, Villona, in dismissive ways: Jimmy by a negative, that he was not "genuinely happy" (*D* 43.12), and Villona by reference to his appetite. Yet this is the pair in which he is seriously invested.

The narrator adopts the rhetorical strategy of deliberately blunting or beveling an apparently predictable pointed effect: an understated bathos. Thus, at the end of paragraph 3, Villona appears merely as an afterthought to Jimmy's résumé, as "unfortunately, very poor" (*D* 44.2). Again, when in the midst of the attention devoted to the serious business entertained by the Doyles, he interpolates the note that Villona feels "a sharp desire for his dinner" (*D* 46.3), he is giving paragraph 8 a rhetorical anticlimax while insinuating yet another misdirection about Villona's true value in the unfolding story.

The subject of the first scene is the establishment of Jimmy's character and circumstances. This it accomplishes by moving the focus of attention from the external (and present) circumstances to Jimmy's reflections (expressed in a series of verbs in the pluperfect tense). It does this in two interesting ways: by gradually raising the proportion of words and phrases from Jimmy's vocabulary in the narrator's account, and by the deft handling of narrative transitions. Therefore, we are only seven lines into the narrator's description of Jimmy when we get the first of the sentences that we subsequently recognize as his: "He [Jimmy's father] had also been fortunate enough to secure some of the police contracts" (*D* 43.18–19).

The confluence of the euphemism "fortunate enough" and the legalism, "secure . . . police contracts" betrays two items in Jimmy's constitution and background: his guilty evasion of an embarrassment over the source of his father's wealth, and his temporary status as a student of law. These and many other imputations enter the narrator's language as the scene develops a portrait of the spoiled son of a socially ascendant butcher.

Another interesting rhetorical strategy in this scene is the manner in which the narrator appears to allow the attention that he should be paying to his story to become waylaid into pursuing the shifts and drifts of Jimmy's feelings. The first two paragraphs conclude on sentences that set up the transition to the next (between the first and second, the French; between the second and third, Jimmy). From then to the end of paragraph 6, we are privy to Jimmy's thoughts; and the paragraph transitions denote that continuity. This sequence has a brief interruption: as Jimmy is considering Villona's poverty, his reflection is put in upon by the roar of the engine, the laughter and banter of the men, and Villona's humming (paragraph 4). From these irritations Jimmy's attention quickly submerges, only to resurface when the tourists reach Dame Street. In other words, when indicating the continuity of the action or of Jimmy's thoughts, the narrator inserts smoothing transitions, and omits them when Jimmy suffers interruption. This formal tactic draws us into an unconscious sympathy with Jimmy.

Stated simply, paragraphs 1–6 of scene 1 inset both essential historical background on the Doyle family and Jimmy's present thoughts within the depiction of Ségouin's driving the car east from Inchicore to Dame Street. These passages are, however, technically and psychologically more subtle than that. When he is in apparent control of the sequence, the narrator lays down clear markers, in the transitions between the first three paragraphs: "the French" (*D* 42.9–10) and "the fourth member. . . . He" (*D* 43.11–13), respectively. Similarly, when pursuing the mélange of Jimmy's reveries and schemes, he inserts a cue sufficient to signal the transition between paragraphs 5 and 6 ("substance . . . investment" [*D* 44.32–34]). He moves our attention from the geography of Dublin's western suburbs to Jimmy's mental landscape by pursuing patterns of association in paragraphs 3–6.[7]

Nonetheless, as if reminding himself to get back to the main task, the narrator twice interrupts Jimmy's reflections in pursuit of the external action. Neither of these resumptions—between paragraphs 3 and 4 (*D*

44.2–3) and between paragraphs 6 and 7 (*D* 45.12–13)—carries a transitional marker, although each sequence of reveries seems to attain an appropriate closure. The first of these redirects our attention from Jimmy's assessment of Villona's pianism and poverty to the narrator's detached description of the car hurtling along "for miles of the road" (*D* 44.6–7). Similarly, the second interjects the narrator's objective account of the car driving down Dame Street into Jimmy's exhilaration at "the bounding courses of the swift blue animal" (*D* 45.12). Rereading the management of these junctures, we see that each conceals an apparent anomaly. In the first, the phrase "for miles of the road" implies that paragraph 4 cannot be a description of Jimmy's view of the car moving between Inchicore and College Green, but of his recollection of how he felt during their journey between Naas and Inchicore some hours previously. And in the second, the narrator's announcement of the car's arrival in Dame Street interrupts, again, Jimmy's mental return to the smooth running of the car's former career "along the country roads" (*D* 45.9–10). In other words, Jimmy's reflections on the satisfactions of automobile travel are not to his current travel through the Dublin City streets between Inchicore and College Green, but are pleasing memories recalled from a previous journey through the roads of counties Kildare and Dublin.

Joyce's careful management of the transitions in these passages, therefore, conceals shifts in chronology and geography beneath the apparently straightforward arrangement of the narrative. This coincidence of the narrator's misdirection of the reader and Jimmy's abstraction are the "objective correlatives" of the thematic silence the narrator accords the memory of Robert Emmet elucidated in chapter 5. Thus, even though it lacks the psychological penetration that we see in the early chapters of *Ulysses*, it argues that from the beginning of his career as a writer of fiction, Joyce was interested in the uses of parallax in the representation of the relationships between different spheres of experience, vividly recalled and attentively assayed.

The central paragraph is the seventh of the story's seventeen (*D* 45.13–25). Its 114 words comprise 5 percent of the whole, falling precisely half way through its 2,272 words. It is the formal centerpiece of the entire work in several coinciding and significant ways: in the location, time of day, and dramatic action that are its subject, and in its rhetorical and thematic design. The chiasmic structure of the story radiates from the images, rhetoric, and tone of this paragraph; and it contains, in microcosm, a compressed version of the action and theme of the entire story. The compact richness of this paragraph constitutes the poetic heart of "After the Race."

In recounting Jimmy and Villona's departure from Ségouin's conveyance, it marks the transition from the motorcar and the elation it confers to the other ("usual") modes of transportation: hereafter, the action occurs on foot, by train, by carriage, and by boat. From this point on, the sensation registered by the motorcar race is fading fast and receives no further mention. The necessary exposition respecting the public sensation of the day over, the real story, Joyce's "epiphany" occasioned by this nonevent, commences. This paragraph describes an axial pause in the dramatic and symbolic movement of the characters as they cross from Dublin's most western point, Inchicore, to Kingstown, its most easterly. A significant aspect of this pause in the pursuit of investment in the guise of international amity and sport, is that it occurs outside the Bank of Ireland, right in the heart of the Hibernian metropolis. The action takes place, moreover, shortly after sundown, as the gas lamps are lit—around "lighting up time"—midway between the dawn at which the race began and the daybreak that brought its "tailgate party" to an end. In its movement from the noise and impatience reported in the first sentence to the "pale . . . haze" of the last, it registers a reduction of pace and reversal of tone from action to reflection, from engagement to detachment, from effects kinetic to aesthetic. Regarding the ostensible subjects of the narrative, the "highs" of commerce and sports competition, it marks a descent into apparent bathos.

It accomplishes these effects by a subtle aggregation of rhetorical and poetic energies. Beginning with a five-word grammatically simple, alliterative, declarative sentence, "They drove down Dame Street," it moves through a sequence of progressively more complex statements about parallel actions and parallax perspectives. This sequence of seven sentences expresses the narrator's increasing range and competence as an observer, first of a discrete and then to an increasing complexity of simultaneous events. Its point of view simultaneously "thickens" from that of a relatively uninformed outsider to a decoder of the body language of the bystanders and on to a more penetrating reading of the privately held attitude (of the joint but unshared "disappointment") of Jimmy and Villona, and finally—in the seventh sentence—to the position of a universal poetic interpreter.

Through this succession of sentences, the tones of the narrative progress from the sardonic to the lyrical and sympathetic.

The most striking narrative aspect of the paragraph is the increasingly complex temporal reportage, from the single simple physical action of the first sentence to the surround-sound ("the horns of motorists and the gongs of impatient tram-drivers") of the second. The fourth and fifth sentences describe two simultaneous actions: the gazers' rendering of homage and the discussion among the young men of their logistical arrangements. The sentence efficiently describing these arrangements is the most temporally complex in the paragraph, indicating four time frames: Villona's continuing visit at Jimmy's home, and the three anticipated actions (walking/driving, dressing, and dining) of the temporarily divided, but parallel pairs of young men. In these ways the sentence situates the action of the paragraph between perspectives fore and aft.

The narrator then follows both pairs of young men, even after they disperse in opposite directions from the front gates of Trinity College. By reinvoking the envy of the gazers at the stylish riders at this point in the narration, the narrator prepares us for the sharp irony of the private disappointment registered by the pair of "alighted" walkers. That not all Dubliners share this envy has already been established by the report of the competition between the motor horns of the visitors and the gongs of the proprietary tram-drivers. In registering the irony of this disappointment, however, the narrator moderates the sardonic humor with which he reported the attitudes of irritation and awe of resident Dubliners, by resorting to the romantic image of the "pale globes of light . . . in a haze of summer evening."

This reversal of attitude, this expansion of sympathy, this enlargement from simple to complex objective to the emotional and universal injects a fresh note of feeling into the narrative. By registering their simultaneous momentary feeling of disappointment, the narrator implies a potential communion between Jimmy and his guest. The narrator's redirection of our attention to the street lamps has the effect of replacing the feelings of envy, hostility, irritation, and disappointment with the particular disruptions of normality, with a powerful emotional invocation of Dublin's tranquil hospitality. More generally, it anticipates the anticlimax in the card games to come, but in addition (and more significantly) injects a note of deliverance by the linkage between the gently phrased image of the gas lamps lighting the city streets at nightfall (ca. 9 p.m.) and the more dramatically developed announcement of the sun lighting the universe at dawn (3–4 a.m.).[8]

The image structure of the paragraph—a complex blend of contraries—is finely designed to support the effect of subtly changing the direction and tone of the story. Just as its last sentence announces the link between the gas lamps and the rising sun, the first sentence, "They drove down Dame Street" recalls the statement with which the story began, "The cars came scudding in towards Dublin, running evenly like pellets in the groove of the Naas Road." Similarly, the repeated references to the "knots of people [and] . . . gazers" recall the repeated images of the "clumps" of sightseers of the first paragraph (*D* 42.4–8). And again, the report that Jimmy and Villona "pushed their way" (*D* 45.21–22) through the crowds on Dame Street foreshadows the image of "[t]he people [making] way for them" later in the evening on Stephen's Green (*D* 46.32). And yet again, the image of the "impatient tram-drivers" in this paragraph revisits and reveals what lies behind "the cheer of the gratefully oppressed" (*D* 42.7–8) at Inchicore: an unsuppressed political anger.

The rhetorical structure of the paragraph reflects other aspects of the opening: the anadiplosis that links the first two sentences, for example ("Dame Street. The street" [*D* 45.13]), recalls the similar trope that bonds the first two paragraphs of the story ("the French. The French" [*D* 42.9–10]). The paragraph re-enacts, in a more intense manner, the flair for poetic effect to which the narrator is intermittently partial. For example, the sentences "A little *knot* of people collected on the *foot*path to pay homage to the *snort*ing *motor*. The party was to *dine* together that *evening in* Ségou*in*'s hotel" are internally bonded by assonance and dissonance. And again, in the full paragraph, the pairs of images reflecting conflicts of movement and direction ("drove down," "drew up") in the first half of the paragraph recur in the "push[ing]" and "walk[ing]" of the pair of friends and the contrasts of hanging and "above" in the final sentence. The integrity of the paragraph is assured by various visual and acoustic motifs: the echo of "gong" in "hung," "gaze" in "haze," "snort" in "knot," "homage" in "home," and "alight" in "light." And further, the metonymies, "The street was busy," "The car steered out," and "the city hung its pale globes," reflect the narrator's more general facility with such devices, as we see in other passages of the story, such as his extension of this last in the subsequent sentence, "That night the city wore the mask of a capital" (*D* 46.29).

In sum, Joyce's placement of this densely imagined paragraph at the coign of his apparently nondescript narrative testifies to his early mastery of classical order and restraint.

Scene 2 (paragraph 9) exhibits a pattern of anticlimax similar to that pursued in scene 1. Beginning with the assertive climax, "[t]he dinner was excellent, exquisite" (*D* 46.4), it makes a gradual descent through a series of mild dissonances to the sharp spat between Routh and Jimmy. Ségouin's gesture of throwing the window open effects a dramatic release, but allows, too, a transition to the night-walk to follow as well as a foreshadowing of Villona's ultimate greeting of the dawn.

Paragraphs 10–13 form a long transition to scene 3. The first of these describes the young men "stroll[ing] along Stephen's Green in a faint cloud of aromatic smoke. They talked loudly and gaily and their cloaks dangled from their shoulders. The people made way for them. At the corner of Grafton Street a short fat man was putting two handsome ladies on a car in charge of another fat man. The car drove off and the short fat man caught sight of the party" (*D* 46.30–47.2). In this passage we read the narrator at his most detached and omniscient, making two observations beyond the attention of our five young men: the ordinary citizens making way for them as they stroll the sidewalk between the hotel and Grafton Street, and the two fat men setting their handsome lady friends upon a (horse-drawn) car and its departure, leaving the shorter by himself at the curb. Whereas the narrator has prepared his readers for Farley by virtue of these unflattering images, his actual presence, so far as our company is aware, is the sound of his voice calling out to Rivière.

As some readers have sensed from the images of indulgence in this transitional scene (the mask, the aromatic smoke, the loud talk, dangling cloaks, and fat men), the handsome ladies are very likely prostitutes taking leave of their customers. (If so, Farley combines support of the American team with ethnic and sex tourism.) This inference is supported by the intelligence that some of these same images appear in one of Joyce's epiphanies from his Parisian sojourn (1902–3), the subject of which is the display and trading of female flesh and affection:

> They pass in twos and threes amid the life of the boulevard, walking like people who have leisure in a place lit up for them. They are in the pastry cook's, chattering, crushing little fabrics of pastry, or seated silently at tables by the café door, or descending from

carriages with a busy stir of garments soft as the voice of the adulterer. They pass in an air of perfumes: under the perfumes their bodies have a warm humid smell.... No man has loved them and they have not loved themselves: they have given nothing for all that has been given them. (Epiphany 33, Scholes and Kain, 43)

To fit the narrative of "After the Race," Joyce has recast this epiphany. He has transferred the images attendant upon the women—their self-advertisement, their false camaraderie, their narcissism—to the five young men; the perfumes become "aromatic smoke," and the "twos and threes" add up to the literal five (a very Joycean touch, that). The last two sentences of the paragraph expand the images of the women's "descending from carriages" and the "voice of the adulterer" into the "handsome ladies" mounting a car with the aid of two fat men. The voice of the shorter of these calling out "André!" completes the harnessing of this epiphany to his narrative requirements.[9]

As Robert Scholes and Richard Kain point out (43), Joyce used parts of this same epiphany in the "Proteus" episode of *Ulysses* (*U* 3.209-15). The only sentence in this elaborate revision that makes its way into "After the Race" is "Faces of Paris men go by, their wellpleased pleasers, curled *conquistadores*" (*U* 3.215), which surfaces as, "The five young men strolled along.... They talked loudly and gaily and their cloaks dangled from their shoulders" (*D* 46.29-32). These comparisons demonstrate that Joyce valued this epiphany sufficiently to press it into separate services. It admits Joyce's ambivalence toward prostitution by contrast with the main theme of "After the Race," economic exploitation and political betrayal.

Scene 3 is composed of paragraphs 14-17. Like scene 2, it begins on a high note: Villona's exclamation "It is beautiful!" (*D* 47.23) and Jimmy's implied exclamation "What merriment!" (*D* 47.27). From there it follows a spiraling descent through a staccato vertigo of punctuated bursts of energy: the dancing (and Farley's "*Stop!*"), Jimmy's long speech (followed by the judgment that "[i]t must have been a good speech" [*D* 48.1]), the series of card games (that Jimmy "wished they would stop" [*D* 48.14]), and the final "great game" (in which "Farley and Jimmy were the heaviest losers" [*D* 48.26]). The coda (last paragraph) emphasizes the finality of this descending spirit, so that Villona's announcement of daybreak "in a shaft of grey light" is the appropriate paradox that sums up the anticlimactic design of the entire work.

Viewed structurally within the last scene, Villona's announcement of the terminating dawn is the final item in a series of anticlimaxes, each of which is dramatically or rhetorically paradoxical. Within the larger design of the story it serves structural and summary purposes. This announcement of the sun's rise over the eastern horizon complements the image of the cars topping the hill at Inchicore with which the story began (*D* 42.3–4, 13–14), even as it rebuts the separate "cheers" of the first and penultimate paragraphs. Villona's announcement, accompanied by the gesture of opening the cabin door and admitting a shaft of sunlight to the small interior, complements Ségouin's previous toast to Humanity and his throwing open the window of the "snug room" in the hotel (thereby mixing the gaslight from the street to the electric illumination from "the electric candle lamps").

The first of this series of anticlimaxes, as we have seen, is Jimmy and Villona's disembarking from the automobile and experiencing the disappointment of their demotion to the anonymity of pedestrians. That this "feeling of disappointment" comes on them just after sunset is implied by the information that their passage through Inchicore took place in sunlight and by the time they disembark at College Green—no more than an hour later—it is lighting-up time, since they walk along Sackville Street beneath the "pale globes" of the gas lights.[10] That these three anticlimaxes form an ordered sequence out of the universal and natural light of the sun is supported by the fact that in his revision of the passages relevant to this design, Joyce changed "descended" to "alighted" (*D* 45.16) and "candle light" to "electric candle-lamps" (*D* 46.8). Ségouin's toast to Humanity accompanied by the gesture that mixes two artificial lights—the gas from the street and the electric from the candle-lamps—contrasts, then, with the light of the evening sun that illuminated the first scene and that of a "shaft of grey light" (*D* 48.32) illuminating its denouement.

Similarly, the three major scenes of the story occur in narrow enclosures—the automobile, the dining room, and the yacht cabin—and the exit from each is marked by a dramatically ironic light. These features of the design serve to contrast night and day, artificial and natural light, human and celestial spaces. They are at the same time aspects in a thematic design that, supporting the ironically stated thesis, "Rapid motion through space elates one; so does notoriety; so does the possession of money" (*D* 44.14–15), demythologizes, respectively, the gods of speed, prestige, and Mammon.

The story begins with an image of the cars rising over "the crest of the hill at Inchicore" (*D* 42.3–4). This symbolic annunciation requires an on-site pause. A visit to Inchicore—in Joyce's time 1 kilometer beyond the city limits—establishes the implied vantage point as looking southwest toward the Naas Road from the canal bridge at the top of Tyrconnell Road and along the upward slope toward the bridge over the Grand Canal. The gentle ascent of this road through the village and on past Bluebell does not reveal any "crest" in Inchicore itself. However, because the road bevels as it traverses the Grand Canal at the village limit, it presents the impression of a crest. Pedestrians clumped at the bridge can therefore see the cars descend past Bluebell and into the village, as can further pedestrians in Inchicore itself see the cars come over the bridge and continue their descent past the Church of Mary Immaculate and downhill to Emmet Road.[11]

Between this terminus and the announcement of the rising of the morrow's sun, paragraph 7 (*D* 45.13–25) is the formal center of the story. This paragraph begins with "They drove down Dame Street" (*D* 45.13), and ends with the image of the "pale globes of light above them [Jimmy and Villona] in a haze of summer evening" (*D* 45.24–25). The action and image in this paragraph, therefore, comprise a microcosm of the world of the story, which begins with the cars topping one crest and ends with the sun rising out of the Irish Sea.[12] Similarly, the tone of this paragraph parallels that of the story—moving from energy and action to disappointment and deflation. Similarly, it marks the lighting-up time (since the "globes of light" are the gas lamps): half way between one sunrise—when the race began—and the next—when the "after-the-race" party ended. This paragraph, therefore, also marks the midpoint in the implied action of the entire story. Finally, the figure at the center of this paragraph is "the snorting motor" (*D* 45.17): the graven image of Mammon to which the natives—and the Doyles—render homage.

Beneath its apparent naturalism and its dramatic anticlimax, "After the Race" has a chiastic structure, evidence of Joyce's control of his materials in accordance with the classical formal tradition. These organizational powers are familiar to readers of *A Portrait*, formally centered on the hellfire sermon, and *Ulysses*, chiastically arranged around its microcosm, the "Wandering Rocks" episode. The simultaneous management of anticlimax and of chiasmus Joyce will refine to higher purpose in the structural ironies of *A Portrait* first noted by Hugh Kenner (*Dublin's Joyce*, 119–23). His invocation of similar devices in "After the Race" supports the contention that even as he treats of the near chaos of the daily lived experience, Joyce was endowed right from the start with an appetite and capacity for the rational and control of widely diverse imaginative materials.

Free Indirect Discourse

The narrator of "After the Race" is a concealed observer of the dramatic action with privileged access to the consciousness of two of the characters, those of Jimmy Doyle and his father. He undertakes to tell the story equipped with knowledge of the Doyle family background and of its scion's limited résumé. To this subject and Jimmy's speculative dabbling, the narrator takes a superior attitude. He approaches the task endowed with a highly ironic, politically and culturally informed sensibility. He is both uninterested and disinterested in automobilism and has a condescending attitude toward those who indulge in this latest craze, and he criticizes those who promote events like the car race because it invents sensational occasions, creates vacuous celebrity culture, and exploits the common good for individual commercial advantage.

The narrator, therefore, approaches his task in a skeptical humor, exhibiting his poetic gifts in flashes of disdain, knowing understatement, and sardonic paradox. He occasionally allows himself—when not dealing with the men of action but with the cityscape—to ascend into brief lyrical flights. He is a man of culture and feeling, whose ostensible task is a description of a celebratory victory party, but whose values draw him irresistibly to the figure of Villona, who, like himself, conceals a rich inner life behind a discreet demeanor. The narrator reveals himself to be morally, politically, and aesthetically superior to the action. He exercises his narrative capacities for deft summary. He does not accord any of the characters sufficient individuation or development, but uses them as ciphers for forces that will do battle in the mechanical age. This narrator reveals himself to be both au fait with Dublin social gossip as well as widely read: his story is studded with knowing allusions to medicine, music, theology, history, literature, and contemporary fads. Thus, while he expects his readers to be familiar with the details of the city landscape (for example, the crest of the hill at Inchicore), he plies them with recherché words like "remonstrative," "torpid," and a series of amusing Gallicisms.

For his purposes in writing "After the Race," Joyce is engaging in an extension of what the classical rhetoricians called "prosopopoeia." He is experimenting with a persona whose engagement in the energy of the task occasionally leads him into pomposity and pleonasm, but whose imitative powers allow him to enter the minds of and ventriloquize the voices of his inventions.[13] The narrative tonalities reverberating through "After the Race" are not those heard by Joyce's acquaintances, but are an artifice of an experiment in rhetorical mimicry.

To appreciate the subtle energy of even this slight story—one of Joyce's minor achievements—readers should pay careful attention to the rhetorical style and diction as the narrative is paid out. Beyond this self-conscious narrator, moreover, can be discovered some organizational or structural elements—silences, aporia, elisions, and chiasmus—for which the narrator is not obviously accountable. This figure, an aspect of Joyce's classical temperament, facilitates the narrator's story within constraints of which he does not betray any awareness. Advanced readers of *Ulysses* are familiar with this figure, the controversial "Arranger": the formal manager of the project under whose rules the narrator tells his tale. A careful analysis of "After the Race" reveals that he came to his major works already a practitioner of these discriminations.

The most prominent aspect of his prose style is his disposition toward phrasing that is rhythmic, alliterative, and assonantal: "The car ran on merrily with its cargo of hilarious youth" (*D* 44.3), "The Frenchmen flung their laughter and light words" (*D* 44.7), "The young men supped in a snug room lit by electric candle-lamps" (*D* 46.7–8), "he aroused the torpid Routh at last" (*D* 46.24), "A torrent of talk followed" (*D* 47.5), and the understated but well-tuned sentence upon which the story concludes, "The cabin door opened and he saw the Hungarian standing in a shaft of grey light" (*D* 48.31–32). Sister Gertrude R.S.M., the former Margaret Joyce, a musically endowed person herself, recalled her brother's habit of composing aloud, even when in Belvedere College, listening to the rhythms of his sentences: "James sang every line when writing his essays" she told Godfrey Ainsworth (10). Since "After the Race" was the single story he wrote in a Joyce family residence (7 St. Peter's Terrace, Cabra: September 19 to October 8, 1904), she may have been the first to appreciate the rhythmical qualities of the language of "After the Race."[14]

As the rest of the first paragraph confirms, the narrator's stance is mildly disdainful, feignedly objective: he presents the scene as if his panoramic view enabled him to see simultaneously both the competitors and the crowds gathered to greet their passage. As the story's title promised, the proportion of space devoted to the onlookers implies that he is more interested in the clumps of watchers—their cheers and gratitude—than in the careering vehicles. He is occupying a bifocal position: his own (panoramic) and that of the onlookers gathered around the junction of Emmet and Tyrconnell roads. From the latter, the succession of cars "topp[ing] the crest of the hill" (*D* 42.14) becomes the image that raises their expectations and provokes their "double round of welcome" (*D* 42.13–14). The effect of the visual and thudding rhythm is to suggest the narrator's discomfort with or condescension to the prosaic task he has undertaken. His appetite for alliteration lends a euphonious authority to the narrative and underwrites its thematic transitions.

A good example of each of these points is the alliteration and iambic rhythm of the phrase with which the first paragraph concludes ("the cars of their friends, the French" [*D* 42.9]) and the clipped assurance that dictates the beginning of the second ("The French, moreover, were virtual victors" [*D* 42.10]). The apparent dispatch of this deft transition conceals their separate ironies (French support for Irish causes was always diffident, never effective; and the claim to be the "virtual victors," when the field has but four competitors, is a euphemism worthy of the age of hype). The brisk pace of the narrative does not allow slower, less attentive, or less informed readers the leisure to unravel the implications of why these "clumps of people" consider the French "their friends" and what disappointments impel them to invoke the wistful formula, "virtual victors."

This phrase exemplifies, indeed, one of the central rhetorical devices at the heart of this story: antithesis ("through this channel of poverty and inaction the Continent sped its wealth and industry" [*D* 42.5–7]). In its variants—the paradox, the oxymoron, the epigram, and the triad—it expresses the narrator's self-regard as an ironist endowed with moral superiority above the subjects of his story, while conspiring to further its major structural device: the anticlimax. We are introduced to this from the very beginning, with the narrator's sardonic oxymoron about the Irish as "gratefully oppressed,"[15] his euphemism about Jimmy Doyle's behavior "within the limits of reasonable recklessness" (*D* 44.28–29), and the narrator's paradoxical characterization of his father's attitude toward Jimmy's extravagance: "covertly proud of the excess" (*D* 43.28).

The narrator affects an urbane condescension, as in his characterization of Jimmy as having "rather innocent-looking grey eyes" (*D* 43.14), of his father as "rich enough to be alluded to in the Dublin newspapers as a merchant prince" (*D* 43.20–21), or of his "curiously" coexistent enthusiasms of music and motoring (*D* 43.25–26). He transcribes Jimmy's thoughts in a "difficult" sentence with a syntactic organization that separates Jimmy's colloquialism from his writerly poise: "Ségouin, perhaps, would not think it a great sum but Jimmy who, in spite of temporary errors, was at heart the inheritor of solid instincts knew well with what difficulty it had been got together" (*D* 44.24–27). He can carry this kind of thing a bit far, as we see in the sentence that follows: "This knowledge had previously kept his bills within the limits of reasonable recklessness and, if he had been so conscious of the labour latent in money when there had been question merely of some freak of the higher intelligence, how much more so now when he was about to stake the greater part of his substance!" (*D* 44.27–32). Here he overreaches himself; for having penned the witty phrase, "reasonable recklessness," he launches into a too-elaborate sentence—the indirect question piled on top of the conditional—in pursuit of an ill-considered and vacuous comparison. It seems to be a parody of a pretentious editorial. The seven-word sentence that follows, "It was a serious thing for him" (*D* 44.32–33), mimicking Jimmy's paucity of wit, betrays the narrator's patronization of his callow creation.

The narrator begins the story with a strangely expressed sentence: "The cars came scudding in towards Dublin, running evenly like pellets in the groove of the Naas Road" (*D* 42.2–3). Can it be an accident, the result of inattention, or obscurely purposeful that five of its sixteen words have double letters? In the brief paragraph that follows, the word "cars" appears four times, supported by the images of "running evenly," "groove," and "channel." Are these repetitions, carried along in a sentence fitted with anapestic and trochaic feet not conducive to onomatopoeia with the repetitive sound of the oscillating pistons and even the patron of automobilism, Gordon Bennett (whose name was at least that day on everyone's lips)? The next two sentences exhibit similar diction choices, leading to the ironical concluding phrase, "the cheer of the gratefully oppressed" (*D* 42.7–8). The force of these examples might suggest that we are in the hands of a narrator who has a circumspect regard for but also a suspicion of the mechanical age, and exhibits in his style a couple of the features that would come to be associated with Futurism.

A closer look at what he and his fellow onlookers are observing presents us with a more plausible justification of this series of double-lettered words. Unlike today's Grand Prix drivers, the competitors in the 1903 Gordon Bennett Cup Race did not drive solo. Whereas today's mechanics occupy the service areas alongside the racing track facilitating "pit stops," the drivers in 1903 were accompanied by their *mécaniciens.* Even the four-seaters (of some of the supporters such as the Rivière-Doyle car) would have had the same visual effect: of two heads appearing together as they topped the crest of the hill.[16] Thus what the onlookers beheld as the cars came into sight was an intermittent succession of pairs of identically accoutered figures—in leather jackets, dusters, goggles, and helmets—breaking the horizon, and even before they saw the actual vehicles upon which they rode (figure 2.2). This uneven succession of similar visual images is matched by a similar succession of acoustic images, "the cheers of the gratefully oppressed." In sum, the sentences describing them contain a literalization of the visual and acoustic repetitions that the narrator sees, hears, and renders in literal metaphors: an astonishing ecphrasis.[17]

This advanced use of free indirect discourse—going beyond diction and syntax and into other formalities of language—is a central feature of the literary style of the mature Joyce. But it is surprising to stumble on evidence of it even at this early point.[18] When Joyce comes to write "Counterparts" (midsummer 1905), he has an otherwise unobservant Farrington, having written the semisentence, "*In no case shall the said Bernard Bodley be,*" reflect on "how strange it was that the last three words began with the same letter" (*D* 90.15–17). This offers the reader a major *clou* to the technique of the story in which repetitions of all kinds technically reflect the theme of depersonalization (see Owens, "Joyce's Farrington"). Like Farrington's attention, fascinated by the recurrence of the letter *b* in his incomplete sentence, the readers' attention is briefly arrested by the series of literal dualisms in the opening sentences. This is the only image in the entire story that refers to the action of the race itself: rendering its visual images into literal and poetic equivalents.

The second paragraph has two principal subjects: a description of the reception accorded the French visitors, and an exposition of the relationships, backgrounds, and motivations of the four young men. The rhetorical structure of the paragraph betrays a pedantic and mechanistic disposition on the part of the implied narrator: moving from two synonyms for "first" ("victor" and "winner"), through "second," and "third," before arriving at what becomes his key phrase, "four young men," which he repeats three times. In these descriptions, the theme of doubling and repetition appears in several rhetorical forms: in the recurrences of "cars," "welcome," and "good humour," and the introduction of the two fully named French cousins and their pair of counterparts, identified only by their surnames.

The third sentence of the second paragraph, "Each blue car, therefore, received a double round of welcome as it topped the crest of the hill and each cheer of welcome was acknowledged with smiles and nods by those in the car" (*D* 42.13–16), besides its explicit announcement of this doubling theme, is especially interesting from a rhetorical point of view. Composed of three clauses describing the welcome accorded the Frenchmen, its location, and its reciprocation, it is appropriately expressed in complementary active and passive verbs ("received" and "was acknowledged") and their identical repeated complement, "welcome." Since the sentence, moreover, begins and ends with the subject "car," it is a chiasmus centered on the word "hill": the point in the action that reveals the drivers to their admirers to one another. This central clause, indicating a series of repeated "double rounds," is, moreover, expressed in a succession of three double-lettered words: "topped," "hill," and "cheer."

This same paragraph ends with the anticlimactic introduction of the protagonist whose name we eventually learn—only after an intervening description of his genealogy—is "Jimmy." We are informed of his surname by but one reference in the story, whereas we encounter his familiar name a total of twenty-six times (corresponding to his number of birthdays). The surname of his friend (and literal double and thematic antagonist) Villona appears but fourteen times: an index of his lower profile in the express action of the story. However, if we take into account how frequently words with double "l" appear in the design of the narrative—for example, "brilliant," "excellent," "fellows," "strolled," "intelligence," "gallantly," "Gallicism"—the total is fifty. This particular combination is easily the most frequent use of words with double letters, etching the visual image of Villona's name into the orthography of the narrative. The comparable words picking up the double "m" of Jimmy's name—"commercially," "humming," "summer" (2), and "immense"—bring that total to thirty-one. This aspect of the literal narrative assays Villona's weightier presence at the story's thematic center, despite his apparent marginalization. That the letters "l" and "m" are the benign twelfth and nefarious thirteenth in the English alphabet suggests, further, that the author of "After the Race" is already practicing the kind of punctilious, symbolic (and even obsessive) literalism that would become one of the marks of his later fiction.[19] When the narrator, in the penultimate sentence of the story, has us behold Jimmy "counting the beats of his temples" (D 48.30–31)—a pointedly futile gesture for one who has suffered indeterminate (and as yet incalculable) losses—he is as well obliquely pointing his readers' attention to this aspect of the literary experience to which they may not have paid adequate attention.[20]

The narrator occasionally waxes lyrical, when he feels called upon to add some local color. Thus, he describes Dublin's hospitality to its Continental visitors as "the city hung its pale globes of light above them in a haze of summer evening" (D 45.24–25). Similarly, he slips into Dickensian mode when describing the passage of the car between Grafton Street and Westland Row as "blended now into soft colors to a music of merry bells" (D 47.9–10), and again in rendering the prospect of the calm sea offered the young men on their exit from Kingstown Railway Station with the observations that "It was a serene summer night; the harbour lay like a darkened mirror at their feet" (D 47.15–16). On other occasions, the narrator appears to lose momentary control, producing pleonastic clauses: "whose spirits seemed to be at present well above the level of successful Gallicism" (D 42.17–18), and "besides he [Villona] was an optimist by nature" (D 43.10–11). These are but samples from the repertoire of a budding parodist.

Throughout the story, the narrator displays his superior wit in ironical plays on mercantile language. In explaining the means by which the Doyle money was accumulated, he implies a relationship between the modification of the father's political views and the securing of police contracts. At the same time, he pretends to accept the spin term "fortunate enough" (D 43.19) as an explanation, the irony of which reappears in Jimmy's privately held regret at Villona's "unfortunate" poverty (D 44.2). The narrator is also partial to medical images: "the torpid Routh" (D 46.24), and the complex metonymy in the sentence, "The journey laid a magical finger on the genuine pulse of life and gallantly the machinery of human nerves strove to answer the bounding courses of the swift blue animal" (D 45.10–12).[21] He converts the "miracle" of technology, whereby the automobile engine—by a rapid succession of electrically ignited explosions—puts inert matter into motion, into a complex double metonymy: the mechanical aspect of the human nervous system is complemented by the apparently equine machine. Jimmy is enchanted by the apparently magical touch effected by the agents of the electrical age: whether whisked along the roads under the spell of André Rivière, the "young electrician" (*D* 43.1) or imaginatively kindled by the light of "electric candle-lamps" (*D* 46.8). The narrator neatly undercuts this futurist hyperbole in his final paragraph when he presents us with the drunk and disillusioned Jimmy Doyle, "counting the beats of his temples" (*D* 48.30–31): a gesture that recalls his recent elation, his financial losses, and the surrender of his self-control.

The narrator's favorite metaphors are drawn from music, religion, and translation. One passage with a few "curious" phrases and repetitions turning upon the topic of translation deserves notice.

> in fact, these four young men were almost hilarious. . . . Ségouin was in good humour because he had unexpectedly received some offers in advance (he was about to start a motor establishment in Paris) and Rivière was in good humour because he was to be appointed manager of the establishment; these two young (who were cousins) were also in good humour because of the success of the French cars. Villona was in good humour because he had had a very satisfactory luncheon; and besides he was an optimist by nature. The fourth member of the party, however, was too excited to be genuinely happy. (*D* 42.18–43.12)

This expository half-paragraph concisely identifies four of the story's six characters and the principal relationships between two of them: of blood, nation, and the business of automobile merchandising. The relationship between them and the other two, Villona and "the fourth member," is unexplained. The bond between the four, while inferentially their common interest in the car race, is their near hilarity.

The peculiar usage of "hilarious"—applying to the subject rather than the object of laughter—was then but "a recent formation," and is now obsolete (*OED*). It makes the similarly odd repetitions—four—of the adverbial phrase "in good humour" characterizing the demeanor of three of the four characters. The contrast between the reasons for the "good humor" of the Frenchmen—the benefits they anticipate from their success in sports and business—and Villona's—his "satisfactory luncheon" (*D* 43.10)—is deliberately anticlimactic. The narrator's comment, "and besides he was an optimist by nature" (*D* 43.10-11), seems apologetically tacked on and, moreover, redundantly phrased. The narrator's apparent ineptitude is belied, however, by the appropriate word he chooses to conclude and dramatically climax the paragraph: "happy" (*D* 43.12). This weighty adjective appears in a negative sentence—the unnamed "fourth member" of the company lacks this genuine quality. Its appearance and anonymous attribution at the end of a paragraph so filled with public, familial, and private detail (the race results, the business deals of the cousins, and Villona's private satisfaction in his lunch), is therefore ironically pointed. It establishes a contrast between the terms around which the paragraph has been turning, hilarity, excitement, and good humour (boisterous laughter and pleasure), and genuine happiness.

The judicious note upon which he ends this paragraph implies that the narrator is not enthralled by the excitement generated in his subjects by the race, its commercial spinoff, or its business-entertainment lunches. The repeated use of the phrase "in good humor" implies a certain loss of rhetorical detachment from his excited subjects (*D* 43.3-11). The isocolon in the long sentences betrays his momentary empathy with each in turn, before he resumes the moral detachment in the progressive repotia of the two concluding short sentences. The narrator's skill in handling free indirect discourse indicates that he at last possesses the ability to distinguish between good humor and genuine happiness.

While admitting some contending tones, the narrator's own voice dominates the account. He occasionally releases flashes of bitter wit as in the litotes of "[Jimmy's] father may have felt even commercially satisfied at having secured for his son qualities often unpurchasable" (*D* 45.31-33). To the sarcastic narrator, the Doyles have accumulated their fortune by the practice of calculation so habitual that it seems a natural virtue. This goes some way to explaining Jimmy's vulnerability to the machinations of Ségouin and company. The half-sentence that conveys this information, combining the narrator's rather pompous tendency to moralize, his cunning reiteration of the Doylism "secured," and the climactic wounding oxymoron, is a rhetorical gem. Considering that what provokes it is nothing more than Jimmy's appearance in evening dress, it is a brilliant combination of over- and understatement.

As he develops his account, the narrator allows the tones of other voices to enter, and especially in the final scene when we hear much from Jimmy. The account is inflected throughout with citations of popular clichés of sports and leisure journalism (presuming his readers' familiarity with them) as well as of contemporary political commentary of the advanced nationalist" press: an odd presumption. The author of "The Holy Office" was similarly cavalier in his ignoring the difference between the readership of the *Irish Homestead* for which the story was written and that of *United Irishman* where it might have won a more sympathetic, if no more comprehending, reception. Joyce's handling of free indirect discourse in "After the Race," his first serious attempt at polyphonic prose, admits intonations from the voices of several characters as well as rival organs of culture, religion, and politics. His technique, sophisticated though it is for a writer at the beginning of his career, is not always adequate to his complex aims. It is no surprise, then, that discerning readers have had troubles with the story and that Joyce himself left it alone, dissatisfied though he was with its final form.

His Master's Voice

The first "living" voice the narrator admits is that of the main character, Jimmy Doyle. Inheritor of the fortune of a self-made, no-nonsense, blue-collar father with business, social, and political pretentions, Jimmy is a college dropout with no work experience, and at the late age of twenty-six is still living with his parents. He is more typical of his potential peers a century later, when prosperity has enabled the coddling of a larger proportion of the youth of the First World than was the norm in 1904. The narrator allows the idioms and tone of Jimmy's callow speech and mental lexicon to enter the language of the story, especially in the final few paragraphs as he becomes inebriated. The euphemism about his irresponsibility—"Jimmy did not study very earnestly" (*D* 43.24)—is the first evidence of his own moral and mental evasiveness. This is followed by his more forthright estimation of Villona—"a charming companion . . . but, unfortunately, very poor" (*D* 44.1–2)—the blunt (but discreetly private) qualifier, "unfortunately," the giveaway.

This opportunism is a part of his paternal inheritance. Mr. Doyle is the one character in the story to whom we are not formally introduced, yet the tones of his voice reverberate through the ruminations of his son and heir. His crass counsel is always on his son's mind, either because Jimmy is deliberately aware that he is emulating his father's example ("Jimmy had a respect for his father's shrewdness in business matters and in this case it had been his father who had first suggested the investment" [D 45.3–5]) or through express citation ("Such a person . . . was well worth knowing" [D 43.33–34]). Indeed, the frequency with which his father's turns of phrase appear in Jimmy's mental language affords glimpses of his continual interior dialogue with his sire and mentor. Examples include the pretentious usage "Dublin University" (D 43.23) (rather than the popular designation, "Trinity College"), the cliché "to see a little life" (D 43.27) at Cambridge (yet!),[22] and the crude monomania implied by the repetitious rephrasing of "money to be made in the motor business, pots of money" (D 45.5–6; this last a metaphor of greed sardonically relished by the superior narrator since it is inherited with a fortune made from butchery).[23]

Again, in attempting to calculate the labor value of Ségouin's car, Jimmy is patently emulating his father's example. In this he does not succeed, since the narrator—without offering any transition—immediately moves our attention to Jimmy's distraction from this mentally demanding task by a less stressful and more sensuous aspect of the car: "How smoothly it ran" (D 45.8–9). By means of this artful aporia, the narrator exemplifies Jimmy's half-heartedness: the mental habit by which he has evaded the discipline of legal studies for the easy pleasures of "musical and motoring circles." These examples demonstrate that the narrative technique of this story includes a fine blending of written, spoken, and mental voices: the narrator's writerly poise registering with mild disdain the tones of Jimmy's interior dialogismus.[24]

Besides this, it is apposite to point out that Jimmy's father is the only character in the story—besides Jimmy himself—into whose mind we are granted anything beyond a momentary entrée.[25] We are allowed but once to witness the father's social demeanor: conditioned by disingenuous commercial practice, his behavior toward Villona is "unusually friendly" (D 45.34). And further, he is the only character whom we see as knowing his own mind (independent of Jimmy's interpretation): his covert pride in his son's excess at Cambridge (D 43.27–29). The dramatic climax of this unarticulated but formative filial bond appears in Jimmy's tiff with Routh: as the narrator implies, this set-to is simultaneously atavistic, "buried," and "personal" (D 46.23–26). Finally, in the anxieties intimated by the words "calculate" and "count" and the oscillation of the words "win" and "lose" in the final scene, we catch the faded but persistent echoes in Jimmy's muddled mind of his master's voice.

The Sounds of Silence

One of Jimmy's proclivities, acquired from his father, but nonetheless indicative of a residual social conscience, is calculative: he repeatedly attempts to work out the cost of his indulgence in terms of its labor value. This suggests a residual guilt about the real cost of his high living: "Jimmy... knew well with what difficulty it [his father's wealth] had been got together" (D 44.25–27), and with regard to the value of a car in man-hours, he was "conscious of the labour latent in money" (D 44.29–30). The narrator's delicious irony attendant upon these observations—that they were indications of Jimmy's inheritance of "solid instincts"—is redolent of a nuanced letter of recommendation that subtracts at least as much as it adds. Such moralizing about labor and value, appearing in the mind of a young man who has apparently never done a day's work but has dabbled at an academy where David Ricardo's economic theories were common coinage amuses the narrator, as we infer from his citation of what is apparently one of Jimmy's favorite phrases: "It was a serious thing for him" (D 44.32–33).[26]

We catch the inflection of Jimmy's untidy impressionability with the intrusion of some of his mental idiom on the narrator's controlled, and sometimes pretentious, language. The narrator repeatedly allows us to overhear three of Jimmy's favorite adverbial tags, "besides," "decidedly," and "of course": indications of his social and intellectual insecurity and his constant need of reassurance. Jimmy's inclination to tag his reflections with afterthoughts appears in a few places, as for example, when he concludes his assessment of the social value of Villona, with the remark that he was "unfortunately, very poor" (D 44.2). Similarly, he rationalizes his feeling of social exclusion in the car with the concluding remark, "Besides Villona's humming would confuse anybody; the noise of the car, too" (D 44.12–13). The imprecise punctuation of this sentence—the omission of the comma after "Besides" and of the verb accompanying "noise"—is the syntactic corollary of the subject of the sentence, and constitutes a purposeful anacolouthon. His deference to Ségouin and Rivière keeps surfacing in his gestures and thoughts: even though he doesn't understand their questions, he shouts back what he hopes are "suitable answer[s]" to the Frenchmen (*D* 44.11), and considers that Ségouin probably considers "the greater part of [Jimmy's] substance" (*D* 44.32) no more than a "mite of Irish money" (*D* 45.2).

Even as his paucity of imaginative energy betrays itself in the repetitions and clichés encumbering his mental language—"play fast and loose" (*D* 45.28), "this was seeing life" (*D* 47.28), "they were devils of fellows" (*D* 48.13–14), "it was getting late" (*D* 48.14–15)—he fancies himself (as does Tommy Chandler) a poet: "Jimmy . . . conceived the lively youth of the Frenchmen twined elegantly upon the firm framework of the Englishman's manner. A graceful image of his, he thought, and a just one" (*D* 46.9–12). In the heat of political argument this passing fancy is dropped, briefly resurrected in the plaudits for his speech, but drowned at last in the succession of toasts and the swirl of the gambling rounds.

As Jimmy's agitations and inebriation rise, so do the proportion of exclamatory remarks beginning with "How" or "What": "How smoothly it ran" (*D* 45.8–9), "What merriment!" (*D* 47.27), "What jovial fellows!" (*D* 48.2–3), "What excitement!" (*D* 48.20).[27] For his part, as if intoxicated by osmosis, the narrator, approaching closure, steers his narrative style into staggering sympathy with Jimmy's lapse into semiconsciousness. This he conveys in several rhetorically conducive ways. We encounter it in the multiply inaccurate sentences, "They drank, however: it was Bohemian. They drank Ireland, England, France, Hungary, the United States of America" (*D* 47.30–32). They are a hodgepodge of catachreses (why the "however"? and what was "Bohemian"?), of asyndeton (why the unidiomatic "drank Ireland"?), and of unaccountable ellipsis (what about Rivière's Canada?).

This farrago of imprecision sets the tone for the three concluding paragraphs in which the narrative style is dominated by single-clause sentences: "The table was cleared," "Routh won," sentences with repetitive syntax ("it was getting late. . . . It was a terrible game"), and an increase in simple-string sentences like "Play ran very high and paper began to pass," and "They were devils of fellows but he wished they would stop." The narrator neglects the logical or syntactic transitions to which he was previously attentive, and he even seems to lose an awareness of his readers, lapsing into Jimmy's unmediated self-address, as in "They drank the health of the Queen of Hearts and of the Queen of Diamonds. Jimmy felt obscurely the lack of an audience" (*D* 48.7–9), and the nonsequitur, "Villona must have gone up on deck. It was a terrible game" (*D* 48.17–18).

These final paragraphs are strewn with such ellipses and syntactic repetitions that betoken loss of concentration: "it must have," "play," "drank," "speech," "someone," "game," "won," "lose," and "glad." This ceding of authorial control reveals itself finally in the apparent slip in the first sentence of the last paragraph, "He knew that he would regret in the morning" (*D* 48.27). The asyndeton is not a compositor's error, since Joyce—no doubt drawing on a practitioner's familiarity with drunkenness—did not emend it in either the 1910 or 1914 proofs. The narrator has enough wit, nevertheless, to convey the same point imagistically in Jimmy's regression through the narrative from recalling "the great sum under his control" (*D* 44.23–24), through the assistance he needed to "calculate his IOU's" (*D* 48.13), to the implication that the last vestige of "solid [businessman's] instinct" is Jimmy's "counting the beats of his temples" (*D* 48.30–31).

Of the other minor characters, we hear but exclamations: Ségouin's ecphonesis, "*Humanité!*" (*D* 46.27); Farley's personal greeting to his fellow North American, André Rivière, and Rivière's impersonal response (*D* 47.3–4); the joint singing of "*Cadet Roussel*" (*D* 47.17–19); and Routh's proposal of "one great game" (*D* 48.16). Farley's other contributions to the vocal tonality of the story are his crying "Stop!," his loud laughter, and his backslapping. Joyce's interest in representing a number of individual voices—some identified, some not (who apostrophizes "Cards! cards!"? [*D* 48.4])—in the midst of an apparent cacophony, which informs the technique of "After the Race," climaxes in the last pages of "Oxen of the Sun."[28]

The one voice that, to coin a phrase, is conspicuously silent is that of the artiste, Villona. While he seems to have been brought along for his pianism, he reveals himself an aesthete. The narrator conveys something of the range of his cultivation in the fluency of his English in praising the achievements of Dowland and Byrd and castigating unhistorical paintings. He does not disappoint: his music supplies the soundtrack for the entire third scene. The record exhibits, moreover, three peremptory examples of his direct speech: "It is beautiful!" (*D* 47.23), "*Hear! hear!*" (*D* 47.33), and the anticlimactic "Daybreak, gentlemen!" (*D* 48.33). Even on these slim interventions, the narrator conveys, through reported speech (in which the word "beauty" appears again), something of his quality of mind. He is roused but once from his role as performer (he hums and plays the yacht piano), to an indignant protest over the loss of the authentic renaissance lute. The narrator has left Villona to himself except for one peculiar departure: the intelligence of the beginnings of his "sharp desire for his dinner" (*D* 46.3). Coming at the end of a paragraph otherwise consumed with exposing the Doyles' attempt to disguise networking as hospitality (the explicit force of the unnecessary "therefore" [*D* 45.34]), it comes as a mild rebuke. This unique report on the private feeling of any character besides the Doyles, father and son, is a silent, but sharp, instance in the general design of deflation in the story.

The narrator's clever arrangement of the narrative order allows attentive readers to tune in on Villona's silences. Consider, for instance, the intelligence, "It was a serene summer night; the harbour lay like a darkened mirror at their feet" (*D* 47.15–16). This prospect, if indeed it registers at all, does not give the young revelers pause: for the next sentence tells us that they march apace downhill toward Farley's yacht, stamping their feet in concert with the chorus of "*Cadet Roussel.*" The tone of the narrator's account and the careful sequencing of the details in this brief scene have purposeful implications, however. First, the narrator has picked up the reflective mood initially invoked by the old ticket-collector's address to Jimmy, "Fine night, sir!" (*D* 47.14). Second, his reflection is interrupted by the young men's raucous song. And third, when he subsequently records Villona's ecphonesis, "It is beautiful!" we are given to understand that his appreciative exclamation is not provoked by the prospect of supper, music, cards, or even by what must have been an impressive yacht. It is a delayed, and convinced response to the placid night scene, as if he alone of the company shared the narrator's enchantment with the "darkened mirror" (*D* 47.15–16).[29] The more likely inference that we are invited to draw from this dramatic ellipsis on the narrator's part is that his emotional response to the scene arises from a preferential sympathy with the introspective and imaginative Villona. The placement of this comment imputes, therefore, an aesthetic consonance between the ticket-collector, Villona, and the narrator: understated by the first, slightly overstated by the third.

Later, as the narrator conducts us through the bold card games and raucous toasts, he scores Villona's contribution as a diminuendo: from some "quietly . . . played voluntaries" (*D* 48.4–5) through his silent departure during the "great game" at the "finish" (*D* 48.16). He is therefore absent during the long passage that ends in the crescendo of the night's revelry as "[t]he cabin shook with the young men's cheering" (*D* 48.23–24). His ultimate appearance to announce the dawn implies, therefore, that during this last moiety he has returned to the nightscape that he had beheld with such rapture during his approach and had proclaimed with such conviction. This conviction had stayed with him through the revelry and drawn him away to contemplate its transition to a morning sunscape. Thus, the contrast that the narrator established between his sensitivity and that of the jovial singers of "*Cadet Roussel*" in the first instance is reaffirmed in the similar contrast between his solo gaze at the sea's mirror and the jubilant gamblers in the second. Each of these delayed reactions—managed by parallel narrative silences—tells much about both Villona's sense and his sensibility. Like the examples of parallax cited from scene 1, these vestigial silences are early indications of a narrative technique of which Joyce was to become a master, in *Ulysses*.

Knots, Belles, and Beaux

As has been already observed at several points, the author of "After the Race" employs a considerable variety of stylistic strategies, some of which have drawn premature criticism from otherwise discerning scholars. The narrator presents himself capable of a range of styles from the periphrasis to asyndeton, and from the delivery of ornate and suspended sentences to their paratactic contrary. These are always functions of the free indirect discourse in which the narrator—occasionally adopting voices other than his own—is disposed to invoke. In this way, the parallelism with which the second sentence concludes—"through this channel of poverty and inaction the Continent sped its wealth and industry" (*D* 42.5–7)—assures readers that the poeticisms with which he opened the account will be balanced by a measured rationality. His use of parentheses is to signify not only an appropriate subordination, but to mark contributions to the exposition deriving from Jimmy's attempts at self-validation by association: with Rivière "(he was about to start a motor establishment in Paris)" (*D* 43.5); "(who were cousins)" (*D* 43.8); "(as his father agreed)" (*D* 43.33–34), et cetera.

Getting into full stride, the narrator cannot hide his proclivity to strike superior and judgmental postures. In consequence, he slips into an unnecessary circumlocution in expressing his condescension to

Ségouin's "cargo": "a party of four young men whose spirits seemed to be at present well above the level of successful Gallicism" (*D* 42.16–18). Similarly, he can produce an antithetical suspended sentence in formal excess of the requirement: "if he had been so conscious of the labour latent in money when there had been question merely of some freak of the higher intelligence, how much more so now when he was about to stake the greater part of his substance!" (*D* 44.29–32).

The narrator is sufficiently assured of his rhetorical mastery to render sentences of poeticized excess from the reveries of the excited would-be poet, Jimmy Doyle, such as, "The journey laid a magical finger on the genuine pulse of life and gallantly the machinery of human nerves strove to answer the bounding courses of the swift blue animal" (*D* 45.10–12). This mélange of mixed metaphor, the misapplication of the notion of gallantry and the deliberate displacement of both "gallantly" (anastrophe) and "bounding" (hypallage) are indications of Jimmy's casual relationship with poetic language.[30] The narrator's tack in belittling Jimmy's emotional and literary limitations—by putting hyperbolic language in his mind—is therefore a complex example of auxesis.

The narrator himself has a finer sense of the appropriate relationship between style and subject than to engage in pretentious periodic prose. Despite some missteps, he displays a keen management of adaptive stylistics. When the occasion demands it—in describing Jimmy's subsidized aimlessness, for example—he fashions a sequence (singular in the story) marked by polysyndeton: "Jimmy did not study very earnestly and took to bad courses for a while. He had money and he was popular; and he divided his time curiously between musical and motoring circles" (*D* 43.23–25). Similarly, he draws his readers into an appreciation of Jimmy's awareness of his regression from mild disorientation to helpless incoherence between the afternoon and late night: "Besides Villona's humming would confuse anybody; the noise of the car, too" (*D* 44.12–13); "The dinner was excellent, exquisite" (*D* 46.4); "There was to be supper, music, cards" (*D* 47.21); "He knew that he would regret in the morning" (*D* 48.27).

This sequence of examples of asyndeton—the omission of elements (a comma, conjunctions, a pronoun) demanded by formal syntax—reveals the narrator's sensitivity to the subject and rhetorical resource.[31] A particularly fine example of this figure is the sentence, "Then an impromptu square dance, the men devising original figures" (*D* 47.26–27). Not only does the missing verb (scesis onamoton) offer a syntactic correspondence to the impulsiveness it implies, but the proximity of the words "impromptu" and "devising" to one another constitutes a virtual oxymoron (itself an "original figure").

More broadly, as Jimmy's evening descends from hilarity and excitement into alcoholic incoherence (unlike its rival hostelry on Stephen's Green, the Russell, the Shelbourne was not a temperance hotel), the narrator's style moves in concert. His account of the events following the dinner (*D* 46.29–48.33) appears in a style that after a passage marked by ecphonesis and epizeuxis—"What merriment! . . . *Stop!* . . . *Hear! hear!* . . . What jovial fellows! What good company they were! Cards! cards!" (*D* 47.27–48.4)—is dominated by parataxis and asyndeton.

Between these rhetorical poles—the periodic and the paratactic—the narrator reveals his capacities as a master of stylistic rhythm and variation. Beginning with the anadiplosis between the first two paragraphs, "their friends, the French. The French, moreover" (*D* 42.9–10), he shows himself a more than competent practitioner of the varied transition (as pointed out previously). One of the distinct features of his style is his partiality to repetition in a variety of forms and for several purposes, whether in the interests of satire or psychological description. These uses of anaphora and isocolon underline its satire: "Ségouin was in good humour because . . . and Rivière was in good humour because . . . Villona was in good humour because he had a very satisfactory luncheon" (*D* 43.3–10). A simpler kind of repetition furthering the narrator's bemusement as the night gets sillier is the ploce of "They drank the health of the Queen of Hearts and of the Queen of Diamonds" (*D* 48.7–8). Other variations on anaphora are, "Jimmy made a speech, a long speech" (*D* 47.32–33), "at present he was glad of the rest, glad of the dark stupor that would cover up his folly" (*D* 48.28–29), and "Jimmy did not know exactly who was winning but he knew that he was losing" (*D* 48.10–11). The emphatic repetition of the same word in close context (the conduplicatio of "speech" and "glad" and the homioptoton in the last example) conveys Jimmy's fitful grasp of his surroundings. Yet another kind of repetition appears in the sentence, "Rapid motion through space elates one; so does notoriety; so does the possession of money" (*D* 44.14–15). The prozeugma (a single verb commanding a sequence of clauses) of the structure has the delicious cumulative effect of parodying the near tautology of the premise: constituting a nice example of the dominant trope of the story, anticlimax.

This trope can be traced to the original *Irish Times* interview with

Henri Fournier. There Joyce had represented this elusive celebrity as arrogant, dull-witted, and ungallant. In the story (whose title derives, literally, from the same interview), anticlimax appears in several places: in Villona's unspoken comment on the effusiveness of Jimmy's father about his "real respect for foreign accomplishments": he "was beginning to have a sharp desire for his dinner" (D 46.3).

And again, the epanalepsis of the sentence, "a short fat man was putting two handsome ladies on a car in charge of another fat man" (D 46.33–34), mirrors the other dominant trope of the story, ironic chiasmus. A more complex example of creative repetition appears in the sequence, "At the control Ségouin had presented [Jimmy] to one of the French competitors . . . he really had a great sum under his control" (D 44.17–24). Since it begins and ends with the word "control," it has a chiasmic appearance. But since the first use of the word is professional jargon for the point from which the race was timed, and the second to Jimmy's presumed financial independence, the repetition (like Jimmy's genuine independence) is a sylleptic illusion: not a chiasmus, but an antanaclasis.

The narrator's handling of literary style embraces a selection of language and idiom that furnishes his account with a rich range of ironic tonalities. The reader encounters one of these almost from the start: in the contentious oxymoron, "the gratefully oppressed" (D 42.8). He follows it with another, two pages later, in the deeply ironic reference to Jimmy's being allowed latitude to "the limits of reasonable recklessness" (D 44.28–29). The manner of his report that "Jimmy did not study very earnestly. . . . He had money and was popular" (D 43.23–25), amounts to a cunningly mild euphemism that the ancients called "paradiastole." The Doyles, father and son, are the objects of his auxesis as he cites their terms, "a merchant prince" (D 43.21), "a big Catholic college" (D 43.22), "some of the biggest hotels in France" (D 43.33), and "pots of money" (D 45.6). His use of this figure is balanced by his less frequent invocation of its contrary or opposites, meiosis, "the mite of Irish money" (D 45.2), or litotes, "This was not altogether pleasant for him" (D 44.9–10), "having secured for his son qualities often unpurchasable" (D 45.32–33), and "not wholly ingenuously" (D 46.17–18). Joyce came to his craft an already advanced ironist.[32]

"After the Race" exhibits many examples of the verbal humors, trivial and quadrivial, for which Joyce would become renowned, even among those who have not read his work with much attention. The text plays on the paronomasia on the word "course," between Jimmy's "bad courses" of study (*D* 43.24), the "bounding courses" (*D* 45.12) of Ségouin's automobile, and one of Jimmy's favorite adverbial phrases, "of course" (*D* 44.34, 48.21): all plays on the French word for the race in which their cars were "virtual victors." We have seen that in the passages describing the conduct of the visitors, the narrative exploits the relationships, consonant and dissonant, between French and English diction and idiom. The narrative indulges in persistent synonymia in weaving a financial motif throughout: "money," "capital," "Bank of Ireland," "sum," "mite," and the "I.O.U's" (*D* 48.13) that Jimmy has "written away" (*D* 48.22).

Joyce's partiality to language play goes beyond such conventionalities, however, and into many interesting and inventive variations. His narrator considers himself above the paronomasia that the sentence, "the Hungarian . . . was beginning to have a sharp desire for his dinner" (*D* 46.2–3), would suggest to schoolboys. He can proffer deadpan the sentence, "the swarthy face of the driver had disclosed a line of shining white teeth" (*D* 44.20–21), allowing the image in the verb to do its quiet work (paronomasia). He indites a similar play in the sentence, "Jimmy set out to translate into days' work that lordly car in which he sat" (*D* 45.7–8). In the wake of his report that Jimmy struggled to grasp the "quick phrase[s]" of the Frenchmen (*D* 44.9), his use of the verb "translate" is an appropriate and ironic syllepsis. He indulges, too, in the classical polyptoton (the repeat of the same word but in different cases), as in the sentence, "What excitement! Jimmy was excited too" (*D* 48.20–21), and in the variant usages, "ran on merrily" (*D* 44.3), "merry bells" (*D* 47.10), and "What merriment!" (*D* 47.27).

More interesting is Joyce's predisposition to etymological wordplay. Indeed, paregmenon (the juxtaposition of words with a common derivation) will become one of the hallmarks of Joyce's literary wit. Consider, for example, the usages of the word "car" in the following succession: "to watch the cars careering homeward" (*D* 42.5), "[t]he car ran on merrily with its cargo of hilarious youth" (*D* 44.3), and "in a car in charge of" (*D* 46.34). These words, "car," "career," "cargo," and "charge" have a common etymological ancestor in the Old Irish word *carr*, one of the very few words found in many modern languages with a Celtic source (which gives us "chariot," "carry," "cart," et cetera). In his reading of Morris's *Elementary Lessons in English Grammar,* Joyce had seen "car" listed among the ten Celtic words bequeathed to modern English. As it came to us via the Norman-French usage (Morris, 9), "cargo" took a Portuguese route (26).

As a subsequent devotee of Skeat, Joyce would have read confirmation of this lineage, and seen, besides, that they are all rooted, further back, in the Sanksrit *char* "to move," which is also the distant ancestor of the word "course" (Skeat, s.v. "current").[33]

In Joyce's story, therefore, these etymological linkages constitute a pleasing complement to the ways in which the word "course" appears in this account of Hiberno-Gallic relationships. A more complex interlinguistic paregmenon appears in the first fourteen lines of the story. We are informed of the action and the place when we read that "[a]t the crest of the hill at Inchicore . . . [e]ach blue car . . . received a double round of welcome as it topped the crest of the hill" (*D* 42.3–14). Now, as already noted, Joyce was clearly familiar with the precise topography of Inchicore, from a childhood visit with Mrs. Conway to weekend perambulations (his primary physical recreation) with his father and friends. He was highly interested in and aware of the toponymics of his native city. He would therefore know that the name "Inchicore" (Ir. *Inse Choir*) derives from two Irish words, *inse*, a "river-meadow," or a "pasture along a stream" (Patrick Joyce, *Origin and History* 3: 392), and *cor,* "a small round hill" (3: 252). Longmeadows Park on the south bank of the Liffey translates the placename, and the modern thoroughfare (the continuous Tyrconnell and Emmet roads) traverses the hill from which the district derives its historic name. Thus, Joyce's ingenious prose does more than simply indicate the place and the action: he first identifies the place and then translates the topographical feature from which it got its name, in twice citing "the crest of the hill" and the "double round" of applause heard from "the channel of inaction" that is modern Inchicore. This historical paregmenon has its chiastic complement in the irony that the action ends in Kingstown (the temporary re-naming of Dún Laoghaire).

From the simile of the opening sentence, the story is rich in the language of expressive ambiguity inherited from the literary and cultural tradition of English poetry. While some of the uses of metaphoric language are transparent, others are deceptively simple, and a few contain an acute knowingness, even in the service of a relatively transparent subject.

We encounter, for example, some metaphors cleverly extended for the purposes of gentle satire or aesthetic satisfaction. The reference in the first paragraph to the Irish natives as "clumps of people [who] raised the cheer of the gratefully oppressed" (*D* 42.7–8) is ironically echoed at the end of the second, in the description of one of them, Jimmy Doyle, as "too excited to be genuinely happy" (*D* 43.12). Since "genuine" descends from *ingenuus*, "free born," this knowing etymological play comments appropriately on the link between the disingenuous cheers of the colonized onlookers and Jimmy's forced good cheer. Again, the sports image in the sentence, "The Frenchmen flung their laughter and light words over their shoulders and often Jimmy had to strain forward to catch the quick phrase" (*D* 44.7–9), is both appropriate to the object of the day's excitement and to Jimmy Doyle's distaff role in the playing of that game. The account of the second scene is inlaid with two contrasting motifs, mechanical and organic. We can thereby easily apprehend the motif linking the "snug room lit by electric candle-lamps," the "kindling" of Jimmy's imagination, and the consequence that "[t]he room grew doubly hot" with political argument (*D* 46.8–25), underlined as it is by the cognates "candle" and "kindle" (Skeat sketches the circuitous etymology of this pair, s.v. "kindle"). We can simultaneously entertain (with Jimmy) the developing image of that argument first from the Frenchman's youth "twined elegantly on [Routh's] firm framework," their standing on apparently "congenial ground," until the discovery of the "buried zeal" of the Doyle Anglophobia (*D* 46.10–24).

Another curious and cleverly developed motif is an extension of the geometric metaphor in the narrator's report that Jimmy "divided his time curiously between musical and motoring circles" (*D* 43.25–26). The "circles" in this sentence comprise a paronomasia encompassing gatherings of enthusiasts, automobile wheels, the circuit upon which the Gordon Bennett Cup Race was run in 1903, and the mathematically based cycles of notes that constitute the musical scale. The image of Jimmy's "dividing" his time recurs in his perception of the "line of shining white teeth" (*D* 44.20–21) in the mouth of the French driver and his own subsequent "giving a last equation to the bows of his dress tie" (*D* 45.31). These visual images of division, balance, taste, order, and judgment, cited in the service of social ascendancy contrast with the manner in which the narrator represents their social inferiors, those "knots" of gazers on Dame Street (*D* 45.16, 22).

It recurs in the subsequent scene in which Jimmy and his friends stride abreast along the fashionable north side of Stephen's Green: these similarly accoutered friends (evening dress, cloaks, and bows) scatter the underclass from the Beaux' Walk. Their encounter with Farley as he parts with his pair of "handsome ladies" (*D* 46.34) subsequently takes the ensemble marching past the obsequious old man to the strains of "*Cadet*

Roussel." When we are informed—close to the end of the narrative—that Farley's yacht bears the name *The Belle of Newport,* we are encouraged to translate this trip in retrospect. If we do, we flit past, in reverse order, the toasts to the Queens of Hearts and Diamonds, "a music of merry bells" (*D* 47.10), Farley's "two handsome ladies," and the knots of gazers on Dame Street.[34] If, then, like the Jimmy Doyle of the first scene, we can "translate" or "catch the quick phrase" (*D* 44.9), we can discern a sequence of references to merely metaphoric presence of *les belles dames.*

Joyce's use of similar conventional metaphoric forms—animation and personification—while appearing simple is, on closer perusal, sometimes far from transparent. As we have seen of the historical circumstances that situate the fiction, Joyce's literary text engages the streets and their furniture and the figures and events with which they are associated in highly complex ways that are simultaneously topographical, historical, and even mythological. In this survey of the rhetorical elements of the story, a few of the less convoluted instances—the building blocks of this elaborate imaginative superstructure—deserve attention. These are the means by which Joyce has enticed us into the suspension of disbelief in anything but the ordinary, material, objective world.

We are not long into his account before we find ourselves accepting these relatively unremarkable figures of speech: the metonymy, "the Continent sped its wealth" (*D* 42.6); the synecdoche, "[e]ach blue car, therefore, received a double round of welcome" (*D* 42.13–14); the animation of the "snorting motor" (*D* 45.17); and the personification in the "street [that] was busy with unusual traffic" (*D* 45.13–14). Such figures are the coinages of ordinary speech, and pass beneath notice, therefore, in plain discourse. Nonetheless, to Joyce's remarkable eye and ear, little or nothing remains a cliché, or even subliminal.

While he can gently satirize Jimmy's poetic fancies (the hyperbolic personification in "the journey laid a magical finger on the genuine pulse of life" [*D* 45.10–11]), he repeatedly animates or even personifies Dublin City, for example, "the city hung its pale globes of light" (*D* 45.24) and "[t]hat night the city wore the mask of a capital" (*D* 46.29). Such figurations, in Joyce's hands, are always designed to carry a force or fulfill a pattern beyond their immediate function in the text. For example, the personified name of Farley's yacht, *The Belle of Newport* (*D* 48.15–16), signifies not only its owner's wealth, prestige, and domicile, but also recalls the first appearance of this "fat man" in the company of "two handsome ladies" (*D* 46.34) (on the Beaux' Walk) and the hypallage adorning the company's travel to Kingstown: "to a music of merry bells" (*D* 47.10).

Similarly, Joyce invests even apparently trite figures with imaginative energy. In describing Jimmy's effort to impress his parents by "play[ing] fast and loose" with the names of "great foreign cities" (*D* 45.28-29), the idiom denotes not only his casual manner, but because of its origins as a gaming trick, implies something nefarious about the companions he has acquired in Paris. Again, looking at the sentences, "He admired the dexterity with which their host directed the conversation. The five young men had various tastes and their tongues had been loosened. Villona, with immense respect" (*D* 46.12-15), we recognize the aptness that has directed the word choices, "dexterity," "tongues . . . loosened," and "immense." While the word "dexterity" compliments Ségouin's social skills, it also echoes his driving skills (partly because the drivers' seats were on the right side). The synecdoche of the loosened tongues facilitates the transition from food and drink to conversation (and confrontation).[35] Similarly, the word "immense" pays efficient simultaneous respect to Villona's good taste and physical bulk (while implying the cause and effect of his healthy appetite).

A similar figure sits in the narrator's auxesis, "[Jimmy] was at heart the inheritor of solid instincts" (*D* 44.25-26).[36] The cogency of this usage in describing Jimmy's avarice has already received comment. It is a fine example of a Joycean metalepsis—the invocation of a remote allusion in conjunction with a close one—which was to become a specialty of his narrative art. Much of the imaginative superstructure of the Joycean universe is constructed out of such double metaphors, what Harold Bloom calls "a metonymy of a metonymy." They are the interstices between the realistic, historical, and allegorical spheres in his expanding universe.

This accumulated evidence supports the conclusion, therefore, that Joyce undertook this story with the intention of making it an exercise in classical rhetoric. This observation helps explain the presence of some flaws, some straining for effect, about which a few critics have complained. We know that Joyce was dissatisfied with it himself; yet he took no steps to assuage this dissatisfaction. From the perspective of its rhetoric, Joyce was apparently content to wait until undertaking the "Aeolus" episode of *Ulysses*.

The art of that episode is rhetoric, and its subject the popular press. Speeches appear prominently in its dramatic action, one of which Joyce himself chose when offered the opportunity to bequeath one selection to posterity in his own voice. "Aeolus" is therefore an exercise in the craft of classical rhetoric: at once a compendium of the craft and a systematic parody of its forms. In demonstrating the indebtedness of this chapter to classical rhetoric, M.J.C. Hodgart's essay on "Aeolus" leads us to an appreciation of Joyce's serious tribute to this aspect of his training as a writer. As Hodgart points out, Stuart Gilbert's catalogue of figures of speech in "Aeolus"—errors and all (194–98)—was probably drawn from a list given to him by Joyce, since it is unlikely that Gilbert or anyone else but the author could have discovered all these figures (Hodgart, 122).[37] We know that Joyce listened to Gilbert's book chapter by chapter before its publication (*JJII* 616). His approval of that pedantic catalogue tells us something about Joyce that may discomfit some modern readers. But it does insinuate that he was exercising there the same kind of writer's penchant that we have documented in its rhetorical antecedent, "After the Race."

As will be discussed, rhetoric's oral cousin, speechmaking, a cherished Irish political tradition, is at the heart of "After the Race" as it is of "Aeolus."[38] The only speech in "After the Race," Jimmy's, we do not hear. The narrator's reticence on this point, therefore, may appear to be a missed opportunity in the development of Jimmy's character. Its omission may be overcompensation for the author's self-consciousness about the rhetorical handbook in his fabrication of "After the Race."

The discernment and naming of rhetorical tropes in "After the Race" is more than a mere pedantic exercise. By applying fine logic to usages of language, classical rhetoricians are analyzing statements that to the untutored appear as "intuitive" or "instinctive," or "imaginative," "fanciful," or "trivial." When Joyce told the sculptor August Suter that from the Jesuits "I have learnt to arrange things in such a way that they become easy to survey and to judge" (*JJII* 27), he is making reference to this classical education. The training he received in making distinctions and connections in language constituted what he later referred to as his own mastery of the "trivial and quadrivial." Joyce's notorious reputation as a "difficult" writer derives from this precise, subtle, and highly informed handling of language. The rhetorical training that accompanied his introduction to the Latin authors and subsequent close reading of Dante at the Royal University regulated and deepened his natural gift of memory. His language is therefore rarely univocal, sometimes equivocal, but more likely to be multivalent. Under the pressure of Joyce's powerful summary command of the literary tradition, what appears as ordinary language deftly expresses the complexity of life's experience in a manner paralleled by advances in other modern fields: psychology, comparative anthropology, and physics.

"O the sons of the fathers!" (*FW* 426.30)

Joyce's classical education made him acquainted at an early age with Ovid. He read some of the *Metamorphoses* while at Belvedere, and excelled in Latin, scoring among the highest marks in Ireland in four successive years (1894–97), and winning a £2 prize for the best translation in 1895 (Bradley, 110–11, 116–17, 130–31; Sullivan, 98). By the time he graduated from the Royal University, he had studied many of the major Latin authors, including Virgil, Ovid, Horace, and Cicero. That this early education in classical rhetoric and mythology left a deep and permanent impact upon his imaginative character is plain. His grandson, Stephen, told me that one of his most vivid memories of his grandfather is listening to him read classical mythology in a French translation of Ovid (personal conversation, July 2008).

Early in his education, then, he found in Ovid classical figures that helped give shape to his imaginative world and ambitions, most obviously Icarus, whom he met in *Metamorphoses,* book 8 (183–235). He encountered another figure around the same time whose impact upon him is not as known, but who antecedes Icarus as a figure assimilated to Joyce's own creative purposes, and in a most intriguing and revealing way, in "After the Race." This is Phaethon.

The story of Phaethon is the longest single episode in the *Metamorphoses.* This dramatic and memorable passage runs from Book 1.750 to Book 2.328. Phaethon is the son of the god Helios and the human Clymene. When one of his schoolmates makes fun of him by challenging his divine paternity, Phaethon asks his mother for the truth. She assures him that Helios is indeed his father. Seeking firsthand verification, Phaethon sets out East to find Helios. Arriving at his palace in India, he is overwhelmed by its decorative grandeur: its walls are adorned with representations of earth, sea, and sky, and around the throne of Helios stand the Day, the Month, the Year, and the Hours. Alongside them stand Spring, Autumn, Summer, and Winter.

Helios confirms that he is indeed his father, and delighted by the appearance of his son, impulsively offers to make good on any wish he desires. Phaethon asks that he be permitted to drive the solar chariot for one day. His father is appalled at this arrogant request because he knows that the control of the immortal horses and fiery chariot requires great strength and experience, far beyond the capacities of a young human like Phaethon. He vainly tries to dissuade him from the task.

Phaethon is enthralled by the Vulcan-made chariot, admiring its style, its jewels, and silver spokes. Seeing his excitement, his apprehensive father cautions him to drive carefully, to keep the middle course, neither to go too high or too low or he would scorch the heavens or the earth. As a personal precaution, he tries to protect him from the enormous levels of heat and light that are ahead by anointing his head with oil. Nonetheless, Phaethon is not long on his course across the heavens before he runs into trouble. Fire-breathing monsters ambush his course: successively, a bull, an archer, a lion, a scorpion, and a crab. Quaking in terror, and failing to control the horses, he allows the chariot to veer off course, high and low, scorching the heavens and drying up the seas. He parches the pastures, sets the forests on fire, turns vast areas into desert, and burns the people black: thus Libya's aridity and the Ethiopians' color.

Apollo is besieged by protests from all quarters to curb the disaster. He hesitates until Earth makes her alarmed appeal to put a stop to Phaethon's career. He finally does this by intercepting his trajectory with a thunderbolt. Dismembered with his chariot, Phaethon and its flaming debris plunge into the River Eridanus. The Heliades, his two sisters, find his remains and lament his death, turning into poplar trees by the river, and dropping amber on its banks.

The best known version of this myth is Ovid's—which became canonical through the Renaissance—as Joyce would have encountered it (William Anderson, 229).[39] From his schoolroom reading of Ovid, Joyce's attention would have been drawn to the obvious similarities between this story and that of Icarus, which was on his assigned curriculum for 1897 (Bradley, 129). And again, in his subsequent study of the *Inferno*, he would have recognized the poetic justice in Dante's comparison of this pair of youthful failures (17.106–14). The earliest usage of the word Phaethon itself is as a Homeric epithet of the Sun (*Iliad* 11.735 ff.), only later becoming the name of his scion.

The name enters English usage (via French) as the name of a particular kind of horse-drawn carriage with four outsize wheels, lightly sprung, and built for speed. In the 1920s several automobile manufacturers developed an open-topped tourer with large wheels that they named a phaethon. The name survives today in Volkswagen's flagship vehicle, the Phaeton (2002).

Amidst the formal assignments that accompanied the study of classical texts—translation, grammar, the composition of verses in proper verse form (Bradley, 129)—Joyce would have been attracted to the myth of Phaethon for two principal reasons: its theme of the verification of paternity, and the youthful fall from pride to death. This close study of Latin verse, its rhetorical forms, meter, and spirit, would have supplied Joyce with a basis for his eventually large appreciation of the qualities of classical literature. The study of Ovid, because it was accompanied by the study of English verse and the writing of weekly essays in English, would have been mutually formative of his growing literary consciousness. There is a direct relationship between these experiences and most specifically between Ovid's account of the myth of Phaethon and one of his first creative efforts, the story "After the Race."

"After the Race" is a story about a young man whose naiveté in the ways of the world leads to his downfall. As with Phaethon, the principal object of his elation is "the swift blue animal/snorting motor" (*D* 45.12/17) of a mechanized adaptation of a horse-drawn vehicle that bore his name. Each of them has gone east "to see a little life" (*D* 43.27)—Jimmy to Cambridge, and later to Kingstown. During his quest for identity, which is his own version of his father's for the power that money gives, he "took to bad courses" (*D* 43.24) and finds himself in an at first confusing and subsequently terrifying world of monsters and fellows he considers "devils." On the one hand, the narrator's account of Jimmy's adventure commences with the sunset, centers on the lighting-up time, and ends with the sunrise. The race that preceded the events of this story began at sunrise. Jimmy, on the other hand, we are twice expressly reminded, loses track of time: on the train between Westland Row and Kingstown Station, a journey of at least thirty minutes, which "seemed to Jimmy [but] a few seconds" (*D* 47.11), and the several hours of card games that Jimmy passed in a drunken stupor, leaving him but "counting the beats of his temples" (*D* 48.30–31). The measurement of time is therefore the salient element that links the race, the story of its aftermath, and the mythological antecedent of both.

Like Phaethon, Jimmy has his father's permission to engage in this one-day experiment with the vehicle whose passage through space changes our notion of time. Given his business success and his son's poor record, Jimmy's father has good reason to be cautionary about the friends Jimmy has acquired at Cambridge and about making any investments in the venture. Nevertheless, having collaborated with Jimmy so far in seeking out the "pots of money" in the automobile business, he does not express any misgivings to which we are admitted about the venture, pronouncing the event "an occasion." Unlike Ovid's Helios, Joyce's Doyle Sr. does not foresee or attempt to forestall the disaster that awaits his son: rather, his sins of avarice and betrayal are visited upon his scion who, for his part, expresses no doubts about his father's judgments.[40]

Again, reading the works in concert, he may vainly think, like his mythological antecedent, that the name of that "merchant prince" (Doyle) may be enough to see his son through his straits (as Helios vainly anointed his son with oil): this sheer jointure of the mechanical and mythological would become a trademark of Joycean trivial-quadrivial literary humor (for example, "Jimmy d'oil"). Jimmy's journey has various elements that are like Phaethon's: made in the teeth of a high wind, swaying on the roads, and through the night. Like Phaethon, he travels in the company of figures who represent the archetypal symbols of earth (Ségouin), water (Rivière), and air (Villona as musician). Like Phaethon, his travel takes several forms of transport: on foot, by train, by automobile, by horse-drawn car, and by boat. Like Phaethon's, these moieties are measured in time. Like Phaethon, Jimmy repeatedly loses track: taking "bad courses" at Trinity College, breaking the decorum of the dinner-party by his conflict with Routh, becoming oblivious to the passage of time as they travel between the City Center and Kingstown, and of his IOUs during the card games. And again, like Phaethon, he allows an evidently historical insult from Routh (as we read, it unearthed in him "the buried zeal" of his "advanced Nationalist" father) to lead to a dispute that became "personal" (*D* 46.26). If something rebarbative ("you butcher's bastard" or "you Fenian fucker") escaped Routh's lips—and it is likely the object of the diplomatic reference to "personal spite" (*D* 46.26) in the spat between them—then considering that the insult that so riled Phaethon at the beginning of his story—Epaphus's questioning the divinity of his lineage—is nicely answered in Ségouin's irenic gesture of raising a glass to "Humanity" (*D* 46.27).

Again, like Phaethon's vain quest, Jimmy's includes personal affront, a vehicular pursuit of elation, and an escalation from domestic to sidereal auspices. The final scenario draws the two trajectories together: Phaethon's plunge from the heavens beneath the waters of the Eridanus and Jimmy's awakening to the consciousness of his failure as he floats in the estuary of the Liffey. The bottom line is that Jimmy, like Phaethon, is "elated" by the technology that seems to give him power over forces that he does not understand, and because of his father's impulsive gesture of paternal pride, takes into his hands reins that he cannot manage. Their common epiphany resides in the announcement of daybreak, which collapses Apollo's lightning strike and the "shaft of grey light" accompanying Villona's announcement of daybreak. The final dawn forces Jimmy to confront his failure—to feel his empty pockets—linking the realistic action to his mythological antecedent's death.

In "After the Race," moreover, Joyce seems to have adopted Ovid's detached, and even contemptuous, attitude toward Phaethon. Whereas Ovid's story has the shape of an epic, its central figure is not heroic, but foolish. His implied narrator concludes his tale in a mood of pity for Phaethon's sisters rather than as his elegist. Similarly, the stance of Joyce's implied narrator toward his naive protagonist is not sympathetic, much less tragic. In this, the moral stance is distinguishable from that in "The Sisters" (in which the narrator identifies with his inquisitive and intelligent protagonist) and "Eveline" (which adopts the stance of an intimate and sympathetic onlooker). It is worth keeping in mind that Ovid's story of Phaethon leads into a series of tales that deal with informers who treacherously pass on incriminating information. The informers are human, betraying their kindred to the deities (William Anderson, 225).

It is not without point that Joyce was similarly inspired in writing that his stories were designed to "betray" the hemiplegia of his fellow citizens to criticism, especially that of the gods. His appreciation of Ovid's narrative and poetic skills in managing the pace and making vivid the details of this long story by contrast with the relative blandness of his version may have been one source of Joyce's dissatisfaction with "After the Race." The brilliance of Ovid's description of Phaethon's journey, first on foot and then across the heavens in a tour-de-force of metamorphic travel, by chariot and figurative ship (*Met.* 2.163–64), has its understated analogue in the various modes of travel by which Jimmy moves east through the microcosm of his native city. Whereas Jimmy Doyle remains a flat character throughout the narrative and Villona's complexity of mind remains unexplored, Ovid's Phaethon passes through phases of psychological change: from doubt to pride, and from pride to terror; from youthful ambition to exercise grand power, and thence to a vain desire to escape the consequences of his proud wish (to paraphrase William Anderson, 227).

One of the qualities to which the young Joyce's attention would have been drawn in his study of Ovid's poetry is its rhetorical versatility. In the course of translating and parsing the Latin text, students would have learned to identify the various figures of speech and rhetorical devices of epic poetry, for example, the ecphrasis of Ovid's description of the Palace of the Sun (*Met.* 2.1–18), the humorous tone in which he catalogues the rivers of the known world (2.239–59), and the pathetic metamorphoses of Phaethon's grieving sisters, the Heliades, into two trees dripping amber by the river (2.340–66). These devices make dramatic appearances in *Ulysses* ("Cyclops") and *Finnegans Wake* (the Anna Livia Plurabelle episode).

More specifically, as Joseph Schork points out (160–61), Phaethon's fall flashes on to a few of the pages of *Finnegans Wake*. An extensive passage describes it in this way: "his ballbearing extremities, by the holy kettle, like a flask of lightning over he careened (O the sons of the fathers!) by the mightyfine weight of his barrel (all that prevented the happering of who if not the asterisks betwink themselves shall ever?) and, as the wisest postlude course he could playact, collapsed in ensemble and rolled buoyantly backwards in less than a twinkling" (*FW* 426.29–35). Here Phaethon is brought to ground by Apollo's thunderbolt because he inherits his father's impulsiveness. This theme is echoed in the senior Doyle's extravagant declaration about the "pots of money" to be made in the car business, the premise of his son's motorized quest. The passage links Phaethon's fall to the risky automobile business: here to "his ballbearing extremities," and elsewhere to his "pramaxle smashed" (*FW* 214.24), and the "navel, spokes [which] felloes hum like hymn" (*FW* 447.4) of the radiant chariot's crash.

Most specifically, and of particular cogency in the present exegesis of "After the Race," is the passage describing the ecological damage to Ireland perpetrated by the invasion of the motorcar:

> We who live under heaven, we of the clovery kingdom, we middlesins people have often watched the sky overreaching the land. We suddenly have. Our isle is Sainge. The place. That stern chuckler Mayhappy Mayhapnot, once said to repeation in that lutran conservatory way of his that Isitachapel-Asitalukin was the one place, *ult aut nult,* in this madh vaal of tares (whose verdhure's yellowed

therever Phaiton parks his car while its tamelised tay is the drame of Drainophilias) where the possible was the improbable and the improbable the inevitable. (*FW* 110.4-12)

This passage sets the interests of the ordinary inhabitants of Ireland ("we middlesins people") who live in the natural world of clover and sunrise, against those who spout neocolonial condescension, "that stern chuckler" Sir John Pentland Mahaffy and his protégé, Oliver St. John Gogarty. Gogarty was well known around Dublin for his primrose Rolls Royce, which had, at the time this passage was written, killed a child. These associations between the myth of Phaethon, Oliver Gogarty, motorcars, sunrise, and Jimmy Doyle seem to have lodged permanently in Joyce's tenacious memory.

Inevitably, therefore, for the student of Ovid, the rhetorical value of handling particular and identifiable figures of speech came as aspects of the same process. The student of Ovid would be familiar with the exercise of identifying rhetorical figures and scanning his lines as ways of ordering, feeling, and judging Ovid's poetic effects. These would include, in his account of Phaethon, some of the following: the near-perfect chiasmus of *sors tua mortalis, non est mortale, quod optas* [you are a mortal: what you want is not for mortals] (*Met.* 2.56); alliteration: *flumineae volucres, medio caluere Caystro* [of the Maeonian banks, sweltered in the middle of the Cayster] (2.253); the personifications of Time (2.23–30); anaphora: *illic frena iacent, illic temone revulsus* [There lay their harnesses, there the axles ripped from] (2.316); paradox: *ultima prona via est et eget moderamine certo: / tunc etiam quae me subiectis excipit undis, / ne ferar in praeceps Tethys solet ipsa vereri* [The last part of the way is sheer and needs a sure control; then even Tethys herself, who receives me in her waters / underneath, tends to fear I'll be brought down head first] (*Met.* 2.67–69); zeugma and oxymoron: *intonat et dextra libratum fulmen ab aure / misit in aurigam pariterque animaque rotisque* [He thundered and balanced the lightning bolt by his right ear / and sent it against the charioteer and drove him all at once from life] (*Met.* 2.311–13). And, throughout, the student of Ovid would read Ovid's preference for balanced, but expressive dactylic lines, such as *sponte sua properant, labor est inhibere volentes* [they hurry of their own accord; as they fly along, the task is to hold them back] (2.128), and the emphatic double spondee with which he ends the catalogue of mountains: *nec prosunt Scythiae sua frigora: Caucasus ardet*

/ *Ossaque cum Pindo maiorque ambobus Olympus / aeriaeque Alpes et nubifer Appenninus* [Nor was Scythia helped by her cold: the Caucasus blazed / and Ossa together with Pindus, and Olympus bigger than both of them, / and the airy Alps, and the beclouded Appenines] (2.224–26); and throughout, his facile management of pace, switches from formal to colloquial language, sensitive rhythmic switches, and knowing citations of Virgil, Lucretius, and himself.

Thus, we can see that in writing "After the Race" as a partial redaction of Ovid's treatment of the Phaethon myth, Joyce is doing more than simply miming some of its narrative moves. He is as well putting to the services of modernist prose fiction some of the rhetorical tropes he learned in his study of this Latin classic. The echoes of Ovidian rhythm and alliteration that can be overheard in such phrases as "unusually friendly with Villona" (*D* 45.34), "The dinner was excellent, exquisite" (*D* 46.4), and "the men devising original figures" (*D* 47.26–27) are but random poetic elements in the large ambitions that Joyce has for even so slight a fiction as this: a design that embraces personal, historical, mythological, and anagogical levels of signification.

Finally, we should recall that in its original version this story first appeared above the name of Phaethon's more famous analogues in the *Metamorphoses*. This was the inventive but foolish son of the gifted Daedalus.

7

The Infernal

Filled though it is with verifiable "street furniture," "After the Race" is moored above infernal fires. Consider this familiar Irish folktale:

"Jemmy Doyle in the Fairy Palace"
My father was once coming down Scollagh Gap on a dark night, and all at once he saw, right before him, the lights coming from ever so many windows of a castle, and heard the shouts and laughing of people within. The door was wide open, and in he walked; and there on the spot where he had often drunk a tumbler of bad beer, he found himself in a big hall, and saw the king and queen of the fairies sitting at the head of a long table, and hundreds of people, all grandly dressed, eating and drinking. The clothes they had on them were of an old fashion, and there was nothing to be seen but rich silk dresses, and pearls, and diamonds on the gentlemen and ladies, and rich hangings on the walls, and lamps blazing.

The queen, as soon as she saw my father, cried out, "Welcome, Mr. Doyle; make room there for Mr. Doyle, and let him have the best at the table. Hand Mr. Doyle a tumbler of punch, that will be strong and sweet. Sit down, Mr. Doyle, and make yourself welcome." So he sat down, and took the tumbler, and just as he was going to taste it, his eye fell on the man next him, and he was an old neighbour that was dead twenty years. Says the old neighbour, "For your life, don't touch bit nor sup." The smell was very nice, but he was frightened by what the dead neighbour said, and he began to notice how ghastly some of the fine people looked when they thought he was not minding them.

So his health was drunk, and he was pressed by the queen to fall to, but had the sense to take the neighbour's advice, and he only spilled the drink down between his coat and waistcoat.

At last the queen called for a song, and one of the guests sang a very indecent one in Irish. He often repeated a verse of it for us, but we didn't know the sense. At last he got sleepy, and recollected nothing more only the rubbing of his legs against the bushes in the knoc (field of gorse) above our place in Cromogue; and we found him asleep next morning in the haggard, with a scent of punch from his mouth. He told us that we would get his knee-buckles on the path at the upper end of the knoc, and there, sure enough, they were found. Heaven be his bed![1]

This story is a fine example of motif F211 in Stith Thompson's *Motif-Index of Folk-Literature*: "Fairyland under a hollow knoll (mound, hill, sídh)," of which there are many variants in Celtic literature and modern Irish and British folk and fairy lore.[2] It is a counterpart to motif F212, "Fairyland under water," which, again, makes many appearances in the written and oral culture. The Celtic Otherworld is imagined as either *faoi thalamh* [under ground] or *faoi thoinn* [under sea], and accessible by entering a cave or *bruidhean*, or by fairy horse or boat (MacKillop, s.v. "Otherworld").

The structural, verbal, and dramatic similarities between this fairy tale and the third scene (and some elements in the second) of "After the Race" argue that the relationship between the folk figure and the literary character is more than coincidence. The fairy tale involves the enthralling of the naive traveler Jemmy Doyle, during the course of a night journey through unfamiliar territory, by the lights of an opulent and exotic abode. By the station gate stands the ticket-collector who evidently recognizes Jimmy (who would have taken this train to his Trinity College classes). His familiar greeting, "Fine night, sir!" (*D* 47.13), would therefore be unremarkable were it not precisely situated between the two counterpart exclamations, Rivière's "It's Farley!" and Villona's "It is beautiful!" (*D* 47.4, 23). One effect of the contrast between the formally expressed exclamations of this Québécois and Hungarian and the old man's metaplasmic Hibernicism is the intimation of the ethnic bond between Jimmy and this servile spokesman for the native oral tradition.[3]

The ticket-collector is at once a sentry at the gate to the underworld and a harbinger of its mysteries. Sure enough, Jimmy soon finds himself an uncomfortable guest among an assembly of strangers and vaguely familiar figures over whom the Queens of Hearts and Diamonds preside. They are engaged in a night-long scene of feasting, dance, song, and drunken revelry. His initial fascination at the company who toast their guest yields to his impression that he is being deliberately embarrassed and deceived. He escapes these apprehensions into a sleep from which he is eventually released by the rising sun.

Besides these formal similarities between the literary and folk stories, the narrative fabric of "After the Race" is flecked with images familiar to the Irish storyteller. It moves from the pedestrian world of streets and labor to a fascinating and frightening sphere where wealth dissolves into wisps of paper. Then, twice as quickly, it moves back again into the gray quotidian daylight. This out-of-life experience whirls the son of a "merchant prince" at a dizzying pace past dull clumps of rooted onlookers, as he attempts to construe his strange company's language and song half-heard and half-understood in strained snatches. First he rides the "swift blue animal" (*D* 45.12) with the "snorting motor" (*D* 45.17), in this context a sly and humorous reference to the fairy *púca*.[4] Then the party of nightwalkers chance upon a short fat man who has made the "pots of money" (*D* 45.6) desired by the Doyles, Farley, a figurative *leipreachán* or leprechaun, known to Munster speakers of Irish as an *fairceallach talmhaí* [the short man—the farley—of the Underworld] (*D* 46.33).[5] A familiar of the company, he leads them to his floating palace where, under a reign of kings and queens, diamonds flash, hearts are bared, and magic portions are proffered. He engages in the exciting otherworldly competition of these companions—whether "good company" (*D* 48.3)[6] or "devils of fellows" (*D* 48.14).[7] The membership of Jimmy's entourage implies the typical diversity found in oral accounts of the trooping fairies. In an orgy of music, drink, food, dance, and gambling, they swirl around him until Jimmy finds himself swept off his feet by the increasing pace, against which his litany of cries of "stop!" are unavailing. Only inevitable dawn, which spells the end of all fairy revels, grants him surcease.

The prospect of the "pots of money" (*D* 45.6) promised by the "charming" Ségouin (*D* 44.1) conjures up the corollary image of the leprechaun's pot of gold, exciting but predictably eluding the night traveler; and suggests, in turn, the vanity of the Doyles' quest for easy riches at the end of the red, white, and blue rainbow. Is this amalgam of clever citations an ironic send-up of sentimental folksiness?[8] Or are we to take it more seriously, as sharing with its fairy counterpart metaphysical and moral cautions about the limitations of the natural order? Is it an elaborate joke or a caution on the need to behave with respect for forces in the universe beyond ordinary observation or offering immediate practical advantage? If the first, it confirms the condescension Joyce displays in executing his official duty as a reviewer of Lady Gregory's *Poets and Dreamers* and as the author of "The Day of the Rabblement" and "The Holy Office." The "senility of the imagination" he discerned in her fairy tales might still serve the needs of a beginner whose long-term ambition was "to become indeed the poet of my race" (*Letters* II: 248).

Joyce's words are an unreliable guide to what might be his actual practice. He had a singular capacity to discern the serious core in a trivial jingle while at the same time is possessed of the intelligence to deflate the sententious in a witty paranomasia. Part of this "jocoseriousness" he inherited from his rhetorically gifted father and part from his Jesuit training. High literacy and orality were not, for him, so much opposites as complementary expressive modes. In the rich anecdotes of John Stanislaus Joyce he recognized an urban and bourgeois version of the rural *seanachaí* [storyteller]: a man possessed of a remarkable memory, a natural, though uncultivated, genius.[9] His witty sociability was the source of much of Joyce's narrative gifts, as he acknowledged. His father's stories represented an often fatuous though deeply felt nationalism: nurturing a long-held sense of political resentment, the "suppressed rage" of Irish Catholics since the Tudors. At the same time, although a skeptic about the exaggerated claims of the Church in the spiritual realm, he was no materialist: he kept silent on the "deep questions," while maintaining an array of superstitions embarrassing to any rationalist. We must keep an open mind on how these forces are likely to reveal themselves even in his apparently least satisfactory and objective fictions.

The interest in Irish fairy lore, as in its European counterparts, is imbued with the spirit of nationalism. It is one of the marks by which the distinctive and local is celebrated. It purportedly provides access to the pre-Christian substratum in regional culture, commemorating the sense of the numinous surviving among the unlettered. While social realists would account for its imaginative force as arising from counsels of caution enjoined upon the young—to avoid this or that place, or this or that deviant person—romantics view fairy lore as articulations of imaginative traditions forced into retreat by urbanization and industrialism, and conventional popular Christianity looked on them as figurations of the vanquished faiths—or "superstitions"—of Celtic Ireland. To the leaders of the Irish Literary Revival, fairy lore served these three premises in various ways; but politically, it served to offer the image of a common imaginative ground before Christian evangelization (which triaged the denizens of the Otherworld into the saints in Heaven, the damned in Hell, and the suffering souls in Purgatory), the depredations of colonialism and the sectarian divisions fomented by the Reformation. Fairy lore offered a popular, oral, and democratic counterpart to aspects of the national imaginative tradition rediscovered in the medieval Irish literary sagas roused from their centuries of linguistic sleep.

Bruidhean Tale

The stories of the two Jimmy Doyles seem to have cousins in the immediate oral tradition as well as a remote common ancestor. The case for an intermediate source closer to home and to the literary and cultural moment at which Joyce is writing, can, however, be advanced: in the *bruidhean* tale of Irish Celtic literature. This tale-type was a standard part of the narrative repertoire of the medieval Irish poet, and would thus be within the competence of a man who would accept the public compliment "that I was going to be the great writer of the future of my country" (*Letters* II: 248, September 5, 1909).[10]

One of the *bruidhean* tales most widely collected in the oral tradition is *Bruidhean Chaorthainn* [*The Fairy Palace of the Quicken or Rowan Tree*]. A translation can be found in a book with which Joyce was familiar, P. W. Joyce's *Old Celtic Romances* (1879: 123–53).[11] Patrick Pearse, whose Irish classes Joyce attended for a period (*JJII* 61), edited a sixteenth-century version of the tale (1908). Irish topographical history lists five or six *bruidne* in early Ireland. Among them is Da Derga's by the River Dodder in Dublin, the focus of the eighth or ninth-century narrative *Togáil Bruidne Da Derga* [*The Destruction of Da Derga's Hostel*]. As John Kelleher demonstrated, this non-Fenian *bruidhean* tale is a structural model for "The Dead."

The *bruidhean* tale is one kind of Fenian narrative in which Finn and his men are invited to a feast in the Otherworld, an occasion that turns into a trap for Finn and his men who find themselves being hosted by their supernatural enemies. Finn is nearly killed, but escapes with new knowledge of the Otherworld, and therefore his excursion can be viewed as a shamanic journey beyond the human world (Nagy, 306).

A shaman can travel to and from otherworlds, especially the world of the dead. His function is to protect members of society from malignant external forces. The shaman is especially knowledgeable; and in his relationships with the Otherworld, the shaman is at first victimized, but later acquires the power to become a true shaman and control his adversaries. In this way, much as the shaman guards the human world's boundary, the Fianna guard the harbors of the country from the violence of foreigners. They are "border guards" defending Ireland from human invaders or expelling malevolent otherworldly beings from the human realm.

Here is the medieval tale type from which the fairy story of Jemmy Doyle among the fairies is descended. The fluid folk memory has dissolved much of the abrasive terror and acidic humor from its ancestor's doughty armor.[12] It is relevant to one of the purposes of the present enquiry that until Whitley Stokes rendered "Find and the Phantoms" into English, it remained for seven centuries, sequestered in the obscurity of Medieval Irish. The publication of such texts, along with the collection of oral tales, comprised two of the foundation stones upon which Yeats and Lady Gregory aimed to construct the Irish Literary Revival. To the extent that Joyce's little story pays simultaneous homage to both of these *Penates*, therefore, it stakes a property claim within that domicile.

Read as three historically discrete forms of *bruidhean*, "Find and the Phantoms," "Jemmy Doyle and the Fairy Palace," and "After the Race" exhibit this sequence of themes: there is a public competition between natives and aliens; this is followed by mutual gift-giving and the invitation to a feast; the hero enters an unfamiliar house into which he is at first hospitably received; initially enthralled, he soon perceives himself to be disoriented and threatened; his mysterious hosts turn minatory; he is offered indifferent food (eaten "for form' sake" [*D* 47.3]) and discordant music; a presumed insult leads to a heated argument; this becomes a deadly combat; only the rising sun saves the hero, who awakens to normality; he lives to tell the tale of his enlightenment. The whole story bears testimony to the existence of an out-of-time world that bears a mysteriously motivated grudge against the sensible order.

This imaginative genealogy switches on some ground lights upon the structure of Joyce's story. Just as the provincial text, *The Book of Leinster*, represents Finn as an antagonist of Munstermen, and as the folktale sees the Wexford countryman Jemmy Doyle almost falling afoul of the fairies, "After the Race" is a nationalist protest against Ireland's sovereignty by Continental mechanicians and the Doyles' dereliction of their posts as defenders of Ireland's claims to nationhood. Each text defends the historical memory of the province of Leinster. In each story the proffered hospitality is a mask for animosity: in the Finn story the fire both warms and blinds the guests, and the virtually raw meat is not really a gift but their own horses. In the oral tale the song and the drink are devices to lure and permanently detain Jemmy in the kingdom of the fairies; and in Joyce's story, the alcohol and card games are the means by which the naive Jimmy Doyle is fleeced: a warning of caveat investor. Similarly, as Finn learns that behind the appearance of the sporting challenge of a horse race lies the treacherous animosity of the Munstermen, and as Jemmy Doyle learns that his apparently jovial and animated fairy hosts are actually custodians of the realm of the dead, so should Jimmy Doyle take warning that his Continental and perhaps Yankee friends may harbor the same colonizing aspirations that history has taught him about the English Rouths.[13]

"Jemmy Doyle and the Fairy Palace" is a South Leinster variant of Thompson's motif F211. As it happened, the 1903 Gordon Bennett Cup Race coursed through the ancient province of Leinster, a point about which its various nationalist critics were exercised. They protested that it rattled the bones of the kings and saints of that province lying in their churchyards. Its linkage with King Edward VII's visit, moreover, celebrated the British usurpation of the ancient native provincial royalty.

This brings into focus one interesting aspect of the symbolic and topographic design of Joyce's story. We revisit, yet again, the relationship between the setting in which the action of the story begins—the "Naas Road" (*D* 42.3)—and the setting in which it concludes, Kingstown Harbour. As we have already noted, the first sentence invokes the town of Naas: *Nás na Rí* [the meeting place of the kings]. Until the tenth century it was the site of the residence of the kings of *Laighin* (Leinster), the O Moores, MacMorroughs, O Byrnes, O Kinsellas, Murphys, and Doyles (MacKillop, s.v. "Nás"; MacLysaght, map insert, "Ireland 1300–1600"). The ancient and medieval town of Naas consisted of a cluster of monasteries and churches, a market place, and at the center, the royal palace.[14] We have seen, too, that the story concludes in a place renamed in honor of the royal visit of King George IV in 1821, Kingstown (Bennett, s.v. "*Dún Laoghaire*"). This renaming—from Dún Laoghaire [Fortress of Leary]—dishonored the fifth-century provincial monarch Lóegaire MacNéill, King of Tara.[15]

These oppositions—between Irish provincial kings and between native and imperial kings—might appear remote from the issue and design of Joyce's story were they not to appear at its formal extremities and were they not mediated by an image that would have been familiar to any Dubliner reading the *Irish Homestead:* the equestrian statue of King William III, the champion of English Protestant colonialism, by which the action momentarily pauses. As we have seen, this pause occurs at the precise center of the narrative. These historically complex references are part of the chiastic design of Joyce's work that, as we have also seen, alludes to the dual monarchy of Austria-Hungary and surfaces in the literal action of the story in the toasts to the Queen of Hearts and the Queen of Diamonds, the Viennese Marie Antoinette, Queen of France, respectively.[16]

The major illumination that arises from the uncovering of this genealogy, however, is on the experience of the metaphysical traveler. Embarking on a journey that at first appears entertaining and harmonious, he passes from the realm of the normal and human into the sphere of the preternatural. In the Fenian tales, a frequent preamble to this crossing over is a horse race. This is a reflection, according to Joseph Nagy, of the widespread depiction, in ancient cultures, of shamanic types riding into the Otherworld (309). The equine images with which the narrator of "After the Race" endows the French car ("the swift blue animal . . . the snorting motor" [*D* 45.12–17]) and the Celtic etymology of "car" support the contention of the imaginative linkages between his story and the *bruidhean* tale.

The violation of the norms of hospitality—commercial exploitation under the guise of social interaction—enables this shift. Thus the story exposes the pretenses of friendship adopted by commercial culture by contrast with the ideal principles of a spiritual world that is not compromised by such engagements. The implied narrator of "After the Race" is not interested in the race or the card games but in what they mask of the voracious appetite of civilized men. The reader who pays attention to the nuances of this apparently dispassionate fiction discovers the traces of Joyce's fictional bite. At the same time, the implied narrator whose alter ego in the story is Villona, offers a hopeful alternative to social Darwinism.

Insofar as he is a persona of the shaman of the *bruidhean* tale, the story offers visionary hope. As Nagy concludes,

> The *bruidhean* tale is distinctly shamanic.
>
> As one who is "elected" or invited into the other world and can leave it unharmed and enlightened, Finn demonstrates his familiarity with the supernatural and his ability to travel in supernatural realms. Finn comes to experience and know the Otherworld in the *bruidhean* contest, and this knowledge is transmitted to the audience of the *bruidhean* tale; the narrative tradition functions as the fictional shaman's organ transmitting a vision of alternate reality. (320)

Even at this early stage of his career, Joyce was beginning to assert his powers of spiritual diagnosis. By observing carefully the postures of contemporary commercial culture and describing its machinations with reference to narrative conventions inherited from Ireland's imaginative traditions, he is able to discern the illness and divine its surcease. He is therefore—to paraphrase Nagy's formulation (321–22)—like the shaman who simultaneously possesses supernatural powers and is possessed by them.

Returning, then, to the historical record, we have this highly apposite aspect from William Bulfin's account of his visit to the Martello tower. Hearing out Samuel Chenevix Trench and Oliver St. John Gogarty, he noticed that the "other poet" [Joyce] listened in silence. Going upstairs, they stood on the parapet to "drink in the glory of the morning." Out of Gogarty's earshot and dominating presence and looking across Dublin Bay, they entered a long conversation:

> We looked out across the bay to Ben Edair of the heroic legends, now called Howth, and wondered how many of the dwellers in the "Sunnyview Lodges" and "Elmgrove Villas," and other respectable homes along the hillside knew aught of Finn and Oisin and Oscar. . . . We stayed far longer than we had intended, and talked of many things, . . . until . . . the shadows were shortening for noonday, when at last we got away from the tower. (Bulfin, 323–24)

In his own comprehensive way, Joyce mythologizes this scene in "Telemachus" and "Penelope": *Ulysses* begins and ends with complementary bifocal views of Dublin Bay: Kingstown/Dún Laoghaire and Howth/ Beann Édair; similarly, *Finnegans Wake* places the sleeping Finn's head in Howth (for example, Danish Hoved, "head" [Bishop, 34–35]). His disparagement of the sentimental Britishism, "Sunnview," may have had an immediate reference to the Gogarty residence in Glasnevin, named "Fairfield." In connection with the story that was forming in Joyce's head at the time, however, it allows us to entertain yet another potential source for its invocation of the Fenian "Daybreak."

Caveat Quester

A notorious incident from the latter days of Joyce's association with Gogarty offers a complementary entrée to the story that was germinating in his mind during the late summer of 1904. It intimates the hypothesis that "After the Race" is deliberately designed to accommodate a parody of a Theosophical allegory of the spiritual order. The evidence for this bold hypothesis is biographical and textual, and both broad and subtle.

It seems that the ribald and dissolute pair one evening stopped by the meeting rooms of the Dublin Hermetic Society, a group of Theosophists assembled under the patronage of George Russell. Among the effects of the absent would-be mystics was a suitcase of commercial samples: ladies' underwear. In a grand gesture of obscene disdain for the otherworldly celibacy of the society, the pair strung up a pair of knickers impaled upon a broom handle. Beneath this display was the legend, "I never did it," signed by John Eglinton (*MBK* 254–55).

We know from the testimony of both AE and Stanislaus that this contemptuous gesture was not spontaneous. From the time of his abandonment of the practice of the Catholic faith of his childhood, Joyce had made some serious forays into alternative spiritual territories. His brother recalls his temporary interest in Theosophy, then fashionable among Dublin's disaffected Protestant elites, including Charles Johnston, Yeats, and AE, who engaged in spiritual experiments (Foster, *Yeats,* 45–51). In 1901 he apparently read Madame (Helena Petrovna) Blavatsky's *Isis Unveiled* (1877) and *Key to Theosophy* (1893), H. S. Olcott's *Buddhist Catechism* (*JJII* 76), A. P. Sinnett's *Esoteric Buddhism* (1883; Curran, 32), Annie Besant, and Charles Webster Leadbeater. Temporarily intrigued, in his own words he "descended among the hells of Swedenborg" (Scholes and Kain, 63), and, recoiling from their stratospheric speculations, turned to Christian mystics whose credentials were less dubious: Thomas à Kempis, and saints John of the Cross, Teresa of Avila, and Catherine of Siena. He reproved his mystified brother's protestations, arguing that these writers were witnessing to "a very real spiritual experience you can't appreciate . . . and with a subtlety that I don't find in many so-called psychological novels" (*MBK* 132).

Joyce was in fact as skeptical about the truth claims of science and psychology as he was of official religion and the socially superior fads that sought to challenge its spiritual authority. As Stuart Gilbert—who knew him much later—records, "he had none of the glib assurance of the late-nineteenth century rationalist" (viii). His partiality to paranormal experiences and preternatural phenomena would embarrass today's readers. Indeed, the fascination with the visionary *Book of Revelation,* which led him to copy the entire text into a notebook, would make most contemporary observant Christians uncomfortable.[17] Long after he surrendered his subscription to the Catholic system of belief, he remained eccentrically superstitious, and permanently interested in attempts to account for the existence of the ordinary universe.

He was therefore sufficiently interested in spiritualism to pay a call on AE in the summer of 1902 and engage him in a protracted cross examination on Theosophical subjects such as spiritual cycles, planes of consciousness, "reincarnation, the succession of gods, and the eternal mother-faith that underlies all transitory religions" (*JJII* 99). He drew imaginative satisfaction from these speculations and the culturally eclectic terms by which they were conjured up, but no consolation for his sagging religious hope. We therefore find him subsequently writing that "words cannot measure my contempt for AE . . . and his spiritual friends" (*Letters* II: 28), apostrophizing the fatuity of Theosophy as if it were "summon[ing] a regiment of the winds" (Scholes and Kain, 64), and portraying himself as facing unpleasant truths while the clique of disconnected revivalists "dream their dreamy dreams" (*CW* 151). Thus, even when not stooping to a sophomoric practical joke, the denigration of Theosophy and its practitioners were never far from his mind during the months before his final departure from Dublin in the autumn of 1904. Even as he was availing of the hospitality of the Cousins household (September 1–2), who were spiritualists as well as vegetarians, he must have found it difficult to suppress his reservations about what he considered the naiveté of his kind hosts.

For all his objections to institutional religion, Joyce's attitude toward the spiritual world is intellectually and imaginatively much closer to a Tridentine view of the human condition than is generally allowed by latter-day Joyceans. Religion was at the bottom of his early education, depositing some permanent layers of trepidation or prejudice beneath the urbanity of his practical apostasy. As a small boy he would have been required to memorize the formulae:

> We are all made partakers of the sin and punishment of our first parents. . . . Our whole nature was corrupted [so that] it darkened our understanding, weakened our will, and left in us a strong inclination to evil. . . . Original sin is so called because it is transmitted to us from our first parents and we come into the world infected with it. . . . This corruption of nature and many other temporal punishments remain after original sin is forgiven. (*Catechism, ordered by the National Synod of Maynooth* [Dublin: Gill, n.d.])

This canonized dogmatic language claims to reconcile the divine origin of the world with the mysterious proclivity to evil in human affairs. It also provides a rationale for the coexistence of the orders of perfection or grace and of an imperfect nature rendering our human understanding murky and our will fitful, suffering mental and physical pain as we await the quenching of our natural self-consciousness.

At the center of the Christian view of the world is this interpretation of our basically good nature as intended and created by God, its flaws redeemable only through the saving grace earned by Christ. This is not so much a historical or mythological statement as an essentialist description of the human predisposition to misjudgment and moral wrong. In this view, the forces of evil are not absolute, but of human making; and to be human, therefore, is to be in need of salvation. Side by side with this image of our irresolute nature there is the picture of the ideal human being revealed and promised in Christ, the likeness of God in human flesh.

It is a central mystery of faith, apparently an absurd sentimentality in the modern age that accepts scientific theories as likely truths. Joyce's personal and intellectual problems with this worldview should not lead us to discount the degree to which he remains in imaginative sympathy with it. He understands and is emotionally sympathetic with the Church's intellectual efforts over two millennia to construct a Christian anthropology and sift from the scriptural evidence the nuggets out of which doctrinal orthodoxy is amalgamated.

An attentive reading of Stanislaus's diaries from the period in his brother's life with which we are concerned here shows that Joyce was dismayed not by the Church's doctrine of grace (which he evidently admired), but by intellectually incompetent, slovenly, and bullying presentations of the Christian dogmas concerning sin, redemption, and divine justice. Thus, although Joyce withdrew his formal subscription to the practices its membership required, it still, in his view, commanded the field belatedly entered into by the Theosophists. The grace necessary for salvation reaches us through three channels: through God's continuous creation of the cosmos, and in His personal relationship with each of us through the sanctifying grace of the seven sacraments and the actual graces that move and accompany individual acts undertaken in the spirit of Christian hope. Spiritualism claims to draw up a cosmology and anthropology that acknowledges no sin, no need for repentance, and no salvation in Christ. It replaces supernatural grace with a naturally cultivated enlightenment, charity with gnosis, and Christian hope with a general optimism in the impersonal processes of metempsychosis.

Catholic apostate or not, Joyce regarded the Dublin Hermeticists with a skepticism deeply inflected by official cautions against amateur dabbling in areas long traversed by orthodox spiritual questers.[18] As Stanislaus recalled (January 1905), "Jim professed a great contempt for the morality of the Irish Mystics. He said their leaving the churches was useless and nominal, for when they left them they tried to become latter-day saints. Even as such they do not compare either for consistency, holiness, or especially charity with a fifth-rate saint of the Catholic Church" (*CDD* 156–57).

Magical Mystery Tour

Modern Theosophy originated in America during the 1870s and was promulgated through the writings of Madame Blavatsky (1831–91), beginning with *Isis Unveiled* (1877). The 1902 London Theosophical Congress gave it publicity beyond its reserved enclaves. Drawing on superficial acquaintance with many fields—Hinduism, Buddhism, Jewish and Christian history, modern science, and Sanskrit—it is easily dismissed for its impressionism and its wild numerological speculation. Despite its patent fraudulence as a system of knowledge, as we shall see, it offered a constellation of poetic symbols and terms to Joyce's spiritually enquiring imagination.

Spiritualism is both a reaction to Darwinian materialism and conventional Christianity. Since established western religions were unable to combat effectively the claims of modern science, and offered transparently mythic visions of salvation, spiritualists felt that it was incumbent upon them to offer an alternative. Spiritualism denies the idols of material progress and the Christian hope of a personal eternal salvation. Based on the assertion that spiritual realities precede, supersede, and survive all material phenomena, it claims to deduce a description of the processes of nature—between cosmic and human—deduced from a set of intuited assumptions about the invisible and divine order. It undertakes an explanation of these processes in a widely syncretic accumulation of ideas and symbols.

Drawing primarily on Hindu and Buddhist religious ideas, spiritualism invokes, in addition, many of the religions of the Middle East preceding Christianity: Mithraism, the Jewish Cabbala, the *Egyptian Book of the Dead*, and the Christian mysticism of Paracelsus and Emmanuel Swedenborg. Rooted in neo-Platonic idealism and Pythagorean symbolic numerology, it is vigorously opposed to atheism and materialism. Theosophy is essentially a modern revival of Gnosticism. It differs from Judaism and Christianity in denying particular divine revelation and a personal god. It differs from comparative religion in that it is not agnostic: hospitable to the insights of all religions, it affirms the absolute reality of the invisible spiritual order. It claims that access to knowledge about the divine can be attained through meditative practice assimilated from its symbol system. Since these insights are only available to initiates, it attracted disaffected Christians or agnostics repelled by modish moralizing and vulgar trading in spiritual goods.

It sees the cosmos as the product of a perpetual conflict of supernatural and impersonal opposites, history as cyclical, and individual existence as an emanation of spiritual evolution through metempsychosis. While inhabiting a material body, the soul appears to be individuated; but like all phenomena declaring themselves to human perception, this is an illusion. After death, it is absorbed into the universal spirit, the Supreme Soul. Disdaining simple faith in the literal realities of the individual soul, heaven, and hell, spiritualism condescends to popular Christian orthodoxy. It aspires to direct access to spiritual realities through occult rituals such as séances. It proposes that true art expresses the tension between eternal oppositions, informed by esoteric doctrines, symbolist speculation, and numerology. It is not readily accessible to commonsense readers whose cultural literacy is bounded by the hegemonies of popular culture, established religion, and the political order.

Turn-of-the-century Theosophy shared some of the paradigms and ideas that prevailed in nineteenth-century science: the evolution of life forms, social Darwinism, and racialism. Although Theosophists advocated toleration of races of lesser accomplishment, their position elevated spiritual enlightenment over charity. In Ireland, therefore, it appealed to disaffected Protestants who could retain their sense of ethnic superiority over the mass of native Irish Catholics while also considering themselves more enlightened than their co-religionists. The cult never had a large following, and was diminished in influence when certain of its leaders—Blavatsky and Leadbeater—were exposed as dishonest in some of their divinatory claims and personal dealings. That their supernatural and preternatural assertions were based on appeals to divine revelation and not amenable to verification was a major weakness that Theosophy shared with all religions. Theosophy, nevertheless, had some temporary influence on the arts—on Yeats's poetry, Piet Mondrian's and Wassily Kandinsky's painting, and Alexander Scriabin's music, for example—and in this respect it enters the present elucidation of the design and theme of "After the Race."

Theosophy holds that what science calls "objective facts" are a "positive unreality," an illusion called *Maya*. They are the reflection—or emanation—of Eternal Reality (Blavatsky, *Key to Theosophy*, 58). There is no original creation, but all existence, cosmic and human, is but a phase in a constant and eternal progressive cyclical oscillation. These cycles provide for, in Blavatsky's words, "the periodical and consecutive appearances of the universe from the subjective to objective plane of being, at regular intervals of time, covering periods of immense duration" (67). Rejecting the stark dualism of Plato and Saint Paul, Blavatsky claims that she has access to a highly systematic knowledge of the real spiritual worlds beyond the appearances available to individual observation or the apprehension of rational science.

> As the sun rises every morning on our objective horizon out of (to us) subjective and antipodal space, so does the universe emerge periodically on the plane of objectivity, issuing from that of subjectivity—the antipodes of the former. This is the "Cycle of Life." And as

the sun disappears from our horizon, so does the universe disappear at regular periods, when the "universal Night" sets in. The Hindus call such alternations "The Days and Nights of Brahma," or the times of *manvantara* and *pralaya* (dissolution). The Westerners call them Universal Days and Nights if they prefer. (57)

What we perceive as a single entity—the sun, our globe—is in reality but a material emanation of a chain of seven occluded suns or globes in the process of evolution.

And just as each of these complementary cosmic cycles evolves in a sequence of seven stages, so does human existence. During evolution on each of the globes of the earth-chain, the human life-wave passes through seven evolutionary stages. These are called "root-races," of which we are at present in the fourth stage of the fifth root-race. Each "root-race" reaches its evolutionary zenith at a midpoint until, or encountering a cataclysm, it begins to sink into decline, meanwhile producing the next root-race (Sinnett, 45–65).

Each human being is the product of seven principles, an Upper Triad and a Lower Quaternary. The Upper Triad comprises mind/intelligence (*Manas*), Spiritual Soul (*Buddhi*), and Spirit (*Atman*). The Lower Quaternary is composed of the physical body (*Sthula Sharira*), the astral double (*Linga Sharira*), principle of life (*Prana*), and passionate nature (*Kama*). The human personality as we each know it is but the Shadow of the Self, the Unknown Root of the perpetually changing apparent identity to which we aspire. The person whom we think ourselves to be or the one we meet in the street is, therefore, but a shade, or astral projection of the invisible spiritual being. To this bodily aspect of the double we actually are as a result of our anthropological descent from pure, celestial Being, the Theosophists give the Sanskrit name of *Chhaayaa* or *Chhāyā* (*Encyclopedic Theosophical Glossary*, s.v. "Chhaya." Cited henceforth as *ETG*).

Throughout our temporary, mortal lives, we are in perpetual psychological flux, while we pass through one of a series of incarnations toward *Atman*. Any notion of a fixed identity is an illusion, either in our present lives or in any condition that we might anticipate in a blissful heaven or tortuous hell. We must not be misled by language into the reification of ourselves or of others: unless our names remind us in some way of these realities—of our celestial descent, that we are doubles—they are likely to be impostures.

It was with a vivid sense of these irrational and counterintuitive fantasies that the author of "After the Race" undertook a clever satire on the "hidden mysteries" behind the public excitements of the Gordon Bennett Cup Race.

Root-Races

As we have seen, the literary technique employed in describing this overt dramatic action leads the attentive and historically informed reader to the revealing silences at its center. The implied action takes a complete solar day to traverse the entire geography of Dublin from west to east: through the most proximate, complete, single cycle of time and space within the experience of Joyce's originally intended readers. As we have seen, the story takes us from the illusions of the material world (*Maya*)—the empires made from meat and money—to the announcement of the Sun (*Atman*) by the single reflective figure in the company. This passage is marked by several motifs representing the metempsychosis or reincarnation of the soul (the recurring circles and doubles), and takes us through the "dark mirror" from day to night, from land to sea, and from the material to the spiritual realms. Whereas Jimmy Doyle may aspire to move from motoring to musical circles, he fails to arrive at the true appreciation of the music of the spheres. The hitherto inexplicably odd numerological patterns, literal doubles, and peculiar Theosophical terms of art suggest the hypothesis that we may be encountering a Joycean parody of an occult parable.

Among the express themes of the story is the projection and unmasking of illusion (*Maya*). We see, for example, Jimmy's parents' misplaced trust in their wastrel son, and Jimmy's consequent delusions about the friendships acquired in the course of pursuing commercial investment and the fast life. We are encouraged, therefore, to share the narrator's condescension to the fraudulent joys of commodified sports, and his exposé of the self-deceptions of constitutional nationalism and the devious machinations of imperial power in its management of public events. The narrative treats us to instances of false victories, disingenuous friendships, and the empty cordiality of speechmaking and fraudulent card games. While the race is putatively between the nations—symbolized by their green (!), white, red, and blue cars—it is more accurately understood as a competition between car manufacturers. Just as the winning German driver is reputedly a Belgian, he bears a Hungarian name, whereas the Hungarian in our story has an Italian. One of our characters is a Franco-Canadian, another an Irish-American, another a Dano-Irishman, and another is an Englishman who could well be an intelligence agent posing as a sports fan. Routh is apparently ignorant of what Dolmetsch has recently revealed of his country's achievement in the musical arts. Further, among the narrator's devices are the interposition of significant silences and several misdirections upon the unsuspecting reader. "After the Race" is not what it seems: it is not about sensational action but about the meditative reaction.

The story pursues Jimmy's movements through motoring and musical circles. In the first half, we are informed of the conclusion of the first of these—which had begun at sunrise that morning—and the second half takes us through its complement in the arguments about music, the choral march to Farley's yacht, and the rest of the night with Villona's playing as its soundtrack. That the Gordon Bennett Cup Race was conducted through seven laps and the musical scale governing Villona's waltzes, square dances, and voluntaries has a cycle of seven notes intimates the complementarity of these circles in the design of the story. These two symbolic circles represent the two halves of the day, during which—from dawn to dawn—our physical globe has passed through a single complete turn. In having his cast of characters moving toward the source of light—to become one of the signatures of Joyce's fiction[19]—surely confirms the archetypal character of a journey to which none but Villona is spiritually sensitive.

Images of multiple circles introduce each of these phases of the day: the "double round of welcome" accorded the French cars at Inchicore (*D* 42.13–14) and the "pale globes of light" suspended above the walkers on Westmoreland and Sackville Streets and ascending along the east side of Rutland Square (*D* 45.24). These images are, in turn, complemented by the report of the sun rising over Dalkey. Now, in his apparently innocent citation of the term "globe" (a Dantean allusion, as we shall see), Joyce is doing more than indicating that the lamplighter has done his nightly duty. In the lexicon of Hermeticism, a "globe" is not simply an object of astronomy, but a phenomenon of astral light emanating from the seven to twelve planes of occluded spiritual force. Every planet or sun is composed of several globes, properly described as a planetary or solar chain. The cosmos as a whole is a living organism composed of celestial bodies each of which forms a unity with companion globes on invisible planes (Sinnett, 29–44).

Thus, in invoking the image of multiple "globes" as mediating between the "double rounds" of the opening of the story and the "daybreak" that is its denouement, Joyce's narrator is raising the implications of Villona's announcement high above and far beyond the appearances of mere daylight. A pedestrian accompanying Villona and Jimmy north along Sackville Street would see just such a "chain" of globes ascending in series before him along the gentle slope of Rutland Square. Instructed by the spiritual intelligence of Theosophy, what Jimmy subsequently perceives as a "shaft of grey light," and Villona as the rising sun, the narrator sees as astral light, itself an emanation of many planes of cosmic force (which the Hermeticists called *Akasa* [*ETG,* s.v. "Akasa"]).

The action of the story conducts us, therefore, in Theosophical terms, through the two phases in a Day of Brahma preceding the dawn of another existence. These two phases are called the *manvantara* and *pralaya.* The *manvantara,* which encompasses the seven rounds of our planetary chain, traces the descent of spirit into matter (daylight), and thence the complementary ascent of matter into spirit (nighttime). This process of material differentiation and dissolution is necessary before the spiritual rebirth of a *pralaya* is possible (Sinnett, 171–84). In broad terms, then, we can observe that "After the Race" follows this structural sequence: its seven scenes following the action through the material culture of the day, and its gradual dissolution in the alcohol and confusion of the nighttime revels, before its termination with the dawn. *Pralaya* is the moment at which a universe or an individual—read Jimmy's illusions of self as a competent investor and man of the world—dissolves. It is entirely within the scope of Joyce's ironic humor that the cabin door admitting the shaft of gray light adumbrating this *pralaya* belong to an emissary of the dominant "race" of the twentieth century, the American Farley.

In view of its international cast of characters, Joyce's story can be viewed similarly as a lampoon of Theosophical theorizing about race. Whereas the sports event of the day and its counterpart, the card games, are metaphors for the struggle for political global dominance—whether about to be enacted in Flanders fields or commemorated in the game of nap—Theosophists view such events as mere shadows of the eternal struggle on the astral plane. The inhabitants of each globe in the eternal evolution of material and spiritual life evolve through a cycle of seven root-races before transferring their life energies to the next globe initiating a similar sequence of seven root-races there.

The characters in Joyce's story are all part of the fifth root-race on the current, temporary, material globe. This root-race, emerging from the Eurasian landmass, is dominated by Aryans, inheritors of the language of Sanskrit. They are about to be superseded by the next root-race, even now appearing in the Americas. American dominance of the age to come, in Blavatsky's view, will be accompanied by certain changes: spirituality will be on the ascendant over materiality, humanity will become androgynous, and the propagation of our species will eventually be furthered not by heterosexual coitus, but by will and imagination (*kriyasakti*). As new cosmic elements enter our sphere, we will develop a new sensory apparatus, the "sixth sense." This will produce many advances, spiritual, intellectual, and physical, so that the attainment of mahatmaship will be notably easier than at present.

In due course, this root-race will concede to the seventh: the mind-born sons, a race of Buddhas. While Farley's presence in the story does, indeed, appear to forecast American dominance of the new century (the results of the day's car race notwithstanding), it is ironic that he is the only character consorting with women. Nothing about Farley, his social habits or his wealth—except perhaps his appearance—resembles the Buddha. In any event, as a harbinger of the sixth root-race, Farley is surely an ironic personification of Theosophical speculation about what happens after the period in human history dominated by the French, British, and Germans, the races Blavatsky (consistent with the former usage of "race" as a synonym for nationality or ethnicity) called Aryans.

On the individual level, Jimmy Doyle is significantly introduced via the biography of his father. He is descended from a man who has "made his money many times over" by opening a chain of butcher shops. Jimmy then moves from "bad courses" at Trinity College to motoring and musical circles at Cambridge. This story shows his latest attempt to enlarge these circles to encompass the international trade in motors. In so doing, he is replicating his father's cashing in his "advanced nationalism" for "pots of money," and accepting "double rounds" of applause for his collaboration in the oppression of his fellow Dubliners. But even while so doing, in his clash with Routh he momentarily allows an atavistic flash of a lost patriotism to reveal itself. Within the bodily form bearing the recycled name of Doyle flutters the transmigrated soul seeking purification but once again deceived by the trinketry of pots, wheels, chains, and coins. In other words, Jimmy is a generational embodiment of a "native strain" that Joyce claimed to recognize in Gogarty, the betrayer of his nation. Jimmy Doyle sells his soul to the excitements of *Maya;* and the narrative appropriately tags his fate with the number thirteen, the mark of Judas.[20]

The Sacred Seven

In regarding the universe as governed by a septenary principle, the Theosophists were adopting one of the most widely held of primeval symbolic numbers (Sinnett, 17–28; Schimmel, 127–55). Permeating the Hebrew and Christian Bibles as representing universality and completion, the number seven embraces myriad instances from the original work week of creation to the rhetorical structure of the Our Father and the Book of Apocalypse. Hindu and Mithraic mysteries bequeathed to Greek and early Christians the notion that the physical and spiritual worlds reflected one another in septenary structures. This is reflected in texts as various as the Vedas, Pseudo-Hippocrates, and Tertullian (Schimmel, 129–42). Theosophical doctrine conceived the universe as existing on seven planes of consciousness (Buddhas), from the atomic to the divine. The human individual is constituted from a quaternary of creative principles: three spiritual (active intellect, passive subconscious, and the ordering power of cooperation) and a quaternity of matter encompassing the four elements and the corresponding sensual powers: air/intelligence, fire/will, water/emotion, earth/morals (Schimmel, 127).

In contemplating a story on the Gordon Bennett Cup Race, Joyce might have been privately amused—and stimulated to numerological fantasy—by the confluence of historical sevens that attended its staging. As noted in chapter 2, the race started at 7 a.m., its competitors igniting their engines at seven-minute intervals as they embarked on a seven-lap course. As we have seen, the other major news event of that seventh month of 1903 was the visit of the seventh King Edward to claim sovereignty over Ireland during the preceding proverbial seven hundred years.

In any case, we are not far into the narrative before we encounter the septenary motif that suggests that these recurrences are more than coincidences in a formless realism. The second paragraph has two principal subjects: a description of the welcome accorded the French visitors, and an exposition of the relationships, backgrounds, and motivations of the four young men. The rhetorical structure of the paragraph is an expression of the implied narrator's pedantic and mechanistic proclivities: moving from two synonyms for "first" ("victor" and "winner"), through "second," and "third," before arriving at what becomes his key phrase, "four young men," which enumeration is repeated three times (D 42.10–43.11). We are thereby introduced, in a deft but nonetheless explicit manner, to the story's inscribed numerological code. The 1-2-3-4 sequence points to the completion of the entire human sphere (seven) and its potential perfection (ten).

The quaternity comprising the material sphere (two squared, the ideal root of the lower levels) is clearly figured by the two pairs of young men, figuring the four material elements in nature: earth (Ségouin, the material man), water (Rivière, the flowing man),[21] air (Villona, the musical man), and fire (Jimmy, the excited man). The car they ride, with its internal combustion engine, "the triumph of the French mechanicians" (D 46.18–19), is the perfect symbol of the dynamic mutual harnessing of energies represented by these radical material symbols. This numerological figure reappears in the yacht scene, with what would become a recognizable Joycean ingenuity, when members of the quintet engage in a waltz followed by a square dance (D 47.24–26). This material quaternity, complemented by the astral triad, comprises the "key-keeper" of all nature, the number seven. Not before the narrative is completed, however, when light and life conjoin in unitary action, are we able to see the complete monadic being on this plane, the septenary individual. A review of the contents of "After the Race" confirms the presence of just such a numerological design.

Its readers follow the plot through a sequence of seven scenes: in the French car, walking the streets, at the Doyle home, in the hotel dining room, along Stephen's Green, during the trip to Kingstown, and floating in Kingstown Harbour. In so doing, we are invited to occupy with the implied narrator a sequence of seven points of vantage: Inchicore, Dame Street, Rutland Square, the hotel, Grafton Street, Kingstown Station, and Farley's yacht. There are seven characters, each distinguished by appearance, speech, action, or motivation: Jimmy, Villona, Ségouin, Rivière, Routh, Farley, and the ticket-collector. A sequence of seven separate onlookers testify to the action of the story: the clumps of people in Inchicore (D 42.4–8), Jimmy's friends who observe him in French company (*D* 44.16–17), the "impatient tram-drivers" (*D* 45.15), the "little knot of . . . gazers" on Dame Street (*D* 45.16–22), Jimmy's parents at the Doyle home (*D* 45.26–46.2), the ordinary citizens making way for them on Stephen's Green (*D* 46.32), and Farley's man who serves the light supper (*D* 47.29). Seven modes of transportation convey the action: car, tram, foot, horse-drawn car, train, rowboat, and yacht.

The narrator allows us to hear the voices of the seven characters through direct and indirect speech. We hear seven separate direct statements: "André!" and "*Stop!*" (Farley); "It is beautiful!" and "Daybreak, gentlemen!" (Villona); "It's Farley!" (Rivière); "*Ho! Ho! Hohé, vraiment!*" (the ensemble); and "Fine night, sir!" (the ticket-collector). We hear the same number of indirect statements: "the winning German car was reported a Belgian" (*D* 42.12–13); "to see a little life" (*D* 43.27) and "Such a person . . . was well worth knowing" (Jimmy's father [*D* 43.33–34]); "the quick phrase" (Ségouin and Rivière [*D* 44.9]); the "three good reasons for Jimmy's excitement" (Jimmy [*D* 44.14–16]); "money to be made in the motor business, pots of money" (*D* 45.5–6); and "pronounced an occasion" (Jimmy's parents [*D* 45.26–27]).

In taking us toward liberation and the light through such a labyrinth invisible to the unaided eye, it appears that Joyce is satirizing Blavatsky's approval of "the Occultist-Alchemist [who] spurning the gold of the earth, gives all his attention to, and directs his efforts only towards, the transmutation of the baser quaternary [which includes the physical plane of human existence] into the divine upper trinity [the spiritual, mental, and psychic planes] of man, which, when finally blended, is one" (*Key to Theosophy*, 201). "After the Race" is, indeed, permeated with citations that reveal it as a parody of the literalized spiritual accountancy of contemporary Hermeticism. Whether out of the habit of an obsessive-compulsive clerk or as a cue to the readers about his parodic purposes, the narrator persists in keeping the count of characters before us: noting that when Routh joins the party, the company was then five (*D* 46.13). This figure enters his subsequent calculations: he notes that after Farley's swelling the company to six, a square dance cannot, without creative effort, engage five participants (Villona's playing leaving him out of the equation).

That Jimmy, toward the end of the story, loses count of the calculations at the card games, and in the end is "counting the beats" of his temples is surely an ironic comment on his loss of bearings in the numerological labyrinth through which the narrator has conducted him and his readers.

A complementary aspect of this theme is that the story is centered on that calculative institution, the Bank of Ireland (*D* 45.15).

The length to which this exegesis has to go to pursue the evidence is a tribute to Joyce's ingenuity. Its obscurity, absurdity even, is evidence of his ability to parody occult theorizing with a sophisticated narrative technique in which there are many levels of reality hidden from plain view. Like Theosophical theorizing, Joyce's story, by its ingenious mechanisms, satirizes the pretensions of the Theosophical claim to "investigate the hidden mysteries of nature" (Blavatsky, *Key to Theosophy*, 28). The critical implications are that both the invention and the exposé of the "mysteries" of the occult are already within the skills range of this apprentice literary forger.

Humming Villona

The most intriguing figure within the Hermetic scheme of "After the Race" is that silent representative of the "spiritual life," Villona. No ascetic or nerd, he sustains his physical immensity by a large appetite: his pleasant recollection of lunch soon yields to his anticipation of dinner. As boisterous as the rest of them, he joins in the revelry with vociferous energy. A man of strong convictions, he is willing to risk social obloquy to vindicate his cultivated sensibility. He is also musically talented and knowledgeable about the history of his art. He is aesthetically sophisticated: from his lips springs the word "beauty." His principal distinguishing features are his silence and detachment.

On the one hand, just as he is singularly unimpressed by the fast car ride and its accompanying repartee, he is totally disengaged from the games of nap. As the single figure in the story lacking in the "solidity" of money (as Jimmy ruefully recalled, he was "unfortunately, very poor" [*D* 4.2]), he is materially unsubscribed to the significant action of the day. As a meditative man, he is not interested in electrical engineering; as a poor man, he is not interested in the card game; and as a Hungarian, he is not interested in the Great Game. His persistent hum voices his bemusement at the triumphant collaboration of mechanicians and electricians. By contrast, his music-making, his silent disappearance during the last great game enables this watcher of the skies to engage imaginatively with the primal source of electricity, listen to the music of the spheres, and appreciate the eternal cycle underlying all the rounds of quotidian existence.

Among the figures in the story he is, therefore, uniquely endowed in body, mind, and soul. He has an imposing physical presence and a cultivated historical sensibility; his response to the rising sun proposes a particular symbolic link between his historical taste for high humanism and his spiritual instincts for universal renewal. He responds to historical music—composed for lute and organ—and to the music of the spheres, as indicated by his sensitivity to the astral light transmitted through the rising sun. His hum, therefore, is both a defense against the tuneless roar of the engine and a sign of his satisfaction in mantric practice.

Representing the fullness of value in the story, a character consonant with the eternal order, Villona, is the only figure whose presence continuously bears the numinous numerological mark of seven. He contributes seven actions to the plot (he hums, alights and walks with Jimmy, dresses, remonstrates with Routh, strolls and talks loudly, plays music for the dances, and performs voluntaries during the card games); seven is the total of his spoken words ("It is beautiful!," "*Hear! hear!,*" and "Daybreak, gentlemen!"). His seven-letter name appears fourteen times.

He bears several marks that Joyce, from his reading of Theosophical works and personal acquaintances, would have associated with Hermeticism. He is an aesthete: associated with the arts of painting, poetry, and especially music. A subscriber to no church or creed, he responds with fervor to two natural serenities: the summer night and the rising sun. In introducing Villona as "an optimist by nature" (*D* 43.11), Joyce is therefore with quiet precision setting this figure apart from the theological tradition, beginning with saints Paul and Augustine, which centers the Christian life on the gratuitous gift of the divine grace of a loving and personal God. Villona is not a figure of Christian love or hope for individual salvation enabled by divine grace, but of benign male friendship ennobled by the arts, the fruits of the natural imagination, buoyed up by a guilt-free optimism unaided by supernatural intervention.

With his counterpart and opposite, Jimmy, Villona shares the distinction of having a double letter in his name (one of the peculiarities of the narrative—already noted—is that an unusually high proportion of the diction, seventy-five different words out of the total of a thousand, have double letters). This device serves the immediate purpose of identifying them not only as the most significant pair of characters in the story, but as singularly carrying the Theosophical mark of the *chhāyā* or "double."[22] In Jimmy's case, there are some signs of a suppressed or unrealized moral or social conscience. In Hermeticist terms, the "double" indicates the presence in the human personality of a temporarily mortal and an immortal soul. But in its own uncanny way, the double *ll* in Villona's name anticipates one of the major literal motifs of *Ulysses*.²³

Throughout the action of the story, Villona is the single character who is seen as if he were in continuous communion with what the Theosophists call the "astral." Throughout the phases of the day consumed with competition, calculation, and dissimulation, he is the sole figure who is continuously in concert with this level of existence at which all are one. Only at the very end does he announce the results of his inner quest confirmed by the appearance of the nearest symbol of this level of spiritual truth. His largely silent but alert presence is a continuous reminder of other fields of intention not expressly reported in the narrative. Not only has he uniquely cultivated in himself the gift that puts the spiritually cultivated soul in contact with the spheres or globes—of sound or music—he is singularly competent to appreciate the approach of our nearest star in the predawn hour, a subtlety to which the cheering gamblers are deaf. His singular gift is his musical talent. The social dimension appears in the music by which the dances are organized; its counterpart is his inner-directed humming that, in Jimmy's estimation, "would confuse anybody" (*D* 44.12–13). The narrator's implied spirit/body contrast here is apt, for Villona's hum might be imagined as bearing more moment than as a mere irritant to Jimmy's physical ear. And indeed, it does.

Acoustically sensitive readers may be inclined to concede that Jimmy has a point, because a humming sound has been subliminally echoing in—and perhaps irritating—their inner ears through the first four paragraphs of the story. The words "clumps . . . clumps . . . humour . . . humour . . . humour . . . humour" precede Jimmy's recorded annoyance; and the same acoustic motif continues its strum among the bass tones of the prose throughout the rest of the narrative: in the words "sum . . . sum . . . human . . . summer . . . instruments . . . triumph . . . summer . . . Humanity." Villona's humming is the dramatic counterpart to this aspect of the reader's subliminal acoustic registration of the tones of the story. It is also an indication of his consonance, despite the noise and silence around him, with a wavelength into which we have not been tuned.

We are allowed to entertain the image of this self-contained figure, continuously humming while sitting composedly in the back seat of the car. To Theosophical initiates, his posture and conduct are revelatory: he is chanting the keynote of a Hindu or Buddhist mantra. The "hum" or "aum" is the Sanskrit term for the mystical triphthong uttered continuously or used as an interjection in the chanting of sacred texts such as the Vedas. It denotes "sounding out loudly" the unity of God, and its practice the effort to put the individual spirit into communion with that of the universal spirit. Theosophical writers elaborate the pleasing speculation that every atom produces a sound, a song, so that had we the power of spiritual hearing (genuine clairvoyance) we would be able to hear an unimaginably grand symphony of sounds permeating the universe.

Closer to home, since each of the seven planets emits a separate note on the scale, together they comprise a complete harmony: the Pythagorean Music of the Spheres (*ETG*, s.v. "Music of the Spheres"). Thus, Villona's meditative humming, despite the immediate surround-sound of the jocular conversations, the car engine, and the applause of the onlookers constitutes an image of his Buddha-like sensitivity to this interstellar symphony. Readers sympathetic to this spirit will be gratified by the aptness of the instrument by which his meditation is interrupted: the gong (*D* 45.14). And at the conclusion of the story, when despite the cheering that accompanies the last great game, the singular tone of the rising sun registers with this "inner man": he is following his own previous injunction to "Hear! hear!" (*D* 47.33).

In this context, one sentence describing Villona's part in the conversation in the hotel deserves another look: "Villona, with immense respect, began to discover to the mildly surprised Englishman the beauties of the English madrigal" (*D* 46.15–16). Here we have the "huge" Villona (*D* 43.2), at another time "the noisiest" of the revelers (*D* 47.7), playing the role of cultural instructor on the subject of the English Renaissance. This role he will replicate and enlarge for the entire company on another level, bearing witness to the sun, the astral image of *Atman*. A Theosophical borrowing from Sanskrit, *Atman* denotes the seventh principle of consciousness, the point at which we are absorbed into universal Higher Self, and become one with the First Logos. In his figurative role, therefore, as a "human being, who through self-directed evolution over many lifetimes, has attained a lofty spiritual and intellectual state" (Blavatsky, *Key to Theosophy*, 101), Villona is the mahatma of "After the Race."

As the story progresses, we see his gradual withdrawal from the world of cars and cards where pots of money are won and lost. Amidst the excitements provoked by the advent of the "electrical age"—represented in the story by the "snorting motor" and the "electric candle-lamps"—Villona's meditative spirit apparently dwells unperturbedly on the source of these effects: on what the Theosophists call *fohat*. This is the cosmic force that emanates from the various suns in the universe, enabling all forms of energy and provoking religious awe. Its lowest forms, from emotional excitement to electricity on the earth-plane, are known to the Theosophists as *daivprakriti*. In drawing the revelers' attention to the sun, therefore, Villona gestures toward *Atman*, the source of the intelligent vitality enabling all phenomena, called *Jiva* (Sinnett, 66–67).

We see that the story sets Villona's aesthetic detachment against the world of competition, political power, and money. Translated into Theosophical terms, as a harbinger of the next phase of spiritual evolution, he is the constant figure through the two phases of cosmic, racial, and personal development represented by the two halves of the story, figuring the *mantanavara* and *pralaya* phases presaging the dawn of the next cycle. It is clear, then, that for all his economy, Joyce has conferred upon Villona each of the seven marks of the complete man. Uniquely in the story Villona exhibits signs of mind/intelligence (*Manas*), spiritual soul (*Buddhi*), and spirit (*Atman*). In his presence, name, and actions he is unambiguously endowed with a physical body (*Sthula Sharira*), an astral double (*Linga Sharira*), the principle of life (*Prana*), and a passionate nature (*Kama*).

From this perspective, then, Villona plays the part of a "Silent Watcher." This figure, as the dominant self in any system, serves as a sentinel on the rim of the circle of darkness, anticipating the arrival of the first signs of the next phase, that of light. Every system, from atoms to globes, is preceded by such eremitic harbingers. Within the small human arena of Joyce's story, Villona plays the role of this "voluntary exile . . . who has succeeded in liberating himself from the bonds of flesh and illusion." In Blavatsky's words, "he stays at his post because the lonely sore-footed pilgrims on their way back to their home are never sure to the last moment of not losing their way in this limitless desert of illusion and matter called Earth-Life" (*ETG*, s.v. "watcher").

"the path of prālāyā"

Stanislaus is correct that Joyce's original interest in Theosophy was serious: he was then looking for a substitute religion (*MBK* 131–32). Richard

Ellmann is close to the truth in the observation that it persisted among his interests for its poetic rather than its religious moment. He was evidently more impressed by its attempt to offer a systematic symbology rather than its pious generalizations (*JJII* 76, 99). Evidence of this interest appears in his subsequent return to the reading of other Theosophical texts, his hilarious lampoon of a séance in the "Cyclops" episode of *Ulysses* (12.338–73), and the invocations of Madame Blavatsky in *Finnegans Wake*.

The scattered references to Theosophy in Joyce's later writing are bemused, never complimentary.[24] The pièce de résistance in this respect is the amusing maltreatment of the séance. Studded with knowing allusions to the Theosophists' pretentious partiality to Sanskrit terms, and delivered as a parody of the circumspect overuse of the passive voice in their published minutes, it satirizes their highfalutin theorizing about (and effective trivialization of) the unknowable forces beyond human witness or verification. Bearing in mind that this is but one voice among many in this episode (and therefore not that of Joyce himself), it serves present exegetical purposes to identify the sequence of images and allusions in this single paragraph that he had already pressed into similar, but subtler, satirical service in the final scene of the story.

The setting of a "serene summer night" (*D* 47.15) becomes the darkness appropriate to a séance (*U* 12.338). The same classic Pauline symbol (1 Cor. 13: 12) conveys the idea of "crossing over" from material to spiritual realms: to Jimmy and his friends, "the harbour lay like a darkened mirror" (*D* 47.15–16), whereas the medium in "Cyclops" "had seen as in a glass darkly" (*U* 12.349). Farley's yacht, the site of dissolution and symbolic renewal, becomes (as already noted) "the path of prālāyā" (*U* 12.346); and the "motoring and musical circles" (*D* 43.26) of "After the Race" become the "devanic circles" (*U* 12.359) embroiling the company at the séance.

The more complex image of the "devils of fellows" (*D* 48.14) whose hands cut, shuffle, and gather in the cards around the table and clean Jimmy out becomes "the spirit hands were felt to flutter" (*U* 12.338) so that the medium "was still submitted to trial at the hands of certain bloodthirsty entities on the lower astral levels" (*U* 12.346–47). Similarly, the "excitement" of the "hilarious youth," with their "cheering," "clapping," and toasts, morph into "Mars and Jupiter [who] were out for mischief on the eastern angle where the ram has power" (*U* 12.359–60). This astrological trio represents the amalgams and conflicts of passion, optimism, energy, argumentation, and bluff that we have seen in the action of "After the

Race." Further transformations include the suspicious Routh, become the police informer, Cornelius Kelleher (codename C.K. [*U* 12.362–66]) and the hotel's pride in the advanced technology of its dining room, "lit by electric candle-lamps" (*D* 46.8), become the departed spirits' boast about "their abodes [that] were equipped with every modern home comfort such as tālāfānā, ālāvātār, hātākāldā, wātāklāsāt" (*U* 12.353–54). The inapposite conjoining of Sanskrit diction and these consumerist trophies of the electric age takes the restrained satire of "After the Race" to an explicit and absurd level.

The clairvoyant medium—whose double-*ll*d "earthname" (*U* 12.345) is Villona—emerges as "the etheric double" (*U* 12.340–41). His superior gifts of a reflective intelligence that enable him to instruct, entertain, and enlighten the company are transcribed as his opening up to the attendees at the séance the "summit possibilities of atmic development" (*U* 12.350). For this transformative denouement, the succession of images of "rounds," "circles," and "globes"—representing metaphorically the successive stages of spiritual purification (motoring, music, light)—has prepared the way for an epiphany of wisdom, bliss, and power. Thus, Villona's watchful scanning of the eastern horizon as he awaits daybreak becomes the medium's "tantras . . . directed to the proper quarter [whence] a faint but increasing luminosity of ruby light became gradually visible" (*U* 12.339–40). The "shaft of grey light" reported by the story's narrator (*D* 48.32) becomes the "orangfiery and scarlet rays emanating from the sacral region and solar plexus" (*U* 12.343–44). By these means, the moral enlightenment of Jimmy Doyle's potential epiphany, that he can repose any faith is the chimera of the "pots of money" to be made from the motor business, is elevated into the medium's exhortation to "all that are on the wrong side of Māyā to acknowledge the true path" (*U* 12.357–58).

These transformations support the contention that, at least in retrospect, Joyce recognized the manner in which "After the Race" was a perhaps oversubtle parody of a Theosophical parable and subsequently reused the material in his travesty of a Hermeticist séance. It implies a criticism of the partiality to esoteric practices by the Anglo-Irish Protestant elites, the self-proclaimed leaders (but usurpers) of the Irish Literary Revival. By the same token, the argument advanced above indicating the relationship between Joyce's story and Jemmy Doyle's visit to the fairy realms and its antecedent *bruidhean* tale from the Irish tradition both precede the modish Hermeticist séance. The burden of these comparisons, in any event, supports the proposition that there is nothing supernatural or even preternatural about Jimmy's experience. Although bearing images drawn from a spiritualist ritual, the complex technique of the story implies that the processes of human imagination—enabled and shaped by traditions of language, myth, religion, folklore, rhetoric, and history—in the hands of a superior artist, expose a fraudulent vein in the Irish Literary Revival and furnish the whole "truth" of the story.

Saint Paul: Christian Shaman

When Jimmy and his friends leave the solid ground of Dublin City and take the rowboat out into Kingstown Harbour, they are moving, like the figure in the folktale, into another world. There they indulge in an orgy of alcohol, music, and gambling where, like Alice in Wonderland, they are conjured into the presence of the Queens of Hearts and Diamonds (*D* 48.7–8). The description of the harbor as a mirror is apt since its enclosure by two beveled piers—a gnomonic frame—might be imagined as giving it the appearance of a hand mirror, but the narrator's simile that "the harbour lay like a darkened mirror at their feet" (*D* 47.15–16), and Jimmy's subsequent sense that his feelings about the company were "obscure" (*D* 48.8) move the figure from the merely fanciful to the theological.[25]

This sequence of images invokes the famous metaphor by which Saint Paul describes the clarity of our apprehension of divine love in the presence of God, by contrast with its obscurity to us in the natural world: "At present we see indistinctly [Douai-Rheims: "obscurely"] as in a mirror, but then face to face. At present I know partially; then I shall know fully, as I am fully known" (1 Cor. 13: 12).[26] The motif of biblical or theological references threaded through the text—"merchant prince" (*D* 43.21), "remonstrative" (*D* 43.28), "profane" (*D* 44.22), "mite" (*D* 45.2), "alight" (*D* 45.16), "homage" (*D* 45.17), disappointment" (*D* 45.23), "graceful image" (*D* 46.11), and "for form' sake" (*D* 47.30)—constitute between them a clearly credible context for such a reading.[27]

We are now in a position to appreciate the figurative force of the odd "impromptu square dance" (*D* 47.26) engaged by the quintet of bohemians. One of Joyce's few revisions of the original text of the story was the insertion of the otherwise superfluous reference to the "five young men" engaged in the dance (*D* 46.13–14). The fifth, or odd participant subverts the congruency, balance, or completeness of the foursome, presenting an image of the geometric gnomon (the fifth point within the square). This emendation seems to serve no narrative purpose other than the underlining of an apparent geometric anomaly that was to become one of the signature motifs of the finished *Dubliners*. The emendation appears to imply, too, that the symbolic significance of the incongruity between the number of dancers and the prescribed dance only struck Joyce as he re-read the original draft.

Joyce's revision, therefore, loaded an originally unintentional plot element with a symbolic weight with which readers of *Dubliners* are but retrospectively familiar. When the figure in this instance is further inscribed within that of the gnomonic Kingstown Harbour, the entire scene constitutes a double inscription of a symbol of the imperfect natural order and of the dimly perceived ideal world from which it descends, and to which it aspires. From this "fallen world," in the vision of Saint Paul, we are only redeemed by the power of the grace earned by Christ's sacrifice on Calvary. In its subsequent appearance in other forms (such as the quincunx of "Grace") and in the revised texts of "The Sisters" it constitutes a significant example of Joyce's progressive self-reflexivity. He develops the gnomon into a major motif in *Dubliners,* a figure of the limitations of our rational knowledge of ourselves and of the world about us, contrasting the realms of science and religion, imperfection and perfectibility: the relationship between the orders of tangible nature and imagined or hoped-for grace. In the figure of Jimmy's dance with his suspicious friends we have, therefore, Joyce's first invocation of the gnomon.

The breathless account of a dance interlude is peculiar in two ways. One (observed by the narrator) is that since there are no ladies present, Rivière is obliged to impersonate a female, and the other (implied) is that since there are five participants in a sequence of dances that require partners (the waltz and the square dance), they are required to "devis[e] original figures." The narrator tells us that this merriment is brought to a sudden halt by the overexerted fat Farley, although we are also allowed to entertain the possibility that the sexually dubious arrangements by which two of the partners have assumed female roles may have exceeded the bounds of propriety their host was willing to permit. The inference that his guests were somewhat reluctant to acquiesce is further supported by their eating the supper "for form' sake." The single word by which the narrator summarizes this sequence of dances, music, food, and drink, "Bohemian," points to a single and intriguing source in Joyce's cultural repertoire: the comic scene that opens the final act of Giacomo Puccini's *La Bohème*.

In the opening scene of act 4, Puccini's characters appear to have evaded these heterosexual threats to their comradely subsistence. During this interlude in the main action of the opera, we see them share a poor meal of bread, herring, and water, imagine themselves as exotic dancers, and chivalric combatants in a battle over personal honor. That this is a fantasy of homosocial escape from engagement in the world of material responsibility and heterosexual love is revealed in a sequence of sharp details expressing the positive value of patient suffering and hope for Christian redemption.

In the high spirits inspired by their mutual dependence, they pretend that the herring and loaves and a bottle of water are salmon, tongue of parrot, and iced champagne. Their straitened condition is aptly dramatized by their single wine glass. If this is a symbolic Last Supper, it is quickly undercut by their rapid clearance of the furniture for a brief pagan orgy of *azione coreografica* [choreographic action]. They rapidly go through a series of spontaneous dances—a gavotte, a minuet, a pavane, a fandango, and a quadrille—taking partners as the improvisations require. The libretto describes Schaunard as "*improvisando, batte il tempo con grande, comina importanza*" [improvising, he beats the time with great comic importance], while Rodolfo plays the gallant, dancing a quadrille with Marcello. When Schaunard takes the play-acting a step further, however, and dances a provocative rondo with his temporary partner, Colline pretends to be insulted at being taken for a lady, and the pair break apart in a mock battle. Arming themselves with tongs and shovel, the turns and jumps of this duel take the forms, in turn, of yet another dance, the rigaudon. All of these demonic high jinks come to an abrupt halt with Musetta's loud knock on the door and her announcement of Mimi's advanced (and soon fatal) illness.

As the summary suggests, this scene informs Joyce's handling of the merriment on Farley's yacht. In its treatment of the sequence of dances, the food and drink, the sexually dubious roles assumed by some of the participants, and the pretext under which it comes to a sudden halt, it is strongly redolent of Puccini's treatment in *La Bohème*. These dramatic similarities argue that Joyce's thematic handling of the limitations of homosocial relations at least subliminally invoked a small debt to Puccini's representation of the same in the counterplot of his operatic masterpiece.

In the present context, then, it figures as a momentary pagan reversal of the figurative Last Supper and the subsequent spiritual deliverance of the Bohemians by the spirit of Mimi's loving suffering and death. The conversion of each of her erstwhile companions from lives of hedonism to charity is borne out by their various donations to relieve her pains and especially Musetta's prayers to the Madonna combine to underline the Christian force of the conclusion to Puccini's opera. Joyce's borrowings from the final act of *La Bohème* imply that he understood it that way, since his story, like the opera, closes with the coincidence of Mimi's death and that great symbol of the Resurrection, the sunrise. In these respects, "After the Race" belongs within the "moral history" of Joyce's native city.

These texts are therefore inscriptions of Joyce's general aspiration for *Dubliners*, as he put it to Grant Richards: "I seriously believe that you will retard the course of civilization in Ireland by preventing the Irish people from having one good look at themselves in my nicely polished looking-glass" (*Letters* I: 64). The contrast between the sophisticated narrator whom Joyce endows with the capacity to handle all of this nuanced theological language is neatly caught in Jimmy Doyle's less instructed but archetypal uncertainty: whether the fellows among whom he was fallen were "jovial" (*D* 48.2) or "devils" (*D* 48.14). Joyce's narrator, familiar with Skeat, knew that the etymology of "jovial" lay in Jupiter and his divine good humor (s.v. "jovial"), whereas the word "devil" originates in the Greek Διαβαλλειν, "to throw across" (s.v. "devil"). The sly and pedantic narrator has twice used the verb "to fling" in describing the manner in which Ségouin and Rivière disport themselves (*D* 44.7, 48.6). This metaphor of the snare, trap, or tripwire of the devil (*insida diaboli*) thrown across the Christian's path by the devil (invoked in the prayer to Saint Michael the Archangel, said after Mass in Joyce's time) derives from citations from two of Saint Paul's letters:

> But they that will be rich fall into temptation and a snare, and into many foolish and hurtful lusts, which drown men in destruction and perdition. For the love of money is the root of all evil. (1 Timothy 6: 9–10)

> The servant of the Lord must . . . be gentle unto all men . . . that they may recover themselves out of the snare of the devil, who are taken captive by him at his will. (2 Timothy 2: 25–26, KJV)

The invisible snare flung across the unsuspecting Jimmy Doyle's trail is indeed the mirage of Mammon, the pot of money, the crock of gold, is the invisible Παγις Διαβολου, the devil's snare.

Personal Parallel

Returning to the biographical record, we can see that when Joyce wrote "After the Race" he had formed what would be the permanent personal relationship in his life. His faith in Nora's love had filled the void left by the death of his mother thirteen months previously. The crisis of faith which that death had provoked was past. It was to become the provocation of *Ulysses*. But in writing "After the Race" as a satire on Theosophical flailings about the spiritual world, Joyce was answering a question closer to his immediate needs. Presenting the figure of Villona in the accoutrements of a mahatma, a man of calm feeling and spiritual vision in a world of agitated action, he was proposing a sympathetic, but highly qualified, alternative to the Christian ideas of grace and love.

As this book has demonstrated, the figure of Villona has many antecedents in the literary tradition. As poet and outsider he is a Villon. And this medieval Villon has his antecedents in the ancient "Greats," Ovid and Virgil. The weight of the numerological evidence adduced in this chapter supports the further contention that by the emblematic double *ll* of his name, Villona represents the eternally parallel lines of rebirth that never converge in redemptive love. This doubled twelfth letter of the alphabet in Villona's name is complemented by the single appearance of the twenty-second letter *v*. Therefore, in the spelling of his name we have the inscription of a doubled double: a cipher of the Theosophical code in the story indicating that he embodies the current metempsychosis of the poetic spirit bearing witness to eternal recurrence.

The burden of evidence, then, is that when he wrote "After the Race," Joyce considered that May and James Joyce would never meet again in "another life." He was to return to these symbols in *Ulysses* in vastly complex ways: in creating the natural optimist, Leopold Bloom, the explicator of metempsychosis, the eternally alone figure marked, like Villona, with "a touch of the artist." For him the symbol of the crossed keys of the New Covenant is but an advertising gimmick. At the writing of "After the Race," however, his hour was not yet come. Meanwhile, in the

Theosophically colored habiliments of Villona we can discern some of the designs of a lately shuffled-off Joycean epidermis.

a riveder le stelle

Villona's announcement of daybreak has, therefore, literal, historical, allegorical, and anagogical referents. It announces the sunrise that ends Jimmy's nightmare. It reflects the image depicted in the poster of Robert Emmet's sacrifice and Arthur Griffith's borrowing of the image in his *Resurrection of Hungary*. It reflects the Christ's resurrection without which Christian belief, as Saint Paul writes, is in vain.

It is worth noting at this point that Joyce imagined political revival in the terms set by the Christian religious imagination. The final paragraph of "Ireland, Island of Saints and Sages" (*CW* 174), for example, indicates that he recognized the same symbolism in the rhetoric of Italian nationalist movements. In urging the Irish to "resurge" or else "descend into the grave forever," he is using the same expression *risorgere* from which the name of the nineteenth-century Italian movement of *Risorgimento* also derives.[28] It is apposite to recall here how the word "daybreak" appears in *Ulysses*. It does so only twice. The first is in reference to the milk woman in her lush field (*U* 1.401), where Stephen is evidently thinking of her as supplier of the morning milk and desiccated mother, the latter an allegorical figure of Ireland as she appears in the *aisling* tradition. The second use of the term appears in "Ithaca" following the answer listing Bloom's dead former companions—Percy Apjohn, Philip Gilligan, Matthew Kane, Philip Moisel, Michael Hart, and Patrick Dignam—with the report of the prospect that greets Bloom: "The disparition of three final stars, the diffusion of daybreak, the apparition of a new solar disk" (*U* 17.1257–58). The narrative language distinguishes between Bloom's objectivity and the implied narrator's sense that the phenomenon represents the mystery of spiritual renewal. And with the narrator's disappearance, the unmediated voice of Molly in her contentious predawn rumination, adds, "who was the first person in the universe before there was anybody that made it all who ah that they don't know neither do I so there you are they might as well try to stop the sun from rising tomorrow" (*U* 18.1569–71).

In citing this popular line of attack on atheism, Molly's amateur theodicy has the merit of documenting the permanence in Joyce's imagination of daybreak as a spiritual epiphany.

"After the Race," therefore, is a primary Joycean exercise in the Dantean mode as he set it forth in his *Epistle to Can Grande*. "Such an allegorical narrative," as Mary Reynolds puts it, "describing his subject under the guise of another which is suggestively similar, is Joyce's characteristic mode" (65). Readers of *Ulysses* will be familiar with this, and some critics have observed some adumbrations in a few of the *Dubliners* stories, notably "Grace." Such a formal principle, adapted from Dante, allows for multiple extended interpretations of the work. My proposition here is that in this, his third in the order of composition, Joyce has written his first Dantean story.

On the naturalistic level, as many readers have seen, "After the Race" exhibits the moral theme of avarice.[29] In this respect, it is a development of the theme of *Inferno* 7 presided over by Pluto the money god. In leading him around this, Circle Four, Virgil says,

Or puio veder, figliuol, la corta buffa
de' ben che son commessi a la Fortuna,
per che l' umana gente si rabuffa;

[Now you can see, my son, the brief vanity of the good things under Fortune's control, for which the human race distracts itself.] (Allan Gilbert trans., 54–55)

He goes on to explain that the goods of the world are distributed unevenly: one nation prospers and another is feeble, as hidden Fortune decrees. While the world pursues the vanity of seeking material advantage, we are unable to see how ultimate justice is served. It seems that Virgil is explaining to Dante that God's ways are not those of the world. In this respect, it casts the images of the "clumps" and "knots" of "the gratefully oppressed" Irish looking on in humble awe at the hilarious and triumphant Continentals in a light that represents the narrator's morally ironic view of these ostentatious visitors.

Joyce's citation of Dante is not merely moral, realistic, or ironic, however. As the foregoing discussion has held, it is technical, structural, and partially theological as well. There is some evidence that from a Dantean perspective, the sin under indictment in "After the Race" is not avarice but the violation of hospitality. If it is true, as many readers agree, that Jimmy Doyle has been inveigled into a business deal beyond his capacities or perhaps even cheated of his money by slick card-sharpers, then his hospitality—and that of the other big loser and owner of *The Belle of Newport*, Farley—has been abused. The slick Continentals have exploited both Irish and Irish-American hospitality. Now, in Dante's *Inferno*, the violation of hospitality is a subcategory of the major transgression, the betrayal of loyalty. This sin—greater than avarice—is punished in the deepest pit of the *Inferno*, in the third zone of the ninth circle.

Now, if the centennial commemoration of Robert Emmet's patriotic rebellion is the model for the advanced nationalism of Jimmy Doyle's father's early political position, his abandonment of it for the fortune to be gained from police contracts is its betrayal. And if, as Arthur Griffith's advanced nationalist position is to view the Gordon Bennett Cup Race as an effort corollary to the king's visit to upstage the centennial commemorations of Emmet's rebellion, Jimmy Doyle's patronage of the Gordon Bennett Cup Race acquiesces in that diversion from the urgent national business to which his father was once committed. Jimmy's flare-up with Routh is an indication that he has at least some residual guilt feelings in this regard; but if he harbors any moral qualms about his and his father's betrayal of their erstwhile nationalism, the narrative does not admit them. The Doyles have purchased their way out of the principle that bound them to their fellow Irish citizens. Their avarice has turned them into imperial subalterns. In this respect, then, there is poetic justice in the exploitation and cheating by his imperial fair-weather friends of a traitor to Ireland's political cause.

This reading of the political moral of "After the Race" accords with several apparent references to *Inferno* 34 in the final scene of "After the Race." In this canto, Virgil has taken Dante through the deepest pit of Hell. There they encounter Satan himself, chewing, with each of his three sets of jaws, the figures of Brutus, Cassius, and Judas, the most infamous traitors in Western history, betrayers of the founders of the political and spiritual orders upon which Christian civilization was founded. Meanwhile, all about this grotesque parody of the Holy Trinity can be seen the flailing legs of innumerable other traitors, fixed forever upside down in an expanse of solid ice. Recoiling with horror from this terrific scene of eternal suffering and despair, Dante hears the voice of Virgil calling him. Despite his weariness, Dante follows his guide upward:

> Lo duca e io per quel cammino ascoso
> intrammo a ritornar nel chiaro mondo;

e sanza cura aver d'alcun riposo,
salimmo su, el primo e io secondo,
tanto ch' i' vidi de le cose belle
che porta 'l ciel, per un pertugio tondo;
e quindi uscimmo a riveder le stelle.

[My guide and I took that dark path in order to return to the world of light, and without thought of any rest we climbed, he first and I second, until, through a round opening, I saw the beautiful things that the sky holds; and we came out from there to look again at the stars.] (Allan Gilbert trans., 294–95)

Thus the pair passes through the center of the earth, into the new world of the *Purgatorio*, whose pains are alleviated by the prospect of eventual redemption. The final scene of "After the Race"—in its exposé and punishment of betrayal—is infused with images, dramatic and textual, from *Inferno* 34.

Like Dante, Jimmy descends into a landscape characterized as a "mirror," which in this context reflects the image of the sheet of Infernal ice. Farley's yacht summons the image of the windmill that the travelers behold on their way. In the three figures of Ségouin, Rivière, and Routh, we have the images of demonic punishment, reverberating in Jimmy's thinking of them as "devils of fellows" obdurate to the repeated pleas from their victims, Farley and Jimmy, to stop (*D* 47.29, 48.14). The historical fact that Jenatzy, the race winner, was known to the Irish public as the "Red Devil," allied to Jimmy's recollection of the "shining white teeth" of the French race driver (*D* 44.20–21), and his already registered strain to keep pace with the conversation in the car "in the teeth of a high wind" (*D* 44.11–12), converge as a motif on (or emerge from) the Dantean image of Satan gnawing on his three victims.[30] Demonic company like this confuses ("uproots") Jimmy and Dante alike, so that they lose count of the hours of the night, and crave release from their respective underworlds.[31] The torment ends with Virgil's call of Dante upward from the abyss:

"Levati su" disse 'l maestro "in piede: / la via è lunga e 'l cammino è malvagio, / e già il sole a mezza terza riede."

["Get to your feet," said my teacher, "the way is long and the road is rough, and already the sun is getting back to mid-tierce."] (Allan Gilbert trans., 292–93)

These lines clearly inform the final paragraph of "After the Race," the only story in *Dubliners* that takes us through the entire night. There are Dantean echoes in Jimmy Doyle's weary reflection that "he would be glad of the rest" (*D* 48.28) as he gazes upward at the Villona-Virgil figure, the poet and guide detached from sin and its punishments, "standing in a shaft of grey light" (*D* 48.32), looking downward from the deck, and announcing the dawn. This moment, the announcement of resurrection and hope in the natural and spiritual orders, proclaims both delivery from the darkness of the night and from the hopelessness of the *Inferno*. Like the concluding lines in each of the three divisions of *The Divine Comedy*, *The Inferno* ends with an invocation of the Psalmist's commonplace, "The heavens declare the glory of God; the sky proclaims its builder's craft" (19: 1; cf. 8: 1; 50: 6; 97: 6): with the word "*stelle*" [star]. This image of the divine order that enfolds the entire universe justifies his highly structured poem in its dramatic form and multivalent poetic language. The manner in which Joyce forges the closure of "After the Race" is poetically, structurally, and thematically similar to Dante's. The invocation of the sun, our nearest star, is significantly linked, in the design of this story and in the opening images of its successor with two complementary and revealing images derived from Dante. We have but three pages before read of Jimmy and Villona's "curious feeling of disappointment [of walking northward] . . . while the city hung its pale globes of light above them" (*D* 45.23–24), and in the opening paragraph of "Two Gallants" will read, "Like illuminated pearls the lamps shone from the summits of their tall poles upon the living texture below" (*D* 49.5–7). These images of the "unpurchasable quality" represented by transcendental stars—the signs of God's grace beyond the reach of Simon Magus—mark the design of Joyce's *Dubliners* in a manner similar to Dante's *Divine Comedy*. "After the Race" concludes the first five of the fifteen stories of *Dubliners*. Just as it began with an invocation of the legend above the entrance to the *Inferno*, so it ends with a citation of the pilgrims' exit. And just as Dante's *Purgatorio* commences with an invocation of the stars, "I turned then to my right and set my mind / on the other pole, and there I saw four stars / unseen by mortals since the first mankind" (1: 22–24, John Ciardi translation), so does "Two Gallants" open the second group of five stories. This purgatorial group concludes, naturally, with "Clay," which, as I have discussed elsewhere, is informed by a Dantean vision (Owens, "'Clay' [1]: Irish Folklore"). The final five stories develop the paradisal themes of *Dubliners*, completing Joyce's tribute in his first prose work to the author of the *Divine Comedy*.

It is evident, therefore, that at least in rereading "After the Race" Joyce recognized in this less accomplished and spontaneous story the unpremeditated presence of Christendom's master poet. His subsequent placement of it confirms the realization that he was following after *il miglior fabbro*.

8

Conclusion

The wide-ranging approach of this book—embracing all of the salient circumstances bearing upon Joyce's writing of "After the Race"—may have at first seemed excessive. But as the painstaking method has set forth, it is necessary if one is to make an adequate assessment of its multivalent language and technical experiment. It shows how his characters are composites of his acquaintances and of historical and mythic figures, as well as projections of his personal fears and aspirations on the eve of his exile. It demonstrates, too, how geographical Dublin—the city streets of his own immediate experience—are transmuted into a symbolic landscape, becoming in the process representations of sensuous and spiritual realities.

This lengthy unpacking of the moment and the text of "After the Race" has the benefit of revealing the Olympian imagination concealed behind its thin human drama (see appendix for a Swedenborg-inspired schematic summary of our travels). By the same token, it exposes another aspect of the weakness of the story: its heavy dependence on private, local, and transient cultural references. While his other works are similarly dense with local allusion, "After the Race," for all the brilliance of its inner world, does not succeed as well as they do in transcending the circumstances of its origins and speaking to a readership beyond the shores of Dublin Bay.

One Final Turn

Too much depends upon the occluded figure of Villona, whose virtual silence implies a melancholy view of the revelry of his boisterous companions. As this book has contended, the artistic precedents for Joyce's personal identification with this figure are François Villon and Arnold Dolmetsch. It was apparently to Dolmetsch that Joyce owed his introduction to the compositions for lute and voice by John Dowland (whom

Stephen Dedalus mistakenly takes to be a fellow Dubliner [*U* 16.1762]). Joyce retained an admiration for Dowland's composite art throughout his life, as attested by his letter to Harriet Weaver (*Letters* III: 138, March 5, 1926). Some of his *Chamber Music* lyrics owe a small debt to the spirit and example of Dowland: in their gentle melancholy, their delicate understatement, and their tonal nuance (Chester Anderson, 140; Russel, 15–19).

The third of the preludial poems in this sequence bears witness to the spirit of John Dowland:

> At that hour when all things have repose,
> O lonely watcher of the skies,
> Do you hear the night wind and the sighs
> Of harps playing unto Love to unclose
> The pale gates of sunrise?
>
> When all things repose do you alone
> Awake to hear the sweet harps play
> To Love before him on his way,
> And the night wind answering in antiphon
> Till night is overgone?
>
> Play on, invisible harps, unto Love,
> Whose way in heaven is aglow
> At that hour when soft lights come and go,
> Soft sweet music in the air above
> And in the earth below.

This nocturnal lyric is more relieved than is Dowland's wont, expressing not only the desire for wholeness, but a trust in the healing powers of music that, through the lonely night vigil, harmonizes with the transcendental music of the spheres. This mystical figure of the "lonely watcher" is, as we have seen, drawn from the Theosophical lexicon. It designates the figure in every system who is set apart from his fellows so that he may light the way and lead adepts to prepare for the next phase of cosmic development (*ETG*, s.v. "watcher or silent watcher"). In Joyce's hands, he is endowed with Dowland's lute to become a concert of Irish and angelic harps praising universal Love. The arrival of dawn seals the troth between earthly and heavenly harpers, between loves carnal and ideal.

It would seem, therefore, that at least in these respects, the silent poet-musician and watcher of the skies in lyric III of *Chamber Music* (written 1901–3) reappears in "After the Race" under the name "Villona." Even as it moves away from the spirit of Dowland, this lyric expresses the complex intersection of the many themes dilated on in this study: the relationship between personal and political, aesthetic and spiritual, folk and mythological. Through the dramatic plot of the story, Jimmy Doyle, the ostensible agent in the "world below," acts as a somnambulist, by contrast with the inner life of the silent bystander Villona and the narrator's vision of the whole.

"After the Race" records the visitation of "future shock" (it is the only story in which both electricity and the motorcar appear) and its accompanying moral conflicts. In a manner of speaking, it registers Joyce's trepidation at what lies ahead as technology and competition for markets drive nations toward the cataclysm of the Great War. At the dawn of this new age, attracted by its investment possibilities (read "possessed by greed"), the characters jostle to find new markets. A timorous participant and victim, Jimmy Doyle is about to serve that new order. Meanwhile, appalled by its philistinism and handicapped by poverty, but observing its machinations with dispassionate detachment, Villona wraps himself in the mantle of high culture and thinks of a delivery represented by a new dawn: "all may be well." On one hand, the story is skeptical about that provided by technology, critical of the old colonialism as it manifests itself in the new forms of global competition in the Great Game. The vision of the story, on the other, balances all the claims of culture and religion: offering their alternative—or competing—spiritual or mythic claims, Vedic or Pauline.

To this end, "After the Race" is a quintessential modernist story: neither naive, entertaining, nor plot-driven, it is subtle, complex, ambiguous, ironical, nondidactic, at once realistic and mythologically informed. It is modern in the obvious way that it is dealing with the incursion of internationalism upon a political culture that for centuries had been preoccupied with Anglo-Irish relations. It is modern in the more penetrating way that moves beyond Victorian discomfort and into a bleaker skepticism. Impenetrable to the casual reader, the technique of this story is densely packed with current, historical, pedantic, and learned reference. An apparently naive narration, it is rather a work of highly selective quotation from the cultural tradition. It implies that just as every word and phrase we employ has been used over and over again, so is every human feeling and experience a revisitation of previous experience, our every dramatic moment previously imagined and composed, by others. Joyce's little characters reenact scenes from Dumas, Dante, Puccini, Villon, Ovid, and the gossip of the Irish oral tradition. In our lives we reenact the dreams of our ancestors.

In its depiction of the evanescence and trivial detail of urban life we recognize some of the marks of the modern. Joyce's mastery of a widely implicative language, its history and rhetorical traditions, so evident in his later works, are here in ur-form, as my many elucidations of the tropes from classical literature demonstrate. His penchant for chiasmus, paronomasia, and especially metaplasm—the most characteristic mark of the language of *Finnegans Wake*—all make early appearances here. We have seen, for example, how in the interests of invoking Griffith's devolutionary policy, Joyce bestowed the name of "Villona," a casual Parisian acquaintance with an obscure Italian name, on his Hungarian character. The strain of this unlikely naming admits, as we have seen, the complex social, political, and spiritual implications of the words "villain," "Villon," and "Virgil" to its metaplasmic embrace. His cunning concealments—the aporia and silences in the narration—conspire in constructing a savvy critique of the deceptions of modern commercialism, its distortions of language, its abuse of friendships, its exploitation of loyalties, argue, by a coherence of form and content to convince us that we should "trust not appearances." This gnomonic method—by which absence is rendered as a "higher form" of presence—is to become a Joycean trademark.

Yet at the same time, even as "After the Race" describes the near chaos of modern life, with its babble of competing languages, it delivers that critique with a fine sense of classical rhetorical and formal control. While it does not invade or explore the recesses of the private mind in a way we have come to associate with the word "Joycean," this story does exemplify its author's definition of the classical. In its objectivity and evasion of what Joyce called "the passive mind" its formal organization, and its depiction of observable life surrounded by an inferred mystery (Power, 74), it is written in the spirit of classical art. Thus, this highly ordered little story stocked with the furniture of daily life, for all its apparent deficiencies, points to the direction its author's work would take: a classical temper pruned and dressed for an astonishing exfoliation.

As this book has also held, "After the Race" is a moral story in its critique of Mammon's presentation of itself in the guise of leisure: wealth-producing business disguised as sports. The story is in addition possessed of a vision of history and salvation: the devices of imperial control and the paralysis of sin. In the author's alter-ego, Villona, we have the personification of the values Joyce is advocating here: that happiness is produced by reflection and composure, the fruits of stability.

The method pursued in this book leads to the conclusion that Joyce is possessed, from the outset, of a serious literary vision: available here in a compressed form, but readily appreciable in his subsequent works, which develop many of its latencies. In his brilliant novel, *At Swim-Two-Birds*, Flann O'Brien satirizes the rhetorical pedantry, the dense intertextuality, the devious narratological strategies, and the representation of the artist as a chameleon: Joycean touches all. If Joyce opens the door out of naive realism into the realms of myth and learned self-consciousness, O'Brien casts a cynical eye on this, regarding it as an elaborate nihilist game. As Joyce's *Portrait* is to modernism, O'Brien's *At Swim* is to postmodernism. But as I hold here, O'Brien, for all his advanced reading of Joyce, mistakes the intention of the technique and the coherence of all that apparent chaos. The reading developed in this book, will, I trust, lead to a better appreciation, even in its apparently least articulation, of the complexity and coherence of Joyce's technical mastery and extraordinary vision. As I trust is now clear, "After the Race" is an exemplary expression of the interior life behind the Joycean mask of "silence, exile, and cunning."

Appendix

Schema for "After the Race"

Historical Figure	Work	Theme	Voice	Touchstone	Symbol	Symbolic Action	Art / Discipline
James Joyce	"Trust Not Appearances," Chamber Music III, Fournier Interview, "The Holy Office"	Rivalry with Gogarty & sympathy with Griffith	Griffith as editor of United Irishman	One of "a series of epicleti" & "the worst"	Thomas Street, Car Race, Kingstown Harbour	Gordon Bennett Cup Race, Royal Visit, Emmet Centennial	Essay, lyric poetry, journalism, satiric broadside
	"After the Race"	Censure of high-end spending & colonial display	Stephen Dædalus, superior ironist	"gratefully oppressed," "pots of money," "Daybreak"	Carr, horse, map mirror, dawn, silence	Silent tour of Emmet's Dublin, game of nap	Modern short story, classical rhetoric
Emily Leslie	"My First Automobile Ride"	Pleasures of wealth	Social tourist	"an intoxicating delight"	Motorcar	Seduction by canny foreigner	Mild escapade
Arthur Griffith	*Resurrection of Hungary*	Devolution of United Kingdom	Political agitator	"the brass band of the denationalised nobles"	Dual crown	Self-reliance	Comparative political history
Rudyard Kipling	*Kim*	The Great Game	Colonial witness	"one great game for a finish"	Great Wheel, Red Bull, River Arrow	Political Intrigue, quest for personal light	Colonial novel
Robert Emmet	Speech from the dock	Personal moral vindication	Patriot & martyr	"my race is run ... the charity of its silence"	Gallows, grave, epitaph	1803 Rebellion	Extempore oratory
Publius Ovidus Naso	*Metamorphoses* I 750–II 328	Perpetual change, the folly of youth	All-knowing poet	"Sors tua mortalis ... non est mortale quod optas"	Chariot, heavens, sun	Phaeton's celestial career, crash, and death	Epic poetry: Latin
Alexandre Dumas, père	*The Three Musketeers*	Gallantry, male bonding	Romantic amuseur	"Tous pour un, un pour tous"	Sword, horse	Intrigue, war, and high jinks	Historical novel
François Villon	*Le Testament*	Social alienation	Social outcast	"Pauvre Villon," "ordure amons"	Poverty	Villon's criminalization	Lyric poetry
Patrick Kennedy	"Jemmy Doyle and the Fairy Palace"	Reality of the world of the sídh	Seanachaí	"Welcome, Mr. Doyle!"	Food, drink, dance, sleep	Fairy seduction of Jimmy	Fairy tale
Madame Blavatsky	*Isis Unveiled*	Atman/Maya	Mahatma	"to unmask mysteries of the universe"	Chhaya, seven, circle, aum	Allegory of the occult	Visionary report and prophecy
Saint Paul	Letters to Romans, Corinthians 1, Timothy	Christian hope & moral discipline	Visionary witness	"I have run the race" "hope does not disappoint"	Mirror, footrace	Witness to Christ's death & resurrection	Theology
Dante Alighieri	*Inferno* 34	Treachery, divine justice	Christian pilgrim	"A riveder le stelle"	Star of dawn	Traitors' punishment, Dante's exit	Epic poetry: Italian
Friedrich Nietzsche	*Daybreak*	Humanistic morality	Refuter of idealism & pessimism	"So many days that have not yet broken"	Recurring dawn		Philosophy

Schema for "After the Race" · 275

Technique	History	Place	Protagonist	Antagonist	Supporting Figure 1	Supporting Figure 2	Supporting Figure 3	Supporting Figure 4	Supporting Figure 5
Genre experiments, classical tradition	1896–September 1904	Clongowes, Joyce family homes, Paris, Martello tower	Oliver St. John Gogarty	James Augustine Joyce	Samuel Chevenix Trench	Thomas Hughes Kelly, Gordon Bennett, Cardinal Farley	Henri Fournier	Camille Jenatzy	William Field
Free indirect discourse	July 2–3, 1903	Inchicore Dame Street Doyle home Shelbourne Kingstown	Jimmy	Villona	Routh	Farley	Ségouin	Rivière	Mr. Doyle
Escapist journalism	1902	The colonies, France					mécanicien		
Argument from historical analogy	1861–1904	Budapest, Vienna, Dublin		Deák	Esterhazy Monarchy				Irish Party MPs
Realistic narrative	1891–99	British India	Kimball O'Hara	Teshoo Lama	Colonel Creighton				
Epidedic speech	July–Sept. 1803: Emmet Rebellion	Green Street Courthouse, Dublin	Leonard McNally		Lord Norbury				
Epic verse: narrative	Mythic Prehistory of the Gods	Greece & North Africa	Phaethon		Anonymous Insulter				Helios
Prose romance	1626: Siege of La Rochelle	France	D'Artagnan	Porthos	Buckingham		Aramis	Athos	
Learned & colloquial verse	c. 1400	Paris							
Irish oral redaction of Celtic *bruidnean* tale	Medieval	County Wexford			Queen of the Fairies	*An fairceallach talmhaí*			
Syncretic Hermetic speculation	Aeon of the Fourth Root-Race	The "Positive unreality" of the world							
Hortatory, epistolary	30 AD–Parousia	Rome, Corinth			Mammon				
Terza rima	Eternity	Ninth Circle of Hell	Satan	Virgil	Brutus		Cassius	Judas	
Aphoristic prose	Eternal return								

Notes

Chapter 1. Introduction

1. This particular campaign had direct impact on the Joyce household, since Stanislaus worked at Telfords, the Dublin organ builders (*JJII* 43). (This is why Harry Hill, Eveline's less-favored brother, is "in the church decorating business" [*D* 38.8].)

2. For the typesettings of this story in the *Irish Homestead*, in the 1910 proofs, and in the 1914 edition, see volumes 3–5 in the *James Joyce Archive*, edited by Hans Walter Gabler (vol. 3) and by Michael Groden (vols. 4, 5) (New York: Garland, 1977–78).

Gabler's collation of these texts in the Norton edition of *Dubliners* has a few omissions (32–38). It should be supplemented by these five emendations:

D 47.30: for form' sake] for form's sake *IH*
D 48.9–10: Play ran very high and] Play ran very high *IH*
D 48.25: They began then] then absent *IH*
D 48.27: He knew] Jimmy knew *IH*
D 48.33: —Daybreak, gentlemen] NO PARAGRAPH *IH*.

3. As the organ of the cooperative movement among Irish dairy farmers, the *Irish Homestead* must have had few readers attuned to Joyce's story. In the latter event, only 532 copies of the first printing of *Dubliners* were sold by the end of 1915 (*JJII* 400).

4. The others are "Araby" (the bazaar at the Royal Dublin Society in May 1894), "Ivy Day in the Committee Room" (the Municipal elections of 1903–4), and "A Mother" (the Grand Gaelic Concert of August 27, 1904).

5. It contrasts with the Anglo-Irish, or Catholic professional, domestic, agricultural, and industrial classes above and below them (Brady and Simms, 263). During the summer of 1905 Joyce briefly entertained the prospect of his following *Dubliners* with another collection, *Provincials* (*Letters* II: 92).

Chapter 2. The Automobile Age

1. John Boyd Dunlop's pneumatic bicycle tire, developed in Belfast, made its debut at the Queen's College Easter Sports in 1889. Known as the "bladder-wheel" and "windbag," it was smoother and lighter than the solid tires that preceded it, and thus facilitated faster rides (Lynch, *Triumph*, 25). That same year the world's first pneumatic tire factory opened on Dublin's Stephen's Street, and within a short time there were twenty-five companies manufacturing bicycles in Dublin (Daly, 48–49). During Joyce's adolescence, then, Dunlop's pneumatic tires were a household name (as the reference to "rheumatic wheels" in "The Sisters" indicates [*D* 17.8]).

When Dunlop moved his manufacturing center to England, the economic benefits of the cycling boom of the 1890s came to an end. With the sudden growth of the motor trade in the next decade, Dunlop's success continued, but abroad. Thus, even though the name of Dunlop provided a nominal incentive in Ireland's case to stage the 1903 Gordon Bennett race (Lynch, *Triumph*, 25), the resentment aroused by his "capital flight" was reignited by the "buy Irish" opponents of the race.

To this resentment against British capital luring Dunlop from Ireland, Griffith periodically returned, as we read in the pages of *Sinn Féin* (e.g., June 6, 1908 and September 24, 1910).

2. Automobilism gave rise to a couple of amusing temporary local usages. A joke had a Dublin shawlie explaining to an unwitting onlooker that the chauffeur got the name from his role as "shuvver" (Lynch, *Triumph*, 79). The conflation of "chassis" and "chaos" gave rise to the Dublin argot invoked by Sean O'Casey's Captain Boyle, "I'm telling you ... Joxer ... th' whole worl's ... in a terr ... ible state o' ... chassis!" (*Juno and the Paycock*, 1925).

3. For example, Mr. Deasy pays Stephen Dedalus the equivalent of £43 per annum. See Gifford, 6–8.

4. The Ford Edge brand of motor oil preserves his memory.

5. In putting this aggressive question, Joyce may have been cannier than he pretended. Fournier was indeed at the time considering defecting to the Mercedes camp (Ward, 33).

6. In the interview, Joyce makes a curious move in describing Fournier as "a slim, active-looking young man, with reddish hair" (*CW* 107), whereas the historical person was muscular and of average height. The French driver to whom the fictional Jimmy Doyle is introduced in "After the Race"—with his "swarthy face" and "shining white teeth" (*D* 44.20–21)—fairly describes the historical Fournier (Ward, 32).

7. The narrator does not identify the hotel. Its up-to-date furnishings, private dining room, formal dress requirements, patronage by the French and British teams, and approximate location all point to the Shelbourne.

8. When Joyce turned to write the story in September 1904, he had an additional reason to associate the name "Gordon" with the "imposture of names": he had recently collaborated with his brother in impersonating one Michael Gordon in the Veterinary Preliminary Examination (July 7–9, *CDD* 86).

9. For their part, the French visitors felt the warmth of Irish hospitality. *Velo*, the Paris racing magazine, reported: "We will never forget the thrilling welcome of the crowd on our return to Dublin, our carriage going at a walking pace past the thousands of persons massed on the pavement and hailing the champions of new locomotion as if they were victorious soldiers returning" (cited by Lynch, *Green Dust*, 26).

10. The campaigns to institutionalize these symbols of Irish identity, long pursued by most advanced nationalist organizations but opposed by shopkeepers and publicans (fearing loss of trade), finally bore fruit in 1904.

11. Arthur Griffith's newspaper ran a regular paragraph citing advertisements in the British press for Protestant or Presbyterian staff in Protestant-owned hotels and businesses in Ireland.

12. This trivial lapse seems to confirm Stanislaus's recollection of his brother's ignorance of the racing schedule and his absence from the race (*MBK* 225).

13. Bill Mason's documentary, *History of Motor Racing: The Heroic Days* (Shell International, 1960), includes two minutes of action footage from the 1903 Gordon Bennett Cup Race: it can be viewed via YouTube. It captures the excitement of that novel event, its heroes raising waves of adulation and dust.

14. Conspiracy theories of Joyce's stories are the contemporary version of the naive "symbol-hunting" of the first generation of readers. They arise from four sources: underestimation of the complexity of Joyce's methods, inadequate historicization of his language and cultural assumptions, selective reading of the texts, and the posture of a modish relativism. This produces what Norris calls "suspicious readings;" and in the case of "After the Race," see 68–78.

The "suspicious reading" of "After the Race" appeared in various publications, before and after Norris's volume of that title (e.g., Cheng, 108; Deane, 23). Despite Shawn St. Jean's eminently sensible protest, many writers advance the argument that Jimmy Doyle is the victim of a coordinated swindle. He loses not only what he gambles, but also his family fortune to the Continental cousins and their collaborators, Routh and Farley.

The textual evidence for these speculations is thin. It is unlikely that solicitors of significant investment would cheat (much less sexually assault) a potential client at a gambling table. They would require readers, further, to accept the prearrangement of the appearances of Routh and Farley, and that Routh's winning at the gambling table and Farley's hospitality are fronts to convert Jimmy's Irish mite into French francs.

15. For his correction of one of Ellmann's few dating mistakes, see Gabler, xviin6.

16. Without actually invoking it, the story illustrates Thorstein Veblen's contemporary term (1899).

17. Deane takes the opposite view that Jimmy's bedazzlement by the "magic" of the fast life and the mirage of "humanity" blind him to the machinations of those who deprive him of "the real thing": money (23–24).

18. "Securities"—documents guaranteeing investments or stock shares—are among the constituents of financial fortunes.

19. The word "villain" was originally a class (not a moral) descriptor: a low-born rustic or feudal serf.

20. Several sophisticated readers misjudge Joyce's cunning parody in "After the Race": for example, Beck, who faults its "clumsy pretentiousness" (126), and Deane its "monotonous grammar" (23). From a deeper sympathy with Joyce's methods, Bowen suspects, but does not pursue, the hunch that the story has a vein of parody ("'After the Race,'" 56n).

21. Bézique is a game for two players, and poker, an American game, was unfamiliar in Ireland or Britain at the time, and is not mentioned in *Ulysses*. Nap makes several appearances in *Finnegans Wake*: one of the "telltale sports at evenbread" (*FW* 550.24–25) appears on the list of popular games (*FW* 176.1–18).

22. Compare with "Declare misery" (*U* 14.1466) and "Messamisery and the knave of all knaves and the joker" (*FW* 202.3).

23. This is the force of the expression "paper began to pass" (*D* 48.10); but it is also a jargon term for passing a bad check when card-playing.

24. The popular identification is owing to the comic illustration by John Tenniel rather than to the character depicted by Lewis Carroll, who was a sentimental royalist.

25. The affair is the subject of Alexander Dumas's royalist novel, *The Queen's Necklace* (1848).

26. This song is based on the legend of Englishman Charles Deville Wells who sailed his yacht to Monte Carlo in July 1891 and in three days parlayed his £400 into £40,000. The proverbial phrase, "breaking the bank," was deceptive: it was actually a publicity stunt whereby the casino closed a single table whenever a bettor won more than its immediate reserves. The table was then ceremoniously draped with black crepe and solemnly closed until the arrival of a fresh infusion from the central office (Schwartz, 312–14). Joyce's bemusement by such a ruse has him endow Bloom with "a prepared scheme based on a study of the laws of probability to break the bank at Monte Carlo" (*U* 17.1694–96); see Bauerle, 5–6.

27. The Roman soldiers' casting lots for Jesus's garments (John 19: 24) signifies despair (after Psalm 22: 18).

28. George Moore protested against the king's visit by having his front door at Ely Place painted green, much to the annoyance of his Unionist neighbors. To express his disdain for the bishops' entertaining the king at Maynooth, in a scornful letter to the *Irish Times* (September 23, the centennial of Emmet's execution) he declared himself a Protestant (Frazier, 331). Writing in the *United Irishman*, Yeats was at his most derisory, asking if he could expect to read in the sporting columns of the *Irish Times* that "Cardinal Logue had 'something on' Sceptre and that Archbishop Walsh has 'a little bit of allright' for the Chester Cup" (August 1).

29. The Dutch tulip bubble of 1637, "John Law's System" in France of 1720, and the South Sea Bubble of the same year in England are among the most infamous (Schwartz, 119–22).

30. Doyle is citing the colloquial usage meaning "a large sum of money" (*OED*, s.v. "pot" 9a), whereas "pot" also refers to "a betting pool in poker and other betting games" such as faro, keno, and poker (*OED* 9e).

31. It accommodated the U.S. Open tennis championships from 1881 to 1914. An architectural relic of the Gilded Age, it is today a National Historic Landmark.

Chapter 3. The Biographical Crisis

1. That Villona is a partial self-portrait and Jimmy a preliminary sketch of Gogarty has been proposed before (Tindall, 23) but nowhere developed.

2. Joyce first signs a letter as "Jim" on September 10, and Nora reciprocates two days later (*Letters* II: 52). Since he was still signing himself "JAJ" through the month of August, the letter on 44–45 is unlikely to have been written in late July. In Joyce's circles of friends throughout his life, only George Clancy (the Davin of *A Portrait*) was permitted to call him "Jim" (fictionalized as "Stevie"). His citation of the familiar name, "Jimmy," by the narrator of "After the Race" only after he has associated the name "Doyle" with the rise of his father's fortunes from butcher to that of a "merchant prince," implies the false familiarity of commercial and advertising culture.

3. This phrase combines Joyce's disparagement of Gogarty's gentlemanly pretensions and his republicanism (as a follower of Wolfe Tone).

4. We do not know the identity of the other. It cannot be Byrne, who was out of town and to whom, in any case, Joyce sent a copy of "The Holy Office" through the post, requesting a "loan." Byrne remonstrated a few days later: "*Miro cur habes satirizatum amicos vestros, num pecunia eorum defuit?*" [I wonder why you have satirized your friends; was it because they had no money?] (*Letters* II: 47, August 19). Joyce and his friends engaged in humorous communications in pig Latin. This game became a practical necessity for Joyce during his sojourn in the Latin Quarter of Paris, when the international orbit of his social relations included a Hungarian with whom Joyce conversed in Latin.

5. We find Gogarty, in a letter of June 26 to G.K.A. Bell, praising the glory of the dawn on the Irish Sea. He had arisen at 3:30 a.m. and traveled from his home on Rutland Square to see daybreak from Howth Head (*Many Lines to Thee*, 7). Gogarty elsewhere observes that the sun's light begins to appear around 4 a.m. (26).

6. This is Joyce's first citation of François Villon, whose "biography" he'd been reading—actually his *Oeuvres Complètes*, edited by M. A. Longnon (Gogarty, *Tumbling in the Hay*, 189). As we shall see, Villon was much on his mind in late summer 1904, casting his first shadow in Joyce's fiction under the metaplasmic signature of "Villona."

7. So Stanislaus reports (*CDD* 86; *JJII* 174–75). In this "temple of neo-paganism" (Scholes and Kain, 97), Nietzsche was the principal prophet, and Swinburne the laureate (*JJII* 172). Nietzsche's most recent work at the time was a critique of friendship and an attack on Saint Paul. Its subscription to the myth of the eternal return and its title, *The Dawn of Day*, suggest that it has a broad relationship with this story.

8. J. B. Lyons offers a stout defense of Gogarty's character and the integrity of his dealings with Joyce, 211–23.

9. Greeting the emaciated Joyce, Gogarty invoked the Greek term φθίσις [wasting away] in a spontaneous Hiberno-Hellenicism, "Jaysus, man, you're in phthisis" (*Letters* II: 230, August 4, 1909). Cf. Joyce's naming of Molly Bloom and Gogarty's poem "Molly" (*Dana* 10, February 1905: 308), and the major scene as the Blooms' recollected tryst on Howth Head. (Gogarty wrote to Bell of just such an occasion in mid-June 1904 [*Many Lines to Thee*, 7–8].)

10. On first meeting Joyce, Nora Barnacle thought her singing suitor a sailor; her image of him, "standing . . . [with] his peaked cap pushed back on his head" (*D* 38.33–34), corresponds with the famous C. P. Curran photo (*JJII* plate 8); Joyce wrote "Eveline" as the couple made arrangements to elope from the North Wall, etc. (see Maddox, 3–6).

11. When in Gogarty's social company, Joyce normally conceded to his brilliant friend's raillery, retreating into a jealous silence ("Telemachus" represents this aspect of their relationship accurately [see Bulfin, 232]). When in his cups, however, Joyce overcame this reticence and would break into long speeches that embarrassed his sober brother (*CDD* 101).

12. The essay, "A Portrait of the Artist" (January 7, 1904; Scholes and Kain, 60–68), was written for the literary magazine *Dana*. It is Joyce's most developed early statement of his artistic ideas and intentions, and thus illuminates several aspects of the figure of Villona.

13. The printer's record is dated ca. August 17. D. J. O'Donoghue, one of the recipients, showed his signed copy (September) to Joseph Holloway on October 18 (O'Neill, 51).

14. This title, pace Mason and Ellmann's gloss (*CW* 149n1), makes no reference to confession, to "the launching of the Inquisition," or to an ostler's service to a stallion.

15. Joyce delights in this kind of excremental deflation. Similar examples of this peculiar combination of tapinosis and paronomasia are the title of his poems, *Chamber Music*, and the description of Bloom reading "Matcham's Masterstroke" in the jakes: "Quietly he read, restraining himself, the first column and, yielding but resisting, began the second" (*U* 4.506-7).

16. According to their joint autobiography (*We Two Together*), James and Margaret Cousins were particular admirers of Joyce's vocal talent, inviting him to their musical evenings, allowing him access to their piano, accompanying him in his song performances (106), and providing him free lodging on September 1-2, 1904 (*Letters* II: lvi). They were interested in the occult, and were founders of the Irish Vegetarian Society. Their feeling for this latter cause was offended daily by the view from their dining room window of a large pasture continuously stocked with cattle awaiting slaughter (Cousins, 106). It was leased by "a prominent suburban butcher" to supply his chain of shops—possibly even William Field, who owned grazing property in the area (Daly, 200). This disturbing sight was unlikely to pass unremarked while Joyce was the house guest of the Cousins couple; and although he was no vegetarian, the breakfast conversation, no doubt uncomplimentary to William Field, may have registered with Joyce as the story of Jimmy Doyle and his father took shape in his imagination during the following month.

Before leaving Dublin, he deposited a copy of "The Holy Office" in his friends' letterbox at 35 Strand Road, Sandymount. Although grateful for the gift, they were disappointed at not finding their names among those whom he excoriated in what they called his "Catharsis." With mixed emotions, they noted that "our musical and mental exchanges . . . had presumably cancelled occult and dietetic eccentricities" (Cousins, 216). They did not notice (nor has anyone else) that Joyce did indeed commemorate their musical relationship. The narrator of "After the Race" identifies the musical circle at Cambridge with which Jimmy is associated by the membership of Rivière and Ségouin, the pair of "cousins" (*D* 43.8). This is yet another small indication of Joyce's inscribing oblique compliments to his friends.

17. Throughout *Le Lais* and *Le Testament*, Villon's characteristic self-descriptor is "*pauvre.*"

18. A letter to Joyce from Gogarty dated July 3, 1904, is signed "Caddie Rouselle" (Lyons, illustration 28).

19. Stanislaus worried about his brother's drinking especially in Gogarty's company. He records that when drunk, James breaks into speeches, makes foolish jokes, harrasses women, and "falling up against and mauling whoever he is talking to . . . sinks down on the floor quite overcome, moaning and venting huge sighs" (*CDD*, September 14, 1904, 101-2).

20. Bell (1883-1958) was subsequently a distinguished Anglican churchman, bishop of Chichester, ecumenicist, and pacifist. During his Oxford days he was a poet and musician: one of his compositions, "Christ is the King, O friends upraise," can be found in the

Anglican hymnal. He may therefore be the object of the allusions to the "musical and motoring circles" and "the music of merry bells" in Joyce's story. That Bell had a "merry" side to his character is conveyed in Gogarty's memorable limerick after his friend's elevation in 1929: "There was a young lady of Chichester / Whose curves made the Saints in their niches stir; / Each morning at matins / The swish of her satins / Made the Bishop of Chichester's britches stir" (*Poems and Plays*, 352).

21. Nor, indeed, two influential critics from the previous generation. Hugh Kenner thinks that Jimmy is "an avatar of Stephen Dedalus and Dublin's-eye parody of Jimmy Joyce" (*Dublin's Joyce*, 55). This same misjudgment appears among a string of errors in Robert M. Adams's cursory discussion of this story (66–68). William York Tindall, however, guesses correctly: "a first study for Buck Mulligan, maybe" (23).

22. The censuses of Ireland for 1901 and 1911 list him as residing with his sister at No. 6, Main Street, Blackrock.

23. Skeat, Joyce's etymologist, traces "torpid" [sluggish] to the Greek τερπειν [to satisfy] s.v. "torpid." When Mulligan refers to Haines "the oxy chap" (*U* 1.154), he may be thinking of Oxford and Saxon (as Gifford annotates it, 16). But since Mulligan thinks of Haines as stupid and dull [μωρος], by contrast with Stephen whom he respects as Kinch (the sharp knifeblade), he is playing off the Greek [οξοσ] for "sharp." This is not as farfetched as it sounds, since these adjectives comprise the familiar synoceiosis, "oxymoron."

24. One of Joyce's notes from 1904 on Gogarty reads: "Doherty's jibes flashed to and fro through the torpor of his mind" (Scholes and Kain, 107). The word "torpor"/"torpid" [inertia/displaying morbid mental and motor inertia] is a term from the lexicon of pathology, and thus probably entered Joyce's vocabulary from Gogarty's oral example. It is a rarity in the Joycean universe, appearing but once in *A Portrait* (188.01), once in *Ulysses* (15.2166), and once in *Finnegans Wake* (530.24).

25. Joyce apparently gave his character this French surname because of its proximity to "*sagouin*" [slob/filthy pig]. In support of the ascription, Jackson and McGinley cite a Paul de Kock story (350). Nearer the mark is the Edwardian association of motor drivers with dust and dusters.

26. The cultural contrast between Routh and Villona is complemented by the etymology of "torpid" in the Greek for "sated" in contrast with the narrator's insight into the Hungarian's "sharp desire for his dinner" (see note 17 above).

27. The brush was subsequently pinched by Trench on his departure from the tower for Oxford in mid-October 1904. The highly irritated Gogarty wrote immediately to Bell, asking him to collect the item on his behalf, explaining that "The only personal extravagance and luxury that I indulge in are summed up in that frond-like brush" (*Many Lines to Thee*, 47). For his part, Joyce appropriated the luxurious image to his characterization of "the cloisteral silverveined prose of Newman" (*P* 176.13).

28. Mulligan's remarks on Dublin's unhealthy food supply (*U* 1.411–14) are an indirect attack on William Field. Its relevance to "After the Race" will be discussed in chapter 4.

29. The classic study is Harold Laski, *The Danger of Being a Gentleman and Other Essays* (London: Allen and Unwin, 1939). For Joyce's invocation of the social convention

of the "gentleman" in *U* and *FW*, see Richard Beckman, "Joyce's Ungentlemen's Club (for Jews and Dandies)" *JJQ* 36, no, 4 (Summer 1999): 799–812.

30. Gogarty never tired of sophomoric quibbling over his former friend's defensiveness about his lack of physical and mental fitness: "I knew Kinch to the bone, and it was not well covered. . . . He knows damn all about Greek, and he hasn't the guts to say so but he tries to laugh it off" (*Tumbling in the Hay*, 188).

Joyce's Greek notebook in the Buffalo Joyce Collection is evidence that he made a serious effort to remediate this deficiency in his formal education. Its pages contain many exercises in an evidently fluent hand (*JJAII*: 288–352).

31. Moore registered his admiration for Dolmetsch and Yeats by entering them—under thinly disguised pseudonyms—as characters in his novel *Evelyn Innes* (1898). The eponymous heroine's father is modeled on Dolmetsch. An accomplished musician, he is dedicated to the liturgical music of Palestrina, the viola de gamba (139), and the music of the Tudor period, particularly that of Henry VIII, Ferrabosco, and Dowland. The "masterly works" of these composers were his "discoveries" in the British Museum (46–48). Like Dolmetsch, he lives in Dulwich in a house named "Dowland," and makes contentious pronouncements such as "The piano has destroyed the modern ear" (207).

32. Joyce had predicted to Joseph Holloway that because of the low level of public taste in England—it did not rise above Negro minstrels—"My tour will not be a success, but it will prove the inadequacy of the English" (*JJII* 154–55).

33. The proper title of this ayre is "From silent night" (Poulton, 302–4). Joyce could readily summon to mind many of Dowland's songs. Writing to Nora in November 1909, e.g., he cites a verse of "I saw my lady weep," adding a comment that admits his occasional identification with this master of moodiness: "You are a sad little person and I am a devilishly melancholy fellow myself so that ours is a rather mournful love I fancy" (*Letters* II: 258–59).

34. Joyce was evidently more impressed by his companions' bulk than their acuity, so that he once found himself declining a duel offered by the German Expressionist poet, Theodor Däubler (1876–1934) who had taken offense at his Celtic impudence (*MBK* 199–200; Gorman, 100).

35. The yacht (or ship's) piano was a compact five-octave instrument version of the drawing-room instrument designed to sit upon a low table. Built in the late Victorian period by J. B. Cramer and Son, London, it was designed for pleasure boats.

36. He might, then, have in mind the well-known portrait by the Hungarian painter János Donát (1744–1830), entitled *Woman Playing the Lute* (1811) (http://www.klassikgitar.net/donat-womanplaying.html). Although painted during the Romantic period, it is a neoclassical work, produced in the style of the Viennese academy: the lady is idealized. Hungarians of Villona's sensibility, viewing it at the National Gallery in Budapest (where it still hangs today), would have been amused by Donát's error in depicting not a lute but a psaltery.

37. There has always been speculation as to the extent of Henry's original contribution to the song, since it is constructed on an Italian convention and became an internationally popular melody when it was first printed in 1529 (Spring, 9). A fine rendition of this

song appears as #13 in the SIRINU ensemble's CD, *All Goodly Sports*, to which Spring supplies the liner notes.

38. Cf. the similar implication in the uses of the word "course" as an allusion to the youth of Prince Hal, supra.

Chapter 4. Arthur Griffith and the Great Game

1. Lecturing the Triestines on the British usurpation of Ireland's political rights, Joyce cited, with evident approval, the hostile manner in which the imperial sovereign was received in his native city: "the old Queen of England entered the Irish capital in the midst of a silent people" (*CW* 165).

2. In 1892 only 33,696 out of a total population of 245,000 were eligible to vote (Brady and Simms, 163).

3. When Dublin Corporation voted to rename Sackville Street in memory of O'Connell in 1884, its decision was ruled out of order by the vice-chancellor of the day, Hedges Eyre Chatterton. The Corporation's response was quick: attempting to rename one of the streets in the notorious red light district Chatterton Street (Brady and Simms, 164–65). The naming of the priest Father Purdon in "Grace" responds, in another (and typically Joycean) turn, on this insulting gesture toward British "syphilization."

4. A very large proportion of offenses appearing in the courts were cases of assault and drunkenness. Domestic abuse and cruelty to children perpetrated by drunken fathers also appears high in the court records (O'Brien, 183–87). For a city remarkably free of serious crime, Dublin was overpoliced, a point persistently made by nationalists.

5. This same visit was the occasion of the famous typographical error (in the Unionist *Evening Mail*) reporting that Her Majesty had "pissed over O'Connell Bridge."

6. Throughout the week, Dubliners could stare in awe at the eight battleships and four cruisers moored along the docks and rub shoulders with the 2,000 marines and sailors plying the streets (O'Brien, 247).

7. Joyce's trenchant criticism of Rooney is not ideological but literary.

8. After his departure from Ireland, Joyce had a considerable range of newspapers and journals to choose from in order to keep abreast of affairs Irish. On the nationalist side, he had the moderate dailies *Freeman's Journal* and *Evening Herald*, while on the unionist were the *Irish Times*, the *Daily Express*, and *Evening Mail*. Of weekly newspapers of opinion or special interest, he had George Russell's *Irish Homestead* (organ of the Cooperative Movement), and the radical *Irish Peasant* (hardly of interest). The cause of urban labor was served by the *Harp* and the *Irish Worker*, while Gaelic Leaguers were accommodated by *An Claidheamh Soluis*. Of the weeklies dedicated to Irish nationalism, there were two: D. P. Moran's clericalist *Leader* and Griffith's independent inheritor of the republican, nonsectarian tradition, the *United Irishman*. Of the periodicals Joyce had the *New Ireland Review* (edited by Father Finlay, SJ) and *Dana* (edited by the socialist Fred Ryan). Joyce wrote for four of these: the *Daily Express, Irish Times,* and *Irish Homestead* (not because of their ideology or constituency, but because they paid), and *Dana* (because he respected the company). It is instructive, however, that of all of these, he "took"

only Griffith's "advanced nationalist," or in the words of the *Stephen Hero* narrator, the "irreconcilable" paper.

9. Stephen Dedalus thinks of Hamlet as "a butcher's son" whose ghostly father "wield[ed] the sledded poleaxe" (*U* 9.131).

10. In 1912, Joyce wrote to Field concerning foot and mouth disease (*Letters* II: 300), fictionalized in Deasy's letter to the *Freeman's Journal* on the same subject (*U* 2.289–344).

11. The record should include the ironic corollary that in his capacity as rate collector (Jackson and Costello, 108), John Stanislaus Joyce helped finance those whom Griffith and the nationalist press regarded as "traitors to their country" and "lackeys of empire," the DMP.

12. In a letter to Stanislaus as he was considering a revision of this story (Summer 1905), Joyce reveals his uncertainty about the conditions under which police contracts were awarded (*Letters* II: 109). His instincts were correct. According to James Herlihy, historian of the DMP, the Kevin Street Depot and each station had a kitchen and wet canteen (74). Provisioning fell to the mess-man in each facility. Canvassing for these lucrative jobs was rife at election time (99).

13. Joyce associates butchery with mercantilism and corruption. He was to return to this theme in the summer of 1905 in "The Boarding House," his attack on conventional marriage.

14. The parallelism between Stephen's portmanteau terms for each of this pair is striking. He thinks derisively of Mulligan's occupation as a pretender to the healing of tribal ills, whereas "milkwoman" embraces her occupations as milkmaid and milkman.

15. See obituary in the *Freeman's Journal* from April 29, 1935 (pace Costello, who reads Joyce's fictional text as historical evidence [106]).

16. Without observing the relationship familiar to Irish citizens of the time, the *London Times*, on the same page as it records the race results, also reports, with unconcealed disdain, this fractious scene of municipal disloyalty (July 4: 8).

17. It is a retrospective historical irony that the two geniuses of Hungarian national music, Zoltán Kodály and Béla Bartók were yet to appear.

18. Villona is not a Hungarian but a rare Italian name (Reggio di Calabria). Joyce did not identify for Gorman the nationality of his Parisian acquaintance of that name (100).

19. She conjectures that the "huge Hungarian" (*D* 43.2) of his story may also be informed by Griffith's image of a "magnificent Hungarian" in one of his Boer War stories, whose passionate indignation at a practical joke could only be appeased by the Irishman's offer of "eternal and unalterable friendship" and a cigar (*United Irishman*, April 28 1900: 5).

20. This imposing statue disappeared in 1937 (Bennett, s.v. "Statues, Equestrian").

21. The fracas avoided in the hotel dining room is reminiscent of many scenes in ethnic bars and restaurants where descendants of Irish emigrants and of the "auld enemy" encounter one another. An ocean away, James Hoban's conflict with the English architect, Benjamin Henry Latrobe, over the building of the U.S. Capitol rose to a level of personal spite that is rooted in the same nexus of Anglo-Irish sensitivity.

22. Bowen in his 1970 essay is the first to discern the relationship between Villona and Griffith's *Resurrection of Hungary*.

23. James Fairhall's foray into this aspect of the story is the most concerted, but it does not pay sufficient attention to the manner in which Joyce's nuanced text registers that highly complex historical moment. His argument is based on the columns of the *Irish Times*, unofficial organ of the race sponsors. Griffith's readers—among them the author of "After the Race"—took a very different view of the competition.

Subsequent "postcolonial" readings of the story, without any re-examination of the textual or historical evidence, offer variations on Vincent Cheng's summary judgment that it is "an Irish parable of racial hegemony in the Gramscian sense" (109).

24. After that war, he issued an expanded version, *Democratic Ideals and Reality* (1919), which has had, directly or indirectly, a wide influence on figures as disparate as Adolf Hitler and Henry Kissinger. Although he did not use the term "geopolitics," his essay is seminal to the thinking of both the foreign policy planners during the Third Reich and the period of the Cold War, and even in that of current American and British Middle East strategists. Robert B. Downs discusses the wide impact of Mackinder's essay (314–16). Zbigniew Brzezinski's 1997 book *The Grand Chessboard* borrows the image in developing the contemporary aspects of the same basic issues. For the permanence of Mackinder's influence, see Gerry Kearns, *Geopolitics and Empire: The Legacy of Halford Mackinder* (New York: Oxford University Press, 2009).

25. A further historical irony here is the role played by a British subject named by his parents after Kipling's character, who recruited from Cambridge by M15, played a major role in the same game: Kim Philby.

26. The Register of Informers and Crime Branch Reports documents the extent of the surveillance. McGee makes extensive use of S files (1890–1910), the DMP files (1882–1900), and DMP and RIC précis (1901–11). Records of the activities of "the G" can be found in two official reports cited by Peter Hart, *British Intelligence in Ireland 1920-21: The Final Reports* (Cork: Cork University Press, 2002), 99n7: "The Report of the Committee of Inquiry into the Dublin Metropolitan Police 1901," HC 1902 (Cd.1008), xlii, 8–11; "Evidence Taken Before the Committee of Inquiry 1901 HC 1902" (Cd.1095), 8–10.

27. An English literary journalist who made his appearance among the Dublin literati during the 1890s, he was the author of *The Whirlwind* (1889–90) supporting the Stuart cause that would have given him an entrée to Irish nationalist circles. He was interested in the Irish language, Theosophy, and vegetarianism. He subsequently traveled widely on the Continent, did odd jobs, was a Russian translator, and wrote some reminiscences (1923).

28. An element in Donald Torchiana's argument that "After the Race" makes a double reference to the Gordon Bennett Cup Race of 1903 and the French landing under General Jean Humbert in 1798 is his note on a certain Colonel Farley (82). He fails to reconcile this observation with a coherent historical reading of the story.

29. Bennett launched this newspaper in 1887, later morphing into the *International Herald Tribune*.

30. The Census of Ireland 1911 lists nine times as many Farrellys as Farleys.

Chapter 5. Robert Emmet Centennial

1. In *Unstoppable Brilliance: Irish Geniuses and Asperger's Syndrome*, Antoinette Walker and Michael Fitzgerald offer considerable biographical evidence hypothesizing that both Emmet and Joyce suffered from this mild form of autism.

2. Cf. "he appeared to his shecook as Haycock, Emmet, Boaro, Toaro, Osterich, Mangy and Skunk" (*FW* 136.14–15).

3. D. J. O'Donoghue's *Life of Emmet*, D. A. Quaid's *Birthplace and Burial of Emmet*, and *The Emmet Song Book*, all under the imprint of James Duffy (*United Irishman*, July 4, 1903). Meanwhile, J. J. Reynolds's *Footprints of Emmet* and R. R. Madden's *The Life and Times of Robert Emmet*, vol. 3 of *The Lives and Times of the United Irishmen* (1844) appeared in 1903.

4. *Sapho* is the title of the Clyde Fitch play (1900) after the Alphonse Daudet novel. Considered salacious and an inducement to immorality because of its representation of extramarital sex, it was attacked by moral crusaders in the United States (1900) and Britain (1902).

5. The International Exhibition was accused of encouraging the importation of goods of foreign manufacture, e.g., Italian stained glass and German organs at the expense of the Irish manufacturers of comparable products promoted by the Home Industries Exhibition, Telfords Organs and *An Túr Gloine* [The Glass Tower], respectively.

6. This statue is the secondary subject of Gabriel Conroy's anecdote about Patrick Morkan's horse. Its conditioned circling of King Billy's statue burlesques the annual Orange parades staged around the bronze monument in early July (*D* 207.9–208.17; Hill, 44). That these commemorations are an aspect of Joyce's tacit allusion in "After the Race" is supported by the narrator's invocation of the payment of "homage" (*D* 45.17) proximate to this statue during the particularly contentious first week of July. Irish national humorists pretended that the statue commemorated the horse rather than the rider, since William met his death following a riding accident. Some nationalists took a less indulgent view: it was repeatedly vandalized, and there were attempts to blow it up until its removal in 1929 (Hill, 40–44).

7. The fictional action anticipates the historical commemoration by two-and-a-half months, whereas Joyce wrote the story within the fortnight following the first anniversary of the Emmet centennial commemoration.

8. In an ingenious argument, Martin F. Kearney discerns Joyce's complex but pointed citation of the final sentence of this same speech in "A Mother."

9. Following the spirit and letter of "O Breathe Not His Name," in his many songs commemorating Emmet, Thomas Moore never identifies the hero. Cf. "O'Breen's not his name" (*FW* 56.32).

10. In a move fairly typical of cultural theorists' attempts to deal with Joyce's treatment of historical events such as the Emmet centennial celebration, Gibbons introduces the appearance of an innovative paradigm: here the contrast of the casual tourist and the flaneur to whom "the hidden histories and unexplained details" yield forth their meanings (149). When he comes to Joyce's text as a presumed illustration of the argument,

however, he treats Joyce's language as if it were univocal and *Ulysses* as a transparent literary monument.

11. The "funeral games" passage in *Finnegans Wake* traces the rebellion and suppression of the United Irishmen. It is sprinkled with a series of references to its Emmet-led phase, its betrayals, foolishness, chaos, cruelty, speech, and false dawn:

> the Kildare side . . . in his riddlesneek's ragmufflers and the horrid contrivance . . . the *Wearing of the Blue* . . so terribly naas . . . and, half hang me, sirr, . . . this is my awethorrorty . . . like the Nap O'Farrell Patter Tandy . . . the first spikesman . . . the last spokesman . . . Tick up on time. Howday you doom? That rising day sinks rosing in a night of nine week's wonder. (516.3–517.34)

As we have seen, several of these references, "horrid contrivance," "the *Wearing of the Blue*," "naas," "sir," "nap," "spokesman," and "rising day" have their precedents in the text of "After the Race."

12. The 1798 Rebellion proper began on May 28 with the Battle of Naas. This might appear merely coincidental with the reference in the first sentence of the story, but that the opening paragraph concludes with the emphatic phrase, "their friends, the French" (*D* 42.9). The French are gratefully remembered in Irish nationalist historiography for their military support of the United Irishmen: General Hoche's attempted landing in 1796, and General Humbert's in August–September 1798. Humbert's rout of the yeomanry at Castlebar (August 27) is popularly remembered as "the Races of Castlebar." The Franco-Hibernian alliance, and the Rebellion, ended with their defeat at Ballinamuck (September 5). The image of Jimmy linking arms with his French guests and singing "*Cadet Roussel*" (*D* 47.16–17) and the ironic reference to the French as "virtual victors" (*D* 42.10), seem like elements in the same historical motif in Joyce's story. Joyce's design does not embrace more than these few, if ingenious, references; but like the centennial commemorations of the Rebellion of the United Irishmen, it begins with Naas, and concludes with the image of the sunrise on the date of Robert Emmet's execution. Torchiana has a proper sympathy with Joyce's historical imagination, but his effort to pursue the relationship between the story and the events of summer 1798 is unsystematic and overstrained (80–84).

13. The precise time (3:26 a.m.) appeared in the same issue of the *Freeman's Journal* as that which reported the results of the Gordon Bennett Cup Race and the victory party held at the Shelbourne Hotel celebrating the French team victory.

14. Kershner cites a couple of literary examples from the proximate culture, but neither bears upon a comprehensive reading of the story, 78–79.

15. For example, Gogarty reports this exchange among a gathering of medical students (and Joyce): "'On one fact you may rest assured,' said Lame Murta. 'The day is not far distant when the Green Flag shall be seen. That day is not far distant.' 'Begog, it's not!' the Citizen shouts. 'Here's the dawn.' 'The sunburst of Erin,' Lame Murta went on, and all that kind of a thing.'" (*Tumbling in the Hay*, 185).

16. The first was made on an Edison 2-minute black wax cylinder (#13143), and the second on a Gramophone and Typewriter Ltd. 7" disc (G&T: Mat.646a; Cat.3–2520). McCormack recorded this song again on September 23, 1904, for the Gramophone and

Typewriter Ltd., 21 City Road, London (Mat.646a; Cat.3–2520). See Worth and Cartwright, 4.

17. Opal CDS 9847. (Pavilion Records Ltd., Sparrows Green, Wadhurst, E. Sussex).

18. This "Grand Gaelic Concert" was sponsored by the Exhibition of Irish Industries and not the Horse Show (as Ellmann implies, *JJII* 168). See Jackson and McGinley, 122.

19. A corollary implication of Ireland's Home Rule rising sun is the denial of its membership in the British Empire. Even though it had its origins in the sixteenth-century Spanish empire, the trope of "the empire on which the sun never sets" was a popular Victorian reference to the British embrace of the globe. A sunburst illumines Mrs. Dedalus's last agony: "A cloud began to cover the sun slowly" (*U* 1.248).

20. Roger Ekirch's encyclopedic book reminds modern urbanites of our distance from the terrors of ancestral night.

21. Joyce's original descriptor of Jimmy Doyle's reaction to Routh's presence (*Irish Homestead* version, replaced by "buried," *D* 46.23) implies a nod to Dublin's millennial Danish origins.

22. The advertiser's slogans interjected through the *Ricorso* passages, "Guld modning, have yous viewed Piers' aube? . . . Genghis is ghoon for you" (*FW* 593.9, 17–18), etc., are the equivalent of the race cars: commodity capitalism capturing the public imagination. He is the voice of the Lord "summoning to their tasks all the officers of the new aeon; they will descend, as though in mystical elevators, to the plane of manifestation" (Campbell and Robinson, 340n2).

23. Nigel Best's study of *Finnegans Wake* 594 assembles much useful data.

Chapter 6. Rhetoric—Modern and Classical

1. It reappears in Stephen's reflection on his three masters: "Horn of a bull, hoof of a horse, smile of a Saxon" (*U* 1.732). The dual images of teeth "of a high wind" (*D* 44.1–12) and of "the swarthy face of the [French] driver" (*D* 44.20–21) that bracket the triad in this story aerate this submerged allusion to an inherited resentment of foreign masters.

2. It is sandwiched between the monetary phrases, "made his money" (*D* 43.16, 18) and "rich enough" (*D* 43.20).

3. An appendix to Alvares's book, entitled "De Figuris" (53–59), defines and exemplifies a catalogue of rhetorical figures, e.g., synaeresis, diaeresis, synaloepha, eclipsis, systole, ectasis (diastole), prosthesis, aphaeresis, epenthesis, syncope, paragoge, apocope, tmesis, antithesis, metathesis. Since he ascribes Stephen Dedalus's acquaintance with "the laws of Latin verse" to this "ragged book," this brief catalogue (all in Latin) seems to be Joyce's model for the rhetorical exhibitionism of "Aeolus" and its modest antecedent, "After the Race."

4. This is one of Joyce's favorite structures in *Dubliners*: e.g., shared by "Counterparts," "Clay," "A Little Cloud," and "A Painful Case." It has a close affinity with the standard five-paragraph essay of English 101.

5. Each of these interludes can be further divided into two discrete subscenes each. Paragraph 7 describes Jimmy and Villona's alighting and walking northward, and paragraph 8 their reception at the Doyle home. Paragraph 10 describes the postprandial walk

westward of the five revelers, and paragraphs 11–13 their trip (with Farley, their augmenting sixth) to Kingstown.

6. The anastrophe of "gallantly the machinery of human nerves strove" helps ratchet up the hyperbole.

7. An interesting example of the deft dovetailing of the narrative voice and Jimmy's interior monologue comes in paragraph 4. Early in this sequence, the narrator reports, with evident appreciation, Villona's "deep bass hum of melody" (*D* 44.6). Jimmy's growing frustration at his inability to follow the exchanges in the car converges on his irritation with this same humming (*D* 44.12). This is a nice example of Joyce's creative handling of the classical epanodos.

8. On July 4, 1903, the sun rose at 3:26 a.m.

9. Revising the description of Jimmy and Villona's disembarking from the car outside the Bank of Ireland, Joyce replaced the verb "descended" with "alighted" (*D* 45.16). The lapsarian implications of "descended"—as its use in the epiphany shows—are inappropriate here; and the word "alight" echoes the assonance of its preceding complement, "elate" (*D* 44.14).

10. On July 2, 1903, it was 9:26 p.m. (30 minutes after sunset).

11. Joyce was evidently familiar with the precise topography of Inchicore, having trodden its roads during weekend excursions with his father and friends. His visual memory would therefore have retained the cresting image formally useful in designing his story. That the cars crossing the canal and to Inchicore are described as passing "through this channel of poverty" (*D* 42.5–6) exemplifies a silent paregmenon, since "canal" and "channel" are doublets (Skeat, s.v. "canal").

He had, moreover, when apparently under the tutelage of Mrs. Conway, been conducted to the Oblate church in Inchicore to see the then-famous wax figures of the Holy Family (Costello, 64). He confers the recollection of this visit upon Molly Bloom who unaccountably associates the simulacrum of the infant Jesus with the pop hit of the 1890s (*U* 18.496–97). This sentimental Tin Pan Alley song about disappointment in love ("many the hopes that have vanished") is remembered, even today, for the first lines of its refrain, "After the ball was over, / After the break of morn." It should therefore come as but a mild surprise that transformations of its first and last images, its initial vantage point, and theme are all inscribed in the design of our story. Whether intentionally summoned or subliminally allowed entry, these ephemera from a bygone era offer intriguing evidence of how, in the creative imagination, random associations coalesce into something new, congruent, and radiant.

12. The verb "raised" in the first paragraph of the story (*D* 42.7), indicating the responsive cheer of the onlookers, has its correspondence in the verb "rose" in the penultimate paragraph, with reference to the card players' gesture toward the "last tricks" (*D* 48.22-23).

13. Formally free indirect discourse, Kenner's "Uncle Charles Principle" (*Joyce's Voices*, 16–19).

14. "The Sisters" and "Eveline" were written in a furnished room at 60 Shelbourne Road, July–August 1904 (*Letters* II: lvi).

15. Griffith's coinage, after Queen Alexandra's remark on her Irish reception in July 1904, that "the poorer they are the more they cheer" (Jackson and McGinley, 35g).

16. This is the image that impressed the journalist who, from the same vantage point as that occupied by the narrator of "After the Race," wrote, "A mile or so away, you caught sight of two human heads topping the screen in front of the body of the car" (cited by Lynch, *Triumph*, 135).

17. Joyce did not attend the race (*MBK* 225). The daily newspapers and magazines carried dozens of pictures of the cars, the drivers, and the race observed from many vantage points.

18. See, e.g., the kinds of literalist and language usages explicated by Roy Gottfried in his brilliant book, *Joyce's Iritis and the Irritated Text*: e.g., that the first sentence of *Ulysses*—the novel designed to exhaust its tradition—utilizes virtually the entire English alphabet (32–34).

19. The major motifs of "parallel," "parallax," and "Parnell" in *Ulysses* bear witness to the persistence of this pairing in Joyce's imagination. As in "After the Race," it comes with its many contrasts and variants, e.g., the "Keyes" and "Kino's 11/= Trousers" motif (*U* 8.90–92).

20. Readers will recall that when Routh joins the party, the narrator keeps the count at "five" (*D* 46.13). When the narrator subsequently observes that the square dance cannot, without creative effort, be performed by an ensemble of five, he is implicitly counting Farley's belated addition to the company (*D* 47.26–27). Consequently, his drawing attention to Jimmy's inability to calculate his bets and debts and compensating attempt to count the beats of his temples is surely an ironic underlining of this motif. That a story whose ostensible theme is business investment is formally centered on that calculative institution, the Bank of Ireland (*D* 45.15), is but another aspect of Joyce's invocation of creative chiasmus.

21. In devising this complex image, Joyce seems to be transforming a phrase he encountered either in a physics lecture at the Old Royal University or in Mary Shelley's introduction to *Frankenstein*. In his treatise on the relationship between the nervous system and electric current, *De viribus electricitatis in motu musculari commentarius* (1791), the Italian physicist and physiologist Luigi Galvani (1737–98) describes a series of bioelectrical experiments in which a spark of electricity can apparently reanimate the legs of a dead frog—or cause the heart to palpitate. This "animal electricity" is known as "galvanism" (*Encyclopedia Britannica*, s.v. "Galvani, Luigi"). Joyce cites the same source, this time without irony, when he has Stephen Dedalus, in his disquisition on the perception of beauty, tell his companion Lynch that a phrase employed by Galvani in that treatise, "the enchantment of the heart" is "almost as beautiful as Shelley's" (*P* 213.24–25).

22. Bloom rebukes the snobbery of the formally educated with another cliché: "University of life" (*U* 15.840).

23. Jimmy's recollection of his father's prediction, cast in these repetitive terms (known to the classical rhetoricians as "exergesia"), suggests something of the mental dullness that accompanied his greed.

The narrator's proleptic sentence, "In Jimmy's house this dinner had been pronounced an occasion" (*D* 45.26–27), presents an interesting puzzle. His use of the passive voice, the pluperfect tense, and the reference to "his parents' trepidation" (*D* 45.27) in the next sentence imply that the word "occasion" ringing in Jimmy's ears as he buttons himself into his evening dress comes from Mrs. Doyle. The narrator's enallage here is doing its work: slyly allowing this single word to break the female silence of "After the Race."

24. In classical rhetoric, the term for conducting a pseudodialogue through taking up a position contrary to one's own. The narrator's report of Jimmy's implied interior language provides several examples that exhibit his partiality to this mental habit. Of the talented Villona we read that he was "unfortunately, very poor" (*D* 44.2). Coming on the heels of his recollection of his father's estimate of Ségouin as "well worth knowing" (*D* 43.34), this calculation implies a familial weighing of commercial interests against aesthetic values. Jimmy's trepidations about his investment in the car business are similarly cast: "Ségouin, perhaps, would not think it a great sum" (*D* 44.24–25).

25. In his opening paragraphs the narrator indulges in a couple of forays into interpretive omniscience: he is privy to the motivations of the bystanders' cheers (their gratitude for British oppression and their sympathy for the French, *D* 42.8–9), and to the particular reason for the "good humour" of each young man riding in Ségouin's blue car (*D* 43.3–12).

26. "The exchangeable value of . . . commodities . . . depends almost exclusively on the comparative quantity of labour expended on each." Ricardo's refinements of Adam Smith's economic theories would have been familiar to even as desultory a student at Cambridge or Dublin University in 1900. "On Value," chap. 1, *Principles of Political Economy and Taxation*, 12.

27. The narrators of "Eveline" and "After the Race"—two of Joyce's first three experiments in short fiction—make the heaviest use of exclamation in *Dubliners*.

28. (*U* 14.1440–1591): see John Noel Turner, "A Commentary on the Closing of 'Oxen of the Sun,'" *JJQ* 35, no. 1 (Fall 1997): 83–111.

29. Joyce devises a similarly delayed response in having Aunt Kate's prayer, "The Lord have mercy on his soul," appear some twelve lines after Gabriel Conroy's mention of "the late lamented Patrick Morkan, our grandfather" (*D* 207.16–29).

30. Jimmy apparently intends to express something about the splendid show the car makes. However, its contemporary chivalric, polite, or amatory connotations—influenced by French usage—are incongruous (*OED*).

31. It should be noted that the tagged-on phrase, "the noise of the car, too," concludes the paragraph that begins with "The car ran on merrily" (*D* 44.3). This nice example of Joyce's use of *inclusio*—by which a passage or work begins and ends with the same word or image—functions here to imply the contrast between the narrator's formal control and Jimmy's distraction. This figure is to become a Joycean specialty, as we see in "The Dead," the "[s]tately" and "yes" of *Ulysses*, Molly Bloom's soliloquy, etc.

32. Testimony to the tone of Joyce's conversations appears in the pages of Gogarty's *Tumbling in the Hay*. They are sprinkled with references to classical etymology (43) and rhetoric, as in this instance, "meiosis" (176).

33. Skeat's dictionary was the standard authority on English etymology in 1904. We know that Joyce consulted it attentively, in either its 1882 or 1898 editions. Skeat's own 1910 edition made many corrections and additions, and his entire enterprise has been since rendered obsolete by subsequent advances. For present purposes, consequently (following Stephen Whittaker's exemplary caution), the 1882 edition is cited.

34. This main thoroughfare acquired its name from a medieval convent, Sainte Marie Del Dam. As that name implies, this establishment was named not after Our Lady (*Notre Dame*), but a mill dam on the River Poddle, which flows under the street at Cork Hill (Bennett, s.v. "St Marie Del Dam").

35. The reference to "loosened tongues" recalls Jimmy's name-dropping in the previous scene. This sequence summons the trite schoolboy joke in which the rhetoric schoolmaster asks how undisciplined sentences, housewives' tongues, and two French cities are alike. The answer: "Toulon and Toulouse."

36. The usage of "inheritor" is interesting here. Before the Renaissance, it referred only to the receiver of property or social position. The first recorded usage with regard to personal qualities recorded by the *OED* is Shakespeare's. This sly sentence, which indicates a parallel between "a great sum under his control" and "the inheritor of solid instincts" while also implicitly back translating "sum" into "*solidus*" (*D* 44.23–27), is another indication of the narrator's superior wit.

37. Gifford's attempt to correct and enlarge Gilbert's list is not among the successes of his annotations to *Ulysses* (642–43). See Jorn Barger, "Rhetorical figures in the Eolus (*sic.*) episode of James Joyce's *Ulysses*" (2000), http://www.robotwisdom.com/jaj/.

38. Hodgart points out that "the art of making persuasive speeches is an ancient and much-loved tradition of the Irish, especially the making of political speeches, whether at the graveside of dead leaders or from the dock" (121). *Speeches from the Dock,* edited by T. D., A. M., and D. B. Sullivan was a best seller and could be found in Irish parlors and bars (1890s); Tom Kettle, Joyce's friend, published *Irish Orators and Oratory* (ca. 1914).

39. Ovid's sources were Euripides, Hesiod, Lucian, Hygenius, and Nonnus; there are references to Phaethon in many other ancient writers, including Homer, Hesiod, Appollodorus, and Virgil. A parallel myth appears in Amerindian folklore. See appendix in J. G. Frazer's Loeb edition of Appollodorus (388–94). See also Wolfgang Galicki, *Phaethon: A Forgotten Myth* (1986), and James Diggle's edition of Euripides's *Phaethon* (2004).

40. In this respect, Jimmy Doyle is one of the least complex or interesting of Joycean sons. Instead of developing the theme of the "doubted father"—in which Joyce was philosophically interested, and which he had already visited in "The Sisters"—he simplifies or naturalizes the Ovidian tragedy. Bequeathing a "fatal gift" upon his son, Helios helplessly beholds Phaethon's destruction. Put another way, whereas Ovid distributes the sympathies evenly between father and son, Joyce casts each of his characters under a penumbra of condescension.

Chapter 7. The Infernal

1. Kennedy, *Legendary Fictions of the Irish Celts* (1866), 116–17. From part 2, "Legends of the 'Good People,'" told by a Mrs. K. about her father.

2. See Cross, *Motif-Index of Early Irish Literature,* 243, and Briggs, *An Encyclopedia of Fairies,* 374, 469.

3. This figure reappears in "Telemachus" in the form of the milk woman who greets Mulligan with, "That's a lovely morning, sir, . . . Glory be to God" (*U* 1.390). He immediately "translates" for Haines the speech of the "islanders" (*U* 1.393).

4. The *púca* (pooka, phouka), name derived from the ON *pukki*, is a fairy in animal form, usually in that of a horse or ass. Its offer of a ride can be benevolent, but is more often not, leading night wanderers astray: its breath or spit renders fruits poisonous (MacKillop, s.v. "pooka").

5. Also known as a "cluricawn" or "lurickeen," this best known and most sentimentalized of the Irish fairies is proverbially short and jolly, but in Kennedy's words "a deceitful old rogue" (129). The only businessman among them, his cobbling trade thrives on his clients' favorite pastime, dancing. As MacKillop records, this figure has a complex descent from the MidIr. *Lúchorpán* [small bodied] (s.v. "leprechaun").

6. The fairies are euphemistically known as *na daoine maithe* [the good people] (MacKillop, s.v. "fairy"). This story is one of Kennedy's eighteen "Legends of the 'Good People'" (79–143).

7. The Irish Christian folk tradition thinks of the fairies as fallen angels (Briggs, *The Vanishing People*, 30; Kennedy, 97, 142–43).

8. The absence of the name "Jimmy Doyle" conceals the folkloric relationship and helps preserve the naturalistic appearance of the story.

9. See Stanislaus Joyce's comments on their father's capacities as an oral storyteller (*CDD* 136–37) for evidence of this gift. Joyce frequently acknowledged this inheritance (*Letters* III: 399).

10. The word *bruidhean* in Modern Irish means a hostel, a castle banqueting hall, or royal residence. It has come to mean—by extension—an Otherworld residence of the fairies. In Old Irish it was spelled *bruidhen*, and had a secondary meaning of a fight, contest, argument, or quarrel (MacKillop, s.v. "*bruiden*"). The linkage is substantiated by the frequency with which *bruidhean* tales concerned a quarrel between a guest and his host over the protocols of hospitality.

11. See Stanley Sultan, *Eliot, Joyce, and Co.* (1987). Writing on Joyce's interest in the Celtic theme of otherworld transformations in *Ulysses*, Maria Tymoczko concurs that this was Joyce's probable original source (292–93).

12. Further, as Patrick Kennedy admits, he bowdlerized the version that he heard in County Wexford in the 1820s, considering that the bawdy song might offend latter-day Victorian (or urban) sensibilities, damaging his reputation as teacher and representative of dignified nationalist aspirations.

13. In this east-west context, Farley is a revenant from the Land of Youth: a "strange" fellow indeed, he has not only returned from the America to which his ancestors fled, but he has foregone the company of an attractive woman to entertain Doyle and his friends. The eastern Continentals, by contrast, are the mysterious deceivers.

14. The great mound or motte just outside the town is all that remains today of that residence (P. W. Joyce, 1: 207). The largest town in County Kildare, it is today's site of the Mondello Park motor racing circuit.

15. Laoghaire (427/8–462/3) built a fort there. The contention between the kings of *Midhe* [Meath, ruled from Tara] and of *Laighin* [Leinster, ruled from Naas] over territorial control of the area around present-day Dublin and Dún Laoghaire led to the death of Laoghaire. Kingstown was renamed Dún Laoghaire in 1920 (MacKillop, s.v. "Lóegaire mac Néill").

16. To reach Farley's yacht, the company traverses Victoria Wharf, where Queen Victoria—derisively known as "The Queen of Hearts"—landed during her visits in 1849, 1861, and 1900.

17. This holograph of the KJV translation can be seen in the archive at Cornell University.

18. Participation in spiritualism is forbidden to Catholics. Considered contrary to Revelation, it is regarded as superstition. Blavatsky's *Isis Unveiled* (vol. 2) is expressly anti-Catholic and anti-Jesuit.

19. This is Joyce's first invocation of the cardinal directions. In *Dubliners* it recurs, with pointed significance, whenever journeys are undertaken or contemplated, e.g. the eastward quest in "An Encounter" and "Araby," and the "journey westward" contemplated by Gabriel Conroy in "The Dead."

20. The number thirteen was ambiguous in the Cabbala and does not figure significantly in Theosophical numerology. Joyce, however, respected the numinous burden it inherited from Babylonian and Christian tradition (*JJII* 517).

21. From among Joyce's acquaintances at the Carrefour de l'Odeon in Paris, he uses the names Routh and Villona. He therefore passes over the Italian Canudo and the German Däubler, evidently in favor of the denotations of these surnames (*adnominatio*). Ségouin and Rivière are, therefore, the only characters in the story whose names are not drawn from the historical record (Gorman, 100).

22. These characters and the implied narrator have their spiritual doubles bearing the names Bennett, Emmet, and Griffith. Elsewhere, Bloom / Ulysses; Finnegan / Finn MacCumhall [MacCool], etc.

23. Bloom associates the words "parallel" and "parallax" with the transmigration of souls (*U* 8.110–13). Stephen is similarly moved to theological reflections on Trinitarian and Christological mysteries (*U* 3.45–54).

24. Joyce's interest in Theosophy persisted: he reread Blavatsky letters in preparing *FW* (Atherton, 236).

25. Following Gerty MacDowell's departure from Sandymount Strand, that agnostic theologian, Leopold Bloom, ruminates: "Saw a pool near her foot. Bend, see my face there, dark mirror, breathe on it, stirs. All these rocks with lines and scars and letters. O, those transparent! Besides they don't know. What is the meaning of that other world" (*U* 13.1260–63). His reflections on the present and hoped-for worlds touch on the ambiguities of the geological and written records, citing Molly, Martha, and St. Paul. The "letters" reference, therefore, could be to those of St. Paul, Martha Clifford, Mr. Deasy, or indeed the kinds of numinous literalism considered here.

26. This powerful image, analogous to that of Plato's cave, undergoes several transformations in Joyce's work. In *Ulysses*, of his task as teacher of algebra, Stephen muses, "Averroes and Moses Maimonides, dark men in mien and movement, flashing in their mocking mirrors the obscure soul of the world, a darkness shining in brightness which brightness could not comprehend" (*U* 2.158–60). He fashions this brilliant amalgam about the "other world" of ideal reality beyond that of phenomena from the language of saints Paul and John and of Giordano Bruno.

27. See Owens, *James Joyce's Painful Case*, 118–19.

28. Mecsnóber notes that Joyce uses the phrase "*risorgimento corporale*" clearly in the religious sense of "bodily resurrection" (345 and 358n12).

29. Ex. Lat. *avarus* [greed]: the inordinate love of riches insofar as the acquisition and retention of wealth is an incentive to injustice (*Catholic Encyclopedia*, s.v. "avarice"). Within the terms of the story, the Doyles are therefore avaricious in the degree to which their fortune was acquired from police contracts.

30. In preparing the 1910 printing, Joyce strengthened these links by replacing "in the face of a high wind" with "in the teeth of a high wind" (*JJA* 4: 3c, 5: 143).

31. The Dantean term "*mi divella*" [uproot me] appears in several synonymous forms in *The Divine Comedy* (Allan Gilbert trans., 345n8) summoning the English word "devil" from Joyce's retentive acoustic memory (he could recite from memory many of its cantos).

Bibliography

Adams, Robert M. *James Joyce: Common Sense and Beyond.* New York: Random House, 1966.
Ainsworth, Godfrey. *James Joyce and Sr. Gertrude Joyce.* 2nd ed. Waverley, New South Wales: Franciscan Friary, 1999.
Alighieri, Dante. *Inferno.* The Italian text with translation and notes by Allan Gilbert. Durham, N.C.: Duke University Press, 1969.
———. *Purgatorio.* Translated by John Ciardi. Introduced by Archibald T. MacAllister. New York: New American Library, 1961.
Alvares, Emmanuel. *An Introduction to the Latin Tongue; or, The First Book of Grammar.* London: Henry Hills, 1689; rpt. Dublin: P. Wogan, 1815; rpt. Cork: Edwards and Savage, 1816.
———. *Prosodia Sive Institutionum Linguae Latinae Liber Quartus: In Usum Studiosorum.* Novi Eboraci: T and J Swords, 1805.
American National Biography. Edited by John A. Garraty and Mark C. Carnes. 24 vols. New York: Oxford University Press, 1999.
Anderson, Chester G. "Joyce's Verses." In Bowen and Carens, eds., 129–55.
Anderson, William S. *Ovid's Metamorphoses, Books 1–5.* Edited, with an Introduction and Commentary. Norman: University of Oklahoma Press, 1997.
Atherton, James. *Books at the Wake: A Study of Literary Allusions in James Joyce's Finnegans Wake.* New York: Arcturus, 1974.
Bauerle, Ruth, ed. *The James Joyce Songbook.* New York: Garland, 1982.
Beck, Warren. *Joyce's Dubliners: Substance, Vision, and Art.* Durham, N.C.: Duke University Press, 1969.
Bennett, Douglas. *The Encyclopaedia of Dublin, Revised and Expanded.* Dublin: Gill and Macmillan, 2005.
Benstock, Bernard. "Telemachus." In Hart and Hayman, eds., 1–16.
Best, Nigel. *Dawn: A Study of the Present Age and* Finnegans Wake *through a close look at FW 594: one page being sufficient for our times.* New Plymouth, New Zealand: Dawn Publishers, 1979.
Bishop, John. *Joyce's Book of the Dark:* Finnegans Wake. Madison: University of Wisconsin Press, 1986.
Blavatsky, H. P. *Isis Unveiled: A Master-Key to the Mysteries of Ancient and Modern Science and Theology.* 2 vols. New York: J. W. Bouton, 1877.
———. *The Key to Theosophy.* London: Theosophical Publishing Society, 1893.
Blayac, Alain. "'After the Race,' ou les avatars d'un texte polysémique." *Cahiers Victoriens et Edouardiens: Studies in the Early Joyce* 14 (October 1981): 39–46.

Bowen, Zack. "'After the Race.'" In *James Joyce's* Dubliners: *Critical Essays,* edited by Clive Hart, 53–61. New York: Viking, 1969.

———. "Hungarian Politics in 'After the Race.'" *James Joyce Quarterly* 7 (Winter 1970): 138–39.

Bowen, Zack, and James Carens, eds. *A Companion to Joyce Studies.* Westport, Conn.: Greenwood, 1984.

Bradley, Bruce, SJ. *James Joyce's Schooldays.* New York: St. Martin's, 1982.

Brady, Joseph, and Anngret Simms, eds. *Dublin: Through Space and Time (c. 900–1900).* Portland, Ore.: Four Courts, 2001.

Briggs, Katherine M. *An Encyclopedia of Fairies: Hobgoblins, Brownies, Bogies, and Other Supernatural Creatures.* New York: Pantheon, 1976.

———. *The Vanishing People: A Study of Traditional Fairy Beliefs.* London: Batsford, 1978.

Bulfin, William. *Rambles in Eirinn.* Dublin: M. H. Gill, 1907.

Campbell, Joseph, and Henry Morton Robinson. *A Skeleton Key to* Finnegans Wake. New York: Viking, 1969.

Campbell, Margaret. *Dolmetsch: The Man and His Work.* Seattle: University of Washington Press, 1975.

Carens, James F. *Surpassing Wit: Oliver St. John Gogarty, His Poetry and His Prose.* New York: Columbia University Press, 1979.

The Catechism, ordered by the National Synod of Maynooth and approved of by the Cardinal, the Archbishops and Bishops of Ireland for general use throughout the Irish Church, etc. Dublin: Gill, 1884.

The Catholic Encyclopedia. New York: Encyclopedia Press, 1907–12. http://www.newadvent.org/cathen/.

Cathorne-Hardy, Jonathan. *The Old School Tie: The Phenomenon of the English Public School.* New York: Viking, 1977.

Cato, Bob, and Greg Vitiello. *Joyce Images.* Introduced by Anthony Burgess. New York: Norton, 1994.

Census of Ireland 1911. The National Archives of Ireland. http://www.census.nationalarchives.ie.

Cheng, Vincent. *Joyce, Race, and Empire.* New York: Cambridge University Press, 1995.

Colum, Mary. *Life and the Dream: Memories of a Literary Life in Europe and America.* London: Macmillan, 1947.

Colum, Mary, and Padraic Colum. *Our Friend James Joyce.* New York: Doubleday, 1958.

Costello, Peter. *James Joyce: The Years of Growth, 1882–1915.* New York: Pantheon, 1993.

Cousins, James H., and Margaret E. *We Two Together.* Madras, India: Ganesh, 1950.

Cronin, Mike. "The Irish Free State and Aonach Tailteann." In *Sport and the Irish: Histories, Identities, Issues,* edited by Alan Bairner, 53–68. Dublin: University College Dublin Press, 2005.

Cross, Tom Peete. *Motif-Index of Early Irish Literature.* Bloomington: Indiana University Press, 1952.

Cuddon, J. A. *A Dictionary of Literary Terms and Literary Theory.* 3rd ed. Cambridge, Mass.: Blackwell, 1991.

Curran, Constantine. *James Joyce Remembered.* New York: Oxford University Press, 1968.

Daly, Mary E. *Dublin, The Deposed Capital: A Social and Economic History, 1860–1914.* Cork: Cork University Press, 1984.
Deane, Seamus. "Dead Ends: Joyce's Finest Moments." In *Semicolonial Joyce,* edited by Derek Attridge and Marjorie Howes, 21–36. New York: Cambridge University Press, 2000.
Dolan, Anne, Patrick M. Geoghegan, and Darryl Jones, eds. *Reinterpreting Emmet: Essays on the Life and the Legacy of Robert Emmet.* Dublin: University College Dublin Press, 2007.
Dolmetsch, Arnold. "The Lute: I"; "The Lute: II." *The Connoisseur: An Illustrated Magazine for Collectors* 8; 9 (April 1904; May 1904): 213–15; 23–25.
Downs, Robert B. *Books That Changed the World.* Chicago: American Library Association, 1956.
Dumas, Alexandre. *The Three Musketeers.* Translated by Jacques le Clercq. New York: Modern Library, 2001.
Dunleavy, Janet Egleson, and Gareth W. Dunleavy. *Douglas Hyde: A Maker of Modern Ireland.* Berkeley: University of California Press, 1991.
Ekirch, A. Roger. *At Day's Close: Night in Times Past.* New York: Norton, 2005.
Elliott, Marianne. *Robert Emmet: The Making of a Legend.* London: Profile Books, 2003.
Ellis-Fermor, Una. *The Irish Dramatic Movement.* London: Methuen, 1964.
Ellmann, Richard. *The Consciousness of Joyce.* New York: Oxford University Press, 1977.
Encyclopedia Britannica. 11th ed. New York: Encyclopedia Britannica, 1910.
Encyclopedia of Rhetoric and Composition: Communications from Ancient Times to the Information Age. Edited by Theresa Enos. New York: Garland, 1996.
Encyclopedia of the Irish in America. Edited by Michael Glazier. Notre Dame, Ind.: University of Notre Dame Press, 1999.
Encyclopedic Theosophical Glossary: A Resource on Theosophy. G. de Purucker, Geoffrey Barborka, Grace F. Knoche, Sarah Belle Dougherty, A. Studley Hart, and Elsa-Brita Titchenell, eds. Pasadena: Theosophical University Press Online Edition, 1999.
Fairhall, James. "Big-Power Politics and Colonial Economics: The Gordon Bennett Cup Race and 'After the Race.'" *James Joyce Quarterly* 28, no. 2 (Winter 1991): 387–97.
Fanning, Charles. "Robert Emmet and Nineteenth-Century Irish America." In Dolan, Geoghegan, and Jones, 138–69.
Flink, James J. *The Automobile Age.* Cambridge: MIT Press, 1988.
Foster, R. F. *Modern Ireland 1600–1972.* New York: Penguin, 1988.
——. *W. B. Yeats: A Life. I: The Apprentice Mage, 1865–1914.* New York: Oxford University Press, 1997.
Frayne, John P., and Colton Johnson, eds. *The Uncollected Prose by W. B. Yeats.* Vol. 2. New York: Columbia University Press, 1976.
Frazier, Adrian. *George Moore, 1853–1933.* New Haven: Yale University Press, 2000.
Gabler, Hans Walter. Introduction to *Dubliners: A Norton Critical Edition,* edited by Margot Norris, xv–xliii. New York: Norton, 2006.
Geoghegan, Patrick M. *Robert Emmet: A Life.* Montreal: McGill-Queen's University Press, 2002.
Gibbons, Luke. "'Where Wolfe Tone's statue was not': Joyce, monuments and memory."

In *History and Memory in Modern Ireland*, edited by Ian McBride, 139–59. New York: Cambridge University Press, 2001.

Gifford, Don, with Robert J. Seidman. *"Ulysses" Annotated: Notes for Joyce's "Ulysses."* 2nd ed. Berkeley: University of California Press, 1988.

Gilbert, Stuart. *James Joyce's "Ulysses": A Study.* New York: Vintage, 1958.

Glandon, Virginia. *Arthur Griffith and the Advanced-Nationalist Press: Ireland, 1900–1922.* New York: Peter Lang, 1985.

Gogarty, Oliver St. John. *It Isn't This Time of Year At All!: An Unpremeditated Autobiography.* Garden City: Doubleday, 1954; rpt. Greenwood, 1970.

———. *Many Lines to Thee: Letters to G.K.A. Bell from the Martello Tower at Sandycove, Rutland Square, and Trinity College, Dublin, 1904–1907.* Edited with a commentary by James F. Carens. Mountrath: Dolmen, 1971.

———. *The Poems and Plays of Oliver St. John Gogarty.* Collected, introduced, and edited by A. Norman Jeffares. Gerrards Cross: Smythe, 2001.

———. *Tumbling in the Hay* . . . London: Constable, 1939.

Gorman, Herbert. *James Joyce.* New York: Farrar and Rinehart, 1939.

Gottfried, Roy. *Joyce's Iritis and the Irritated Text: The Dis-lexic Ulysses.* Gainesville: University Press of Florida, 1995.

Griffith, Arthur. *The Resurrection of Hungary: A Parallel for Ireland.* Dublin: James Duffy; M. H. Gill; Sealy, Bryers and Walker, 1904.

Gudgin, Peter. *Military Intelligence: The British Story.* London: Arms and Armour Press, 1989.

Hardiman, Adrian. "The Trial of Robert Emmet." In Dolan, Geoghegan, and Jones, 227–41.

Hart, Clive. *Structure and Motif in* Finnegans Wake. Evanston, Ill.: Northwestern University Press, 1962.

Hart, Clive, and David Hayman, eds. *James Joyce's* Ulysses: *Critical Essays.* Berkeley: University of California Press, 1974.

Hayes-McCoy, Gerald Anthony. *History of Irish Flags from the Earliest Times.* Dublin: Academy Press, 1979.

Herlihy, James. *The Dublin Metropolitan Police: A Short History and Genealogical Guide.* Dublin: Four Courts Press, 2001.

Hill, Judith. *Irish Public Sculpture: A History.* Dublin: Four Courts, 1998.

Hodgart, M.J.C. "Aeolus." In Hart and Hayman, eds., 114–30.

Holloway, Joseph. *Joseph Holloway's Abbey Theatre: A Selection from His Unpublished Journal, Impressions of a Dublin Playgoer.* Edited by Robert Hogan and Michael J. O'Neill. Carbondale: Southern Illinois University Press, 1967.

Honey, J. R. de Symons. *Tom Brown's Universe: The Development of the English Public School in the Nineteenth Century.* New York: New York Times Book Co., 1977.

Irish Catholic Directory and Almanac. Dublin: James Duffy, 1909.

Jackson, John Wyse, and Peter Costello. *John Stanislaus Joyce: The Voluminous Life and Genius of James Joyce's Father.* New York: St. Martin's, 1998.

Jackson, John Wyse, and Bernard McGinley, eds. *James Joyce's* Dubliners: *An Illustrated Edition with Annotations.* New York: St. Martin's, 1995.

Jacobs, Joseph. *Celtic Fairy Tales*. New York: World, 1971.
Joyce, Patrick Weston. *Old Celtic Romances: Tales from Irish Mythology*. London: David Nutt, 1897; rpt. New York: Devin-Adair, 1962.
———. *The Origin and History of Irish Names of Places*. 3 vols. Dublin: Educational Company, 1920.
Kearney, Martin F. "Robert Emmet's 1803 Rising and Bold Mrs. Kearney: James Joyce's 'A Mother' as Historical Analogue." *Journal of the Short Story in English* 37 (2001): 49–61.
Kelleher, John V. "Irish History and Mythology in James Joyce's 'The Dead.'" *Review of Politics* 27 (1965): 414–33.
Kennedy, Patrick. *Legendary Fictions of the Irish Celts*. London: Macmillan, 1866; rpt. New York: Blom, 1969.
Kenner, Hugh. *Dublin's Joyce*. Boston: Beacon, 1956.
———. *Joyce's Voices*. Berkeley: University of California Press, 1978.
Kershner, R. B. *Joyce, Bakhtin, and Popular Literature: Chronicles of Disorder*. Chapel Hill: University of North Carolina Press, 1989.
Kinealy, Christine. *A Death-Dealing Famine: The Great Hunger in Ireland*. London: Pluto, 1997.
Kipling, Rudyard. *Kim*. Edited and introduced by Edward W. Said. New York: Penguin, 1989.
Leslie, Emily. "My First Automobile Ride." *Wide World Magazine* (March 1902): 542–48.
Liddell, Henry George, and Robert Scott. *A Lexicon. Abridged from Liddell and Scott's Greek-English Lexicon*. Oxford: Clarendon Press, 1966.
Litz, A. Walton. *The Art of James Joyce: Method and Design in "Ulysses" and "Finnegans Wake."* New York: Oxford University Press, 1964.
Lynch, Brendan. *Green Dust: Ireland's Unique Motor Racing History, 1900–1939*. Dublin: Portobello, 1988.
———. *Triumph of the Red Devil: The Irish Gordon Bennett Cup Race 1903*. Dublin: Portobello, 2002.
Lyons, J. B. *Oliver St. John Gogarty: The Man of Many Talents: A Biography*. Dublin: Blackwater, 1980.
MacKillop, James. *Dictionary of Celtic Mythology*. New York: Oxford University Press, 1998.
Mackinder, Sir Halford J. "The Geographical Pivot of History." *Geographical Journal* 23, no. 4 (April 1904): 421–37.
MacLochlainn, Alf. "*Pyper? Un homme de pois!*" In *James Joyce: ce cahier a été dirigé par Jacques Aubert et Fritz Senn*, 503–7. Paris: Editions de l'Herne, 1985.
MacLysaght, Edward. *Irish Families: Their Names, Arms, and Origins*. New York: Crown, 1972.
Maddox, Brenda. *Nora: The Real Life of Molly Bloom*. Boston: Houghton Mifflin, 1998.
Manganiello, Dominic. *Joyce's Politics*. Boston: Routledge, 1980.
Maume, Patrick. *The Long Gestation: Irish Nationalist Life, 1891–1918*. New York: St. Martin's, 1999.
McCartney, Donal. "The Sinn Féin Movement." In *The Making of 1916: Studies in the History of the Rising*, edited by Kevin B. Nowlan, 31–48. Dublin: Stationery Office, 1969.

McCormack, Count John. "When Shall the Day Break in Erin?" Music and words by Aynsley Fox and Denis Downing. London: Gramophone, 1900. Reissued in *The Complete Surviving Early Recordings* (Vol. 7: 1904–6). Sparrows Green, E. Sussex: Pavilion Records, 1991.

McGee, Owen. *The IRB: The Irish Republican Brotherhood from the Land League to Sinn Féin*. Dublin: Four Courts Press, 2005.

McNichol, Dan. *The Roads that Built America: The Incredible Story of the U.S. Interstate System*. New York: Sterling, 2006.

Mecsnóber, Tekla. "James Joyce, Arthur Griffith, Trieste, and the Hungarian National Character." *James Joyce Quarterly* 38, nos. 3–4 (Spring–Summer 2001): 341–59.

Montagu of Beaulieu, Edward John Barrington Douglas-Scott-Montagu, Baron. *The Gordon Bennett Races*. London: Cassell, 1963.

Moore, George. *Evelyn Innes*. New York: Appleton, 1898.

Moore, Thomas. *A Selection of Irish Melodies with Symphonies and Accompaniments by Sir John Stephenson, and Characteristic Words by Thomas Moore, Esq*. Edited by Francis Robinson. Dublin: H. Bussell, 1850.

Morris, Richard. *Elementary Lessons in Historical English Grammar Containing Accidence and Word-formation*. London: Macmillan, 1874.

Nagy, Joseph Falaky. "Shamanic Aspects of the *Bruidhean* Tale." *History of Religions* 20, no. 4 (May 1981): 302–22.

New Grove Dictionary of Music and Musicians. Edited by Stanley Sadie. 20 vols. Washington, D.C.: Grove, 1995.

Norris, Margot. *Suspicious Readings of Joyce's "Dubliners."* Philadelphia: University of Pennsylvania Press, 2003.

O'Brien, Joseph V. *"Dear, Dirty Dublin": A City in Distress, 1899–1916*. Berkeley: University of California Press, 1982.

O'Connor, Richard. *The Scandalous Mr. Bennett*. New York: Doubleday, 1962.

O'Connor, Ulick. *Oliver St. John Gogarty: A Poet and His Times*. London: Mentor, 1967.

Ó Lúing, Seán. *Art Ó Gríofa*. Baile Átha Cliath: Sáirséal agus Dill, 1953.

O'Neill, Michael J. "The Date of 'The Holy Office.'" *James Joyce Review* 3, nos. 1–2 (1959): 50–51.

O'Nolan, Brian (pseud., Flann O'Brien). *At Swim-Two-Birds*. New York: Walker, 1966.

Ovid. *Metamorphoses*. http://www.thelatinlibrary.com/ovid.html.

Owens, Cóilín. "'Clay' (1): Irish Folklore." *James Joyce Quarterly* 27, no. 4 (Winter 1990): 337–52.

———. *James Joyce's Painful Case*. Gainesville: University Press of Florida, 2008.

———. "'A Man with Two Establishments to Keep Up': Joyce's Farrington." *Irish Renaissance Annual* 4 (1983): 128–56.

Peake, C. H. *James Joyce: The Citizen and the Artist*. Stanford: Stanford University Press, 1977.

Polmar, Norman, and Thomas B. Allen. *Spy Book: The Encyclopedia of Espionage*. New York: Random House, 1997.

Poulton, Diana, ed. *The Collected Lute Music of John Dowland*. Berkeley: University of California Press, 1982.

Pound, Reginald. *Mirror of the Century: The Strand Magazine, 1891–1950*. South Brunswick, N.J.: Barnes, 1966.
Power, Arthur. *Conversations with James Joyce*. Edited by Clive Hart. London: Millington, 1974.
Rafroidi, Patrick. *James Joyce,* Dubliners: *Notes*. Beirut: York, 1985.
Reid, B. L. *The Man from New York: John Quinn and His Friends*. New York: Oxford University Press, 1968.
Reynolds, John J. *Footprints of Emmet*. Dublin: Gill, 1903.
Reynolds, Mary T. *Joyce and Dante: The Shaping Imagination*. Princeton, N.J.: Princeton University Press, 1981.
Ricardo, David. *Principles of Political Economy and Taxation: The Works and Correspondence of David Ricardo*. Edited by Piero Sraffa. Vol. 1. Cambridge: Cambridge University Press, 1951.
Rooney, William. *Poems and Ballads*. Edited by Arthur Griffith. Dublin: Gill, 1901.
Rose, Danis, and John O'Hanlon. *Understanding* Finnegans Wake: *A Guide to the Narrative of James Joyce's Masterpiece*. New York: Garland, 1982.
Russel, Myra Teicher. *James Joyce's "Camber Music": The Lost Song Settings*. Bloomington: Indiana University Press, 1993.
Schimmel, Annemarie. *The Mystery of Numbers*. New York: Oxford University Press, 1993.
Scholes, Robert, and Richard M. Kain, eds. *The Workshop of Daedalus: James Joyce and the Raw Materials for* A Portrait of the Artist as a Young Man. Evanston, Ill.: Northwestern University Press, 1965.
Schork, R. J. *Latin and Roman Culture in Joyce*. Gainesville: University Press of Florida, 1997.
Schwartz, David G. *Roll the Bones: The History of Gambling*. New York: Gotham Books, 2006.
Silva Rhetoricae: The Forest of Rhetoric. Edited by Gideon Burton. http://www.rhetoric.byu.edu.
Sinnett, A. P. *Esoteric Buddhism*. London: Trübner, 1883.
Skeat, Walter W. *An Etymological Dictionary of the English Language*. Oxford: Clarendon Press, 1882.
Slocum, John J., and Herbert Cahoon. *A Bibliography of James Joyce (1882–1941)*. New Haven: Yale University Press, 1953.
Somerville, Jane. "Money in *Dubliners*." *Studies in Short Fiction* 12 (1975): 109–16.
Spring, Matthew. Liner notes to *All Goodly Sports: The Complete Music of Henry VIII*. Performed by SIRINU, Ensemble for Early Music. Oakhurst, N.J.: Musical Heritage Society, CD 515306Y, 1999.
St. Jean, Shawn. "Readerly Paranoia and Joyce's Adolescence Stories." *James Joyce Quarterly* 35–36, nos. 4–1 (Summer/Fall 1998): 665–82.
Sullivan, Kevin. *Joyce among the Jesuits*. New York: Columbia University Press, 1958.
Symons, Arthur. *Plays, Acting, and Music*. London: Duckworth, 1903.
Terrinoni, Enrico. *Occult Joyce: The Hidden in* Ulysses. Newcastle, United Kingdom: Cambridge Scholars Publishing, 2007.

Thompson, Stith. *Motif-Index of Folk-Literature: A Classification of Narrative Elements in Folktales, Ballads, Myths, Fables, Mediaeval Romances, Exempla, Fabliaux, Jest-Books, and Local Legends.* 6 vols. Bloomington: Indiana University Press, 1955–58. Electronic edition: Charlottesville, Va.: InteLex, 2000.

Tindall, William York. *A Reader's Guide to James Joyce.* New York: Farrar, Straus and Giroux, 1959.

Torchiana, Donald. *Backgrounds for Joyce's* Dubliners. Boston: Allen and Unwin, 1986.

Tracy, Robert. "Leopold Bloom Fourfold: A Hungarian-Hebraic-Hellenic-Hibernian Hero." *Massachusetts Review* 6, no. 3 (1965): 523–38.

Tymoczko, Maria. *The Irish* Ulysses. Berkeley: University of California Press, 1994.

The United Irishman (newspaper) [Dublin] 1899–1905.

Villon, François. *The Poems of François Villon.* Translated and introduced with notes by Galway Kinnell. Boston: Houghton Mifflin, 1977.

Walker, Antoinette, and Michael Fitzgerald. *Unstoppable Brilliance: Irish Geniuses and Asperger's Syndrome.* Dublin: Liberties Press, 2006.

Walzl, Florence. "*Dubliners.*" In Bowen and Carens, 157–228.

Ward, David F. "The Race Before the Story: James Joyce and the Gordon Bennett Cup Automobile Race." *Éire-Ireland* 2 (Summer 1967): 27–35.

Weldon, Helen. "The Motor Cup Course." *New Ireland Review* 19, no. 4 (July 1903): 278–84.

Whittaker, Stephen. "Joyce and Skeat." *James Joyce Quarterly* 24, no. 2 (Winter 1987): 177–92.

Williamson, C. N. and A. M. "The Goddess in the Car." *The Strand Magazine* (March 1902): 262–71.

Woodham-Smith, Cecil. *The Great Hunger: Ireland 1845–1849.* New York: Harper and Row, 1962.

Worth, Paul W., and Jim Cartwright. *John McCormack: A Comprehensive Discography.* New York: Greenwood, 1986.

Wyndham, Guy Percy, ed. *Letters of George Wyndham, 1877–1913.* 2 vols. Edinburgh: Constable, 1915.

Yeats, William Butler. *The Collected Letters of W. B. Yeats.* Edited by John Kelly and Ronald Schuchard. Vol. 3: 1901–4. New York: Oxford University Press, 1994.

———, ed. *Fairy and Folk Tales of Ireland.* New York: Macmillan, 1888.

Index

Page numbers in italics refer to illustrations.

Abbey Theatre, 3, 75, 96, 114
Act of Union, 73, 116, 121
Adams, Robert M., 283n21
Adventure stories, 9, 13, 47–49, 178
Aeríochtanna, 24, 145
Afghanistan, 129–31
Agnosticism, 70, 102, 239, 296n25
Ainsworth, Geoffrey, 194
Aisling, 170, 261
Alexandra Dock, 30
Alice in Wonderland, 45, 256
Alighieri, Dante, 66, 219, 243, 270, 297n31; Dante's vision in Joyce, 9, 97, 262–65; *Epistle to Can Grande*, 262; *Inferno*, Canto 7, 262; *Inferno*, Canto 34, 10, 263–64; Joyce's reading of, 10, 63, 217; *Purgatorio*, 264–65
Allegory: after Dante, 261–66; of the Great Game, 45, 134; of Griffith's politics, 116, 170–74, 261; of Hermeticism, 235; of Irish and Hungarian politics, 8–9, 116, 123
Allen, Thomas B., 135
All Goodly Sports (Spring), 285n37
Alliteration, 195, 224, 225
Allusion: to the 1798 Rebellion, 289n11, 289n12; biblical, 256; biographical, 66, 77, 283n20; classical, 80; to Dante, 243, 263; to Dolmetsch, 93; to Emmet's speech, 159–60; to the Famine, 124; gnomonic, 256; to the Great Game, 124, 133; historical, 290n1; to King William III's statue, 288n6; local, 267; to money, 40; musical, 283n20; Pauline, 10, 157; to Queen Alexandra, 53, 291n15; to the *Resurrection of Hungary*, 8; Shakespearean, 73, 285n38; Theosophical, 9, 254
Alvares, Emmanuel, 179, 290n3
American National Biography, 139
Amerindian folklore, 294n39
Amiens Peace Treaty, 143
Anderson, Chester, 268
Anderson, William, 219–23
Angers, 65
Anglo-Irish Treaty, 109

Anti-climax, 9; in Fournier interview, 20, 211; narrative, 187–88, 191; rhetorical, 195–96; structural, 182–83, 189, 192–93
Antinous (character), 73
Apjohn, Percy (character), 261
Appollodorus, 294n39
Argyll (automobile), 21
Aristotle, 10, 63, 64, 65
Arnold, Benedict, 134
Arranger, 194
Aryans, 245
Ascot Gold Cup, 43
Asperger's Syndrome, 288n1
Assonance, 188, 291n9
Atheism, 239, 261
Athena, 78
Atherton, James, 296n24
Athy, 25, 31
At Swim-Two-Birds, 271
Augustine, Saint, 250
Aunt Kate (character), 293n29
Australia, 30
Austria-Hungary, 129, 233. See *Resurrection of Hungary*
Automobiles: age of, 12–49; cost of, 16, 21–22; cultural impact of, 3; environmental objections to, 26; Joyce's attitude toward, 3, 4, 20–22; manufacturers of, 14–16, 30; marketing of, 16; models, 15–16; races, 16, 19, 48, 99. See also Gordon Bennett Cup Race
Automobile Age (Flink), 14–18

Bach, Alexander, 123
Bach, Johann Sebastian, 85
Baden-Powell, Robert, 135
Bank of Ireland: center of narrative, 49, 153–55, *154*; monetary center, 155, 186, 212, 292n20; symbol of Home Rule, 155, 170
Barney Kiernan's, 115
Baron Renfrew (pseudonym), 47
Barry, Madame du, 45
Bartók, Béla, 286n17

B-attitudes, 74
Battles: Naas, 289n12; "Races of Castlebar," 289n12; "Rotunda," 98; Veszprém, 122; Waterloo, 44–45, 129
Bauerle, Ruth, 88, 91–92, 280n26
Beaufoy, Philip (pseudonym), 180
Beaux' Walk, 121, 155, 214, 216
Beck, Warren, 6, 180, 279n20
Beckman, Richard, 284n29
Belgium, 15, 30–31, 45, 243, 248
Bell, G.K.A., 55, 60, 68, 281n5, 281n9; biography, 282n20; and Trench, 283n27
Belle of Newport, 43, 49, 67, 263; as trophy, 78, 134, 180, 215
Belvedere College, 105, 141, 179, 194, 218
Bennett, Douglas, 121–22, 233, 286n20, 294n34
Bennett, James Gordon, Jr., 139–40
Benstock, Bernard, 70
Benz, Carl, 15
Beresford, Lord Charles, 100
Berlioz, Hector, 85
Besant, Annie, 235
Best, Nigel, 290n23
Betrayal: in Dante, 10, 73, 263–64; of Emmet, 165, 289n11; of Fenians, 136; of friendships, 69; Gogarty's, 52, 57, 246; Jimmy's, 51, 54, 69, 110, 157, 221; Joyce's paranoia about, 135; Mulligan's, 70–73, 176; in Ovid, 222; political, 172, 190, 263
Bible: Hebrew, Psalms, 265, 280n27; Acts of the Apostles, 122; Apocalypse, 129, 246; John, 280n27, 296n26; Luke, 73; Douai-Rheims, translation, 256; King James, translation, 259, 296n17. *See also Book of Revelation*; Paul, Saint
Bicycle, 14, 17, 21, 25, 106, 277n1
Big Wind, 23
Birthplace and Burial of Emmet (Quaid), 288n3
Bishop, John, 173, 235
Bismark, Otto von, 129
Blackrock, 110–11, 283n22
Blavatsky, Madame, 240, 245, 253; in *FW*, 254, 296n24; *Isis Unveiled*, 235, 238, 296n18; *Key to Theosophy*, 235, 248, 249, 252
Blayac, Alain, 41
Blight: The Tragedy of Dublin (Gogarty), 114
Bloom, Leopold (character), 1, 43, 136, 141, 180, 296n22, 296n23, 296n25; critic of meat trade, 112–15; and Emmet, 161–65; and Griffith, 109, 123, 172, 261
Bloom, Molly (character), 109, 141, 261, 281n9, 291n11, 293n31, 296n25
Blücher, Gebhard Lebrecht von, 44–45
Bluebell Estate, 192
Boer War: Anti-war movement, 2, 112, 135, 146–47; and British intelligence, 135; Griffith's anti-colonial parallels, 101, 118, 120, 150; Queen's visit as recruitment for, 95, 119
Bohemian, 84, 90, 123, 205, 257
Bonaparte, Napoleon, 44, 45, 54–55, 142, 162
Book of Revelation, 236
Bowen, Zack, 39, 110, 128, 181, 279n20, 287n22
Boylan, Blazes (character), 59
Bradley, Bruce, 141, 218–20
Brady, Joseph, 23, 277n5, 285nn2–3
Bream, Julian, 89
Briggs, Kathleen, 294n2, 295n7
Brigid, Saint, 28
British Museum, 85, 90, 284n31
Bruno, Giordano, 296n26
Brutus (character), 263
Brzezinski, Zbigniew, 287n24
Buckingham Palace Conference, 5
Buddhism, 173, 176, 238–39, 252
Buddhist Catechism (Olcott), 235
Budgen, Frank, 46
Bulfin, William, 106; account of Martello visit, 55–56, 78, 166, 234, 281n11
Bull, John, 87
Bung, 151
Butler, Father (character), 170
Buy Irish campaign, 3, 102 169, 278n1
Byrd, William, 87, 206
Byrne, John Francis, 51, 54, 58, 146, 281n4

Cabbala, 239, 296n20
Cabra, 194
Calabria, 68, 286n18
Call of the Wild (London), 22
Campbell, Berkeley, 36
Campbell, Joseph, 176, 290n22
Campbell, Margaret, 84–92
Cambridge University, 293n26; for aspiring espionage agents, 132, 137, 287n25; for aspiring gentlemen, 59, 124, 132, 137; for networkers, 37, 68, 82, 127, 203, 220–21, 245, 282n16

Canada, 37, 123, 205
Captain White (pseudonym), 47
Card games: analogy with Great Game, 124, 134, 138; bézique, 43, 279n21; gambling and business cultures, 48–49; Jimmy a loser, 156, 190, 248; nap, 43–44, 244, 249, 279n21, 289n11; parallel with car race, 42–49; parallel with Waterloo, 45; poker, 44, 279n21, 279n23, 280n30; Villona's disengagement from, 83, 249
Carens, James, 57–58
Carlow, county, 25, 27, 156, 165
Carlyle, Thomas, 153
Carpaccio, Vittore, 88, 91
Carrefour de l'Odeon, 90, 296n21
Carroll, Lewis, 280n24
Carson, Sir Edward, 1, 24
Cartwright, Jim, 290n16
Casey, Joseph (character), 18
Cash nexus, 18, 49
Cassius (character), 263
Catachresis, 205
Caters, Baron de, 34
Catholic Encyclopedia, 297n29
Catholicism, 1, 2; gambling condemned, 46; and "The Holy Office," 62–63; Joyce's position on, 10, 61; and King Edward VII, 47; modernism condemned, 140; and Theosophy, 235–36, 238, 296n18
Cavan, county, 140
Celtic Archeology, 173
Celtic etymology, 212–13, 233
Celtic literature, 227, 230; *Book of Leinster*, 232; *Bruidhean Chaorthainn*, 230; bruidhean tale type, 9, 227, 230–34; Fenian narrative, 175, 230, 231, 233; "Find and the Phantoms," 231; *Tógáil Bruidne Da Derga*, 230
Celtic myth, 76, 230
Celtic Otherworld, 227, 295n10, 295n11
Celtic Tiger, 2
Census of Ireland: of 1901, 283n22, 287n30; of 1911, 283n22
Central Bank, 41
Chamberlain, Austen, 112
Chandler, Thomas (character), 176, 205
Chassis, 15, 278n2
Chatterton, Hedges Eyre, 285n3
Chauffeur, 15, 19, 278n2

Cheng, Vincent, 279n14, 287n23
Chester Cup, 280n28
Chiasmus, 9, 270, 292n20; in Ovid, 224; in *Portrait* and *Ulysses*, 192; structural, 185, 192–94; syntactic, 198, 211
Chichester, 282n20
Ciardi, John, 265
Cicero, 218
Civil War, Irish, 2, 5
Claidheamh Soluis, 25, 147, 167, 285n8
Clancy, George, 51, 135, 280n2
Clann na Gael, 101
Claudius (character), 73
Clément (automobile), 14
Clongowes Wood College, 179
Clough, Arthur Hugh, 80
Clymene, 218
College Green, 29, 153–54, 181–82, 185, 191
Colline (character), 258
Collins, Michael, 57, 138
Colloquialism, 196, 280n30
Colohan, Dr. John, 17
Colonialism, 13, 94, 101, 178, 287n23; "After the Race" as a critique of, 22, 30, 42, 70, 128, 232, 269; Anglo-Irish colonials' support of the Gordon Bennett Cup race, 21; Dublin as a colonial center of, 2, 23, 100, 128; and espionage, 134, 136, 155; famine and poverty as the outcome of, 125–26; Gordon Bennett Cup race propaganda for, 46–47, 166; Griffith's anti-colonialism, 22, 103, 142, 146; Joyce's moderate anti-colonialism, 58, 75; the Land Question and, 27–28, 126; and Mackinder, 130–34; Martello tower as a bastion of, 54, 171; and Routh, 127; statue of King William III as a symbol of, 155, 233; Trinity College as an outpost of, 80, 155, 224. *See also* Royal visits
Colum, Mary, 46, 79, 140
Colum, Padraic, 36, 46, 52, 64, 79, 140
Congregatio pro Doctrina Fidei, 62
Connolly, James, 101, 104
Connor, Jerome, 152
Conroy, Gabriel (character), 288n6, 293n29, 296n19
Conspicuous Consumption, 39, 134, 182
Cooney's tobacco shop, 106
Cork, city, 134
Cork, county, 24

Cork Hill, 294n34
Corley (character), 59, 75, 176
Cosgrave, Vincent, 51, 54, 146
Cosgrave, W. T., 34
Costello, Peter, 36, 111–12, 134, 286n15, 291n11
Cotin, Guillaume, 65
Cousins, Gretta, 36, 87, 92, 236, 282n16
Cousins, James, 36, 87, 92, 236, 282n16
Crimea, 130
Croke Park, 20
Cromwell, Oliver, 28
Cuchulain, 102
"*Cúirt an Mheán Oíche*" (Merriman), 63
Cumann na nGaedhal, 104, 122, 150
Curragh Mutiny/Incident, 5
Curran, Constantine, 46, 88, 235, 281n10
Curran, Sarah, 143–44, 146
Cusack, Michael, 106

Daedalus, Stephen (character), 5, 225
Daimler (automobile), 15, 21, 28
Daimler, Gottlieb, 15
Dalkey, 36, 55, 243
Daly, Mary, 113–14, 277n1, 282n16
Dandy Fifth, 2
Danes: Doyles as, 173–74; and Dublin, 165
Darwinism, 233, 239, 240
Däubler, Theodor, 284n34, 296n21
Daudet, Alphonse, 288n4
Davitt, Michael, 117, 127
Dawn (Gonne), 167–68
Dawn of Day (Nietzsche), 281n7
De Dion (automobile), 28
Deák, Ferenc, 8, 118, 120
Deane, Seamus, 279n14, 279n17, 279n20
Deasy Act, 127
Deasy, Mr. (character), 278n3, 286n10, 296n25
Dedalus, Mrs. (character), 290n19
Dedalus, Simon (character), 60, 68
Dedalus, Stephen (character): in *Portrait*, 3–4, 122, 280n21, 290n3, 292n21; in *Ulysses*, 61, 66, 71, 75, 268, 278n3, 286n9
Depression, 2
Devil, 31, 72, 160, 228, 254; in Dante, 264, 297n31; Jenatzy as, 31–33, *32*; Mulligan as, 72; in Saint Paul, 259–60
Devlin, Anne, 144, 146
Dickens, Charles, 199
Diesel, Rudolph, 15

Digges, Dudley, 152
Dignam, Patrick (character), 261
Dillon, John Blake, 170
Dillon, Leo (character), 170
Doherty (character), 59, 72, 283n24
Dollard, Ben (character), 161, 162, 164
Dolmetsch, Arnold, 8, 84, 284n31; biography, 84–87; concert program, *86*; and Joyce, 67, 87–89, 267; as model for Villona, 89–93
Donát, János, 284n36
Double-lettered words, 196–99, 250, 260, 296n22
Doubles, Astral, 241–51, 253–55, 260, 296n22
Dowland, John, 84, 87, 206, 284n31, 284n33; "Come [From] Silent Night," 89; and *CM*, 267–69; "Weep You No More, Sad Fountains," 91
Down, county, 24
Doyle, Bernard, 167
Doyle, Jimmy (character): classical precedent, 218–25; versus Emmet, 156–57; after Gogarty, 51, 56, 59–61; gullible loser, 67; Irish folk precedent, 9, 226–30; materialist, 36–38, 41; and Mulligan, 69–79; precedent in "The Old Watchman," 36–38; quarrel with Routh, 124–28; and Shaun, 59, 173–74; Trinity College dropout, 47, 202; Villona's rival, 7, 121–24; wealthy investor, 38, 48l
Doyle, Mr. (character): "advanced Nationalist," 156, 214; and auto industry, 48, 223; butcher, 65, 110–14; Danish descent, 174–77; after Field, 68, 110–15, 282n16; and Gogarty, 68, 72; language, 202–4; Mammon worshipper, 36, 38–39, 48, 192, 199–201
Doyle, Mrs. (character), 293n23
Drogheda, Earl of, 104
Dublin Castle: administrative center, 103, 147; and Emmet, 143, 145, 154, 155; surveillance center, 134, 135
Dublin City:
—Buildings: Ancient Concert Rooms, 169; Church of Mary Immaculate, Inchicore, 192; City Hall, 2, 3, 116; General Post Office, 1; Gresham Hotel, 29; Kilmainham Gaol, 1, 144, 145, 147, 153, 154; Metropole Hotel, 51, 120; Rotunda, 98; Russell Hotel, 210; Saint Catherine's Church, 144, 154; Saint Michan's Church, 145, 151; Westland Row Station, *154*, 156, 199, 220. *See also* Bank of Ireland; Dublin Castle; Shelbourne Hotel

—Places: Bluebell, 192; College Green, 29, 153–54, 181–82, 185, 191; Dodder River, 230; Goldenbridge, 153; Howth, 234–35, 281n5, 281n9; Sandymount, 122, 282n16, 296n25. *See also* Inchicore; Kingstown Harbour; Rutland Square; Saint Stephen's Green

—Roads: Emmet, 153–54, 192, 213; Naas, 143, 153–54, 188, 196, 232; Old Kilmainham, 154; Saint Peter's Terrace, 194; Sydney Parade, 142; Tyrconnell, 153, 192, 195, 213

—Statues: Robert Emmet, 142, 152; Holy Family, 291n11; George II, 122, 155; William III, 155, 233, 286n20, 288n6

—Streets: Bridgefoot, 144, 154; Christchurch Place, 155; Cork, 143; Cornmarket, 155; Dame, 38, 154–55, 184–88, 192, 214–15, 247–48, 294n34; Grafton, 1, 53, 121, 142, 154–55, 189, 199, 247; Granby Row, 1; High, 155; James's, 154; Kevin, 112, 114, 286n12; Lord Edward, 154–55; Marshalsea Lane, 143, 154; Mount Brown, 153–54; Patrick, 143, 154; Sackville, 243, 244, 285n3; Thomas, 143, 144, 147, 150, 151, 154; Werburgh, 155; Westmoreland, 1, 243. *See also* Beaux' Walk

Dublin Corporation, 31; opposition to Unionist dominance of, 100, 104, 106, 110, 285n3; patronage and public health, 112–14; and visit of Edward VII, 95, 116

Dubliners: "Araby," 116, 277n4, 296n19; and biography, 35, 57, 59, 277n1; "The Boarding House," 172, 286n13; "Clay," 265, 290n4; "Counterparts," 117, 197, 290n4; "The Dead," 230, 269n19, 293n31; "An Encounter," 170, 172, 296n19; "Eveline," 37, 222; "Grace," 59, 112, 257, 262, 285n3; and *Irish Homestead*, 37, 50; "Ivy Day in the Committee Room," 47, 107, 108, 120, 277n4; " A Little Cloud," 59, 176, 290n4; "A Mother," 105, 277n4, 288n8; "A Painful Case," 290n4, 296n27; "The Sisters," 222, 257, 277n1, 291n14, 294n40; technique, 181, 293n27; "Two Gallants," 59, 176, 26; writing of, 87, 281n10, 291n14

Dublin Hermetic Society, 235, 238

Dublin Metropolitan Police (DMP), 148, 148–49, 286n11; penetrated by IRA, 136–38; presence and surveillance, 112–13, 287n26

Dublin University. *See* Trinity College, Dublin

Dudley, Lord Lieutenant, 95

Duffy, James, 288n3

Dulwich, 284n31

Dumas, Alexandre, 270; *The Queen's Necklace*, 280n25

Dunciad (Pope), 63

Dun Guaire Castle, 55

Dunleavy, Janet and Gareth, 79

Dunlop, John Boyd, 14, 103, 277n1

Earlsfort Terrace, 24, 34

Earwickers (characters), 173–74

Easter Rising (1916), 2, 8, 138

East India Company, 48

Edge, Selwyn, 18, 19, 24, 32, 33, 278n4

Edgeworth, Richard Lovell, 25

Edison Gramaphone and Typewriter Company, 168, 289n16

Eglinton, John, 65, 235

Egyptian Book of the Dead, 173, 239

Ekirch, A. Roger, 290n20

Electric age, 2, 172, 255

Elementary Lessons in English Grammar (Morris), 212

Eliot, T. S., 295n11

Elliott, Marianne, 145–46, 150, 162, 164

Ellipsis, 205, 207

Ellmann, Richard, 279n15; on Gogarty, 58–59; on "The Holy Office," 282n14; on Joyce, 36, 87, 254, 290n18; on Joyce's library, 132

Elwood, John, 51, 68

Emergency (World War II), 2

Emmet, Dr. Robert, 142, 157

Emmet, Robert: Asperger's syndrome, 288n1; biography, 142–44; centennial, 9, 95, 98, 104, 111, 142–53, *163*, 265, 280n28, 288n7, 288n9; and Arthur Griffith, 57, 101, 104, 150; and Jimmy, 156–61; Joyce his memorialist, 10, 57, 153–56; and McNally, 145–46; rebellion, 143–44; in popular culture, 144–53; and Saint Paul, 159; speech, trial, and execution of, 54, 158–61; in *Ulysses*, 161–65

Emmet Song Book, 288n3

Emmet, Thomas Addis, 54, 142, 146

Encyclopedia Britannica, 292n21

Encyclopaedia of Dublin (Bennett), 121–22, 233, 286n20, 294n34

Encyclopedia of the Irish in America (Glazier), 140

Encyclopedic Theosophical Glossary, 241, 244, 252, 253, 268

English Renaissance, 8, 84, 90, 91
Epaphus (character), 221
Epiphany, 173, 186, 222, 255, 261, 291n9; epiphany #33, 53–54, 190
Eridanus, river, 219, 222
Esoteric Buddhism (Sinnett), 235, 241, 244, 246, 253
Espionage, 9, 131–38, 243
Etymological Dictionary of the English Language (Skeat), 42, 79, 213, 214, 259, 283n23, 291n11, 291n33
Etymology: car, 212–13, 233; "channel," 291n11; "Farley," 141; "gentleman," 79; "genuine," 214; "jovial," 259; "kindle," 214; "pot," 42; "solid," 40; "torpid," 283n23
Euphemism, 295n6; about business, 39, 41, 184; about Jimmy, 179, 195, 202; journalistic, 40, 195
Euripides, 294n39
European Union, 2, 90
Exhibition of Irish (Home) Industries, 51, 104–5, 149, 169, 288n5, 290n18

Fairhall, James, 128, 287n23
Fairy tales, 226–30
Famine, Great, 25, 110; and Gonne, 103; and Griffith, 103; and Joyce, 126–27; resentment over, 1, 8, 23, 126, 146; and Routh, 124–28
Fanning, Charles, 146, 158
Farley (character): gambler, 44, 49, 128, 214–15; historical models, 64, 139–41; and an Irish-American political alliance, 8, 124, 139–41, 159; Irish-American wealth, 40, 78, 139, 179, 215; as a leprechaun, 140–41, 228, 295n5; representing a root race, 244–45; representing the U.S. in the Great Game, 138, 245; sex tourist, 53, 139, 180, 189; surprising entrance, 141
Farley, Fr. Charles, 141
Farley, John Cardinal, 139–40
Farman, Henry, 33
Farrington (character), 74, 117, 197
Feis Ceoil, 169
Feiseanna, 24, 145
Fenians (IRB): and Farley, 139; and Field, 110–11; and Griffith, 147; and Joyce, 18, 135, 170; in popular memory, 144, 146; rising, 1, 135; spies among, 135–36; symbol of, 78–79, 170, 175, 235
Ferrabosco, Alfonso, 284n31
Ferrari (automobile), 17

Field, William J.: biography, 110–12; butcher, 22; and Emmet centennial, 151; Fenian, 137; Griffith's attacks on, 111, 115; Irish Party MP, 73; Joyce's relationship with, 115, 282n16, 286n10; and public health, 112–15; and royal visit, 98, 116; single, 68
Fili, 76
Finley, Fr. Peter S.J., 28
"Find and the Phantoms," 231
Finn Mac Cumhaill, 167, 230–34, 296n22
Finnegans Wake, 44, 101, 134, 165, 166, 218, 279n21, 279n22, 284n29, 288n2, 288n9; Phaethon's fall in, 223–24; *ricorso*, 9, 172–77, 290n22
Flags: American, 139, 148–49; Austro-Hungarian, 118, 122, 133; Fenian sunburst/sunrise, 149, 166–68, 175, 289n15; French, 151; Harp, 149; Union Jack, 46, 128, 148–49
Folklore, 18, 78, 118, 265, 294n39; Irish, 9–10; "Jemmy Doyle and the Fairy Palace," 226–32; leprechaun, 228, 295n5; *púca*, 228, 295n4; ticket-collector, 227–28. *See also* Celtic Literature
Fomorians, 167
Footprints of Emmet (J. J. Reynolds), 288n3
Ford, Henry, 3, 16, 17, 278n4
Fordism, 21
Foreshadowing, 181, 188, 189
Fort of the Plains, 28
Foster, R. F., 87, 136, 235
Fournier, Henri, interview, 7, 18–20; into "After the Race," 95–97, 104–5, 152–53; anti-climax trope, 211
Foxford tweeds, 107
France, 35, 233, 280n29, 294n35; automobile industry, 14–16, 22; in Gordon Bennett Cup race, 19–22, 29–30, 33–34, 99; in Great Game, 23, 128–31; language, 79, 82, 211–12, 219. *See also* Bonaparte, Napoleon; Dumas, Alexandre; Emmet, Robert; Fournier, Henri, interview; Paris; Ségouin; United Irishmen; Villon, François
Frank (character), 35, 51, 59
Frayne, John P., 146
Frazier, Adrian, 280n28
Free indirect discourse, 9, 70; in "After the Race," 153, 193–218, 291n13
Freeman's Journal, 1, 98, 148, 285n8; and Field, 286n15, 289n13; and Joyce, 169, 286n15;

masthead of, *167*, 169–70; promoting the race, 17–18, 25–26, 286n10
French Revolution, 45
Friendship, 281n7, 286n19; in "After the Race," 28, 38, 69, 233, 242, 250, 270; in Joyce's biography, 50–56
Futurism, 197

Gabler, Hans Walter, 37, 277n2, 279n15
Gabriel, Fernand, 19, 33, 288n6, 293n29, 296n19
Gaelic Athletic Association, 102, 106, 117, 136, 150
Gaelic culture, 64, 77, 104
Gaelic League: and 1798 centennial celebrations, 2, 150; and Griffith, 102, 169; Joyce's skepticism about, 108, 136; publications, 25, 167, 285n8
Galicki, Wolfgang, 294n39
Gallaher, Ignatius (character), 59, 176
Gambling: and business, 48–49; culture of, 46–47; and Edward VII, 47; and George IV, 45; and Gordon Bennett, 42; Griffith on, 46; images of, 41; Irish vice, 37; Joyce's indifference to, 43, 46; and Newport Casino, 49; and sports, 7, 43, 47–49. *See also* Cards
General Post Office, 1
Gentleman, 31, 46, 71, 283n29; education of, 79–82; sporting and wealthy, 178–79; term, 79–80. *See also* Gogarty, Oliver St. John
Geoghegan, Patrick M., 157, 159, 160
"The Geographical Pivot of History" (Mackinder), 8–9, 129–34, 287n24
Germany: automobile manufacture in, 14–19; church organ manufacture in, 3, 277n1, 288n5; and Gordon Bennett Cup Race, 29–35, 96, 242; Joyce's personal acquaintance with, 90, 284n34, 296n21; Mackinder's analysis of, 128–35; rising global power, 5, 21–23, 117; and Waterloo, 44–45
Gibbons, Luke, 161, 288n10
Gifford, Don, *Ulysses Annotated*, 79, 137, 161, 278n3, 283n23, 294n37
Gilbert, Allan, 262, 264, 297n31
Gilbert, Stuart, 217, 236, 294n37
Gilford, Miss E., 35
Gilligan, Phil (character), 261
Glandon, Virginia, 101–2

Glasnevin Cemetery, 115, 235
Globes: Dantean, 243, 244, 265; gas lamps, 187, 188, 191, 192, 199, 215; geographic, 290n19; Hermetic, 241–45, 251–55, 265
Gnomon, 156, 256–57, 270
Gnosis, 238
Gnosticism, 239
Gogarty, Oliver St. John: automobilist and sportsman, 17–22, 74, 224; and Bell, 282n20, 283n27; classical education, 58, 79–81; and Collins, 57; estrangement from Joyce, 7, 51–54; and Griffith, 57, 81; Joyce's necessary antagonist, 57–59, 135, 246; Martello sojourn, 53–56, 281n5; politics, 61, 82, 289n15; profession, 22, 114; rivalry with Joyce, 17–22, 81–82, 281n11, 284n30; Trinity gentleman, 79–82, 281n3; vindication of character, 58, 281n8; wit and humor of, 58, 67, 77, 235–36, 281n9, 293n32
—In Joyce's works, 59, 283n24; "The Holy Office," 61–66; as Jimmy Doyle, 51, 59–68, 280n1; as Mulligan, 68–79, 114
—Works of: "Ballad of Joking Jesus," 74; *Blight*, 114; limerick, 283n20; *Many Lines to Thee*, 55, 60, 281n5, 283n27; *Tumbling in the Hay*, 281n6, 284n30, 289n15
Goggins (character), 59, 72
Gonne, Maud, 45, 100–101, 136, 167; *Dawn*, 168; at king's visit, 98, 119; protest at queen's visit, 45, 103, 126
Gordon Bennett Cup Race, 7; aftermath, 24, 34–35; as cover for intelligence agents, 134–38; Irish press and public response, 25–31; Irish staging of, 24–25; Joyce's relations with, 18–25; links with the king's visit, 8, 94–95, 98, 104–5, 118–19, 131; race report, 31–33, 179n13; and tourist industry, 29; upstaging Emmet centennial, 98, 104, 147–53
Gordon Bennett Yachting Cup, 42
Gorman, Herbert, 72, 138; and Joyce's Paris circle, 90, 121, 124, 284n34, 286n18, 296n21
Gottfried, Roy, 292n18
Grace, doctrine of, 237–38, 250, 257, 260, 265
Grand Prix, 19, 30, 34, 48, 49, 197
Great Game, 8–9, 23, 45, 128–39, 249, 269
Greek language, 171; etymology, 259, 281n9, 283n23, 283n26; and Joyce, 81–82, 284n30
Gregory, Lady Augusta, 18, 36, 58, 231; *Poets and Dreamers*, 18, 229

Griffith, Arthur: "advanced nationalist," 31, 46, 81; biography, ideas, and political organizer, 94–105; "buy Irish" campaign, 3, 102, 104, 169, 278n1, 288n5; critic of the Irish Party, 73; and Emmet centennial, 152, 263; as gryphon in *FW*, 109–10, 172, 175; ideas and language in "After the Race," 110–16, 121–28, 291n15; influence on Joyce, 32, 35, 52–55, 105–10; opposition to Gordon Bennett Cup Race, 8, 22, 34, 46, 155, 156; opposition to royal visits, 47, 98–101, 147–51; relations with Joyce, 105–10; relations with Oliver Gogarty, 57, 81; relations with William Rooney, 101–2; *Resurrection of Hungary*, 8, 51, 116–24, 261, 287n22, 287n23; *United Irishman*, 8, 101–5, 285n8
Groden, Michael, 277n2
Gudgin, Peter, 138
Gurden, Sir Brampton, 17

Haines (character), 78, 137, 283n23, 294n3; as transformation of Routh, 71–72, 170–71
Hamburg, 47
Hand, Robert (character), 59
Hardiman, Adrian, 145
Harrington, Tim, 98
Hart, Clive, 174
Hart, Michael (character), 261
Hart, Peter, 287
Hauptmann, Gerhart, 36
Healy, Tim, 24
Hearst Corporation, 42
Heliades, 219, 223
Helios, 218, 221, 294n40
Hellenizing, 77, 122, 170, 171
Herlihy, James, 286n12
Hermeticism: "After the Race" as burlesque of, 243–55; Joyce's attitude toward, 9–10
Hesiod, 294n39
Hiberno-English: "advanced nationalist," 57, 95, 102, 104, 120; "Bung," 151; "chassis," 278n2; "Fine night," 227; "Land Question," 126; "office," 62; "tinpikery," 149, 151; "Trinity gentleman," 80; "West Briton," 103, 147
Higgins, Francis, 134, 146
Hill, Judith, 288n6
Hinduism, 173, 238–39, 241, 246, 252
History of Irish Flags (Hayes-McCoy), 166, 175
History of Motor Racing: The Heroic Days (Bill Mason), 279n13

Hitler, Adolf, 287
Hodgart, M.J.C., 217, 294n38
Holloway, Joseph, 87, 282n13, 284n32
Holohan, Hoppy (character), 105
Holyhead, 29
"The Holy Office," 202, 229; biographical moment, 51–52, 61, 281n4, 281n16; after Villon, 62–66
Home Rule, 5, 126; Irish aspiration toward, 23, 101, 140; Joyce's attitude toward, 108–9; reflected in "After the Race," 110, 169–70, 290n19
Homosocial relations, 51, 258
Honey, J. R. de S., 79, 80
Hong Kong Jockey Club, 46
Horace, 179, 218
Horse, 221, 248; and apocalypse, 172; and the automobile, 13–19, 179, 189; and British imperialism, 109, 130, 133, 155, 288n6, 290n1; and Celtic myth, 232–33; Dublin Horse Show, 27, 105; horse racing and gambling, 46; horse racing and the Grand Prix, 20, 49; and the myth of Phaethon, 219–20; and the *púca*, 227, 295n4. *See also* Statues
Hospitality: commodification of, 29, 207, 233; in Dante's *Inferno*, 262–63; an Irish and Irish-American virtue, 28, 95, 187, 199, 236, 278n9, 278n14; Joyce's availing of, 58, 236; violation of, in Celtic myth, 232, 295n10
Hudibras (Butler), 63
Hughes, Archbishop Joseph, 140, 141
Humber (automobile), 14, 16
Humbert, General, 287n28, 289n12
Hungary, 284n36, 286n17; and Dolmetsch, 84; flag of, 122, 132; Jenatzy and, 30–31; and Mackinder, 133; Saint Stephen of, 116, 122–23. *See also The Resurrection of Hungary*; Villona
Hyde, Douglas, 79, 102, 104, and deAnglicization, 117, 170
Hygenius, 294n39

Iliad, 219
Implied narrator, 73, 133, 222, 247, 261, 296n22; antagonist, 59; in "Holy Office," 63–65; moralist, 153, 233; pedantic parodist and rhetorician, 180, 198, 247; in "Sirens," 164; superior, 91–93; in "Telemachus," 171
Inchicore, 38, 181, 247; and design of "After the

Race," 153–55, *154*, 191–92, 194, 291n11; and technique, 184–88, 243
India, 48, 218; in the Great Game, 129–35
Inferno (Dante), 10, 31, 219, 262–65
Influenza, 2
International Exhibition of Industry, 51, 104–5, 149, 288n5
Irish Automobile Club, 15, 18, 25, 34, 46, 99
Irish Catholics: Doyles as representing, 82; Gogarty and Joyce, 58, 61, 81; prejudice against, 1, 31, 81, 240; suppressed rage of, 229
Irish Cattle Traders and Stockowners' Association, 112
Irish Fortnight, 24, 34
Irish Free State, 2, 8, 34, 82, 109; and daybreak, 173–75
Irish Homestead, 51, 59; Joyce's submission of "After the Race" to, 35–37; publication of "After the Race," 4–5, *5*, 50, 69, 277n1, 290n21; readership of, 36, 50, 202, 233, 277n3, 285n8
Irish language: *aeríocht*, 24, 145; *bruidhean*, 9, 227, 230–34, 255, 295n10; *camán*, 150; *carr*, 212; *ceathair*, 175; *dubh ghall*, 174; *fairceallach*, 140, 141; *fairceallach talmhaidhe*, 228; *feis*, 24, 145; *fili*, 76; *Inse*, 213; *púca*, 228, 295n4; *seanchaí*, 229; *seóinín*, 56, 151; *sídh*, 227
Irish Literary Revival: "After the Race" as an expression of, 256; Anglo-Irish leadership of, 10, 62–65, 255–56; and Celtic sagas, 230–31; and fairy lore, 230; Joyce's antagonism toward mystics of, 62–63, 236, 255; Joyce's criticism of language revival, 103–6; Joyce's criticism of the mediocrity of, 52, 65; and Kelly, 140
Irish National Foresters, 150
Irish National Theatre Society, 22
Irish Party: criticized by Griffith, 73, 101, 103; Doyles as representatives, 110–16; and Gordon Bennett Cup Race, 24, 26; and king's visit, 94, 98–99; Joyce's views of, 107–11; policies pursued by, 24–26, 94, 98, 101, 126
Irish Republican Brotherhood (IRB), 102, 134–38, 167. *See* Fenians
Irish Times, 1, 3, 168, 280n28, 285n8; and Joyce's interview with Fournier, 7, 20–21, 95, 97, 210; promoter of the Gordon Bennett Cup, 18, 24–25, 27, 148, 287n23
Irish Transvaal Committee, 101, 136
Irish Volunteers, 5, 166
Irish War of Independence, 2, 109

Isle of Wight, 42
Italians, 288n5, 292n21; Villona as an Italian name, 68, 286n18, 296n21
Italy, 43, 261; and lute, 88–90, 284n37

Jackson, John Wyse: and Peter Costello, 107, 111, 134–35, 286n11, 295n9; and Bernard McGinley, 41, 111, 169, 283n25, 290n18, 291n15
Japan, 23, 51, 178
Jarrott, Charles, 33
Jenatzy, Camille, 19–20, 30, 31–34, *32*, 264
Jesuits, 105, 296n18; Joyce's education by, 64, 141, 179, 217, 229
Jews, 22, 81, 123, 238–39, 284n29
Johnson, Claude, 25
Johnson, Colton, 146
Josef, Emperor Francis, 118–19
Journalism, 8, 9; Joyce's, 18, 51; Weldon, 28; Williamson, 12–14. *See also* Griffith, Arthur; Parody
Joyce, James: Fournier interview, 18–20; and *James Joyce Archive*, 284n30, 297n30; Paris sojourn, 18, 36, 50–54, 89–94, 104, 109, 126; relationship with Nora Barnacle, 29–56; writing and submitting "After the Race," 35–36, 53–54; writing "The Holy Office," 52, 61, 65. *See also* Bulfin, William; Cousins, James and Gretta; Gogarty, Oliver St. John; Griffith, Arthur; McCormack, Count John
—*Letters* I: *Dubliners* as a looking glass, 259; Elizabethan music, 87; odour of offal, 62, 114
—*Letters* II: AE's invitation, 50; ambitions as poet, 229, 230; approval of Sinn Fein, 108; criticism of Griffith, 104, 107–8; criticism of Hermetic Society, 236; criticism of Irish Revivalists, 104; devotion to Nora, 50, 52, 280n2; dissatisfaction with "After the Race," 69; Dowland, 284n33; Elizabethan music, 51, 87, 92; Field, 286n10, 286n12; Gogarty's Greek, 281n9; Griffith's friendship, 108; negative estimate of Gogarty, 54, 57, 61, 135, 146; Paris epiphany, 53; poverty and homelessness, 84, 281n4, 282n16; reservations about *The Resurrection of Hungary*, 120; Stanislaus's criticism of Kipling, 131–32; submitting "After the Race," 35–36; writing and defense of *Dubliners*, 62, 291
—*Letters* III, 295n9; Dowland, 89, 268; Monte Carlo, 46

—Works of: *Chamber Music*, 268–69, 282n15; "A Curious History," 108, 110; "The Day of the Rabblement," 229; *Exiles*, 57, 59; "Home Rule Comes of Age," 108; "Home Rule Comet," 108; "Ireland, Island of Saints and Sages," 176, 261; "Poets and Dreamers," 18, 229; *Stephen Hero*, 53, 57, 106, 108, 286n8; "Trust Not Appearances," 270. *See also Dubliners*; *Finnegans Wake*; "The Holy Office"; *A Portrait of the Artist as a Young Man*; *Ulysses*

Joyce, John Stanislaus, 18, 43, 111, 134, 229, 286n11

Joyce, Margaret (Sister Mary Gertrude, R.S.M.), 51, 194

Joyce, Mary Jane (May), 50–51, 67–68, 95, 260

Joyce, Nora (Barnacle), 4; displacing prostitutes, 50, 54; emigrating with, 35–36, 56; and "Eveline," 51, 281n10; Joyce's courtship of, 50–54, 92, 92, 280n2, 284n33; Joyce's meeting with, 29; replacing his male friends, 51–53, 72; replacing his mother, 50–51, 53, 260

Joyce, Stanislaus, 141, 279n12, 281n7, 295n9; on Joyce's career counseling, 38; on Joyce and Catholicism, 238; on Joyce's drinking, 68, 282n19; on Joyce and Griffith, 105, 107–8; on Joyce and Hermeticism, 235, 238, 253; on Kipling, 131–32; on sports, 20

Joyce, Stephen James, 218

Judas, 73, 146, 160, 246, 263

Jupiter (deity), 254, 259

Kandisky, Wassily, 240
Kane, Matthew (character), 261
Kearney, Martin F., 288n8
Kearns, Gregory, 287
Kempis, Thomas à, 236
Kelleher, Corny (character), 136, 255
Kelleher, John V., 230
Kelly, John, 134
Kelly, Thomas Hughes, 64, 139, 140
Kempthorpe, Clive (character), 71
Kennedy, Patrick, 294n1, 295nn5–7, 295n12
Kenner, Hugh, 193, 283n21; "Uncle Charles Principle," 291n13
Kerry, county, 24
Kershner, R. B., 166, 289n14
Kettle, Tom, 102, 120, 294n38
Kildare, county, 140, 185, 289n11, 295n14; and 1798 rebellion, 27–28, 165; and Emmet's rebellion, 143–44, 153–54, 165; and Gordon Bennett Cup Race, 25, 29, 99, 133, 156

Kilmainham Gaol, 1, 144–45, 147, 153–54, *154*
Kilwarden, Lord, 143, 155, 159
Kinealy, Christine, 124–26
Kings: Arthur, 175; Edward VII, 26, 34, 79; 1903 visit and controversy, 3, 116, 94, 118, 147; 1904 visit, 51, 105; and automobiles, 27; Joyce and visit, 47, 107, 120, 160; reputation, 47, 108; visit celebrated, 23, 123, 15–51; visit linked to race and centennial, 147–50, *148*; Fergus, 74; Francis Josef, 118–19; George II, 122; George IV, 45, 12, 132, 233; Henry VIII, 51, 84, 87, 91–92, 284n31; Leopold I, 172; Lóegaire MacNéill, 123, 233, 295n15; Louis XV, 45; Louis XVI, 45; Solsking the First, 176; Stephen, 116, 122

King's Inns, 142

Kingstown Harbour, 83, 121, 139, 186, 216; in "After the Race" and "Telemachus," 54–55, 70, 75, 78, 106, 153, 174; as darkened mirror, 75; and Edward VII, 123, 156, 232; and gambling, 45, 49, 256; and George IV, 45, 78, 233; as gnomon, *76*, 257

Kinnell, Galway, 64
Kipling, Rudyard, 8; *Kim*, 131–33, 138, 287n25; *Plain Tales from the Hills*, 131
Kissinger, Henry, 287n24
Kitty Hawk, 133
Knyff, Rene de, 33
Kock, Paul de, 283n25
Kodaly, Zoltán, 286n17
Kossuth, Lajos, 118

Land Acts, 8, 95, 126–27, 152
Land Conference, 94
Land League, 102, 109, 145, 167
Land Question, 126
Laois, county, 25
Larne, 29
Last Supper, 258–59
Latin language, 81, 82; Joyce's conversational use of, 90, 281n4; Joyce's education in, 179, 217–25, 290n3
Lautrec, Toulouse, 15
Lawrence Collection, 1
Leadbeater, Charles Webster, 235, 240
Leader, 1, 26, 120, 147–51, *148*, 285n8
Lee, Robert E., 158
Leinster, Province of: folktale, 9, 232; historical

territory, 28, 232, 295n15; site of Gordon Bennett Cup race, 25, 28, 97, 154
Lenehan (character), 176
Leo XIII, Pope, 22
Leprechaun, 228, 295n5
Leslie, Emily, 13
Life and Times of Robert Emmet (Madden), 145, 288n3
Life of Emmet (O'Donoghue), 288n3
Liffey, river, 28, 213, 222
Light Locomotives (Ireland) Act, 24
Lincoln, Abraham, 158
Little Review, 69
Liszt, Franz, 85
Litz, A. Walton, 69, 72
Locarno, 69
Logue, Cardinal Michael, 280n28
Lucian, 294n39
Lucretius, 225
Luddites, 26
Lúgh Lámhfhada, 167, 176
Lute, 76–77, 207, 284n36; Dolmetsch's essays on, 88–92; Dowland's songs for, 267–68; Joyce's interest in, 8, 67, 84–88, 91–92
Lynch, Brendan, 15, 17, 277n1, 278n1, 278n2, 292n16; on the Gordon Bennett Cup Race, 20–34; on Irish hospitality, 29, 139, 278n9
Lyons, J. B., 281n8, 282n18

MacDermott, Red Jim, 134, 136
MacKillop, James, 227, 232, 295n5, 295n6, 295n10, 295n15
Mackinder, Halford, 8–9, 129–34, 287n24
MacLochlainn, Alf, 137
MacLysaght, Edward, 141, 174, 232
MacMorroughs, 232
MacNally, Leonard, 61, 134, 135
MacNéill, Eoin, 109
Maddox, Brenda, 52, 281n10
Madrigal, 76, 84, 90–91, 252
Maeterlinck, Maurice, 15
Mahaffy, John Pentland, 79, 224
Mahatma, 245, 252, 260
Mammon, 36; Bank of Ireland as, 41; commodified sports as, 191; Griffith cites, 97; in "Holy Office," 52, 62–63; a mirage, 260, 271; and Saint Paul, 259
Manchester Martyrs, 136, 146
Mangan, Henry Connell, 152

Mangan, James Clarence, 89
Manganiello, Dominic, 120
Marcello (character), 258
Marie Antoinette, 45, 233
Marquess Conyngham, 21
Marriage, 286n13
Martello tower, 59, 67, 69, 115, 234; Bulfin's account of, 78, 166, 234; construction of, 54–55; and daybreak, 166–70; as displaced basis for "After the Race," 77–79; Griffith's visits to, 106; Joyce's departure from, 35, 65; Joyce's sojourn at, 52–56; link with Emmet rebellion, 152
Martyn, Edward, 98
Mason, Elizabeth, 142
Mason, Ellsworth, 282n14
Mass, 72, 73, 171, 259
"*Matcham's Masterstroke*" (Beaufoy), 180, 282n15
Maume, Patrick, 102–3, 136–37
Maynooth College, 47; *Maynooth Catechism*, 237, 280n28
McCartney, Donal, 103, 109, 117
McCormack, Count John, 168–69, 289n16
McGee, Owen, 111, 136, 287n26
McSwiney, Terence, 120
Meat trade, 38–39, 112–14, 242
Meath, county, 27, 139, 140, 144, 295n15
Mecredy, Richard, 25–26
Mecsnóber, Tekla, 104–5, 107, 117, 121, 297n28
Mercadante, Saverio, 161
Mercedes (automobile), 15, 19, 21, 30–34, 278n5
Metaphysics, 229, 233
Metempsychosis, 10, 238–39, 242, 260
Metropole Hotel, 51, 120
Meyerbeer, Giacomo, 161
Michelin brothers, 14, 30, 34
Milk trade, 114
Mimi (character), 258–59
Mirror: and Dante, 264; gnomonic, 256; and other world, 296n25, 296n26; Pauline, 75, 256; and spiritual order, 242, 254; in "Telemachus," 74–75; and Villona, 61, 199, 207–8
Mirus Bazaar, 23
Misdirection, 38, 181–83, 185, 243
Mitchel, John, 102, 117, 125–26, 127
Mitchell, Susan, 64
Mithraism, 239, 246
Model T (automobile), 3, 16, 21
Moisel, Philip (character), 261
Moling, Saint, 28

Monasterevan, 25
Mondrian, Piet, 240
Money: from automobiles, 22, 38–41, 48, 98, 203, 245, 248; Doyle fortune, 220, 242, 245; Farley's, 228; forms in "After the Race," 39–40, 212; and gentlemen, 48; Gogarty's money, 58, 60, 71, 81; and Griffith, 115; as illusion, 253–55, 259–60; Jimmy's guilt about, 196; Jimmy's loss of, 25, 39, 262; Joyce's lack of, 36–37, 43, 58, 66, 81, 281n4; Ségouin's, 40, 228; from tourism, 29; Villona's poverty, 66–69, 184, 282n17. *See also* Mammon; Meat Trade; Pluto; *Solidus*
Montagu, Edward: on French auto production, 19; on the Gordon Bennett Cup race, 17, 24, 32–34; on Jenatzy, 31; on opposition to the race, 26; on price gouging, 29
Montagu, Hon. John Scott, 24–25
Montagu Trophy, 33
Moone, 28
Moore, George, 58, 87, 280n28; *Evelyn Innes*, 87, 99, 90, 284n31
Moore, Thomas, 144; "The Harp that Once," 77; *Irish Melodies*, 144; "O, Breathe Not His Name," 144, 288n9; "She Is Far from the Land," 144; "When He Who Adores Thee," 144; "The Wine Cup Is Circling," 166
Moran, D. P., 116, 285n8; critic of colonial propaganda, 46; critic of Emmet centennial, 147, 151; critic of Gordon Bennett Cup race, 26; critic of Griffith, 120, 122; critic of *Irish Independent*, 148–49, 148; and Joyce, 127; critic of Trinity gentlemen, 80
Morris (automobile), 14
Morris, Richard, 212
Morris, William, 87
Mors, Emile, 19, 30, 33
Motif-Index of Folk Literature (Thompson), 227, 232
Motif-Index to Early Irish Literature (Cross), 294n2
Mulligan, Buck (character), 59, 114, 176; compared to Jimmy, 60, 68, 283n21; and public health, 170–71, 283n28; in "Telemachus," 68–78, 283n23
Multivalency, 217, 265, 267; *for example*, globe, 243, 265; race, 159–60, 245; Villona, 121, 270, 278n19
Murphy, D. B. (character), 37

Murphy, William Martin, 103, 104, 105, 148
Murphys, 232
Musetta (character), 258–59
Music: Bell's talent, 282n20; folk, 102, 118, 286n17; Jimmy's interest in, 196, 209; Joyce's interest in Elizabethan song, 8, 69, 85–93; Joyce's performance of, 92–93, 282n16; Joyce's talent and taste in, 51, 144, 169; metaphor in "After the Race," 76, 180, 199–200, 214, 216, 243; music hall vulgarity, 46–47, 67, 103, 127, 147; Routh's ignorance of, 67, 124, 243; in "Sirens," 162–64; Symons's essay on, 87; and theosophy, 240; Villona's talent for, 89, 90, 121, 172, 206–7, 247–51. *See also* Dolmetsch, Arnold; Dowland, John; Musical Instruments; Music of the Spheres; Opera; Songs
Musical instruments: harp, 74–77, 149, 167, 268; harp lute, 91; harpsichord, 85; mandolin, 88; organ, 3, 90, 250, 277n1, 288n5; piano, 85, 87, 88, 168, 282n16, 284n31; psaltery, 87, 284n36; viola d'amore, 85; viola de gamba, 93, 284n31; yacht piano, 31, 83, 90, 180, 207, 284n35. *See also* Lute
Music of the Spheres, 242, 249–50, 252, 268
Mustang (automobile), 17

Naas, 28, 185, 232, 289n11, 295n15
Naas Road: and 1798 rebellion, 143, 154, 289n12; in "After the Race," 153, 154, 188, 192, 196, 232
Nagy, Joseph Falaky, 231, 233–34
Nap (card game), 43–44, 244, 249, 279n21, 289n11
Napier (automobile), 30, 33
Narrative techniques. *See* Allegory; Allusion; Arranger; Etymology; Free indirect discourse; Implied narrator; Multivalency; Parody; Satire; Structure
National Council, 104, 107
National Yacht Club, 139
Naturalism, 192
Nazism, 2
Neoplatonism, 239
Nero, Emperor, 48
New Grove Dictionary of Music and Musicians, 87, 89, 91
New Ireland Review, 28, 285n8
Newman, John Henry Cardinal, 176, 283n27
Newport, R.I., 49, 180

Newspapers: *Claidheamh Soluis*, 147, 167, 285n8; *Daily Express*, 18, 285n8; *Daily Mail*, 26; *Derry People*, 150; *Evening Herald*, 285n8; *Evening Mail*, 285n5, 285n8; *Fáinne an Lae*, 167; *Harp*, 285n8; *Irish Independent*, 103; *Irish Peasant*, 285n8; *Irish People*, 26, 27; *Irish Worker*, 285n8; *Leader*, 1, 26, 120, 147–48, 148, 151, 285n8; *Middleburg Courant*, 101; *Morning Post*, 31; *Nation*, 167; *New York Herald Tribune*, 18, 42; *New York Times*, 26; *Northern Whig*, 24; *Pall Mall Gazette*, 29; *Il Piccolo della Sera*, 117; *Sinn Fein*, 22, 107, 108, 111, 278n1; *Sporting and Dramatic News*, 26; *Weekly Irish Times*, 3, 168. *See also Freeman's Journal; Irish Homestead; Irish Times; Times of London; United Irishman*
Nietzsche, Friedrich, 153, 281n7
Nonnus, 294n39
Norbury, Lord, 144–45, 158–59, 162
Norris, Margot, 4, 279n14
Northern Unionists, 24
Numerology, 238–42, 246–48, 250, 260, 296n20

O'Brien, Joseph V., 123, 136, 150, 285n6; automobiles in Ireland, 15–21; public health in Dublin, 23, 112–13, 285n4
O'Brien, William, 26, 126
O Byrnes, 232
O'Casey, Sean, 114; *Juno and the Paycock*, 278n2; *The Plough and the Stars*, 157
O'Connor, Richard, 139
O'Connor, Ulick, 21, 57, 114; Gogarty-Joyce relationship, 52, 66–68
O'Donovan Rossa, Jeremiah, 135
O'Hara, Kimball (character), 132
O'Hara, Matthew, 18
O'Healy, M., 148
O Kinsellas, 232
Old Celtic Romances (P. W. Joyce), 230
Old Kilcullen, 25
"The Old Watchman" (Berkeley Campbell), 36–37
O'Leary, John, 135, 152
Ó Lúing, Seán, 98, 102, 104, 105, 116
Olympic Games: Paris, St. Louis, 23
O Moores, 28, 232
Omphalos, 56, 171, 176
O'Neill, Henry J., 136

O'Neill, Michael J., 282n13
O'Nolan, Brian (Flann O'Brien), 271
Opel (automobile), 14
Opera, 2, 38, 258–59
Ordure, 62, 64
Origin and History of Irish Names of Places (P. W. Joyce), 295n14
Original Sin, 237
Ossa, 225
Otherworld: in Celtic literature, 227–34, 295n10; in Joyce, 9, 228, 295n11
Otto, Nicholas, 15
"Our Father," 246
Ovid, 9, 179, 260, 270, 294n39, 294n40; *Metamorphoses*, 218–25
Owens, Cóilín: on "Clay," 265; on "Counterparts," 74, 117, 197; on "A Painful Case," 296n27
Oxford English Dictionary, 15, 40, 62, 90, 122, 200, 280n30, 293n30, 294n36
Oxford University, 52, 59–60, 67–68, 81, 282n20, 283n23, 283n27

Palestrina, 91, 284n31
Panhard (automobile), 14–15, 19, 28, 30, 33
Paracelsus, 239
Parallax, 10, 185, 208, 292n19, 296n23
Paralysis, 156, 271
Paranoia, 55, 65, 134
Paris, 23, 26, 34, 43, 46, 200; automobile industry in, 14–16, 208; Emmet in, 143; Griffith in, 136; Joyce's circle in, 121, 124, 216, 270, 281n4, 286n18, 286n21; Joyce's epiphany of, 53–54, 189–90; Joyce's sojourn in, 18, 36, 50–54, 94, 104; newspapers, 106, 140, 278n9; Villon in, 64–65
Parnell, Charles Stewart, 111, 117; Griffith's model, 102–9, 136; and Joyce, 81, 105, 115, 292n19; and rising sun, 148, 169, 170
Parody, 1, 46, 66, 263, 279n20, 283n21; of gentlemen's magazine writing, 160, 178–82, 199; of Hermeticist writing, 9–10, 235, 242, 248–55; of pretentious editorializing, 196, 210; of sports writing, 7, 9–10; in *Ulysses*, 151, 217
Paronomasia, 229, 270; "circle," 214; "column," 282n15; "course," 211; "disclosed," 91; "Farley," 141; "Hungarian," 212; "translate," 212; "Villona," 82

Patrick, Saint, 102, 128, 146, 176
Paul, Saint, 9, 250, 257, 261, 296n25; Blavatsky's rejection of, 240, 269; "darkened mirror" (1 Corinthians), 75, 254; devil (1 Timothy), 259; "disappointed" (Romans), 256, 296n27; Emmet's citations of, 159; my race is run (2 Timothy), 10, 159, 160, 259; Nietzsche's criticism of, 281n7
Peake, C. H., 39
Pearse, Patrick, 25, 152, 230; Emmet and 144, 147; and Griffith, 102, 103, 109
Peel, Sir Robert, 124
Perfection, 237, 247, 257, 296n26
Periodicals: *Allgemeine Automobil Zeitung*, 34; *Autocar*, 26; *Automobile Club Journal*, 31; *Automotor Journal*, 25; *Blackwood's*, 178; *Connoisseur*, 88–91; *Dana*, 281n9, 281n12; *Field*, 26; *Gentleman's Magazine*, 178; *Little Review*, 69; *Motoring Illustrated*, 96; *New Ireland Review*, 28, 285n8; *Strand*, 13, 15, 178; *Titbits*, 180; *Velo*, 278n9; *Wide World*, 13
Phaethon (deity), 294n39; in "After the Race," 220–23, 294n40; in *FW*, 223–25; Joyce's encounter with, 9, 220
Phaeton (automobile), 220
Philippines, 22, 129, 131
Phoenix Park, 23–24, 34, 106, 123
Piggott, Richard, 134
Pilate, Pontius, 159
Pindus, 225
Piper (character) 137
Pitt, William, 171
Places: Angers, 65; Mondello Park, 295n14; Newport, R.I., 49, 180; Pola, 4; Scollagh Gap, 226; Trieste, 4, 22, 69, 107–8, 132. *See also* Dublin; Paris
Plato, 75, 240, 296n26
Plunkett, Horace, 17, 34
Pluto, 262
Pola, 4
Polmar, Norman, 135
Pope (automobile), 14
Pope Leo XIII, 22
Portrait of the Artist as a Young Man, A: chiasmus in, 192–93; *Dana* essay, 281n12; and Joyce's biography, 22, 59; and modernism, 271; Villona and Stephen, 61

Pound, Reginald, 15
Power, Arthur, 62, 63, 270
Presbyterians, 278n11
Prostitution: Joyce's attitude to, 50, 54, 190; Farley's women, 189; social problem, 23, 113
Protestants: and Hermeticism, 235–36, 240; and Irish Literary Revival, 10, 65, 255; Irish ruling class, 1, 27, 100, 278n11; kings, 47, 155
Prussia, 44, 119
Pseudo-Hippocrates, 246
Pseudonyms, 288n2; AE, 36; Baron Renfrew, 47; Captain White, 47; Cunningham, 143; Daedalus, 5; Dedalus, 4; Flann O'Brien, 271; Hewitt, 143; John Eglinton, 65; O'Breen, 288n9; Robert Ellis, 143; Trebor, 143; Whiskey, 136
Púca, 228, 295n4
Puccini, Giacomo, 270; *La Bohème*, 258–59
Purcell, Henry, 84
Purgatory, 230
Pyper, J. Stanton, 137
Pythagoras, 239, 252

Quaid, D. A., 288n3
Quebec, 227
Queens: Alexandra, 148, 291n15; of Diamonds and Hearts, 31, 45, 123, 206, 210, 215, 228, 233, 258; Marie Antoinette, 45, 233. *See also* Victoria, Queen
Quincunx, 257
Quinn, John, 140

Rafroidi, Patrick, 181
Rambler (automobile), 14
Raoul (character), 12
Rathcoole, 154
Red Devil, 31–35, 32, 264
Redmond, John, 24, 98
Reid, B. L., 140
Reincarnation, 236, 242
Relief Commission for Ireland, 124
Renunciation Act, 116
Renvyle, 55, 61
Resurrection, 10, 173–74, 259, 261, 265, 297n28
The Resurrection of Hungary (Griffith): in "After the Race," 120–24, 261; cited, 103, 118–19; debated, 106; policies adopted, 109; publication, 104–5, 116–20

Reynolds, John J., 158, 288n3
Reynolds, Mary, 262
Reynolds, Thomas, 61, 135, 146
Rhetorical figures: Anadiplosis, 188, 210; Anaphora, 210, 224; Anastrophe, 209, 291n7; Antanclasis, 83, 221; Antithesis, 108, 195, 290n3; Aporia, 194, 203, 270; Asyndeton, 205, 206, 208, 209–10; Bathos, 181–82, 183, 186; Ecphonesis, 206, 207, 210; Elision, 194; Ellepsis, 205, 206, 207; Epanalepsis, 211; Epigram, 85, 182, 195; Epizeuxis, 210; Homioptoton, 210; Hypallage, 209, 216; Hyperbole, 200, 215, 291n6; Isocolon, 201, 210; Litotes, 171, 201, 211; Meiosis, 211, 293n32; Metalepsis, 40, 216; Metaplasm, 227, 270, 281n6; Metonymy, 188, 199–200, 215, 216; Onomatopoeia, 196; Oxymoron, 40, 65, 195, 201, 210, 211, 224, 283n23; Paradiastole, 211; Paradox, 40, 65, 165, 182–83, 190, 191, 193, 195–96, 224; Parataxis, 210; Paregmenon, 212, 213, 291n11; Parenthesis, 66, 208; Periphrasis, 208; Pleonasm, 179, 194; Ploce, 210; Polyptoton, 212; Polysyndeton, 209; Prolepsis, 292; Prosopopoeia, 194; Prozeugma, 210; Synoceiosis, 283n23; Synonymia, 212; Triad, 179, 195, 290n1; Zeugma, 224. *See also* Chiasmus; Euphemism; Paronomasia
Ribbonmen, 144
Ricardo, David, 204, 293n26
Richards, Grant, 62, 114, 259
Riordan, Mrs. Dante (character), 43
Risorgimento, 261, 297n28. *See* Resurrection
Rivière (character): acquaintance of Farley's, 190, 227; automobilist, 197; Cantabrigian, 137; devil, 259, 264; entrepreneur, 48; female impersonator, 257; flowing man, 221, 247; French Canadian, 205; representing the electric age, 200; Ségouin's cousin, 282n16
Rivière, Dr. Joseph, 36
Roberts, George, 4, 65, 108, 115
Robinson, Henry Morton, 176, 290n22
Rock of Dunamase, 28
Rodolfo (character), 258
Rolls Royce (automobile), 21, 74, 82, 224
Romans, 47–48
Rooney, William, 101–2, 285n7; *Poems and Ballads*, 105

Root races, 241–46
Rothschild, Henri de, 30
Routh (character): biographical origins, 56, 68, 89, 124, 296n21; British agent, 134–38, 255; Englishman, 8, 45, 70–72, 123, 160, 189; gentleman, 82; Jimmy's spat with, 61, 214, 221, 245, 263; link with Corny Kelleher, 255; link with Haines, 71–72, 171; misreading of, 35, 279n14; Philistine, 67, 76, 82, 91, 243. *See also* Great Game; Routh, Sir Randolph
Routh, Sir Randolph, 124–28
Rover (automobile), 14
Royal Assent, 24–25, 94
Royal Irish Automobile Club (RIAC), 18, 25, 46, 99
Royal Irish Constabulary (RIC), 112, 138
Royal Irish Yacht Club, 139
Royal Saint George Yacht Club, 139
Royal University (Dublin), 38, 81, 106, 135, 217–18, 292n21
Royal visits: and "After the Race," 152–53; and Boer War recruitment, 95, 146–47; Edward VII (1903, 1904), 8, 94–95; George IV, 123; Griffith's leadership in opposition, 98–99, 104, 107, 118–20; and Joyce's "Ivy Day," 120; linked to Gordon Bennett Cup Race, 23, 95, 99, 100; opposition to, 94–95, 151; support of, 29, 47, 95, 107, 126; upstaging Emmet Centennial, 104–5, 147; Victoria (1849, 1861, 1900), 94–95, 126, 285n5; and Wyndham Act, 126
Russell, George (AE): benignity, 36, 52, 55, 57, 58; editor, *Irish Homestead*, 50, 285n8; mystic, 62, 235–36
Russell, Lord John, 124, 127
Russia, 22, 34, 178, 287n27; in Great Game, 23, 129–31; Russo-Japanese War, 23, 51
Rutland Square: in "After the Race," 172, 243, 244, 247; Gogarty's residence on, 60, 72, 281n5

Saint Michan's, 145, 151
Saint Stephen's Green: and the Beaux' Walk, 121–22, 154, 155, 214; Emmet's birthplace, 142, 150; and George II's statue, 122; Irish-Hungarian parallel, 132; and the Shelbourne Hotel, 34, 121, 155

Saints: Andrew, 128; Augustine, 250; Brigid, 28; Catherine of Siena, 236; David, 128; George, 128; John Chrysostom, 77; John of the Cross, 236; Moling, 28; Stephen of Hungary, 116, 122–23; Stephen the Martyr, 116, 122; Teresa of Avila, 236; Thomas Aquinas, 63, 65. *See also* Patrick, Saint; Paul, Saint
Salvation, doctrine of, 237–39, 250, 271
Samuel Whyte's English Grammar School, 142
Sanskrit, 173, 238, 241, 245, 252, 254–55
Sapho, 148, 149, 288n4
Sarajevo assassination, 5
Satire, 180; "After the Race" on commodification, 7, 41, 242; on gentlemen's presumptions, 178; on Hermeticism, 10, 255–60; "The Holy Office" on unworthy Irish poets, 62, 176; on Irish Party hacks, 111–12; on vulgarization of Emmet's memory, 151
Schaunard (character), 258
Schimmel, Annmarie, 246
Scholes, Robert and Richard Kain, 72, 190, 235–36, 281n7, 281n12, 283n24
Schork, Joseph, 223
Schwartz, David G., 46–48, 280n26, 280n29
Scriabin, Alexander, 240
Seanachaí, 229
Séance, 10, 239, 254–56
Ségouin (character): Cantabrigian, 37; car owner, 41; devil, 259, 264; diplomat, 45, 76, 191, 206, 221, 216; entrepreneur, 48; Frenchman 40; gambler, 148; materialist, 73, 247; name, 73, 221; wealth, 40, 196
Seven stages, 241–53
1798 Centennial: celebrations, 111–12, 144–49; Joyce cites, 161, 162–63, *163*, 168–70; poster, 162–64, *162*
1798 Rebellion, 54, 102, 287n28; Leinster, 27, 162, 165, 287n28; and Robert Emmet, 142, 155. *See also* United Irishmen
Shakespeare, William: *Hamlet*, 71, 73, 75, 111, 286n9; *Henry V*, 285n38; *Macbeth*, 73; *Merchant of Venice*, 48–49
Shaman, 9, 132, 231, 233–34, 256
Shaun (character), 59, 173, 174
Shaw, George Bernard, 87
Shelbourne Hotel: accommodating the British Automobile Club, 29, 124; and the French drivers, 34, 289n13; imagined location of dinner in "After the Race," 121, 124, 155, 172, 210, 278n7
Shelley, Mary, 292n21
Sídh, 227
Silence: Emmet's request for, 9, 152, 158–66; Joyce's mask of, 8, 55, 65–67, 166, 234, 271, 281n11; in technique of "After the Race," *154*, 155–56; and theme, 249–53, 270; Villona's, 8, 67–74, 206–8, 249–51, 267
Silent Watcher, 253, 268
Simms, Anngret, 23, 277n5, 285n2, 285n3
Sinn Féin (newspaper), 11, 107, 278n1; Joyce's reading of, 108
Sinn Féin party, 138, 139, 167, 174; election of 1918, 123, 136, 174; founding, 104, 109; and Gogarty, 57, 81; Joyce's approval of policies, 81, 108, 135; Joyce's citation of, 78, 175; policies, 22, 57, 68, 122
Sirr, Major Henry, 143, 145, 289n11
Skeffington, Francis Sheehy, 36
Smith, James Walter, 178
Soares, MP, Mr., 17
Solecism, 183
Solidus, 40, 294n36
Somerville, Jane, 39
Songs: "After the Ball Was Over," 291n11; "Ah, the sighs that come from the heart," 92; "Bold Robert Emmet," 145; "The Boys of Wexford," 2; "*Cadet Roussel*," 66, 93, 206–8, 289n12; "Come [From] Silent Night," 89, 284n33; "The Croppy Boy," 164, 169; "Dawning of the Day," 167; "God Save Ireland," 145–46; "God Save the King," 147; "The Green Isle of Erin," 169; "The Irishman," 169; "Killarney," 169; "The Man That Broke the Bank at Monte Carlo," 45–46, 280n26; "The Night Before Larry Was Stretched," 152; "The Old Green Isle," 169; "The Ould Plaid Shawl," 169; "Pastime and good company," 87, 92–93; "Turpin Hero," 87; "Weep You No More Sad Fountains," 91; "When He Who Adores Thee," 144; "When Shall the Day Break in Erin?," 168–69, 289n16. *See also* Moore, Thomas
South Africa, 101, 130, 135
South Seas Company, 48

Speeches from the Dock (T. D., A. M., and D. B. Sullivan), 145, 294n38
Sports: bowls, 20; boxing, 46; cricket, 20, 46, 178; cycling, 20, 106, 178n1; gaelic football, 24, 106, 147, 150; horse racing, 20, 46, 49; hunting, 13, 178; hurling, 24, 106, 147; soccer, 46; tennis, 280n31; yachting, 42. *See also* Gordon Bennett Cup race; Olympic Games
St. Jean, Shawn, 279n14
Statues: Emmet, 142, 152; George II, 122, 155, 286n20; William III, 155, 233, 288n6
Stokes, Whitley, 231
Stonyhurst College, 59
Story of Ireland (A. M. Sullivan), 145
Stradbally, 25
Structure, 9, 84; of "After the Race," 181–208; of *Dubliners*, 262–66; of *Portrait*, 192–93; septenary, 246–53; thematic, 42–43, 132. *See also* Anti-climax; Chiasmus; Fairy Tales; Silence
Sullivan, A. M., 145, 146
Sullivan, Kevin, 218
Sullivan, T. D., 145
Sultan, Stanley, 295n11
Suter, August, 217
Swedenborg, Emmanuel, 235, 239, 267
Swift, Jonathan, 63, 102
Swinburne, Algernon, 75, 78, 281n7
Switzerland, 4, 35
Sykes, Claude, 69
Symons, Arthur, 87
Synge, John Millington, 3, 64; *The Playboy of the Western World*, 3

Tandy, Napper, 145
Tara, 123, 233, 295n15
Tenniel, John, 280n24
Tertullian, 246
Theatre Royal, 2, 168
Theology, 125, 193
Theosophy: *Akasa*, 244; *Atman*, 241, 242, 252–53; *Aum*, 252; *Buddhi*, 241, 253; *Chhaayaa*, 241, 250; *Daivprakriti*, 253; *Fohat*, 253; Four material elements, 247; *Jiva*, 253; *Kama*, 241, 253; *Kriyasakti*, 245; *Linga Sharira*, 241, 253; Lower Quaternary, 241; *Manas*, 241, 253; Mantra, 252; *Manvantara*, 10, 241, 244; *Maya*, 240, 242, 246, 255; Music of the Spheres, 242, 249–50, 252, 268; *Pralaya*, 10, 241, 244, 253, 254; *Prana*, 241, 253; Reincarnation, 236, 242; Root races, 241–46; Seven stages, 241–53; Silent Watcher, 253, 268; *Sthula Sharira*, 241, 253; Upper Triad, 241. *See also* Blavatsky, Madame; Globes; Leadbeater, Charles Webster; Russell, George; Swedenborg, Emmanuel
Times of London, 97, 127, 131; and Gordon Bennett Cup Race, 19–20, 33, 139, 286n16; and king's visit, 94–95, 98, 286n16
Tindall, William York, 6, 280n1, 283n21
Tinpikery, 149, 151
Tógáil Bruidne Da Derga, 230
Tone, Wolfe, 145, 281n3
Toponymy: Dún Laoghaire, 233, 295n15; Inchicore, 213; Kilcullen, 28; Kingstown, 45; Naas, 28, 232; Timolin, 28
Torchiana, Donald, 287n28, 289n12
Tourist industry, 25, 29, 189
Tournament of Shadows, 129
Tracy, Robert, 123
Trans-Siberian Railroad, 130
Transvaal, 101, 150
Treaty of Vereeniging, 147
Trench, Samuel Chenevix, 55, 56, 68, 234, 283n27
Trevelyn, Charles, 127
Trieste, 4, 22, 69, 107–8, 132
Trinity College, Dublin, 187, 203, 293n26; British colonial institution, 79–80, 132, 155; and Emmet, 142, 157; and Gogarty, 59, 81; Jimmy a dropout from, 47, 59, 221, 227, 245
Tuberculosis, 23
Tudors, 93, 229, 284n31
Tully, Stanislaus (character), 114
An Túr Gloine, 288n5
Turner, John Noel, 293n28
Tymoczko, Maria, 295n11
Tynan, Brandon, 152
Typhus, 1

Ulster Volunteer Force, 5
Ulysses: "Aeolus," 216–17, 290n3; "Circe," 77, 123, 136, 137, 172; "Cyclops," 10, 151, 161, 165, 223, 254; as a development of "After the Race," 7, 9, 54, 69–79, 294n3; "Eumaeus," 37; "Ithaca," 261; "Oxen of the Sun," 31,

Ulysses—continued
206, 293n28; "Penelope," 234; "Proteus," 190; "Scylla and Charybdis," 68; "Sirens," 161–64; "Telemachus," 57, 59, 61, 234, 281n11; "Wandering Rocks," 137, 192

Unionists: and Dublin politics, 1, 98, 100, 106; endorsement of the Gordon Bennett Cup race, 25–26, 99; opposing Home Rule, 5, 104, 148; supportive newspapers, 18, 148, 285n5, 285n8; welcoming the king, 107, 116, 280n28

Union Jack (comic book), 170

United Irishman, 1; advanced nationalist organ, 31, 111–12, 116, 128, 138, 285n8; and Emmet centennial, 146–55, 288n3; Gogarty and, 57; Gonne in, 103, 168; Joyce's reading of, 8, 105–7; opposition to Gordon Bennett Cup race, 34, 95–99; organ of Irish Revival, 24, 106, 116; readership, 102, 202; and *The Resurrection of Hungary*, 116–20, 286n19; and Rooney, 101, 105; Yeats in, 280n28

United Irishmen: British response to, 134; and Emmet, 9, 142–45; French support for, 33, 54, 289n12; in *FW*, 289n11; informers among, 135; in *Ulysses*, 163, 163–64

United States of America: American tourists, 29, 98, 139, 140, *148*, 148–49; automobile production, 14, 16, 21–22; Clann na Gael in, 101; and Emmet, 142, 146, 152, 157, 160; and Famine, 124, 127; Farley as unique representative of, 128, 139, 189; gambling in, 47, 180; Gordon Bennett, 139–40; and Gordon Bennett Cup race, 30–33; in Great Game, 128–34, 287n24; Interstate Highway System, 3; Joyce and Irish-America, 138–39, 151; Kelly, 140–41; and Theosophy, 234, 238, 245; Wright brothers, 22

Upper Triad, 241

Ussa, 78

Veblen, Thorsten, 134, 279n16

Vedas, 246, 252

Victoria, Queen, 45, 85–86; and famine, 123, 126; visits, 94, 103, 123, 296n16

Victry, Thibault de, 65

Vico, Giambattista, 173–75

Vikings. *See* Danes

Villain, 40, 106, 121, 145, 270, 279n19

Villon, François: informing Villona, 8, 65; Joyce's reading, 65, 281n6; *Le Lais*, 64–66, 282n17; *Le Testament*, 64–65, 282n17; ordure in "The Holy Office," 64–66

Villona (character): after Dante's Virgil, 265; after Dolmetsch, 89–93; anticipating Shem, 173–74; anticipating Stephen Dedalus, 70–71, 77–79; artist, 51, 61, 66; becoming the "Eireweeker" of *FW*, 176; Calabrian name, 68; detached, 39, 65–66; Joyce's self-portrait, 56, 59, 61, 67–69, 177; Jimmy's antagonist, 7, 83; a mahatma, 249–52; non-Magyar villain, 120–21; poverty of, 66–69, 184, 282n17; silent, interior man, 61, 66, 83; a Silent Watcher, 252–53; social character, 82; the voice of Griffith's Sinn Fein, 121–23, 165; after Villon, 8, 65–66, 134

Virgil, 10, 294n39; Dante's guide, 262–65; in Joyce's rhetorical education, 218, 225, 260

Volta Cinematograph, 43

Voluntaries, 83, 90, 207, 243, 250

Vulcan (god), 219

Wagner, Richard, 85

Walsh, Archbishop William, 280n28

Walzl, Florence, 6, 110

Ward, David F., 20, 278n5, 278n6

Wars: Anglo-Afghan, 129; Cold, 287n24; First World (Great), 2, 23, 120, 129–30, 287n24; Franco-German, 33; Irish Civil, 2; Irish Independence (Anglo-Irish), 2, 109, 138; Napoleonic, 54–55; Philippines, 22, 129, 131; Russo-Japanese, 23, 51; Second World (Emergency), 2; Williamite, 125. *See also* Boer War

Waterford, 29

Waterloo, Battle of, 44–45, 129

Watson, Cathcart MP, 26

Weaver, Harriet, 89, 268

Weldon, Helen, 28

Wellington, Duke of, 44–45

Wellington (nap), 44

Wells, Charles Deville, 280n26

West Britonism, 103, 147

Westrumite, 32

Wexford, county, 2, 28, 144, 232, 295n12

Whiteboys, 134

Whittaker, Stephen, 293n33

Wicklow, county, 143–44, 170, 176

Wilde, Oscar, 75

Williamson, A. M., 12

Williamson, C. N., 12

Winch, Terence, 158
Winton (automobile), 14, 28, 30
Winton, Alexander, 139
Woodham-Smith, Cecil, 125
Woolwich Arsenal, 22
Workers' Strike (1913), 1–2
Worth, Paul W., 290n16
Wright brothers, 22
Wyndham, George, 147–48
Wyndham (Land) Act, 8, 28, 31, 94, 126–27, 147

Yacht piano, 90, 180, 207
Yeats, W. B., 58, 62, 140–41, 146, 231; and Boer War, 101, 280n28; and Dolmetsch, 87; and Joyce, 50–52, 57, 64, 69–70; and Moore, 28n31; opposition to king's visit, 98–104; *The Shadowy Waters*, 22; and Theosophy, 235, 240; "Who Goes With Fergus Now?," 74
Young Ireland, 102, 110, 144

Zborowski, Count Eliot, 25
Zurich, 4, 35, 69

Cóilín Owens is professor emeritus of English at George Mason University, Fairfax, Virginia. He is the editor of *Family Chronicles: Maria Edgeworth's Castle Rackrent,* coeditor of *Irish Drama, 1900–1980,* and author of *James Joyce's Painful Case.*

THE FLORIDA JAMES JOYCE SERIES
Edited by Sebastian D. G. Knowles

The Autobiographical Novel of Co-Consciousness: Goncharov, Woolf, and Joyce, by Galya Diment (1994)
Bloom's Old Sweet Song: Essays on Joyce and Music, by Zack Bowen (1995)
Joyce's Iritis and the Irritated Text: The Dis-lexic Ulysses, by Roy Gottfried (1995)
Joyce, Milton, and the Theory of Influence, by Patrick Colm Hogan (1995)
Reauthorizing Joyce, by Vicki Mahaffey (paperback edition, 1995)
Shaw and Joyce: "The Last Word in Stolentelling," by Martha Fodaski Black (1995)
Bely, Joyce, and Döblin: Peripatetics in the City Novel, by Peter I. Barta (1996)
Jocoserious Joyce: The Fate of Folly in Ulysses, by Robert H. Bell (paperback edition, 1996)
Joyce and Popular Culture, edited by R. B. Kershner (1996)
Joyce and the Jews: Culture and Texts, by Ira B. Nadel (paperback edition, 1996)
Narrative Design in Finnegans Wake: *The Wake Lock Picked*, by Harry Burrell (1996)
Gender in Joyce, edited by Jolanta W. Wawrzycka and Marlena G. Corcoran (1997)
Latin and Roman Culture in Joyce, by R. J. Schork (1997)
Reading Joyce Politically, by Trevor L. Williams (1997)
Advertising and Commodity Culture in Joyce, by Garry Leonard (1998)
Greek and Hellenic Culture in Joyce, by R. J. Schork (1998)
Joyce, Joyceans, and the Rhetoric of Citation, by Eloise Knowlton (1998)
Joyce's Music and Noise: Theme and Variation in His Writings, by Jack W. Weaver (1998)
Reading Derrida Reading Joyce, by Alan Roughley (1999)
Joyce through the Ages: A Nonlinear View, edited by Michael Patrick Gillespie (1999)
Chaos Theory and James Joyce's Everyman, by Peter Francis Mackey (1999)
Joyce's Comic Portrait, by Roy Gottfried (2000)
Joyce and Hagiography: Saints Above!, by R. J. Schork (2000)
Voices and Values in Joyce's Ulysses, by Weldon Thornton (2000)
The Dublin Helix: The Life of Language in Joyce's Ulysses, by Sebastian D. G. Knowles (2001)
Joyce Beyond Marx: History and Desire in Ulysses *and* Finnegans Wake, by Patrick McGee (2001)
Joyce's Metamorphosis, by Stanley Sultan (2001)
Joycean Temporalities: Debts, Promises, and Countersignatures, by Tony Thwaites (2001)
Joyce and the Victorians, by Tracey Teets Schwarze (2002)
Joyce's Ulysses *as National Epic: Epic Mimesis and the Political History of the Nation State*, by Andras Ungar (2002)
James Joyce's "Fraudstuff," by Kimberly J. Devlin (2002)
Rite of Passage in the Narratives of Dante and Joyce, by Jennifer Margaret Fraser (2002)

Joyce and the Scene of Modernity, by David Spurr (2002)
Joyce and the Early Freudians: A Synchronic Dialogue of Texts, by Jean Kimball (2003)
Twenty-first Joyce, edited by Ellen Carol Jones and Morris Beja (2004)
Joyce on the Threshold, edited by Anne Fogarty and Timothy Martin (2005)
Wake Rites: The Ancient Irish Rituals of Finnegans Wake, by George Cinclair Gibson (2005)
Ulysses *in Critical Perspective*, edited by Michael Patrick Gillespie and A. Nicholas Fargnoli (2006)
Joyce and the Narrative Structure of Incest, by Jen Shelton (2006)
Joyce, Ireland, Britain, edited by Andrew Gibson and Len Platt (2006)
Joyce in Trieste: An Album of Risky Readings, edited by Sebastian D. G. Knowles, Geert Lernout, and John McCourt (2007)
Joyce's Rare View: The Nature of Things in Finnegans Wake, by Richard Beckman (2007)
Joyce's Misbelief, by Roy Gottfried (2007)
James Joyce's Painful Case, by Cóilín Owens (2008)
Cannibal Joyce, by Thomas Jackson Rice (2008)
Manuscript Genetics, Joyce's Know-How, Beckett's Nohow, by Dirk Van Hulle (2008)
Catholic Nostalgia in Joyce and Company, by Mary Lowe-Evans (2008)
A Guide through Finnegans Wake, by Edmund Lloyd Epstein (2009)
Bloomsday 100: Essays on Ulysses, edited by Morris Beja and Anne Fogarty (2009)
Joyce, Medicine, and Modernity, by Vike Martina Plock (2010; first paperback edition, 2012)
Who's Afraid of James Joyce?, by Karen R. Lawrence (2010; first paperback edition, 2012)
Ulysses *in Focus: Genetic, Textual, and Personal Views*, by Michael Groden (2010; first paperback edition, 2012)
Foundational Essays in James Joyce Studies, edited by Michael Patrick Gillespie (2011)
Empire and Pilgrimage in Conrad and Joyce, by Agata Szczeszak-Brewer (2011)
The Poetry of James Joyce Reconsidered, edited by Marc C. Conner (2012)
The German Joyce, by Robert K. Weninger (2012)
Joyce and Militarism, by Greg Winston (2012)
Renascent Joyce, edited by Daniel Ferrer, Sam Slote, and André Topia (2013; first paperback edition, 2014)
Before Daybreak: "After the Race" and the Origins of Joyce's Art, by Cóilín Owens (2013; first paperback edition, 2015)
Modernists at Odds: Reconsidering Joyce and Lawrence, edited by Matthew J. Kochis and Heather L. Lusty (2015)
The Ecology of Finnegans Wake, by Alison Lacivita (2015)
James Joyce and the Exilic Imagination, by Michael Patrick Gillespie (2015)

www.ingramcontent.com/pod-product-compliance
Lightning Source LLC
Chambersburg PA
CBHW021848230426
43671CB00006B/311